DATE DUE			
JUL 2 8 1980			

America's Backpacking Book

America's Backpacking Book

Raymond Bridge

CHARLES SCRIBNER'S SONS   NEW YORK

1 3 5 7 9 11 13 15 17 19   v/c   20 18 16 14 12 10 8 6 4 2

Printed in the United States of America
Library of Congress Catalog Card Number 73–1342
SBN 684–13370–9 (cloth)

To my Father,
who taught me to love walking in high places.

Contents

Contents

Contents

Introduction

This book is a guide to some modern techniques of foot travel in the wilderness areas of North America. I hope that it will be of particular use to some of the many people who have become interested in camping in the last few years, and who would like to take up backpacking but don't know where to start. It is not just a beginner's guide, however. I have tried to make it a fairly complete discussion of the techniques and equipment needed for successful travel in all kinds of terrain and conditions that can be traveled without highly specialized skills and equipment. Hopefully, some of the discussions here will be useful to those who are already backpacking.

Although the book is intended to be complete in one sense, it is quite limited in another. American wilderness and semiwilderness areas differ greatly and any one person's experience in them is bound to be limited by the situations he has encountered, by his preferences for particular kinds of country, and by plain prejudice. The methods discussed in this book are those I have found effective and which have resulted from my own experiences and those of many friends and acquaintances. In the final analysis I can only say that they have worked for me. They are not the only techniques, and frequently they may not be the best. As the beginner gains experience, he will probably diverge at many points from the advice given here.

Since the experience with wilderness travel on this continent is quite extensive and has produced plenty of literature, the need for books on "modern techniques" may well be questioned. One justification lies in the great improvements in equipment that have been made in the last few years. The modern backpacker has a much easier time of it than any of his predecessors in dealing with average conditions, if he knows how to use the equipment available to him. He also can safely undertake many types of trips that would have involved serious risks or much more elaborate preparation in earlier years. For the beginner or intermediate backpacker, though, the boom in equipment has resulted in considerable confusion both in selection and use. This book attempts to lend some help in these areas.

There is a much more serious need for "modern techniques," however, resulting from a combination of the capabilities of modern equipment, the great popularity that outdoor recreation has gained in recent years, the increased accessibility of remaining wilderness areas to weekend and vacation use, and from the nature of many of these areas. The long and honorable tradition of camping in this country copied from the Indians and modified by trappers, guides, and other woodsmen has become entrenched in the programs of many youth groups, in summer camps, outdoor magazines, and general mythology. Unfortunately, this tradition is suitable only for a particular type of wilderness camping, a type completely inappropriate for most use of the wilderness and outdoors today. There is a pleasant nostalgia evoked by cutting poles for tents or lean-tos, building bough beds, and the use of similar skills redolent of campfires deep in the north woods, but continued teaching and practice of these methods of camping is destroying a lot of fine camping country.

This style of wilderness living was based on small numbers of campers in vast, heavily forested country. It was always destructive when it was used in areas not meeting these conditions, and for most campers today it should be a thing of the past. If you get a chance to explore heavily wooded regions that are rarely traveled, you may still have a chance to camp in this manner without putting an excessive load on the wilderness, but you'll have to go a long way to reach such an area today.

Most wilderness and semiwilderness areas that can be reached by the average backpacker fall into one of two categories. Either they are subject to heavy use or they are very harsh environments. The beautiful regions surrounding the Appalachian Trail are in the first category. If they don't look heavily used, it is because people have tried hard to leave few signs of their own passage and to clean up the debris left by others. At any rate, if each hiker traveling the trail hacked down a few live trees, trips along it would soon have all the wilderness feeling of a garbage dump.

An even less desirable sort of place to practice traditional forms of woodcraft is in the hard climate of the high mountains, the desert, and similarly harsh surroundings. Such wild and beautiful environments are the most interesting places to backpack, but the living conditions in such places make life precarious for the permanent inhabitants, a fact often missed by the casual human visitor. A small, gnarled alpine tree, half snag and half alive, is not like a low-altitude shrub that will grow back in a few years. It is hundreds, sometimes thousands, of years old. In country like this the backpacker must learn to be self-sufficient. He must not rip up delicate tundra to form a mattress or tear up brush for shelter. Only a boor would use the beautiful snags for firewood, but ignorance often causes people to do all these things.

Modern technique demands that the backpacker be aware of his responsibilities for leaving the wilderness as he found it. Many more people are now making use of a dwindling supply of wilderness. There is room for all of them without a feeling of overcrowding or the destruction it can cause, but only if they use camping methods appropriate to their numbers.

Old-timers will find that in many cases I emphasize the use of stoves over fires and other such unaesthetic substitutions. This is not because I am too lazy to build a fire, but because I think that many of us have to revise our thinking about appropriate methods of camping. In country where there is adequate deadwood, fires are always pleasant, but what happens when the camper relying on fallen deadwood can't find any? Does he eat a cold meal or go hungry? The answer is evident in well used campsites. Every dead branch within reach is broken off the trees, and then work starts on the live ones. In many areas we will have to stop building campfires if we want to preserve both reasonable access and the quality of the land. There are numerous similar examples which will be discussed here and there, but the point is simply that some of us who have been camping for a while need to rethink our own practices. Then we need to teach newcomers how to enjoy the back country without disfiguring it.

The book is arranged in five parts. The first discusses basic camping and trail techniques, the standard repertoire of the backpacker. The second part of the book deals with equipment, and includes general advice on purchasing and making various kinds of gear, together with detailed plans for some items. The third part has chapters on various special problems and skills, some of which are generally applicable, like first aid and route finding, and some of which are much more specialized, like the sections on mountain travel and backpacking with children. The fourth section has a chapter suggesting trips that might be especially interesting and a chapter about preserving some of the wilderness you will need for continued enjoyment of the sport. Finally there are appendices listing suppliers of equipment, some useful books, and other assorted compendia.

The author's debts are particularly difficult to pin down in a book like this one, since the writer draws on a general fund of information that passes among backpackers largely by example and word of mouth and occasionally through magazine articles and books. Some acknowledgments are implicit in the bibliography at the end of this book. For the rest, I would like to thank all the companions and chance acquaintances who have taught me, argued with me, and laughed at or with me on the trail and at home. All of them are really coauthors of this book.

Part 1

The Art and Folklore of Backpacking

Why Go Backpacking? 1

Like many similar activities, backpacking and its particular attractions are difficult to explain to the unbiased listener. One is usually talking either to a fellow believer—a kindred soul even though he may never have ventured into the woods—or to a dubious questioner whose values or prejudices seem to preclude the possibility of common ground for discussion. Hence the wilderness traveler cast up in society and trying to explain his passion customarily retreats either to banal statements ("I like it") or high-flown dissertations on the moral and spiritual superiority of experiences in the backcountry over any that civilization could possibly provide.

Those who already know in their heart of hearts that wilderness tramping is for them can skip immediately to the main portion of this book, which attempts to tell how they can engage in the sport with reasonable comfort. The curious may want to stay with me for a little, while I endeavor to explain some of the attractions of wilderness travel on foot.

Nearly everyone seems to be familiar with Mallory's famous explanation for wanting to climb Everest: "Because it is there." It has always seemed to me that this must have been the desperate reply of a man besieged by the hundredth little old lady at a cocktail party rather than the cryptic and profound statement of eternal verity which it is often taken to be. So, pressed for an explanation of my lust for wandering around the backcountry, I feel it would be cheating to give a similar response. The real reasons vary from person to person and from trip to trip, but there do

3

Why go backpacking? The beautiful and peaceful setting of this typical backpacker's camp in the Rockies is answer enough for many of us.

seem to be some common experiences and motives in heading for the woods, deserts, and hills.

Before stumbling along any farther, it may be well to talk about what backpacking is. I think of it as a way to travel in the wilderness, carrying everything necessary to live in reasonable comfort for the duration of the trip (or leg of the trip) in the country you are visiting. In his chosen environment, the backpacker is a free spirit, subject to all the harsh laws of nature, but otherwise going where and when he will. This is not a definition, but an idea, and its appeal lies in its simplicity. It is a very basic way of traveling—you want to go somewhere, you walk. You go there not because the law says you have to, because it may get you a contract, or because your boss said to, but because you feel like it, or because it looks like a good place to sleep, or because you think you may find water there. If you're prevented from getting there it will be because a cliff too steep to climb bars the way, because you're not strong enough, or because the weather is bad—that is, for very simple and elemental reasons.

I think the fascinating quality of all sorts of wilderness and backcountry travel lies in the reduction of life to its essentials: food; shelter; beauty; the confrontation with forces and circumstances which are at once comprehensible, mysterious, and so powerful that they will not be denied. The technological gadgets we carry with us are sufficient to keep us comfortable but elementary enough to leave us aware of the true dimensions of things; we are protected from the elements but remain acutely aware of them.

When you go backpacking you leave enough of the paraphernalia of civilization behind to make it just possible to achieve some real contact with the rest of the world, the nonhuman part—contact, that is, of a different kind and quality than the kind a bulldozer has with the topsoil it is pushing around. Such experiences can range from a Wordsworthian contemplation of natural beauty to a struggle with precipitous mountain walls in inclement weather, depending on your mood and inclination. The touchstone for all these experiences is that nature sets the terms. Whether you are basking or struggling, you are in contact with the sun, the wind, and the rain, and you must come to terms with them and live with them. If your trip is in the desert, the scarcity and the importance of water become a fiber of your being. It's not possible to unthinkingly turn on a tap, bringing in water from eight hundred miles away, or to turn on the air-conditioner when you get hot.

For me, at least, all this provides a very satisfying atmosphere. There is a harmonious feeling about living and traveling in country that you're not trying to change or conquer. Being at peace with the world around you instead of at war, you can develop a feeling of connection with the natural cycles that go on all the time, but from which civilization usually insulates us. If you insist on finding a utilitarian purpose for traveling in the wilderness, look at it this way: by living with minimal equipment in a wilderness situation, you gain an intuitive understanding of the basic economies of nature, an understanding which man must clearly achieve in a hurry if he is not to make the planet uninhabitable.

On a less weighty level, it's nice to get off to places where you can

5

look at the snow and the flowers, breathe air which is still relatively clean, hear the birds and the wind in the trees, feel the roughness of sandstone or the smoothness of glacially polished granite, enjoy the companionship of people where there aren't too many of them, and taste the cool crispness of mountain water that doesn't have to be chlorinated to make it drinkable. It's even nice to meet a big bear and realize that the only reason he even cares about your existence is that you're in the middle of *his* trail. (Better get out of the way.)

Finally it's good for your ego to get the feeling that you can take care of yourself with minimal help from civilization, computers, nursemaids, politicians, or policemen. Of course, normal backpacking uses a lot of the products of civilization. It must, for reasons that are discussed elsewhere in this book, but the skills used in backpacking are easily transferred to the problems of living off the land, the techniques of which are fun to try once in a while. Even if the feeling of self-sufficiency is only self-delusion, it's a nice illusion to experience, and one that is getting increasingly rare in the modern world. The *freedom* of the wild places is one of their great attractions and always has been. Whatever its overtones of romanticism, heading for the wilderness enables you to go where you want, when you want, circumscribed not by tensions or contrived rules, but only by the realities of mountains, storms, waterholes, and your own abilities. By the time you come back to the everyday world, you should have gained a sense of perspective about your surroundings and yourself, which will serve you in good stead during those surrealistic encounters with what your city-bound friends will refer to as "reality." Put a pack on your back and join those of us who think we know better.

Aside from the many heavy reasons I've talked about, most practitioners of the sport go backpacking because it's fun. Enlightenment, when it comes at all, usually arrives unexpectedly, so I generally leave it to find its own occasion and head for the hills to have a good time. You can find incomparable scenery, get away from everyday pressures and drudgery, and just have some jolly good fun by getting to the nearest trailhead with your pack and taking off. All the things like good fellowship and pleasant surroundings go along with this, as does the perpetually rediscovered pleasure that goes along with physical activity.

Some of the characteristics just mentioned have a lot in common with the reasons that people engage in any sport, but trivial as they may seem at first glance, I think that on reflection you will find that they form an essential basis for part of a whole life. I, at least, find I become slightly unbalanced by unyielding pursuit of more serious activities for too long a time, especially in the uptight atmosphere of our urban centers. Though certain little voices from my cultural background keep telling me it's immoral to do something just because it's fun, I don't really believe them anymore.

CAMPING AS AN ART

In the last few years the word "camping" has been appropriated by the promoters of various styles and sizes of mobile homes, trailer parks, and associated paraphernalia. Now an efficiently designed small house which can be driven or dragged from place to place, hooked up to the standard public utilities, and used as a convenient spot in which to watch Johnny Carson undoubtedly has its place, but living in one is not camping. This is pure prejudice on my part, but it happens to be one of the prejudices I'm fond of and intend to keep. I have no objections to someone spending thousands of dollars on equipment for the privilege of being squeezed like a sardine into a "kampground" which looks like a parking lot with a swimming pool—*if* that's what he really wants. However, I am annoyed when people who would really like to learn to enjoy wild places are conned by the entrepreneurs into thinking that they can't possibly go camping without carrying a ton of junk that will tie them forever to their car and the commercial gravel pads. I become irate and start to froth at the mouth when the same promoters use their ill-got gains to lobby for more roads, more parking, and more development in the remaining wilderness and semiwilderness public lands.

With each type of camping there is a point where an increase in the amount and variety of equipment you carry no longer brings with it a corresponding increase in comfort or enjoyment. Where that point is, of course, varies with many factors, including subjective feelings. In general, whether you're car-camping, canoeing, backpacking, or whatever, the more equipment you have the more you sacrifice mobility and the freedom to see what's over the next hill. Backpacking represents a fairly extreme compromise in the direction of mobility. Equipment is cut down in weight or bulk so much that you can carry it comfortably on your back, so you're free to travel anywhere you can walk.

Because of this, backpacking is one of the best ways to learn the art of camping, which is the art of living comfortably in primitive conditions with a minimum of effort. If you learn to do this with equipment you can carry on your back, you'll never have trouble doing it with a car, canoe, or raft available to carry your gear. In most parts of the country, you'll also be freer to choose where you want to go. Car camping is predicated on the existence of a road where you want to go and on a fairly low population density there, and the latter condition is getting rarer every day. The backpacker needs only a trail, and in many regions not even that. An area can tolerate more backpackers than cars, yet still leave the visitors feeling less crowded and the natural setting less affected (a principle discussed in more detail later in the book). Hence the backpacker has more freedom than most other travelers and campers. The main exception to this rule is in those areas of the country replete with waterways and impenetrable brush, but low on trails—there, the canoe is the free man's means of transport.

BACKPACKING AS A SPORT

As I hope I've managed to indicate, backpacking is a fine way to approach the wilderness, to experience nature. It's also a good sport, partly because it can be enjoyed at so many levels. Families with small children can make leisurely trips, perhaps covering only a few miles a day, with side trips to satisfy more ambitious members. At intermediate levels, you can vary your trips from easy to difficult, depending on your mood and aspirations. The ardent athlete will have no trouble at all concocting trips to bring him near or past the point of total exhaustion. Difficulties requiring skill, experience, and daring are easy to find if they're wanted, and these can be nearly independent of the athletic prowess or conditioning required. A young hustler may be able to easily outperform his more experienced companion in the number of easy trail miles he can cover in a day, but their roles may be completely reversed when the two confront the route-finding problems of an intricate set of desert valleys, the balance and confidence needed on a steep snow field, or the difficulties of building a fire in a soggy forest after weeks of rain. Both the challenges and the simple pleasures of backpacking are so infinitely varied that their interest never wanes, especially when all the accessory pursuits of nature watching, mountaineering, skiing, swimming, and several dozen others are added.

Sports in general are commonly pursued for many reasons and at many levels, and wilderness travel has many advantages as a recreational activity. It is inexpensive, since a good collection of backpacking equipment lasts a long, long time, and since there are essentially no additional costs except transportation to and from your favorite spots. Any number can play. Depending on your taste, you can travel alone or with a party of sixty. You can (ugh!) even make a competitive game out of it, if that sort of thing gives you satisfaction. Backpacking is the best and least boring way I know to get into shape or stay there, and for those who like to fiddle with perfection of equipment or technique, there is always plenty of interest.

A MEANS OF GETTING TO REMOTE AREAS

I think very few people backpack because they have to, at least not much of the time, but for some, backpacking is simply a means of transportation. People who have to or want to get into wilderness areas often have to backpack in, because of the nature of the terrain, its remoteness, or regulations prohibiting other means of transportation. Various occupations from geology to forestry may require backpacking into some regions, as may avocations from fishing to technical climbing. Most people I know whose occupations require extensive wilderness travel have picked the jobs for that reason, and so require little advice from me. Participants in various outdoor activities may find their horizons widened considerably with the acquisition of the skills needed to travel and live farther into the backcountry than day hikes, jeeps, or horses can take them. They may also find, like many before them, that wilderness travel itself will become as interesting as the activity that initially prompted it.

Presumably, if you've read this far you're either already addicted or are interested enough to think you might want to try getting away from the roads for a little while to see what it's like. Those who have already been on a few backpacking trips and have most of their equipment may want to skip the following section, which discusses . . .

HOW TO GET STARTED

As I've already said a few times, backpacking doesn't really have to be very hard, though it's open-ended in that you can make it as difficult as you

9

want to. It doesn't hurt to be in good shape when you start, but it's unlikely that you will be, so the best thing to do is to pick a trip you think you can manage and *go*. If you've never done any camping before, pick a very easy trip, then stop in the middle of the afternoon to give yourself plenty of time to make camp and fix supper. These things take about five times as long at the beginning, but you'll find that they go more smoothly on each trip.

I think that if you pay close attention to the details of planning, avoid excessively ambitious projects at first, and try to arrange your first few trips in good weather, you'll find that your troubles will be minor, even if you have to teach yourself everything. The easiest way to start, of course, is by going with an experienced friend a few times. A club is another good way to start, especially at most universities, though the trips run by some clubs are absurdly expensive. You must also make sure the trip you go on is within your abilities. In either case, try to get your friend or the other people on the trip to show you what to do rather than just let them do it themselves. Otherwise you may find when you go off on your own that you know no more than you did before you started.

The main problems for beginners, however, aren't really a matter of acquiring esoteric skills, getting in shape, or that sort of thing. They usually break down into two difficulties: the lack of equipment and the psychological barrier that we all tend to have about doing something we've never done before. This book is an attempt to give you some help with the latter problem; hopefully, by reading it you will no longer feel quite so intimidated by the prospect of walking off into a wilderness or semiwilderness area for a few days or weeks, since you will know a little more about the problems involved. The first difficulty, the lack of equipment, presents a number of facets, which will vary somewhat according to your particular situation. You may not be able to afford proper equipment, at least not all at once, or, if you can afford it, you might not be convinced yet that you're going to like backpacking enough to justify the cash outlay. Even if you have plenty of money and don't mind spending it, you are still left with the problem of deciding what you need.

Obviously, one of the functions of a book like this is to help you solve some of these problems. Part II is devoted to a detailed discussion of equipment, and I hope it will help you to make an intelligent choice among rapidly multiplying commercial lines. This section also devotes quite a bit of

With the exercise of restraint in your ambitions, backpacking is a fine family sport. Children enjoy having their own packs.

attention to the problems of getting things at the lowest possible prices, making them yourself, and other cost-cutting alternatives. Incidentally, making your own gear will often give you better equipment than the most expensively equipped banker, so don't despair if you're a poverty-stricken student. The boom in commercially available equipment is of pretty recent origin, and for a long time the majority of climbers' and backpackers' equipment was scrounged or homemade.

For those who have reasonable funds but want to make sure of their tastes first, there is an easy alternative in many areas—rental. These days many stores specializing in lightweight gear will rent most of the major pieces of equipment like tents, packs, and sleeping bags at fairly reasonable prices. (Availability of items like boots and sleeping bags varies a good deal according to health codes.) Renting equipment allows you to avoid a large cash outlay for major items until you are sure you want them. In addition you will get some experience along the way, and you'll be able to make a more intelligent purchase when you get around to it. If you rent several times, try to get different types of gear each time so that you'll get wider experience. Incidentally, if you plan to rent, get in touch with the store well in advance and find out whether you need to reserve equipment to assure its availability when you want it.

Those a bit harder up will prefer to avoid the rental route as much as possible, to avoid draining their limited funds without being any better off next trip. And of course, if you don't live near any stores dealing in lightweight equipment you won't have the option available.

The most inexpensive alternative is to limit your trips, at first, to areas where limited equipment and makeshift alternatives will do the job while you gradually accumulate your outfit. Special sales, making your own gear, judicious secondhand purchases, and plain scrounging can cut the costs of an adequate outfit way down. The various methods of cutting equipment costs are discussed in more detail in the second part of the book.

Once you do get started, it won't take you long to decide whether you like the sport or not, but if you do want to like it I suggest that you take it easy on your first few trips. If you're tough and game, by all means ignore this advice, but make sure the other beginners you're taking along are that way, too. This advice applies especially to those traveling with spouses, boyfriends, girlfriends, and children with whom they want to take other trips in the future. If the first one is an ordeal, you may never get your companions to go again.

Watching Your Weight   *2*

If there is one key rule in the technique of successful and enjoyable back-packing it is to keep the weight of your pack to the minimum which is consistent with safety and comfort. This is especially important for the average backpacker, who is rarely in top condition, but even the athlete in perfect shape will enjoy a trip much more with a thirty-pound pack than one tipping the scale at seventy. Since modern frames make it much easier to pack brutal loads, people often make the mistake of doing so for no good reason. Only a few special kinds of trips warrant this kind of hard, tedious work.

The greatest virtue of modern equipment is that it allows the average weekend refugee from the city to hike pleasantly with enough equipment to make him comfortable for a weekend or a fortnight. If you succumb to the urge to stuff your pack with more and more of the proliferating arsenal of gadgetry aimed at the camping market, you will soon find that your load is as heavy as it would be without the boons of convenient dehydrated food, lightweight clothing, and so on. The essence of a good backpacking outfit must be its simplicity and the multiple uses to which each of its components can be put.

The trick in assembling your gear is to take everything that you *need*, but to leave the things that "just might come in handy" at home, in the car, or on the shelf in the store. Most things in your pack should come in for heavy use, and even emergency items should be multipurpose whenever it's feasible. Proper equipment design and many other factors will affect the

Near the beginning of the Appalachian Trail on the Katahdin Plateau. The key to enjoyable backpacking is keeping the weight of your pack down.

weight of your pack, but the most important method of reducing weight is ruthless paring.

TAKING ONLY WHAT YOU NEED

Suppose you are planning a trip; your first step would probably be to make a list of the things you need to take. Clearly, all the equipment should be as light as possible, a matter which is discussed in some detail in the second part of the book. Before you even purchase, rent, or dig out the gear, however, you should go through the entire list, asking yourself whether you really need each item. Most lists, like the ones in this book, err on the side of completeness, since their authors cannot know the country and season in which you will be traveling. You will not need three extra wool shirts while walking through Massachusetts in August, or your long johns, down parka, or ice ax. If there are no problems in building fires where you are going, you can leave the stove, gasoline, and fuel can at home, and if easily broken deadwood is available, the ax and saw can stay with them.

By the time you have eliminated enough items in this way, you may find that the remainder can be carried comfortably in your two-pound rucksack instead of the four-pound frame pack—another thirty-two ounces eliminated. With the lighter load you may also find that you no longer feel the need for your heavy boots and can wear your light trail boots instead, taking a pound off each foot, which helps even more than two pounds off the back.

The difference between a sixty- and a forty-pound load, or between one that weighs twenty and one hefting at thirty-five, is difficult to describe in words. The distance you can travel, the way you feel at the end of the trail, the sense of freedom and ease of movement that a light pack can bring, are so fine that they are worth quite a bit of care and thought to achieve.

A rest stop. Your trip will be more pleasant if you pare your pack down to essentials.

BORING HOLES IN TOOTHBRUSHES

Once you have mentally eliminated what you can from the list, the next step is to assemble your equipment—all of it—into a heap on the living room floor. If you are wise, this will be done at some reasonable time. If it is now two o'clock in the morning the night before the trip, you may have to weigh the value of further paring against that of a few hours of sleep. For your first few trips at least, it's really a good idea to work this out well ahead of time.

Having assembled all that stuff, put on the clothes you would expect to wear on the trail, pack the rest of it up, and then pick up that pack. Heavy? You haven't finished chopping yet. Dump it out on the floor again and get to work. A whole cake of soap? How long is this trip going to be, anyway? Break off a little weekend-size piece. A complete roll of toilet paper? Come now, take the remains of the roll in the bathroom instead. Put that family-sized tube of toothpaste back in the cabinet and take a little plastic bag with some tooth powder. The stub of a candle is probably quite adequate for a supplemental fire-starter, and it weighs less than that full-sized candle you have. You will be amazed at how much weight you can eliminate with this kind of examination, at least until you've gotten down to your standard pack. When you find yourself sitting up one night boring holes in the handle of your toothbrush to make it lighter, go into the bathroom and look in the mirror. Do you see the gleam of the fanatic in your eyes? Congratulations, you're now a confirmed weight-watcher!

THE LIMITS OF PARING WEIGHT

Though the process of reducing the weight of your pack never really ends, there are certain factors which set the limits for each person and trip. Some of them have to do with the locale and the season in which you do your traveling. The greater and more uncomfortable the range of conditions in the places you frequent, the more extra weight you will probably have to carry to meet them. The next chapter discusses these factors in more detail, but the basic principle is simple. In the high mountains or in the far north, for example, you have to carry more clothing for safety, even when it's hot, than you would ever have to take in more temperate regions. The reason is simply that in some places it can get cold in a hurry.

Safety always has to take precedence over the elimination of a few ounces, so that first-aid and emergency supplies are subject to reduction only when their adequacy won't be diminished. Just what *is* adequate is partly a matter of personal judgment, but most of the principles are straightforward and will be taken up in various later chapters. The circumstances of your particular outing will be the main determinant. The clothing needed under survival conditions in the Yukon weighs a good deal more than that required in Missouri.

The remoteness of your trip is as much a part of the conditions as the weather and the terrain, at least insofar as the emergency equipment you have to carry is concerned. Consider your situation in the event of a broken leg on one of two trips under identical conditions except that on one you will never be more than a half-day's walk from help and on the other a week's walk. In the first case one of your party could be out and back with help or supplies within a day, while in the other you would face a one- or two-week delay. Obviously the weight of equipment required for a given level of safety is very different in the two situations.

In a similar category with the remote trip is the solo trip. In most areas used by backpackers these days it's rare to find a trip that is a genuine week of hard travel from help. On a two-week trip you might follow a range of wilderness mountains or wild canyonland, but by heading out at right angles to your line of travel, civilization is usually not so far. Hence a *group* is never *that* isolated. A man or woman traveling alone is in a different situation, however. A hard day's walk through rough country is a long, long crawl. Breaking your leg when you are alone leaves you in a survival situation similar to that of the party a long way from civilization. This is one reason why most solo travelers prefer to leave word with a friend giving their route and a reasonable date for return. Then, instead of having to carry enough equipment to survive till they can get out under their own steam, they need only carry enough to last until the friend comes looking. In well traveled country, of course, the solo traveler is not so isolated from potential help.

EXTRA-LIGHT TRAVEL

One odd feature of your pack if you really start to go light is that its weight converges with that of a basic emergency kit. For example, I find that my   *17* figure things out like a beginner.

Once you've rid your winter pack of the mosquito repellent, your desert gear of the long snow gaiters, and your high-altitude sack of the double-bitted ax, you still have the problems of choices that really do affect your comfort. You have to decide how big a tent you're willing to carry for extra headroom when you're sitting out the rain, or if it's worth carrying a tent at all. Do you want to carry a full complement of rain gear, or will a few makeshift items do? How warm a sleeping bag do you need?

Items like this will require you to balance a number of considerations, many of which will be discussed in detail in the second part of the book. You will sometimes be forced to choose between a light load on your back and a light load on your wallet. Also, though quality and light weight tend to go together these days, even if you should decide to buy very high-quality equipment, you are unlikely to want to buy or make half a dozen different outfits for the different conditions you may encounter. The best equipment is quite versatile, but you may sometimes have to pay for that versatility by carrying a heavier pack than would otherwise be necessary. If you can only afford one sleeping bag, it has to be adequate for the coldest conditions you may encounter. Clearly, a bag even barely adequate for winter conditions on Mount Washington or Long's Peak is going to be a lot heavier than necessary for summer hikes on the Appalachian Trail. If you want versatility at a reasonable cost, you will occasionally have to put up with a few extra pounds.

When balancing the demands of comfort, you should choose equipment to meet the worst conditions which you will *usually* encounter. In considering emergency gear, you have to prepare for real extremes, but in planning for comfort your guide should be the golden mean. You *may* be surprised by a storm dropping three feet of snow in the Rockies in early September, and you should be prepared to survive it, but if you prepare to be comfortable in it, you'll be miserably uncomfortable lugging a heavy pack through the pleasant weather which is far more likely. At the same time, some snow frequently falls in this place and season, so warm clothes and shelter ought to be standard equipment.

Using this principle, I carry a minimum of rain protection for summer trips in the Sierra Nevada—a water-repellent parka and a plastic tube tent would be one lightweight and satisfactory combination. In case of a week of rain, I'd get soaked through the parka, and I'd wish for a real tent even though keeping moderately dry at night, but the week of rain is pretty un-likely. For the high peaks I'd take a waterproof cagoule as well, just to be on the safe side. In New England, however, where a week of rain would be as likely as not, I'd be sure to carry both a full rainsuit—say, a cagoule and chaps—and a good shelter. A poncho serving as both shelter and rain clothing might be a good choice for California summer conditions, but it would be miserable where rain is common and prolonged, because once you pitched your shelter, you'd get soaked every time you had to leave it.

A FINAL WORD

The freedom of the backpacker inheres in his ability to travel at will over all sorts of country, carrying everything that he needs. His equipment must be as durable and as versatile as possible, and one of the most important conditions it must satisfy to be truly versatile is that it must be very light. Its other characteristics will vary somewhat, but they should be chosen to be adequate for any circumstances they may be called on to meet and as nearly ideal as possible for those they will usually meet. A desert rat's equipment will differ somewhat from the mountaineer's, but since each will have items which serve as many purposes as possible, chances are that either kit could be adapted to function fairly well in the other domain. One of the most basic requirements for enjoyable backpacking of all kinds is a light and versatile pack. It is amazing how many purposes a really simple outfit can serve. A few sweaters and a cover turn a medium-weight sleeping bag into a winter one. Many layers of good but inexpensive clothing can be taken or left home depending on the needs of the moment; and skis, saw, ice ax, or water bottles are strapped on the outside to meet the fantastically varied climate and terrain of North America. The freedom of the backcountry belongs to those who keep their weight down.

3 Nature Makes the Rules

One of the great pleasures of backpacking is the direct contact with the larger environment which it both permits and enforces. Realities from which we shield ourselves in daily life press themselves upon the attention of the backpacker. The common delusion of our species that it is master of all it surveys is quickly dispelled when the city and the automobile are left behind.

The wilderness foot traveler has to come to terms with his environment on peril of discomfort or worse, and this adjustment to the larger world begins at the planning stages of any trip. Equipment, ambitions, and attitudes must all take into account the conditions in the country and season where you are going. Clothing which is quite suitable for the moderate conditions of the lowlands is likely to be dangerously inadequate in the fickle weather of the mountains. An itinerary which might be so simple as to seem trivial in areas with good trails and easy slopes will become an endurance trial with the addition of rough terrain, steep grades, or dense cover. Lightweight footwear which is a pleasure to wear on well maintained paths becomes painfully inadequate for extended talus hopping and scrambling. The list could go on forever.

An example from my own experience may serve as a typical illustration of the need for careful advance consideration of the environment in which you are planning to travel. My first trip in the California Sierra was a ten-day backpacking tour in the northern part of the range, where the

A winter backpacking camp in New Hampshire. The backpacker has to learn to accommodate himself to the environment.

mountains are too low to support year-round snowfields. All my previous mountain experience had been acquired in higher or wetter ranges where water is never far away, and I was woefully unprepared for the conditions at the end of a dry summer in the Sierra Nevada. Two of us carried a 1½-pint water bottle and packs rather heavy with equipment and food for two weeks. As it turned out, the five-thousand-foot climb with which the trip began was completely devoid of water, the springs shown on the map having dried up. By the time we reached the lakes on the other side of the hill we were parched, having had a long and sunny lesson in the ecology of the area and in the California rainfall pattern.

The environment is not, of course, an enemy to be conquered or tamed, but it sets the ground rules which will become the facts of life you

23

will live with on your trip. Some consideration of those facts will make the living an enjoyable and worthwhile experience rather than a pointless ordeal. The thoughtful backpacker will be prepared to meet situations that can be anticipated, avoiding survival struggles except in genuinely unpredictable emergencies.

The environment in which you plan to travel will impose the dominant conditions affecting all the decisions you make about a trip, from the equipment you need to carry to conclusions you will draw about dangers and difficulties. This intimate involvement with the world around you is one of the attractions of backpacking. By going into the wilderness with minimal equipment, you accept the terms it dictates and you become more aware of the forces shaping the world around you than you could ever be when your experience of them was filtered through machines. The awareness should start at the planning stages of the trip with a brief consideration of the nature of your destination.

WATER

The availability or scarcity of water, its patterns of precipitation and drainage, its form and potability, give it such importance that it tends to overshadow other factors. In dozens of different ways water sets the conditions of travel and of life for you and your fellow creatures.

Consider a trip in the desert as an example. Observation of the world around you will reveal erosion patterns of both wind and water, but the lives of plants and animals seem dominated by the scarcity of water. Plant life is structured to waste as little water as possible through evaporation and to absorb and store any moisture that comes. Some forms of animal life lie dormant for long periods and burst into brief and frenetic activity when the hard rains of the desert fall. Your own dependence on your water supply will have long since become evident to you.

The importance of water is just as great in regions where it abounds. It may present impassable obstacles like large, fast-falling rivers, or it may provide the easiest means of access, as stream beds in densely forested areas often do. The type and density of the vegetation is, of course, dependent in large part on patterns of rainfall, as is the erosion that governs many of the landforms. The great glaciers in the Pacific ranges from the

Cascades to Alaska are the result of the heavy precipitation that those mountains receive. Ranges further inland receive less snow and thus have glaciers only at higher altitudes and latitudes.

Water as a dominating factor is most apparent to the backpacker in its role in sustaining his own life and comfort. In regions where plenty of potable water is available in many places, he can carry dehydrated food and only the water and containers he feels are needed for his convenience. Where drinkable water is available less widely, containers and foresight are required to have water when it is needed. In most parts of this country, water taken directly from streams, rivers, and lakes is not suitable for consumption until it is boiled or chemically treated. In some regions, though water is plentiful it may be impossible to make fit for drinking by any practical means. This is primarily true where people have fouled the water with chemical contaminants. In desert and ocean regions all available water may be too saline or alkaline for consumption without distillation. Finally, of course, there are desert regions where all the water you require for days or weeks must either be carried or cached in advance.

The absence of available drinking water severely limits the mobility of the backpacker, since the body requires large quantities at frequent intervals, and because the stuff is pretty heavy. A two-week supply of dehydrated food doesn't need to weigh very much, and it can be carried without much difficulty even by an unathletic person. A two-week supply of drinking water would weigh somewhere between 100 and 150 pounds, even without considering the extra requirements imposed by high altitudes or very hot, dry regions—so the availability of drinking water obviously sets a rather short limit to the distance that you can cover carrying your own water.

TERRAIN

No environmental factor is really isolated from all the others, not even such a seemingly fixed entity as the terrain through which the backpacker walks. It results both from the action of great terrestrial forces and from the nibbling of small pushes and pulls over the great reaches of geological time. The backpacker will generally consider the terrain to be set in its features, though occasionally he may become profoundly, perhaps unpleasantly,

25

aware of the processes of change. Watching a landslide, sitting out a sand-storm, or climbing a scree slope will probably convince him of the imper-manence of even the landscape.

In planning his trips the wilderness wanderer has to concern himself with both the fixed and the changing aspects of the country he hikes through, and as his understanding of the terrain of a particular region grows, so will his appreciation and his imagination in devising routes. A steep ravine of identical contour will have an altogether different meaning in two different places: in one it may provide a highway of talus blocks from top to bottom, while in another it may present difficult slabs of smooth granite or treacherous heaps of crumbling rubble.

The usual way of getting advance information about the terrain of a particular region is to consult a contour map. The technique of map read-ing is discussed in detail in a later chapter, and with practice the back-packer will find that an amazing amount of information can be deduced from modern government maps. Supplementary information on the geol-ogy, climate, and other features of an area fill in the details on the basic outline provided by the map.

Of course, the amount of information the trip planner wants or needs varies a good deal with the trip he is planning. For a weekend in a new segment of a familiar mountain range he may do no more than glance at a map of the area. A long trip through infrequently traveled and unfamiliar country, however, may require many hours of map study to determine the feasibility and requirements of the proposed route.

CLIMATE AND WEATHER

Climatic influences dominate life in the wilderness and provide much of its interest. For the backpacker, accommodation to the patterns of weather and climate are at once the most challenging and difficult problems of the sport. Since the weather can change in a few hours or minutes, the wilder-ness walker must be prepared to adapt to widely ranging conditions in a short time. The fickle nature of the weather is the main reason why back-packing equipment needs to be so versatile, suitable for wide ranges of temperature, sun or rain, wind or calm, precipitation changing from rain to sleet to snow.

Climate and weather on the North American continent have an amazing variety, and familiarity with their vagaries is the ambition of everyone seriously interested in wilderness travel. Climate and weather influence everything; the number of possible examples is infinite.

As one instance, consider the influence of snow on your trip. Along the coast ranges in California, you can plan a conventional backpacking trip at any time of the year. In winter you will carry warmer and more weather-proof clothing if you are wise, but except for river crossings, the weather will affect your comfort and speed, not your ability to travel. A couple of hundred miles farther inland in the mountains of the Sierra Nevada the story is quite different. Sierra Nevada means snowy range, and the heavy winter snowfall in the high country often makes travel without skis or snowshoes not just difficult but impossible. The snows in winter make a smooth highway for the passage of the cross-country traveler equipped with skis, covering boulders, small trees, streams, and houses. The same snow arrives in storms of quite amazing ferocity, sometimes trapping even the well equipped traveler for days. The backpacker encountering the first big snowfall of the year in the wilderness had best be prepared for a tough trip out.

In regions where the climate permits snow to rest on the ground throughout the year, permanent snowfields and glaciers may provide the traveler with easy paths or formidable obstacles. Such a climate always leaves us a gift of spectacular and wildly beautiful scenery. Other ramifications range from the fantastic geological effects produced by glaciation to the impenetrable thickets that often result from the fine watering of lower valleys by the snowfields.

Of the many environmental factors which will influence your trip, climate and weather are, along with the availability of drinking water, the most important matters for advance investigation in planning a trip. A misjudgment of terrain may mean that you won't get nearly as far as you expected, but this is usually not particularly important unless you are heading for a cache or rendezvous. A real misjudgment of climatic conditions will probably result in your being pretty uncomfortable, and it may be really serious. There are many instances of campers unfamiliar with severe climates getting into trouble in the high mountains and in the far north, because they were inadequately equipped for a sudden onset of storm and cold.

I always try to carry adequate equipment to keep me comfortable in any weather that I might reasonably expect to encounter on a trip and to keep me alive in any conditions that might possibly occur. In order to make judgments like this, however, you must know something about the area to which you are going. Such knowledge must include both average and extreme conditions. Average temperature in arctic and subarctic regions in the summer is pretty high, for example, because the sun is shining most of the time. Things can change in a hurry, though, and you had better be ready if they do.

VEGETATION

The plant cover in a particular region is dependent on many factors, including those already mentioned, and it in turn plays an important part in storing water, holding down erosion of the landscape, and so on. For the backpacker, the vegetable cover is of particular interest for still another reason; it affects his mobility as much as the terrain does. Anyone who has ever bushwhacked through really thick forest or bush will know immediately what I mean. Others may take this as a warning. In some areas working through a few miles of forest may take days, while in others the obstructions presented even by heavy woods may be only minor.

In practical terms the plant cover will determine whether the backpacker can plan to travel cross-country with comparative freedom, or whether he must confine his travel to established trails. Where there are no trails and the cover is thick, route-finding problems center on ways of avoiding brush. Under such conditions even a very long detour may often prove to be a shorter route in time than a seemingly direct way.

THE BACKPACKER AND HIS SURROUNDINGS

Only a few of the many environmental factors which affect the backpacker have been mentioned. There are others, and all of them together are woven into a fabric so complex that the individual threads cannot always be distinguished from one another. The success and ease of the wilderness traveler depend on his ability to understand this pattern and to follow the warp

28

of the weave rather than trying to go against it. As his understanding of a particular sort of country grows, he will learn how to find water, how to make the easiest way across the terrain and through the brush, and how to keep track of his wanderings easily. The greatest aid to understanding a particular environment is an open and observant mind.

This understanding begins long before a properly planned trip, whether through previous knowledge, observation of a nearby area, or investigation of the area of the proposed trip through books, maps, friends, or even a look from the roadhead before you decide what you will need.

Of the many sources of information available to the backpacker, the topographic map is the most useful. Reading one is discussed in a later chapter. An experienced map reader with a little knowledge about the geography of an area can pick out campsites and gauge the length of a day's walk from a topo map.

Some other sources of information are listed in the appendix. Important facts are the average minimum and maximum temperatures in the place and season where you plan to travel, the extreme highs and lows that have been reported there over the last ten years or so, rain and snowfall patterns, and so on. Obviously, the need to look up these items is only important for areas which are strange to you. If you live in Ohio and are planning a backpacking trip a hundred miles from your own home, you don't need climatic summaries to tell you what sort of weather to expect. On the other hand, if you are making your first trip to the British Columbia coast range, you'd better get all the information you can.

In some parts of the country, you can be fooled by very short distances. This is particularly true in and near the mountains, which often make their own weather and drastically influence the weather of other areas. By traveling up the side of a mountain, you can get into a completely different climate very quickly. The climate at high altitude bears great resemblance to that of regions far to the north. For example, the vegetation on the plateau of Maine's Mount Katahdin is similar to that of Greenland. Though effects vary to some extent, a rise of a thousand feet in altitude brings one to a climate similar to that three hundred to five hundred miles farther north. The backpacker can change climatic zones faster by climbing a mountain than he could by flying north in an airplane. He will miss the midnight sun, but may have an even better chance to be caught in a summer snowstorm.

In the mountains the weather can change completely in a very short time. Storm clouds building in the Rockies.

Mountains cause many other effects that concern the backpacker. By driving a short distance across even a minor range, the traveler may pass from a fairly wet zone with easily available water into a desert in the rain shadow of the mountains. There are many cases like this where major geographical features produce great discontinuities in climate. The backpacker should be wary of assumptions that a short drive or walk will make little difference in conditions.

The tremendous variety of the American landscape provides challenge and interest to the backpacker that would be hard to equal. A day's hike can take him from lush forests to alpine meadows and snowfields, and another day can have him well out into the desert. Mountains and ocean beaches stand side by side. The wilderness traveler who remains keenly aware of the necessity of accommodating himself to his surroundings can spend a long lifetime sampling these possibilities without even coming close to knowing them all.

30

The Art of Travel 4

The backpacker travels by walking, an art which is in a severe state of decline these days. Beginners at backpacking are even likely to find themselves in the embarrassing position of having to *learn* how to walk. It is important to admit the need, however, at least to oneself, in order to consciously develop the habits necessary to get you farther than the garage without completely exhausting you. Young people in reasonably good shape can get away with inefficient walking while they unconsciously acquire the habits needed for negotiating miles of rough terrain comfortably with packs, but if you are in mediocre shape, you had better use your physical resources as economically as possible.

LEARNING TO WALK

Walking on even moderately rough terrain can be very tiring to those who have not become used to it. Once some practice has given you the knack, you may find that miles in the wilderness are less of a strain than an equal number on the hard pavement. In any case, the first trick in walking long distances is to develop a reasonable stride. Most people accustomed to walking only to the file cabinet or the refrigerator get used to taking very short steps. Swing your legs out in front and put your body into your walk. Of course, your stride shouldn't be exaggerated, and it is always subject to

Even on a good trail like this one, obstacles are the rule rather than the exception. Footing is likely to seem rough to those used to city walking.

the demands of pace, which will be discussed shortly. Even a very slow walk, however, should have rhythm and spirit—get a little spring in your knee and toe. Picking up your feet is most of the work, and adding six or eight inches to your stride can add up to a lot of extra miles by the end of the day.

Obstacles are not the exception in wilderness walking; they are the rule. Prepared trails wind through many extra miles to avoid them, and for good reason. The constant presence of rocks, fallen trees, stumps, roots, mudholes, and other barriers makes it very important that the hiker trying to conserve strength avoid wasting energy on each obstacle. In general, anything large enough to break your stride should be circumvented if this is reasonably convenient. Stepping over the obstruction is second choice, lifting your body and pack weight as little as possible; and stepping up and climbing over ranks a poor third. It is usually much less tiring to walk around fallen trees than to clamber over them, especially when you are wearing a heavy pack. The combined heights of all the rocks and trees you could have walked around can add up to a lot of climbing by the end of the day. In addition to this energy factor, such obstacles often provide insecure footing and invite accidents.

Obstacles tend to shade into the category of generally rough footing, especially in rocky country. This is where the matter of breaking stride as the dividing point comes into the matter. In rocky areas a trail is often defined simply by a cleared route through the brush or a line of ducks crossing a talus fan, and the hiker must pick his footing over the rocks. Practice will enable the backpacker to balance his way along such routes without breaking stride, picking the route ahead with his eyes to avoid more up and down than necessary.

The key to this and other kinds of walking is *pace*. One of the most conspicuous marks of the beginner is his inability to pace himself properly. An experienced walker, even one who is out of shape, knows how to pace himself to make the most efficient possible use of his muscles (though vanity may occasionally make him forget). The object of pacing is to keep the individual hiker or group going steadily at the fastest speed that can be maintained, giving walking a rhythm which keeps the muscles working well and eats up the miles. The most common mistake of the novice is to try to go too fast, forcing his muscles to work jerkily and necessitating frequent stops for breath and for rest.

The start-stop routine is tiring, inefficient, and unenjoyable. It is characterized by brief spurts and panting halts along the trail, especially an uphill one, and by long and frequent rest stops collapsed by the side of the trail. There are a lot of reasons to avoid this routine. It is slow. Extended and repeated stops will hold you back much more than a slow pace that is fairly steady. In addition, your muscles cannot work at their best with this kind of pace. Long rests allow the muscles to stiffen, so that it is hard to get started again. Pushing on too hard in between stops, though it may temporarily convince you that you're getting somewhere, taxes your muscles in a way which you cannot afford if you're out of shape and trying to get somewhere without having to call for helicopter service.

When the muscles are pushed beyond their ability for continuous effort, waste materials accumulate in the tissue. As the concentration of excess wastes builds up, you get tired and you have to stop until some of them have been carried off. The body cannot get rid of these wastes very efficiently, so you have to rest a long time. Roughly, the harder you push yourself past the capacity of your body to handle these wastes as they are made, the less efficiently your muscles will operate. So unless you are in good enough shape to be well on top of the situation, when you get to that hill don't dash madly for the top and stand there panting; go up it slowly and steadily, using your shortness of breath as a guide that you're pushing too fast.

Though you should avoid going too fast and though this is the most common beginners' mistake, I don't mean to imply that you should avoid making any demands on the body. The push should be in the form of sustained effort, and a pace should be considered too fast precisely because it cannot be maintained. Leisurely walking is fine some of the time, but the body must also work hard to develop reasonable muscle tone and endurance. If you expect to get into decent condition within a reasonable length of time, you'll have to put up with a little discomfort occasionally. See the chapter on physical conditioning for more details.

WALKING UPHILL

Climbing hills requires a slower pace than moving on even ground, and for the most part this just means that you shorten and slow your stride somewhat. Try to maintain a rhythm rather than get into the habit of spurting up a few steps to hang panting on a tree and then repeating the process up to a rock a bit farther up. On really steep and strenuous grades, especially at high altitudes, you may find that you can't maintain a normal rhythmical pace. At this point you should switch to the *rest step,* which enables you to incorporate a rest in each step while still maintaining a steady, even pace.

It's hard to get a feel for the rest step except in hard climbing where you need it; then it becomes quite natural as soon as you get the knack. Suppose you are stepping up with your weight on your right leg. When you put your left foot down, lock your right knee and leave all your weight on the right leg. Pause and rest for a short time before shifting your weight to the left leg and stepping up. After stepping up, lock the left knee, and leave your weight on your left leg for the rest interval. The length of each rest interval will depend on how hard the slope is, but the important thing is to maintain a regularity of pace.

When you are walking in rough country, especially with a heavy pack, learn to walk with your eyes well ahead of your feet. Use the ground to your advantage whenever possible. Watch the trail ahead; climbing two steps here may save five uphill steps a few yards farther along. Balancing along some rocks may save some up and down. Cutting to the left may avoid a fallen tree. Walking with your eyes will eventually become an established habit, but you have to cultivate it at first.

TAKING CARE OF YOUR FEET

Whatever violence you're willing to endure in the rest of your body either on trips or in exercising, you cannot afford to brutalize your feet. As the injunction goes, "Be kind to your ass, for it bears you." The backpacker's bearers are his feet and they will make him rue any unkindnesses. In real wilderness areas, whether in summer or winter, the mark of the "tenderfoot" is his sore, blistered, or frostbitten feet, which result from improper care.

The first rule in taking care of your feet is simply to prevent common foot ailments from occurring. Corns, bunions, and ingrown toenails are really serious matters on the trail, the more so because there's not much you can do about them the night before the trip. All these ailments can be prevented and cured, and it is foolish to allow them to occur or to neglect them if they do. The most common cause is improper footwear. Fallen arches are a different problem, and they may require special arches in your hiking boots. If you ever have trouble with painful arches, try your boots well in advance, and get special arches put in if you need them. The strain on your feet is much greater on long walks with a heavy pack, though wilderness footwear is generally better for the feet than city slickers' pointy shoes.

Getting your feet into shape is at least as important as preparing any other part of your body, especially if your first trip in the season is to be a long one. Breaking in a new pair of boots (discussed in a later chapter) will help toughen your feet as well. In general, walking with proper footwear is the best way to toughen your feet, but many people also find it helpful to bathe them in alcohol or alum solution as an aid to toughening. If they are tender, bathing them when the opportunity arises, using foot powder, and

35

changing the socks frequently are all helpful measures. If you bathe your feet at rest stops, an excellent and refreshing practice, be sure they are dry before putting your boots back on.

BLISTERS

However tough your feet ought to be, proper care during trips is mandatory. A hot spot or chafing feeling on your foot is a warning that a blister is forming, and it must be heeded soon in order to head the blister off. Blisters should be prevented rather than treated. If the chafing is caused by loose boots or by wet or dirty socks, tightening boots or changing socks may solve the problem. Otherwise, the irritated spot should be covered, preferably with moleskin, which can be obtained at any drugstore and which ranks as one of the hiker's best friends. Adhesive tape may also be used. If you wait too long and get a blister anyway, don't break it unless you have to—that is, unless you've let it get so bad that you can't fit it and your foot both into the boot at the same time. In this case lance it with a sterile needle or knife point, making only a small hole at the side for the liquid to drain. Whether the blister is intact, broken, or lanced, wash the area well, paint it with antiseptic, cover with a small, thin piece of sterile gauze or cotton made slippery with ointment or Vaseline, and then cover with moleskin or adhesive tape. On a long trip keep this spot scrupulously clean, since if you get an infected foot you may really be in trouble.

At the risk of being pedantic, I reiterate: don't get blisters in the first place. Prevent them by keeping your feet clean, taking care of them on the trail, carrying enough socks to be able to change them when necessary, and using proper socks and boots.

SORE FEET

Unless you have been doing a lot of hiking and backpacking recently, you can expect your feet to be tired at the end of a day on the trail—you might even consider them sore, under any reasonable definition of the word. Really sore feet, though, are bruised badly enough to prevent your walking on them without a good deal of pain, and they can be avoided with boots that fit properly and are sturdy enough for the terrain. Wearing footgear that is too light over very rough country with a heavy pack is a good way to get sore feet. The chapter on footwear in the equipment section goes into detail on the choice of boots and socks. A backpacker wearing sneakers on the trail should be wary of punishing his feet too much, unless they are well toughened.

Keep your toenails trimmed to a reasonable length for hiking. Downhill walking with long toenails can create some very painful bruises. It is also a good idea to tighten your boot laces a bit before starting long downhill sections to prevent your feet from sliding about too much.

Your feet will be much more comfortable if you change socks frequently. Dirty socks are uncomfortable, and they provide less insulation in cold weather. Usually it is convenient to wash your dirty socks out when you change them, hanging them on the outside of your pack or somewhere in camp to dry. In wet weather wring them out as much as possible and hang them in the peak of the tent. Of course, where water is scarce, as it is in desert and winter camping, you may be unable to wash socks, and under these conditions you may want to carry a few extra pairs.

EATING ON THE TRAIL

Whenever you're demanding that your body produce a lot of energy, especially in sustained effort, don't neglect its need for food. Hauling yourself and your pack to the top of a ridge requires a good deal of work, and your muscles won't do that work without fuel any more than your car would without gasoline. The fuel can come either from recently digested food or from the body's reserves of fat. Even though most of us can easily afford to lose some of our fat reserves we should recognize that they are not readily available to the muscles on an instant's notice. If you starve your body in order to force it to use up last month's beer, you'll have to pay the price of a slower climb up the hill and slightly shaky knees at the top.

If your main concern is to make your body run as efficiently as possible between the roadhead and camp, you will have to see that it has fuel available the whole way. Most backpackers do this by eating small snacks throughout the day, beginning at breakfast and nibbling at rest stops or sucking on candy along the trail. This is a particularly efficient way to keep the muscles supplied with energy, since it both maintains the level of immediately available nutrients in the blood and avoids the need to eat large midday meals, which require that much of the blood supply be shifted from the muscles to the stomach. Instead of a major repast, lunch becomes a slightly larger snack eaten in a longer rest period than the others before and after.

The body is really quite capable of adjusting to widely varying styles of eating, so my advice of frequent snacks is merely suggested because it seems particularly suitable for the weekend backpacker whose system is not tuned for sustained effort day in and day out. Frequent small snacks keep usually sedentary muscles operating in an efficient way on the trail. On long trips it's easy to get your digestive system used to whatever regimen seems desirable.

Food is discussed in more detail in Chapter 6, along with various ways of keeping your body fueled without too much trouble. In choosing trail food remember that when you are pushing your muscles hard, you are less likely to become fatigued if you keep your blood sugar up, which is easily done by drinking a sweet beverage or sucking on a piece of hard candy. Fats and proteins "stick to your ribs" because they take longer to digest, but they are less useful for quick energy.

WATER AND SALT

Drinking water is much more critical for the backpacker than food, since the body can function with no food for much longer than it can do without water, and since the weight of a day's water is much more than that of food for the same period. Fortunately, in many backpacking areas finding drinking water presents no problem. Frequent stream-crossings often bring the wilderness walker into almost continuous contact with better drinking water than that available from the tap at home. Where this is true, there is no problem, and you can simply have a drink when you feel like it.

The blissful situation of having readily available pure water is confined to quite limited regions, however, and in large areas of the country there is virtually nowhere left with a pure stream. Any vestige of civilization upstream makes all water (except tap water intended for drinking) suspect. Besides the problem of contamination, in many regions surface water is un-

Drinking water is more critical for the backpacker than food.

common enough to make you pretty thirsty between creeks and springs.

General precautions about the potability of water and methods of purification are given in Chapter 6. It is important to remember that one drink of bad water can ruin your trip, and it may get you in serious trouble if you are far away from medical care when you come down with the bug you drank. In some kinds of places the water can safely be assumed to be pure, but when there is any doubt it must be purified. In areas with suspect water this generally means carrying a water bottle with treated water. When you reach a stream, drink your fill from the bottle, refill it, and drop in the required purification tablets. Don't try to drink the water before the chemicals have had time to work.

Travel in dry country requires carrying enough containers for an adequate water supply between resupply points, including provision for emergencies. The actual quantities you will need depend very much on temperatures, humidity, the difficulty of the terrain and weight of your pack, and various individual factors like physiology and personal stoicism. See Chapter 6 for details.

One of the best ways to save yourself from having to pack too much

39

weight in dry country is to learn to "tank up" when water is available. People used to nearby water faucets generally drink only until their thirst is satisfied, but the body can comfortably absorb a good deal more water than that. Once you get in the habit it is a simple matter to sip your way through a quart or two of water while you are puttering around in the morning or at a lunch stop near a waterhole. After I learned this trick I found myself more comfortable after a day carrying only a quart of water when I used to be carrying a half-gallon.

Other tricks for conserving water are well known: sucking on hard candies or pebbles, taking sips and washing them around rather than drinking in swallows, and so on. You can learn to get along on less water, but there is definitely a limit to this. For one thing, most of these methods assume you'll reach water at lunch or the end of the day or some time soon. Tanking up isn't a way to get along with much less water, but simply a way to consume it at more convenient times. Your body needs a lot of water in hot weather, and except in survival and endurance situations, it is senseless to deprive it unnecessarily or to experiment too precipitously with reduced supplies. In hot weather evaporation is the way your body cools itself, and without enough water it can overheat dangerously quickly. Also, as a practical matter, if you become too dehydrated, you will have to spend some time restoring your body's water reserves. You'll travel faster by carrying more weight in water than if you carry less but have to stop for several hours when you come to a spring just because you've allowed yourself to get too dry.

It is obvious that in country where water is scarce, its location pretty well governs one's line of travel, stopping places, and general view of the trip. One travels from Big Water Spring to Little Fork Creek to Jackson's Well. Trail food in country like this should be chosen to go down easily with small quantities of water. Save the peanut butter and Logan bread for a wetter trip.

Not all thirst in dry country indicates a need for water, though. Whenever you do a lot of perspiring, whether aware of it or not, you need to replace the salt lost in perspiration as much as the water. Heavy perspiration uses up more salt than you normally get in your food, and the deficit has to be made up. Oddly enough, one of the signs of a need for salt is often an insatiable thirst. More advanced signs include muscle cramps. In general, you can expect to need extra salt if you are drinking a great deal of water.

Some people like the simple expedient of taking salt pills to replace what they sweat away. These are hard on the stomach, though, and I prefer to just use ordinary table salt, putting extra in my food, sprinkling a little in my water, or licking it in small amounts from the back of my hand. If you use tablets, take them just before drinking or eating to avoid nausea.

CLOTHING

The importance of your clothing depends mainly on the kinds of places where you plan to go. In other words, it depends on whether the main function of your garments is to protect your anatomy against the elements and the hazards of the trail or to satisfy the needs of propriety and your ego. I know very little about either your ego or propriety, so I will confine my remarks to those situations where protection is important.

You may want your clothes to protect you from scrapes with brush, thorns, rocks, and the like, to ward off the rain, to shade you from the sun, to keep you warm, to break the wind, or any combination of these. The equipment section of the book goes into considerable detail on choosing and making clothes to do these things, so all we're really concerned with here are a few principles for making the best use of your clothes when your body needs shelter from one of the beasties just mentioned.

There's not really much to say about protection from cacti, scrub oak, sharp volcanic rock, and such. The first principle is to stay away from all that stuff, and if you can't, have smooth, tough clothes that keep you from getting all scratched up and which don't get immediately torn to shreds. Move slowly and smoothly through brush so that when your clothes do snag you'll be able to stop before you rip the seat off your pants. Good luck!

WALKING IN THE RAIN

Much of the time, rain really doesn't present much of a problem to the backpacker, providing he is properly equipped and has the right philosophical attitude. On some occasions, however, wet weather makes a state of reasonable comfort so hard to achieve that the most skillful wilderness traveler is likely to be challenged.

The main problem with rain is, of course, that it tends to get you wet. Worse, as the days and weeks of rain wear on, it gets everything you are carrying with you wet, too. It requires a true act of will to smile and hold forth on the joys of backpacking without heavy sarcasm when, after slogging through two weeks of rain, you set about pitching your soaked and muddy tent at least high enough above the water line to ensure against your drowning that night, all the while trying to decide whether it would be warmer inside or outside your sodden sleeping bag.

Aside from the misery it can inflict, rain can also be really threatening under certain conditions. Probably the most dangerous kind of storm one can encounter in the wilderness is cold rain driven by high winds, followed by a drop in temperature. If the rain destroys the insulation value of your clothing, the cold wind can easily kill you unless you find shelter.

The methods of handling rain are: (1) avoid it, (2) stay dry despite it, (3) at least keep your spare clothing and sleeping equipment dry, even though you get wet, (4) maintain an ability to dry yourself and your gear out, even if you get soaked, or (5) endure it. You may select your own order of preference. Conditions will probably dictate the choice anyway.

Whether and how hard you try to avoid traveling in the rain depends on your aesthetic sense, the depth of your masochism, and the area you travel in. When you get caught, of course, you have to be prepared with the right equipment and philosophical attitude. Some areas get so much rain that there simply isn't any question of picking a dry weekend—there aren't any. Similarly, on long trips you just have to take the weather as it comes, after the first few days. All this being true, let's suppose you have carefully chosen storm gear appropriate to the place and season—what to do when the rains come?

The first thing to do is to *do something*, even if it is only to decide that you are dealing with an afternoon shower and would just as soon get wet. Don't walk along for a while waiting to see whether it's really going to rain and allowing your clothing to be gradually soaked because you're too lazy to get out the poncho. If you need rain gear, get it out when those first few drops start coming down, or before. Staying dry is generally easier than getting dry. If your pack needs some kind of special cover to protect the contents, it's important to take care of this right away, lest your spare clothes and sleeping bag get wet.

If the weather is warm enough, the simplest way to keep your clothes dry is to put them in the pack, and just wear your boots and a bathing suit, shorts, or whatever, enjoying the shower. It isn't always warm enough for this method, so generally you'll have to put on your poncho, cagoule, parka, or whatever. Try to allow as much ventilation as possible, since all waterproof garments tend to condense moisture from your body on their inside surfaces, soaking your clothes with your own perspiration. This problem is particularly acute in cold weather, precisely when you can least afford to get your clothes wet. Don't draw the openings at the neck, bottom, and sleeves of a rain parka tight unless this is necessary because of wind-driven rain. Avoid sweating when you are wearing rain gear by slowing down if necessary.

Don't forget about your pants when it starts raining. Weather permitting, shorts work well in the rain, with long pants staying dry in the pack for the evening chill. A similar effect may be achieved by simply rolling up the trouser legs. If you're wearing long pants, though, you'll probably need to put on rain chaps or pants. Wet brush, water dripping from cagoule or poncho, and wind-driven rain will often soak your pants in no time unless they are protected.

When the rain first starts it is time to think about fires if you're in wooded country and you want a blaze later. It's much easier to gather kindling for an evening or lunchtime fire before everything on the ground gets wet than to wait until later. By the same reasoning, if you build a lunchtime fire, use it to dry some kindling for the evening one.

Reasonably comfortable travel in the rain demands the same foresight and common sense that is the secret of all effective wilderness travel. On a Sunday walk it is largely a matter of taste how much trouble one bothers to take to keep dry, since wet clothes can soon be shed for a hot bath. You may just not worry about keeping dry during a summer afternoon thundershower in the southern Rockies if you are sure that the dry evening winds will take care of your wet clothes anyhow. On the other hand, on long trips in humid areas where the duration of rain is unpredictable, a great deal of care is often needed to avoid getting any wetter than necessary, and this is particularly true at high altitudes or in spring and fall when falling temperatures may follow the rain. For mountain travelers especially, staying dry is very important. Backpackers who travel in adequately wooded areas may want to use fires to dry themselves and their clothes out. Fire building is discussed elsewhere, but it is worth mentioning here that a small fire in front of a tarp or poncho quickly pitched as a lean-to can do wonders to raise flagging spirits on a rainy day. A little hot soup for lunch is never more welcome.

WALKING IN COLD WEATHER

Except for deep snow, which is discussed elsewhere, the only real problem presented by backpacking in cold weather is the need for special care in the choice and the use of equipment. Warm clothing and shelter must be carried and they must be kept as dry as possible. The principles of insulation and the choice of clothing will be detailed later in the book, but the best available equipment may become quite useless if it is allowed to get wet.

The first principle of cold weather walking is *don't sweat*. The colder the weather, the more important this injunction becomes. The most common mistake of the beginning cold-weather walker is to steam up a hill with all his warm clothes on, not realizing that he is working up a good lather. When he reaches the top of the hill, ready for a rest, he is hit in the face by an icy wind which chills him to the core because of his sweat-soaked clothing. The cold-weather traveler has to maintain adequate ventilation to carry away any perspiration and to keep adjusting the layers of his clothing to keep his body from becoming overheated or chilled. As soon as you start to warm up on the morning trail, take off your hat or unzip your parka. When you stop to rest put on the hat and zip up the parka, since you will cool down as soon as you stop working.

Food is more important in cold weather. If your blood sugar supply runs low in normal temperatures, you will probably find that you are tired and have less stamina. In cold weather when your body runs out of easily available fuel you may not be able to maintain your body temperature properly, so make sure to keep yourself supplied with food.

The rules and techniques for cold-weather travel are discussed in detail in Chapter 20, and there is a long discussion in Chapter 9 of the body's thermostat and the clothing it needs for help in cold weather, so no more detail is given here. Remember, though, that cold weather requires somewhat more careful preparation for safe travel. Cold is deceptive because some cooling factors can change so quickly. *Rain and wind combined with cold are very dangerous to the unprepared.* Don't be caught by surprise.

CARRYING A PACK

Traveling easy terrain with a pack of reasonable weight is not very different from walking without it, except that you will go more slowly and get tired sooner. It is important to choose your pack carefully if you want to be comfortable on your first few trips, though if you're willing to make the effort you can train yourself to carry any kind of suitable pack. The chapter on packs discusses this choice in detail, but most beginners will finally decide on a contoured aluminum or magnesium pack frame with a mated bag. The key to using this type of pack effectively is the waist belt. Make sure you have a good one, and then learn to use it. Get into the shoulder straps first and hunch your shoulders up to raise the pack; then cinch the waistband just above the hips. When you let your shoulders down, most of the weight of the pack should rest on your hips. If it doesn't or if the waistband is uncomfortable, either the pack needs adjusting or something is wrong with it.

Most of the time the weight of the frame pack should rest almost completely on the hips, and the shoulder straps should serve mainly to balance the pack. If you tip the top of your body back and forth a bit you should pass a balance point where no weight at all is on the shoulders. Of course, in a day's walking you will shift the load to the shoulders on occasion for relief of the hips or for other reasons. The fact is, though, that the hips are much better supported for load carrying, providing the load can be got on them without forcing the rest of the body into an unnatural position, and this is what the contoured frame pack permits. The shoulders and the neck require a lot of training to develop the musculature needed to haul heavy loads.

One of the purposes of the contour frame pack is to raise the center of gravity high on the frame, which makes for easy carrying but also for unstable balance. In most situations this is really not much of a problem, and you will soon get used to it, but there are occasions when you will not appreciate this characteristic of modern frames. This high center of gravity makes balancing across slippery log bridges even more delicate than such maneuvers already are. Successfully negotiating these obstacles with a loaded contour frame requires that you develop a new set of reactions, keeping the top of your body carefully erect and making any violent adjustments of balance with your legs and arms. Do your fancy footwork while keeping your torso sedately poised directly above the place you want to be.

A difficult choice faces one in places like this: whether to remove the waistband or not. Leaving it on generally ensures surer footing in slips, but if you are crossing a dangerous spot, you may want to unhitch the belt so that you can get rid of the pack in case you fall in.

The most awkward spots for the wearer of a contour frame are places that require ducking forward, because the high center of gravity is then trying to pitch you on your nose, while at the same time the top of the pack is trying to catch on every available nubbin and branch. This often occurs in bushwhacking, and in passing under fallen trees and boulders overhanging the trail. It is often easier in situations like this to take off the pack and carry it ahead of you.

Carrying rucksacks, older types of frames, and other kinds of packs presents no particular problems other than getting your shoulders strong enough to carry the required load. More care is needed when placing equipment in those packs which don't have a frame holding them away from the back. A pot edge digging into your spine will become intolerable very quickly. Make sure things are packed comfortably before you leave, or you will have to repack on the trail. All packs should be loaded so that the center of gravity is as close to the back and as high as possible. The only exception is that very high packs like contour frames may need the center of gravity lowered for difficult terrain. Special care is needed in packing old-fashioned large rucksacks which hang low and protrude far out at the bottom. Skill is required to get the load close to the frame in such packs, since the big, heavy objects always gravitate to the projecting bottom. If this is permitted to occur, the load will pull you backward, requiring you to lean so far forward that you'll be doing more work holding the pack over your legs than carrying it up the trail.

Some types of frame rucksacks allow some of the weight to be shifted to the hips with the frame and perhaps a waist strap, but most of the load must usually be carried by the shoulders. Waistbands on rucksacks are generally intended to keep the pack from shifting and throwing you off balance on difficult terrain.

LAKE, STREAM, AND RIVER CROSSINGS

Since prehistoric times, one of the great problems of foot travelers has been the crossing of streams, lakes, and rivers, and such crossings remain one of the most formidable difficulties for anyone traveling away from areas frequented by bridge builders and tunnel diggers. If you are following a standard trail, you can usually expect at least crude bridges to exist where there are no good fords or stepping stones. If you are traveling across country without benefit of trails, though, you have no such guarantees. Even the trail traveler in an unusually wet year or in an off-season may find that the usual crossing of a difficult river has been washed away or is under several feet of very fast, cold water. Finally, there are many trails which include fairly difficult stream crossings that may be beyond the skill of many backpackers.

The most obvious way to get past a body of water is to walk around it, a method suited mainly to lakes but sometimes necessary with fast mountain streams in spring. A look at the map may give a helpful hint on the practicality of such an enterprise. In difficult wilderness travel, days or weeks of travel may be needed to get around water obstacles.

A lake on a large river may in fact be the best place to cross, since the problem of fast currents is eliminated. Lake crossings can be accomplished with rafts or by swimming, or through some appropriate combination dictated by the temperature and size of the lake, the availability of materials for a raft, and the skill and ambition of the traveler. In any case, a conservative attitude should prevail, especially if the lake is large. A lake that looks only a mile or two across may actually measure ten, and an improvised raft is not the best vessel to get caught with on a windy afternoon in the middle of a large lake. Improvised rafts are not suitable for crossing really big bodies of water.

Rafts may range from full-sized platforms big enough to carry everything and everyone high and dry to a two-log affair which will keep the top of your pack dry and with which you can swim across a warm lake. For the two-log kind lash the pack between the logs with the logs spread far enough from one another to prevent tipping. Rafts made with three or more logs should have a cross-pole lashed diagonally across as a brace.

On any trip where possible rafts or float crossings are anticipated, a sturdy air mattress should be preferred as a bed to a foam pad, because it can be blown up to make a good float if you choose to swim your pack across. It should be inflated and tied to the pack on a raft trip in case of accident. Large plastic bags closed with rubber bands will protect your sleeping bag, clothing, etc., inside the pack and will also make the whole load quite buoyant.

Long poles are usually more effective for propelling rafts than paddles, but some sort of improvised paddle should be taken in case the lake gets too deep for poling. Lashing the raft should be done with nylon parachute cord, and you should make sure that it is absolutely secure before risking your life by trusting it. Similar care is necessary in preparing a float for your pack if you plan to swim across. Depending on a cheap plastic air mattress that might be punctured halfway across, for example, would not be very prudent.

Rivers can sometimes be crossed using a raft or swimming your pack across, but even more care must be exercised than in lake crossings. Don't rely on your estimate of the speed of the current. Smooth-flowing water is often very deceptive. Throw in pieces of wood and watch how fast they go. Throw some of them as far out as you can—the current may be much faster on the other side. Be particularly wary if there is a cutbank on the other side or if you are on the inside of a curve. Whenever feasible, you should walk far down the river before attempting a crossing, in order to find out about any dangerous spots you might be carried into by the current. The inspection may also reveal a ford that will enable you to walk across. Don't be in too much of a hurry to get across; floating or swimming big rivers is serious business.

Under no circumstances should you attempt a raft or float crossing unless you are a strong swimmer; it is foolhardy. No matter how good a swimmer you are, be extremely careful, and don't go unless you are sure of the safety of the crossing. Improvised rafts are not good white-water craft. Be particularly wary if the water is cold. No matter how good a swimmer you are, really cold water will reduce you to numb incompetence incredibly quickly. If the water is cold, don't make any crossings that might result in a spill.

Raft and float crossings of large rivers and of lakes can make a trip into a real adventure, but they demand a lot of extra care. If the water is too fast, the wind too high, or the rapids too close, spend an extra day or week making a safe crossing, or turn back.

More common ways for the backpacker to cross moving water are to leap across on stones, ford at a shallow spot, walk across on fallen trees, or use some combination of these. In winter or spring snow bridges may be used. The great advantages of stones and logs are evident, especially when the snowmelt streams of the mountains are encountered—you don't have to get your feet wet. As you become more experienced, you will become more adept at leaping across on rocks. With a big, fast stream this can be a real test of confidence and balance. The main trick is to plan your route ahead of time so that you can keep moving during the actual crossing. A continuous series of linked jumps is easier than separate leaps and gives you a better chance to recover if a rock rolls or proves slippery.

With relatively small creeks, the decision on whether to try a series of boulder jumps is really a matter of taste, since a slip just means a cold bath or perhaps a broken leg. As streams get larger and colder, however, this is no longer the case. Especially in the high mountains in the spring, established trails often cross quite dangerous torrents. A fast, deep, frothing meltwater stream is one of the most dangerous features of many a mountain, all the more so because it may not look as hazardous as a cliff.

Remember that rock and tree crossings are likely to occur where the stream is fastest and deepest. If you are not reasonably confident about the safety of a crossing, it might be safer to look for a better crossing or a ford. If you are nervous about walking a log, straddling it may be wiser, although less elegant, especially if the log is greasy. Snow bridges are discussed in a later chapter.

Fording is often the safest way across fast mountain streams, and even in relatively simple creeks, you may speed your progress by fording instead of walking a half-mile through the brush looking for a dry crossing.

The best fords are usually at wide spots in the river, where the current is least forceful and the channel shallowest. At bends expect the fastest current along the outer bank. On an easy crossing of clear water with a good bottom, you may just take off your boots and hang them from your pack or your neck. (Don't just drape them; tie them so that they won't be lost in a slip.) However, if the crossing is hard, if there are sharp rocks on the bot-

And then there are log crossings. Get your practice on easy ones like this, and you'll be ready for the slippery ones inclined over raging spring torrents.

tom, or if the footing is insecure, it's best to take off your socks and wear the boots. This prevents foot injuries, and it gives you better grip on treacherous bottoms.

A lot of rivers can be waded with little problem, but many are difficult because of the current and depth. The waistband of the pack should be taken off and the straps loosened so that you can dump it if necessary. If the weather is chilly, it will probably be warmer to roll up your pants legs or to carry your trousers across in the pack and have them dry at the other side. Beware of fast water swirling above your knees; fast water deeper than this is dangerous. Move very carefully on difficult crossings, and use a pole or an ice ax for a third leg on the upstream side. Try to shuffle across, but don't push too far. A very unpleasant situation can develop in which you can retain your stability with both legs where they are—in the middle

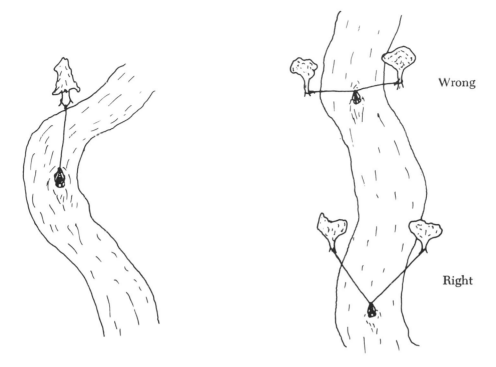

Crossing fast water with the aid of a handline. Light nylon line is strong enough, but only if used correctly. In the left-hand illustration the line is rigged so that the pull is as direct as possible, making footing easier and putting minimum stress on the line. In the right-hand drawing, one person has gotten across and rigged the line for the others. The top method is very bad—perpendicular force on a tight line creates tremendous stress, and the line may break. In the lower example, the slack in the line will greatly reduce the stress. The cord should be padded where it goes around rough objects like trees to prevent abrasion from cutting it.

of the river—but you cannot move either of them without upsetting yourself.

A party may be able to cross safely when a single man could not by firmly linking arms, each man holding the wrist of the next. This is useful mainly when only a few feet of channel are really difficult, but it may allow

51

one person to gingerly test a stream while the end of his chain of companions remains firmly attached to a tree on the bank. Mountaineering parties can often make good use of their rope to make crossings safe which would be impossible without it. (Belay the leader from as far upstream as possible.) Nonclimbers should not place too much reliance on such aids, but with a bend in the river, a length of parachute cord may serve as an aid to balance and provide a safety factor, as shown in the diagram. Do *not* rig parachute cord as a tight handline across the stream; it is not strong enough. If you use a handline for members of a party after the first, it must be very slack. See the diagram.

Finally, remember that rocks are buoyed up by the water, and therefore their effective weight is much less in the river than on the bank. Very large rocks may be easily dislodged, so watch your footing.

Most stream crossings are not difficult at all, involving damp feet at the worst. Like other aspects of backpacking, you can find the degree of challenge that you want. A look at the map before you go will usually warn you of the possibility of difficult crossings, which would be more likely after heavy rains or when a heavy winter snowpack is melting quickly in the spring. You need rarely worry about crossings on well-traveled trails except under special circumstances like these. Remember that special conditions can often be waited out. A stream which starts in melting snow is lower in the morning and higher in late afternoon. A creek swelled by rain will drop a day after the rain stops. Sometimes a camp in the afternoon will allow an easy crossing next morning.

Walking in the wilderness is largely a matter of physical conditioning and practice. On your first few trips you may find even easy boulder fields and stream crossings tiring and perhaps a little scary, especially toward the end of the day. By the end of the season you'll be hopping across them without a care, wondering what you thought was so hard. Acquiring this assurance is definitely worth the effort.

Living on the Trail 5

Camping for the backpacker is necessarily a fairly simple affair. Since all the equipment he uses has to be carried along, he has an incentive to stave off the gadget onslaught, a motive which most of us lack in everyday life. Even among backpackers, however, one finds a great variety in life-styles and their practitioners; they range from the vagabond who never carries more than a poncho for shelter and a tin can for cooking to those who would not think of being caught without an expensive tent and a reflector oven for baking apple pie and blueberry muffins. In fact, an attractive aspect of backpacking is its offer of so many alternative ways to approach open spaces and wilderness. There are enough techniques and modes of living to suit the most diverse personalities and the strangest landscapes.

Camping moods and methods result from an interaction between the personality of the traveler and the nature of his environment rather than from either of them alone. The blueberry muffins demand both an ambitious cook and adequate firewood. The techniques that you develop will depend on your own tastes and on whether you camp in the New England woods or the southwestern desert.

Many of the basic principles of wilderness living are the same for any environment and any style of camping, though there are numerous possible variations on the main theme. In general, as surroundings become harsher, they allow less room for individual choice of methods, with the most efficient possible technique and equipment demanded for the most severe conditions. Even the most confirmed poncho camper would not try to use this sort of shelter in regions where rain and snow driven by extreme winds are prevalent.

Within limits technique can be substituted for equipment, and to reverse the same coin, reducing the amount of equipment you carry below a certain level demands improved camping skill. A campsite for pitching a closed tent does not require so artful a choice as one where a poncho or tarp is to be used for shelter. Another less desirable substitute for equipment is fortitude in the face of discomfort, but personally I prefer to endure misery only when it is forced on me by circumstances or difficulty.

The requirements for living in reasonable comfort when you stop walking at the end of the day are an adequate water supply, a good meal, a comfortable bed, and shelter from whatever elements nature might bring along to disturb your night's rest. Water and food will be discussed in the next chapter; bed and shelter are our main topics in this one. In addition to these essentials there are certain amenities like campfires that are so pleasant as to be worth considerable effort when circumstances permit them. Finally the camper has always to concern himself with the problem of leaving his site in the best possible condition for himself and others to use in the future, and the importance of this matter should make it *the* overriding consideration for all of us whenever we are camping.

CHOOSING A SITE

The first order of business in setting up camp for the night is to find a good campsite. The amount of thought that goes into the choice may range from long, advance study of maps in search of suitable spots to simply collapsing in the nearest clearing when it's time to stop, the standard method in open, dry-floored pine forests well supplied with streams. More commonly, the situation is at neither extreme. Good campsites are easily found, but they may be infrequent enough to require that you start looking an hour or two before you definitely want to stop.

It is usually a good idea to decide on quitting time well in advance to ensure that you start looking for a good place early enough. Some situations dictate the need to get to a certain spot. If water is scarce, for example, you may be planning to camp at the crossing of a particular creek, and you might feel the need to get there even if you have to travel after dark. On long trips, planning may have to be tight enough to require that you make a certain number of miles each day. If the primary objective of your trip is a mountain or some other spot, you may have to get to a particular campsite in order to be within striking distance of your goal the following morning.

Barring special circumstances, however, it is almost always best to plan on making camp before dark, and it is definitely more pleasant to be able to hunt up firewood, cook, and get through other camp chores while there is still light. Circumstances may not always permit this, especially with the tight schedules of many weekend trips made by people trying to squeeze long distances into the space between Friday evening and Monday morning. You should beware of just continuing your city habits in the wilderness, though. "Early to bed and early to rise" may not make you healthy, wealthy, or wise, but it will allow you to travel farther, more pleasantly than late starts and late arrivals. Whatever the exigencies of a weekend trip beginning and ending with a long drive, when you go off for a few weeks in the summer, try to cultivate the habit of making your schedule compatible with that of the sun. Among other advantages, you won't have to carry as much power for artificial lights. I used to use my headlamp to wash dishes every night and often to cook supper, too. Now I find that I often go on several trips in a row without ever using a flashlight at all. By the time dark rolls in I try to be sitting back lazily with camp all fixed and stomach full, leaving me free to poke the fire and watch the stars come out.

A good procedure is to figure out how long it will take you to set up camp and do whatever else you want to do before dark. Subtracting this time from the hour of twilight, you have a stopping time you don't want to pass. You may want to stop earlier, of course, and beginners particularly should allow themselves plenty of daylight to set up camp.

The actual mechanics of choosing a site are simply a matter of considering your needs, comfort, and equipment, and matching them with the terrain around you. Easily available water is usually one of the determining factors. Quite aside from convenience, the aesthetic qualities of campsites near brooks, streams, rivers, and lakes are often enough to justify an extra effort in pitching a tent or clearing stones for your sleeping spot. Practically speaking, it's a pain in the neck to have to carry water long distances up- and downhill.

Certain care has to be observed about choosing campsites close to water, however. If there is a chance of rain, it is unwise to bed down either in the drainage system from higher ground or on spots over which your stream or lake might rise when it begins to accommodate the larger flow of water. Such spots are easily recognized if you look for them. Lakes and marshy spots are often breeding areas for insects, and since they may also be poorly ventilated, it's best to be wary of camping in a mosquito hollow. A breezier spot on the slightly higher knoll may be free of pests that infest the bowl just below.

In thickly wooded regions you may also need to exercise care in avoiding noctunal disturbances by larger local fauna. If there is only one clear path down to the water, it is often tempting just to bed down in the middle of it. Before you do, take a look and see whether it is the main highway to the old waterhole for every deer, moose, and bear in the region. Narrow game trails are not likely to provide you with uninterrupted rest.

In some areas, one rarely finds good campsites at convenient distances from water. If you anticipate this situation, carry a couple of big jugs (gallon bleach bottles are light, convenient, and free). When the time comes to start looking for a campsite, fill the jugs at the next watering place, and you will have your water available when you find a place to camp.

Obviously it is advantageous to camp near potable water rather than polluted or questionable sources, if you have a choice. The problem of the purity of drinking water is discussed more thoroughly in the next chapter.

A good campsite should have a fairly flat spot for sleeping, as free as possible from large projections that cannot be smoothed out, such as the pointed tops of large buried boulders. Be particularly careful of sharp objects if you are pitching a tent with a floor, since they will leave holes as a lasting memento to your neglect. Whether your sleeping space also needs to be soft depends on the adequacy of your sleeping pad. If you are sleeping without a pad or air mattress, test the ground carefully. With a good mat, small irregularities are not important, but a level spot is. A tilt that seems slight on cursory inspection is likely to wake you up a half-dozen times during the night to climb back up the hill.

The site itself should be as dry as possible, and if there is any possibility of rain, make sure it has good drainage. Even a good, coated tent

This erosion scar began when someone dug a small trench around his tent near a sub-alpine lake. It has only begun to erode; it will get bigger and uglier until it becomes a gully. Please don't trench a tent unless you know it won't damage the environment.

floor is going to fill up eventually if it is sitting in the middle of your own private lake. In most places you are likely to camp, trenching is *not* an appropriate way to ensure drainage. On forest floors with deep beds of pine needles or humus, trenching may be perfectly all right, and it certainly is on sand or similar surfaces. However, trenching mountain meadows, grassland beside lakes, the sparse soil near trees around timberline, vegetation on dunes, hillside plant cover, and similar spots is foolhardy, irresponsible, and often illegal. Particularly in alpine regions, such trenching, even if it is filled in, may result in severe erosion damage, and at best leaves scars that take a long time to heal. Shortsighted abuse of this type often necessitates the closing of backcountry areas to camping by the responsible authorities, since there is no way to police backpacking campers.

If you are going to pitch a tent or other shelter, you will have to examine prospective sites with your anchoring needs in mind. A tube tent requires two fairly tall objects with a good sleeping spot on a direct line be-

57

tween them. Alternatively, poles must be available for holding a line up. If you were using a tarp or poncho instead, you might prefer a spot farther down the trail with a well-placed boulder against which the tarp could be easily pitched. With a mountain tent you would probably be more influenced by the ease of driving stakes or the presence of strategically placed natural anchors. One simply learns to examine a possible camping place with his own shelter in mind.

If you plan to build a fire, whether for cooking, warmth, or general good cheer, this may be the most critical factor in the choice of a site. Availability of fuel is an obvious factor, and availability will be determined by your equipment as well as by external matters. A saw will enable you to get wood from large pieces of deadfall, while an ax will make it possible to split dry wood from the centers of wet chunks. A suitable spot in which to build a fire is also needed. Fires must never be built on ground which consists mainly of built-up vegetable matter. Former bogs and forest floors with heavy accumulation of debris are the most common examples. A fire built on such a base will often establish a deep bed of coals and continue to burn no matter how carefully you attempt to put it out later. It may flare up and cause a forest, brush, or grass fire weeks after you have gone. If you intend to build a fire, your site must have a spot with a good mineral base.

There is some discussion in the next chapter of limiting fire building because of limited fuel, but there are now also many areas where you should confine your campsites to established spots if you want a fire. In an effort to leave things unspoiled for others, many of us for years have built our fireplaces and then carefully scattered the rocks before we left. In some places this is a good idea, but in many areas it is becoming a self-defeating tactic. Around the attractive campsites surrounding many lakes in the Sierra Nevada these days, there is not a loose stone to be found that is not fire-scarred, nor a boulder without its smoke stains. Clearly, before this point is approached, it is best to leave fireplaces built, and for anyone who wants a campfire to use those already made.

A final point on the influence of fires in the choice of campsites is simply to note that in many wilderness areas there are regulations on both the permissibility of fires and their required location. In some areas you may camp where you choose if you use a stove for cooking, but you may use only designated sites for wood fires. It is important to obey these rules when they apply, both because they are often made for good reason, ena-

A perfect campsite. It has clean water nearby, a view, dry, level ground, and a breeze to carry off the mosquitos. Please don't build a fire unless there is dead wood on the ground, though. This sub-alpine environment is fragile, and plant growth is slow.

bling fire lookouts to identify your column of smoke as a campfire, and be-cause too many violations will force the rangers in charge either to close the area or to impose a host of unpleasant regulations and restrictions on access.

You should also examine your prospective campsite for advantageous situation. There is often an amazing amount of variation in temperature, wind, and ventilation between two spots which are very close together. The most obvious example of this is the sheltered side of large objects. Less widely recognized are the differences resulting from the fact that cold air sinks and tends to follow drainage patterns like water. If you expect the night to be cold, and your sleeping gear is somewhat inadequate, don't bed down in a low hollow—it will probably be the coldest spot. In the moun-tains, aside from storms and large weather patterns, each night the cold air from the high hills usually rolls down the slopes. This cold wind tends to concentrate in gullies and ravines. On cool nights you would be warmer if you camped above the valley and gully bottoms, but on hot, still nights, you might want to seek out these same places.

Shelter from wind is even more important than temperature if you want to stay warm. Both weather-system winds and the local winds mentioned above will chill the camper with marginal equipment. Many shelters are not suited to withstand high winds either.

PITCHING CAMP

Having settled on a campsite and perhaps taken a swim or a walk if the hour is early, you have to get your camp ready. The order of tasks will depend on whether you are alone or with friends, on the lateness of the hour, and on your own proclivities. If I am building a fire, I prefer to gather enough wood for the night and the next morning as a first order of business, because it's easier to pitch my tent in the dark than to find good pieces for the fire. Next, I get water, unless the source is close and the footing easy. If it is almost suppertime, I may start heating some water while I prepare my bed and pitch any required shelter. Obviously circumstances change the order of preference. In rain you might want to pitch a shelter first, allow the ground under the shelter to dry off a bit, and get your things out of the downpour. In winter the first priority may be to stamp out a platform in the snow for your tent.

Depending on the situation and your preferences, you may have to decide whether to set up a shelter at all or to sleep out under the stars. Some people always sleep in tents or under tarps as a matter of habit, and this may be necessary if your sleeping bag is not quite warm enough. I never sleep under a shelter unless I have to. If the weather is good I always sleep under the open sky, which is far more interesting to watch than any tent roof. I want to be able to lie in my nice warm bed and watch Orion climb up into the October sky. On a good night I also save myself the trouble of setting up a tent at night and the trouble of breaking it down the next morning. Of course, this saving may be counterbalanced by the need to get up and pitch a shelter in the middle of a freak rainstorm at 2:00 A.M., but the risk is worth it.

One can always pitch a tent and then sleep outside, of course, with a readily available retreat in case of rain. I do this occasionally when the weather is threatening. An easy hedge is available to those using tube tents, tarps, or ponchos for shelters. Simply prepare your bed and use the shelter for a ground cloth, but string out all the necessary pitching lines to the surrounding trees or bushes. If rain does come up, it nearly always begins with mild sprinkling, which is sufficient to wake you before you even get damp. All you have to do is toss your sleeping bag and belongings inside, pull the lines tight, and crawl into bed before the cloudburst starts in earnest. This method is really quite effective and not much trouble.

Whether you are putting up a shelter or not, spend some time getting the spot ready for your bed. Pick a level place, or one as level as possible. Pick up all the rocks, branches, pine cones, stones, and other hard, irregular objects, and toss them somewhere else. It takes less time to do this *before* you lay out your ground sheet or tent, and is much less irritating than searching for the lump under your spine after you have gone to bed. Remember that small, sharp objects are hard on tent floors and ground cloths. If you are sleeping without an air mattress or pad, or if you are using a thin, closed-cell pad, pay particular attention to the ground underneath you—you have to live with it all through the long night. A mattress of dry pine needles, well smoothed and spread out, is very pleasant when available. So is sand, but be careful to smooth and shape it well before laying out your bed.

If you use a ground sheet, one side will get dirty, especially when the ground is damp. Always lay the dirty side down and keep your sleeping things clean. If it is windy or gusty, weight the edges of the sheet so it won't blow away, and do the same with your pad and sleeping bag. Fluff the sleeping bag so that it will recover its loft and warmth. If it is still afternoon and is not too damp, it's a particularly good idea to get your sleeping gear out for airing while you go about fixing camp.

Pitching tents easily and quickly is largely a matter of practice. Circumstances vary, but as a general rule the entrance should be pitched into the prevailing wind in order to reduce flapping in the night. If your tent has a floor, simply stake it out around the edges first, or attach floor ties to available anchor points. Most tents are provided with more anchor points than are normally needed, but they should all be secured in windy conditions. A tent without a floor does not have a shape built in to determine the position of the stakes. So with this type you must be particularly careful to check the angles when you stake out the bottom, otherwise the tent will be distorted, wrinkled, and less stable when you raise it. With most tents the next step is to secure all pullouts, side ties, and guy lines to appropriate anchors. Sometimes the proper length for lines can be determined even before the tent is up, but normally these are tied with some sliding tension knot or mechanical fastener and left loose until the tent is raised. Finally, the poles are inserted and raised, and everything is tightened properly.

In forested areas be careful not to pitch the tent under any large dead branches which might be brought down by wind during the night. Such branches are ruefully known as "windowmakers." The great number of available anchor points provided by the woods will often make it possible for forest campers to dispense with carrying of poles. Generous lengths of parachute cord tied to the anchor points of a tent will substitute, except with some of the newer tents that depend heavily on curved poles to hold their shapes. One problem often encountered in using a line to hold up the ridge of a tent is that the center of the line and hence the ridge show a pronounced sag. A second line attached to the center of the first can often be tossed over a tree branch and used to straighten the curve. A guy line which needs a high anchor can be directed across an appropriate tree fork or branch by tying the end to a stone and throwing it over.

Open-fronted tents and shelters are often pitched facing fires for good cheer, comfort, and convenience, especially in bad weather. This is a good and time-honored practice, but care is required to prevent stray sparks from damaging the tent. Usually, the most effective arrangement is to build the fire against a good back reflector, large enough to control the smoke and draft. (See the discussion of backlogs, stones, and such in the next chapter.) Very small cooking fires are usually not much of a problem except in bad wind, but a larger warming fire should be a safe distance in front of the tent. Be conservative in using this technique until you gain experience with it.

Judicious use of natural anchors and weather breaks is important when you are establishing any camp, but it is of especial concern to those who use tarps, ponchos, or plastic shelters. Tarps and ponchos are most comfortable when they are used to form an extra wall in combination with a large log, a natural rock overhang, or other natural shelter. This combination will give you more room and better protection than the tarp alone. Don't get carried away when you find a nice roof, though. Not all overhanging rocks shed water; on some it just runs down along the inside of the roof, pouring off everywhere. Streams draining under the rock or log aren't very pleasant to discover in the middle of a nighttime storm either. A careful inspection before you settle down will avoid most such errors.

Try to determine how the prevailing winds blow when you set up camp. If you pitch your tarp as a lean-to, and have the open side facing into the driving rain, you'll be soaked in no time. The same consideration applies to large ventilation openings in tents, and to the ends of tube tents. The latter can be controlled to some extent if you bring along some spring-loaded clothespins for controlling the opening and anchoring the tent to the line. The best method is to place your shelter well, to begin with. Pitching in a naturally protected spot makes any shelter work better. Lean-tos don't get soaked inside or blown away, plastic shelters are less likely to tear, and tents will not have to shed so much rain and are thus less likely to leak.

GETTING YOUR BED READY

Whether you pitch a shelter or just throw out a ground cloth, it's usually a good idea to get your bed laid out as soon as possible. The insulation in your sleeping bag will work better if you give it time to recover from the compression of packing, and if the air is warm and dry enough an airing will allow some of the previous night's body moisture to evaporate from the bag.

In extremely moist and humid conditions, as in a snow shelter or in a wet tent after a week of backpacking in the rain, it is better to keep the sleeping bag in a waterproof stuff sack or plastic bag except when you are in it. It will stay drier if it is not allowed to cool off in damp conditions, so in these circumstances it is best to get the bag into the stuff sack as soon as you are out of it in the morning.

When you get your ground cloth down or your tent pitched, lie down on your proposed bed, and make sure that there aren't any unpleasant bumps you missed or a slope you didn't notice. Remember that a good night's sleep is important for an enjoyable trip, and it's worth a lot of trouble to make your bed comfortable. Do an especially good job if you are not using a pad. Get the cones out of a pine-needle bed. Scoop or find hip holes if you will sleep directly on the ground. If you are camping on the sand, you will have a comfortable mattress, but only if you shape it well beforehand. It's not as easy as it seems to scrunch the sand to your shape through the sleeping bag and tent floor.

If there is some question about the adequacy of your sleeping bag for cool evening temperatures, try to have some shelter from the clear night sky. If you are not sleeping in a tent or under a tarp, sleep under the branches of a tree. The intervening surface cuts your radiated heat loss, which can be quite high if you sleep out under the heavens on a clear night.

CAMP ROUTINE

There are a lot of details that have to be managed in a backpacking camp. None of them are very difficult under normal circumstances, and in good weather even the beginner will have a pretty easy time taking care of them. What throws some novices into a state of confusion is simply the large number of small tasks that have to be organized. Unsystematic beginners are usually best advised to make things easy on themselves by taking their first few trips with someone who knows what he is doing or with another beginner who has a knack for handling details. Programmatic types have less difficulty adjusting to the new routine of living from a pack.

The experienced backpacker works all the chores and necessities of camping into a routine, so that he is free to enjoy the experience at a leisurely pace when it suits him and he is capable of getting everything done in a hurry when he needs to. He can put up his tent almost unconsciously while keeping his cooking fire fed, dropping ingredients into the supper pot, or whatever. This facility is simply a matter of practice, technique, and organization, but these should be cultivated by anyone who wants to enjoy the sport. Sooner or later nearly anyone who travels a lot in the wilderness is bound to have to put up a late camp in miserable weather, and when he does he will appreciate being able to do it quickly and well.

Developing an efficient camping method is first a matter of getting the necessities straight in your mind. Get used to pitching your shelter in various circumstances, and think about what you need to do at any particular sort of site. Add ties to your tent if they will make it easier to pitch in some places. Get used to setting up your shelter efficiently when there isn't any wind, so that you won't have a lot of trouble when there is. When you use fires, accustom yourself to lighting them with the first match and without fire-starters, so that you'll be able to get them going in bad weather. (Fire-starters are not immoral, but if you get used to using them in relatively easy circumstances, you'll never develop the skill needed to start a fire in a difficult situation, with or without aids.)

Systematic packing is also a great help when you get to camp. When you're tired it's very annoying to have to dig through the pack for twenty minutes to find the salt. With good packing everything you need will be at your fingertips. There isn't much room in a rucksack, but it's amazing how well you can lose something in such a small space if you just toss it in without thinking. It is ordinarily best to try to pack things so that the items you will need first are on top, providing you can do it without unbalancing the pack. In general, trail items go into the most accessible spots, and the camp gear goes in so that the last-needed equipment is buried the deepest. Food especially, which becomes the heaviest and bulkiest part of the load on long trips, should be parceled into packages by the meal, day, or week, and the meals for later in the trip should be at the bottom. This avoids the necessity of unpacking your whole load at every stop, a particularly unwelcome chore when the rain is pouring down while you are trying to fix supper.

If you can develop a more or less unconscious procedure for unpacking, getting your camp up, fetching water, and cooking supper, you will have more time to enjoy the lake and the sunset, and you will also get more pleasure out of the physical activity involved in the chores themselves. Dozens of small matters contribute to this efficiency and confidence. If you always put your flashlight and glasses in the same place, you'll be able to find them easily and without irritation when you need them in the middle of the night. Best of all, you'll feel at home on the trail, not like an unwelcome guest in a strange house.

RUBBISH DISPOSAL

The problem of keeping the wilderness clean is one of the most obvious difficulties presented by the new influx of people into the backcountry. Trash,

An efficient camp routine will leave you more time to horse around. The author mugs for the typical summit picture.

66

litter, and pollution are already very real problems in many wilderness areas, even in some that are remote. The offensiveness of the junk that is left almost everywhere is obvious. Much of the litter from modern packaging is practically impervious to the natural processes of disintegration, except over a long time. Shreds of plastic from discarded wrappers or ground sheets keep whipping around for years. Tin cans at least rust away eventually, but their aluminum replacements stay shiny through the seasons. The only way to avoid having our woods and mountains turn into monstrous junkpiles is to leave none of our trash in the backcountry. This means either burning or packing out every single bit of your debris.

If you use fires, you can burn up paper and plastic bags. Don't bury the rest—carry it out. Animals dig up buried cans and trash, and erosion often uncovers it. If you can manage to carry a full container into the wilderness, you can certainly carry it out empty! Fixed camps and ski cabins may require refuse pits to be dug, but this is a different matter. Such pits can create various erosion and pollution problems, and anyone placing them should acquire sufficient knowledge beforehand to be able to do it right. For backpacking situations the answer is to burn it *thoroughly* or pack it out. Remember that wrappers made partly of foil, orange peels, and cans don't burn and must be carried out.

Long-distance travelers using caches, rendezvous, relays, or airdrops for supply have a slightly different problem with trash, but this is not an excuse for littering either. Unfortunately, expeditions have long considered themselves privileged to dump in a way that they would allow no one else to do close to home. Where fires can be used, good planning will simply dictate packages that can be disposed of by burning. With a rendezvous, you can always have your support team carry out your junk, an extension of the principle that you can carry out empty anything you can carry in full. Only with caching and airdrops do problems become more difficult, since both methods often require metal containers to prevent damage from the drop or from visiting animals. In the case of caches, you can always plan to revisit the sites at the end of the trip to get the junk out. If you do, don't just *plan* on the return—*make* it.

There are still a few situations where burying rubbish may be justified, perhaps at some semipermanent camps with Forest Service or other approval, or on long trips in some regions. Even in these circumstances everything possible should be burned. Anything to be buried should be burned   67 or washed thoroughly, because if food remains on containers, animals will dig them up. Cans should be flattened so that they take up less space. Tin cans or containers should be burned before burial to melt off the tin; the cans will rust out much faster if this is done. The dump itself should be dug as deep as possible, away from water, some big rocks should be thrown in to make animal excavation less likely, and the vegetation cover must be replaced as well as possible. Anyone traveling in alpine, arctic, or desert environments should be particularly reluctant to leave junk, since natural processes of degradation operate very slowly in such conditions. There is no excuse for dumping in areas within the range of a weekend trip from civilization.

SANITATION

The problem of trash is a simple matter of people accepting responsibility for their own junk. Some pollution problems result as much from ignorance as irresponsibility. Heavy use of many wilderness areas, particularly those in fragile environments, places pressure on natural cleaning systems that they are not capable of sustaining. Besides actual pollution, there are problems of aesthetics that should be a concern of everyone who does much backpacking and which require some changes in current attitudes. Around some popular high-country lakes, one can hardly turn over a stone anymore without finding someone's latrine. Some people don't even bother with the stone. This kind of behavior is simply not tolerable anymore. Where there is earth, take the time to dig a decent hole, well away from any water runoff. For a latrine at camp, the hole should be of a size commensurate with the length of time you plan to stay. For one-time use, the hole obviously should be filled when you leave, but at camp, a moderate amount of dirt after each use will be adequate until you vacate. If you are using a wood fire in camp, bring some of the ashes up and use them in the hole to speed up deterioration of the waste. In places where adequate holes can't be dug, try to find the best possible spot, and carry matches to burn up your toilet paper, which deteriorates rather slowly.

The distance of a latrine from camp should be far enough away to prevent circulation of flies when they are in season, but with a deep enough hole and the use of dirt or ashes for cover, this won't be too much of a problem. The main requirements are that it be well away from water (not just downstream from you!) and that it be in a spot where no one else is likely to want to camp. It is an advantage to have it at a convenient distance from camp so that no one will be tempted to neglect it at night, but self-discipline is a remedy for that problem. Anyone camping on snow should be particularly careful in locating a spot and in firing toilet paper, since the contents of snow holes merely freeze until the summer melt drops them in pristine condition on the ground below the spot where they were deposited.

For the backpacker, garbage should be minimal or nonexistent, because it represents wasted weight and probably wasted food. Burning is the best way to handle any that you have. Small bits of food can be scattered for animals and birds. When this isn't feasible, it's generally all right to bury garbage, but not together with trash. Animals may dig up the garbage and will scatter any trash that is with it.

Washing out clothes and dishes is fairly straightforward, but it should not be done in streams or lakes. Take a pot down to the lake if you are washing in cold water, and do the actual washing and dumping of soapy water at least a few yards away, and farther with a small water supply. It's even better, especially in heavily used areas, to take the water back to camp and do the washing there. Dishwater disposal is not usually much of a problem in backpacking camps, since quantities are small and stays usually short. One or two stray noodles are not going to hurt anything, and they will probably soon be picked up by a bird or chipmunk. Long stays, large parties, or heavy use may dictate more care, though, and so would large amounts of grease from frying bacon or something similar. For better disposal dig a hole, put some rocks and large gravel in it so that it will drain well, and cover the top with dead grass or pine needles. Dishwater is poured into the hole, and the grease and detritus is caught by the grass or needle trap, which is then burned and replaced by a fresh one. Fill the hole before breaking camp.

WASHING

Your own tastes and those of your companions will be the main determinant in the frequency and thoroughness with which you wash yourself and your utensils, but the climate and the length and difficulty of the trip should also be considered. Except for socks and underwear, there is rarely any need for laundry except on trips of more than two weeks.

The face and hands tend to get pretty dirty, except on winter trips in the snow, but beware of too much washing. Removal of the natural oils from the skin promotes chapping and sunburn. People with sensitive skin may need to bring along a skin preparation to replace some of that oil. On dusty trips you may find that you need a bath, or at least want one, every day, while on jaunts across nothing but rock and snow you may well find that you stay cleaner than you would at home. Except where water is scarce and in really cold weather, there really isn't any problem bathing as often as you want to, although you'll probably have to get used to sponge baths. Luxury lovers with adequate fuel can heat up water for theirs, while more Spartan souls can search for fresh snowmelt and top off their bath with a dive into a mountain tarn where ice cakes still float. In either case, though, do your washing and rinsing away from water to keep your contribution of detergent and soap to a bare minimum. Lakes take a long time to turn their water over, and in many of the best backpacking areas, biodegradation takes a very long time. Keep your suds out of the lakes and streams.

What soap you use is partly a matter of your own preference, but if you're washing much in cold water, find a soap that will work up a decent lather at that temperature. Some campers like to carry a very small bottle of liquid detergent for both the pots and their hands, and it works very well. I like a small piece of soap for sponge baths and something stronger for sooty hands. For the latter, you can use a little hunk of gritty laundry soap, some powder like the kind you find in gas stations, or some mechanic's hand cleaner, which works without water and has the extra advantage of leaving an oily film on your hands to prevent chapping.

Scrubbing pots and pans is one of the less attractive chores in wilderness camping, and quite a few backpackers don't usually even bother until they get home. Except in winter I prefer to scrub mine, but I am lazy enough to try to keep the work to a bare minimum. There are a number of tricks to doing this, and one of them coincides with keeping your weight down; that is to use as few pans and dishes as possible. In cooking for any reasonably sized party I rarely use more than two pans, never more than three. One of those pots is usually used only for water, so the inside doesn't get dirty. Parties relying on stoves won't have to worry much about soot, but for others it is very helpful to have an individual sack for each of the nesting pots. Each sack keeps the sooty outside of the pan from soiling the inside of its larger neighbor, obviating the necessity of cleaning the outside of the pots. If you must clean off the soot, a layer of soap spread on the outside of the pan before it goes on the fire will make your job simpler.

There are several kinds of scouring pads which make the pot-scrubbing job easier, though sand and crusty snow also do a fair scouring job. Water should always be heated for dishes if you are using soap, especially in very cold weather. A lot of cold-weather campers would rather scour their pots with some granular snow and forget them on the assumption that a little grease carried over to the next meal won't hurt. This is reasonable, because if you use soap without a thorough rinsing it will mix in with the grease for an unpleasant and unhealthy addition to tomorrow's menu. If you're going to be sloppy about dishwashing it's best to leave detergent and soap out. A small amount of hot water can be used for all your dishes, pouring it from the largest vessel to the progressively smaller ones, and this is the usual dishwashing method for individuals and small groups. Large groups usually prefer a big pan for dishwashing. Remember, if there is much waste in the dishwater it should be burned, and a grease trap should be used if there is much oil.

SLEEPING IN COMFORT

I've already mentioned the importance of preparing a comfortable sleeping spot, but it's hard to overemphasize the point. The art of backpacking is in making yourself comfortable with a minimum of equipment and effort, not in seeing how much misery you can stand. Save the discomfort for extremely difficult trips where it is impossible to avoid, and learn how pleasant most seemingly hostile environments can be.

It is a continual source of amazement after long sojourns in the civilized world to find just how few things we really need to be comfortable and happy. This is the discovery always awaiting the backpacker along the trail. The farther down the path you go, the more clearly those essentials will stand out. One of them, you will find, is a good night's sleep. You'll probably never learn to enjoy long backpacking trips unless you learn how to sleep comfortably.

The first priority for a decent bed is a spot which is reasonably level and free from hard projections digging into your anatomy. In some kinds of country you may sleep with your bag separated from the ground only by a waterproof sheet, but it is usually more sensible to use a foam pad or an air mattress, unless one is included in your sleeping bag. This subject is discussed in the equipment section, so for now I'll just say that with most sleeping bags economy of insulation and comfort dictate the use of a pad of some kind. Springy carpets of pine needles and some meadows may be comfortable, but they are not always available. The famous bough bed of legend cannot even be considered in most places these days—it requires a great volume of live boughs—and besides, it takes quite a bit of time to put together and often gets rather uncomfortable at around three in the morning.

Air-mattress users should beware of inflating their beds too much; this will make them uncomfortable, easy to fall off, and more prone to puncture. Proper inflation will barely keep your hips from touching bottom when you are lying in the bed. Check all your favorite positions when you are testing. I generally fill the air matress and then lie on it, releasing the air slowly until I sag to the proper level. Pads just need to be rolled out early so they will have time to expand completely before bedtime. Thin, closed-cell foam pads are good insulation, but they provide minimal padding, so if you have one, be particularly careful when fixing your foundations.

Most backpacking pads and air mats are the short type, extending from the hips to the shoulders or head. You should take a little time fixing a pillow, if you need one, and providing padding and insulation for your feet and calves when the spot calls for them. On a soft forest floor, your feet probably won't need padding, but they will on gravel, and insulation is needed in cold weather no matter what the surface. Use your pack, spare clothes, and the like to make the lower part of your bed. I make a pillow from some of my clothes rolled in the sleeping bag stuff sack.

Some people like to wear all their clothes to bed, and some do not. It doesn't matter unless the weather is cold enough to push your sleeping bag to its lower limits. Dry clothes may be used to keep you warm and comfortable. If you're wearing damp clothes and it's chilly, though, better change to dry ones. It's true that you can dry off your clothes inside the sleeping bag, but the heat needed to evaporate the water has to come from your body, and if you're cold you won't be able to spare the warmth during the night, when your body produces its smallest quantities of heat. A good night's rest will make you better equipped to dry them out on the trail tomorrow, and wet or frozen clothes in the morning are preferable to a night of wakeful shivering. If you're warm enough you can suit yourself on the question of whether to dry clothes inside your bag. The advantages are obvious; the penalties are some discomfort and some extra moisture in the bag, which will result in reduced efficiency and greater weight. In general, the colder the weather, the more circumspect you should be about drying clothes in your sleeping bag.

Putting on any available dry clothes is an obvious measure to take if you are cold in your bag. Other important steps for a warm sleep on a cold night are to stay warm before you get into bed, to have some food before going to bed, and to fluff your bag up well. If you are cold when you climb into the sack, you will take a while to warm up, because you'll stop most of your heat-producing muscular activity. The food helps because you produce heat in digesting it, and the fluffing gets the maximum amount of insulating dead air into the bag. Pull all your drawstrings tight to prevent the air you do warm up from escaping, but keep your mouth and nose free to breathe outside the bag—you don't want all that moisture in the insulation. If you need more clothes, put on a hat first, since your head radiates a lot of heat.

Isometric exercises are good for getting warm, allowing your muscles to generate heat without stirring up air currents to carry it away. They are especially useful just after you get into the bag on a very cold night, because it takes a few minutes to warm up the inside so that it can start insulating. If you wake up cold in the middle of the night, have a candy bar and do some more exercises. (Isometric exercises are done by tensing up muscles against each other, without moving them significantly. Any muscles will do, but for warming up, tense one set for a few seconds, then another. The abdominal muscles are the most effective for getting warm.)

You won't actually be very likely to need any of these warm-up tricks unless you start doing cold-weather camping or bivouacking with minimal equipment. Backpackers with adequate sleeping bags generally sleep better in camp than at home. The only precaution I usually take when I go to bed is to leave my glasses on for a while so that I can watch the stars from the comfort of my warm bed.

Before you turn in at night, try to put everything you may want to get from the bag within easy reach and in a place where you can find it. Boots beside the head of your bed make handy repositories for pocket items, glasses, and a flashlight. Clothes you need for the next day should be placed within easy distance too. Leaving the pack outside your shelter is all right, providing everything in it is adequately protected against the weather. Try to avoid leaving everything strewn all over camp, though. A surprise rain coming up in the night will leave you the miserable job of stumbling around with a flashlight, trying to find it all. (You won't—the matches will be discovered in a puddle the next morning.) Don't leave out anything that will be damaged by rain or blown away in a hard wind. In cold seasons don't leave things where they might be covered by snow.

MIDNIGHT MARAUDERS

After licking your lips over the last morsel of your gourmet supper, you should spend a few minutes thinking about local residents that might have an interest in your remaining supplies. The possibilities for uninvited evening guests range from mice to bears. As you are the prospective host, you would be discourteous and unwise not to prepare for your visitors.

The safest way to make sure of undisturbed slumber and a full larder next morning is to get all your food out of reach of the local denizens. Some fairly elaborate safety devices are often needed in semipermanent camps, but the backpacker rarely needs to worry about really devious attempts. I usually put all my food in a stuff sack, tie the top to a length of parachute cord, and suspend the whole business from a tree branch well out of reach from the ground, tree, or branch. To get it up, all that is needed is to tie a stone to the other end of the cord, throw it over the branch, and haul the sack up to a convenient height.

In deciding whether you actually need to take this precaution, you simply make an informed guess. Factors to be considered are the amount of use of your campground, availability of other food, the season, and the consequences of losing your larder. On a long trip with tight provisioning, the prospect of an extended trek without food should make you conservative enough to take all possible precautions. In general, animals are more likely to come around looking in frequently used camps than rarely visited ones.

They also become less wary of people and more clever at getting into containers, though at big campgrounds they may prefer the garbage cans to more widely dispersed food caches. Be particularly wary in spring and after early fall snows, when animals need more food and the supply is scarce.

Whether or not you hang your food, there are a few precautions you should always take. Don't let your pack become soaked with food remains. Wash it if a chocolate bar melts through. Small rodents will eat a hole right through the stain, an efficient cleaning job, but one that creates some other problems. Don't put your food in a place that would force a bear to go through you or the wall of your tent in order to get it. The foot end of your sleeping bag or tent is not a good place for a food cache. It will discourage some bears, but will make your encounter with a more determined one rather trying. If you want to risk having a bear carry away your store, leave it where he can get it without bothering you.

Leather boots tempt some rodents, and they should be kept close at hand. Where this seems to be a real problem, watch out for your pack, too. Porcupines hungry for salt will sometimes eat up your sweat-soaked pack straps, whether they are leather or nylon. Swing the whole pack if they are a problem. Where there are procupines there are trees, but remember to suspend the parcel well out in the air, since porky can climb the trunk.

Where there are no trees, marauders tend to be less of a problem. Small rodents are foiled by simply putting the food in a covered pot, and wiring it shut will stop a raccoon but not a determined bear. Trees too small for limb-suspension systems may still foil bears if they are high enough to get the package out of reach and too skinny for the bear to climb. Steep-sided boulders may also suffice for bear protection.

INSECT STUFF

Smaller marauders, which are more interested in eating you than your supplies, have already been mentioned in connection with the choice of a campsite. In areas and seasons where they cannot be avoided mosquitoes and their allies must be dealt with. If there aren't too many bugs and you're not especially sensitive, you may choose to ignore them. A warning, though—my own worst nights have resulted not from the heaviest concen-

Another kind of backpacking campsite. The salt marsh is beautiful, but in some seasons you had better be prepared for the local insects or you may fail to appreciate the beauty the next morning.

tration of bugs, but from occasions when they didn't seem to be thick enough to require repellent; by the time I woke up covered with bites proving my poor judgment, it was too late to salvage a comfortable night's sleep.

The old standby for insect control is a net bar, either on the tent door or draped over the sleeper. These are satisfactory for most insects if they are made and draped properly. Take the time to kill everything already in the tent before bedding down. Bars over the sleeping bag should be held up away from your skin, or the little monsters will just sit outside while they feed.

Recently, fairly effective insect repellents have become available which are also relatively inoffensive to humans. Government studies have shown that these work not by smell or taste, but by being unpleasant to the insects' touch. The same studies show that for a given amount of compound, the most effective repellent is diethyl toluamide, so I would recommend picking whatever stuff gives you the greatest amount of this substance for the least money. Aerosols are generally poor buys for carrying on a trip, but they are useful for spraying clothing before you start. Repellent applied to clothing lasts quite a while, but on the skin it goes much more quickly. Personally, I rely almost solely on repellent now, rather than bothering with insect bars. In the worst places and seasons you will need to use both. Some kinds of flies pay little attention to repellents, requiring the use of head nets by day and netting by night.

In tick country you can prevent becoming an involuntary host by arranging a seal between pants legs and boots—with anklets for example. Then add repellent around the ankles and check your clothes every half hour or so. Alternatively, you can strip down and inspect each other a couple of times a day. Children should always be checked carefully, since they periodically charge through the bush, and often a lot of bushwhacking adults need the same treatment. Hair and ears should receive special attention. Ticks take a couple of hours to really attach themselves, so remove them before they have a chance.

BREAKING CAMP

If you have a destination or distance in mind for the day's hiking, you should remember that an efficient departure is as important as economy in setting up camp. Think about the time you can spare for morning sluggishness the night before. Then pack up and get ready to go before you start lying around in the sun; breaking camp always takes longer than you think it will. When your pack is tied up next to the trail, you can look at your watch and decide whether you have time for another half-hour of basking. This may sound merely puritanical, but every experienced backpacker knows (whatever his practice) that a lot of energy and pleasure is wasted by getting into camp late at night because of a dilatory start.

How long you actually spend getting going will depend a lot on your morning routine, a very subjective thing. The ambitious souls who have scrambled eggs and muffins just have to get up earlier than the vagabond who munches a piece of Logan bread while he packs up. This is very much a matter of personal taste, one about which it is wise to reach an understanding when traveling with new companions.

If the sun is up and you have other chores, open your sleeping bag and air it on a sunny rock or log so that it will dry as much as possible before packing. The same advice may apply to tents also, although this is much less important. In good weather roll your sleeping bag as the last item before leaving in the morning. If the air is damp and soggy, roll it as soon as you get up, before it loses your body heat.

Eating on the Trail 6

Food for backpacking can be about as simple or complicated as you like, and tastes vary in this area of lightweight camping more than in most others. I like to keep things simple most of the time, so if you would prefer to prepare six-course dinners in the backcountry, you can take the advice given in this chapter with a grain of salt. Your pocketbook is also likely to influence your attitude toward camp cooking a good deal. A good sleeping bag is worth making sacrifices for, but expensive freeze-dried meals aren't. Meals for backpacking don't have to be expensive.

FACTS OF LIFE FOR THE CAMP COOK

Regardless of the style of cooking that attracts you, there are certain basic requirements for cooking from a pack that you will have to get used to. Weight is a problem. On a weekend trip you can ignore it if you want to and carry almost anything. Your pack will be heavier than necessary, but it won't be unmanageable. On longer trips, however, it is quite impossible to tote along cans of beef stew and marinated artichokes for your basic diet. The weight of the containers and the moisture in the food rapidly add up to prodigious weights. Next time you come home with a full-week's groceries, think about tossing them into your pack and heading down the trail. For trips of a week or more, bulk can also be a problem. A reasonably compact pack is necessary for efficient walking, and very bulky items won't usually withstand much banging around.

Backpacking foods have to be protected from spoilage. On a weekend trip you may be able to use some fresh foods without much thought to preservation, but in general this is not the case. Only foods which will keep for some time without refrigeration can be carried for consumption after the first day or two of a trip. Winter trips in cold weather can be an exception to this rule, but it applies to most backpacking trips.

Ease and method of preparation have to be considered in planning your menu. If you want to bother to make an apple pie, you can manage it, but you'll have to bring a reflector oven. Length of cooking time can be an important factor, especially at high altitudes, where water boils at a lower temperature than at sea level so that food cooks more slowly, when it cooks at all.

Waste should be kept to a minimum in any foods chosen for backpacking. Carrying ten pounds of garbage a hundred miles into the woods only to be faced with the problem of getting rid of it is rather silly. You might even have to carry it all the way out again.

Finally, food for backpacking has to meet the same nutritional requirements that any other food does, especially since it is usually fueling bodies doing work to which they aren't accustomed. On short trips, a little common sense usually takes care of balancing meals, but on long journeys the need for eliminating all waste and avoiding cumulative deficiencies requires more careful planning.

BASIC COOKING FROM A BACKPACK

The heart of most meals for the backpacker is a casserole-type dish which is boiled rather than baked. Call it stew, soup, or glop, the basic method is to combine a starchy base (rice, noodles, potatoes, etc.) with some vegetables, a source of protein, and some flavorings, and cook it in a single pot until it is done. Sophisticates carefully regulate the timing of each addition and may add touches like dumplings, but the idea is to cook everything in one pan whenever possible, or to use two at the most.

A dish like this can provide everything you need for supper, even if you choose to add side dishes. I nearly always stick to the basic one-pot meal unless I'm having trout or eggs for dinner. When I feel creative, I try to make it a very imaginative one-pot meal, but I stay with the method because it is so well suited to the problems of fixing meals for backpacking.

My own preparation goes like this. Before the trip, I scoop out the ingredients of my meal from my box of camping food, mixing everything that can be mixed, and packaging things that have to go in the pot at different times in different plastic bags. The whole thing goes in one plastic bag, along with a slip of paper telling me any directions I need, like the amount of water to use or cooking time. I have a bag for each cooked meal. On most trips things like coffee go into single bags for the whole trip, but on a long journey, daily rations can go into the meal bags.

At the same time that I pack up my meals I fill my salt and pepper shakers, replenish my bags of sugar, coffee, tea bags, hot chocolate, bouillon cubes, and cream substitute. I make sure that I have the right number of breakfasts and suppers, and that I have enough trail food for lunches. On a long trip I might ration lunches, but usually I don't bother. I'm generous with trail food, and that also provides my emergency reserve. If I am using a stove, I fill my gasoline containers with enough fuel for the trip.

Tea, coffee, and the like go into my cook kit, along with the stove, soap, pot-scrubber, matches, pot handles. The other things are packed in order so that the first day's rations are on top. That way they aren't too hard to find even in the dark, and I don't have to rearrange the whole pack during the first couple of days.

When I get into camp, I get a full pot of water and put it on to boil. When it gets hot I dip water for some drinks right away, pour any extra into the second pot, and start the meal cooking in the remaining water. If I have a fire, I'll start two pots, but with a stove I'll have some soup or something to sip while the meal is cooking by taking the hot water out before adding the meal ingredients to the pot. With instant suppers I may only have to pour hot water from the pan when it has begun to boil.

If I am alone, I eat directly from the pan, putting the second pan on the stove with water for drinks and washing, or moving it to the side of the fire where it can simmer. If I am with others, I dish the food into bowls. With one-pot meals each person needs only a mug and a bowl. Some people just use a mug.

There are lots of special dishes and tricks which can be used in backpack cookery. Some of them will be talked about later in this chapter, but I think the one-pot meal is basic. It allows preparation of appetizing meals in an orderly way on a single stove. Most of the preparation—measuring, mixing, and figuring—is done at home. Only a small fire is necessary if one is used. The amount of liquid can be increased if the party needs liquids, as in winter camping. Both preparation and cleanup are simplified. The method is easily adapted to any size group. It is also adaptable to widely varying tastes and pocketbooks. You can throw some stuff together or make a gourmet meal, according to your propensity.

COOKING UTENSILS

Another advantage in cooking in this way is the simplicity and light weight of the equipment needed. A couple of pots holding around two quarts each will serve a party of four very nicely. Lids should be included to conserve heat, especially for cooking over a stove. If you plan to do much frying, you should take a spun-steel fry pan, which is much superior to aluminum. Some cook kits have lids meant to double for frying made of steel, but most are thin aluminum, good for nothing but burning. A spatula should also be included for frying.

Normally, a soup spoon is all that is needed for tending a one-pot meal. I use a pot gripper available in backpacking stores, and swear by it, but some people manage quite nicely with the cuffs of their shirt sleeves. Pots with locking bails are easy to handle, but they are generally more expensive.

The only other necessities are a spoon, a cup, and a bowl for each person. Avoid aluminum for these purposes: it burns your lips when the contents are hot but cools the food too quickly. The stainless-steel Sierra Club cups are nice and are multipurpose. Enameled ware also works well. However, although I have always hated plastic eating equipment, I have finally become a convert. It doesn't burn you, it packs easily, it doesn't dent, and food and drinks stay hot for a reasonable period of time. A plastic cup can be marked to double as a measuring cup with the aid of a hot knife. The only defects of the plastic items are that they can't be used for cooking and they must not be left too close to the fire. If you opt for plastic get the soft kind that will bend in your pack without breaking, and try to find a design that nests well, so that two bowls or cups take only a little more room than one.

If you are cooking over fires, a grill and a couple of pot-hangers are useful. The grill should be a very light kind made for backpacking, and it should have a case. Sooty pots are more easily taken care of if each has a fabric or plastic bag, keeping the carbon away from other items in the pack, and from the inside of the neighboring pot. Many people who cook over fires like to carry a single cotton work glove for handling sooty pots.

FIRES AND STOVES

I feel very strongly that the attitude of wilderness travelers toward fires has got to be changed. With proper use even delicate wilderness areas can stand quite a bit of human traffic, but subjected to the pressures resulting from the combination of numbers and misuses many areas are suffering badly. Some of the worst abuses are connected with fires. Hacking live trees with hatchets because of a mistaken notion that that is what camping is all about is inexcusable. It is possible as well as desirable to camp without burning everything in sight.

In some areas of heavy use, especially in alpine and subalpine environments, fires are simply inappropriate—any fires. I know how nice it is to sit around the fire, but if you cannot get wood without ruining the spot, use a stove. There is simply no excuse for the kind of self-indulgence that breaks off every beautifully weathered snag and mutilates every tree, just so that someone can toast marshmallows by a lake in the Rockies.

Modern equipment and modern food allow the backpacker to do his cooking on small fires—the kind that old-time woodsmen used to build for making tea in the afternoon. You can make fires from small dead sticks that can be gathered and broken without the aid of saws and axes—fires large enough to cook your supper and give you good cheer without burning up a cord of hickory. Older camping methods used fires to keep people warm all night, to cook beans all day, and for other similar purposes. Such methods still have occasional place, but as a general rule they should be relegated to the past.

In frequently used campsites with established fireplaces and plenty of wood, the camper can build a fire to suit his taste. But in relatively unspoiled sites, he should leave no sign of his passage, and that usually means a small fire, carefully built and eradicated with just as much care.

83

FIRE BUILDING

For small fires designed for boiling water and being put out fairly soon, there is little need for the elaborate structures which fill the literature. Care is needed for safety, but otherwise, the building can be a simple thing. Fires should not be built on peat, forest duff, or other soils filled with flammable vegetable matter. They should be built on an absolutely fireproof mineral base or on wood laid on snow. Fire can smolder and travel in peat, duff, and tree roots for weeks before bursting out twenty feet from the original site. Sand or gravel near water is a good place to build a fire. In forested areas it may be possible to remove the duff in a circle and set it aside for later replacement. Be sure to get down to mineral soil if you are building a fire on the forest floor.

One can always build a fire on a rock base, but this practice should be used only when good taste will permit it. Too many areas have been defaced by having every natural rock formation covered with fire scars. Pick a flat rock that is largely concealed, cover one with sand or soil to protect the rock, or use someone else's spot. Remember that fire scars last a very, very long time. Soot and charcoal are practically indestructible. If the only available fireplace is a beautiful rock formation which is unscarred, have the grace to move on, use a stove, or eat a cold supper.

In a reasonably dry forest, building a fire is so simple as to be almost trivial, even if an afternoon thundershower has wet the wood lying in the open. One has merely to get a few rocks to contain the fire and to hold up the grill and the larger pieces of wood. Kindling can be collected along the last few miles of trail if it is at all scarce. Start picking up dry twigs when you start thinking about stopping. A few dry pieces of deadwood which are protected under the branches of trees can be whittled into fuzz sticks, two or three of which make excellent kindling. A collection of broken up pieces of deadwood (not rotten) ranging in size from the diameter of a pencil up to the largest size you can break completes the fixings. These should be arranged in a loose pile with lots of air space and plenty of wood above the point of ignition in progressively larger sizes.

Practice makes perfect. If you don't know how to build a fire, practice lighting them with a few matches in all kinds of weather. Spend plenty of time laying the fire. That is the key. Once it is burning well, even most wet and green wood can be burned—within reason. Candles make good fire-starters, as do various chemical tablets and pastes, but practice without them.

Fire building only really becomes a test in wet weather that lasts long enough to soak things down. Saving kindling over from one fire to the next is a help, and usually dry wood can be found in protected spots, but it must be admitted that when the weather is wet enough for long enough, you'll only get dry wood by standing it in front of your fire or splitting it out with an ax. If you have an ax and the use seems reasonable, there is always dry wood in a standing dead stub that isn't rotten.

As a general rule, it is far better to collect wood with your hands than with an ax or saw, which leave their telltale marks and add weight that isn't usually necessary. Except in wet weather there is almost always enough wood lying around for a cooking fire, if fires ought to be built at all. If there isn't enough deadwood, then there either isn't enough wood growing or the camping use in the area is too high. Use a stove.

In windy weather don't build a fire unless you are sure it is safe, and if the forest is dry it probably isn't safe, especially with softwoods that spit large sparks. During the day, the sparks may not be noticeable, but take a look at your fire at night to see how far the sparks can travel. If the fire is safe despite the wind, you will probably need to build a small windbreak to protect it.

Beginners commonly make the mistake of not providing for enough air. They pack their wood too tightly and protect the flame from the breeze that would fan it to life. Remember that the fire needs oxygen to burn as much as it needs fuel.

FIRE DISPOSAL

If you make a fire, you must also put it out, and unless a permanent fireplace is to be left, you must also eradicate the signs of your fire. The most important step is putting the fire out, especially in true wilderness areas. In Alaska and wilder parts of Canada like the Yukon Territory, there is no hope of fighting large fires except where they menace settlements. The fires simply burn themselves out, destroying tens of thousands of acres of forest, wildlife, and soil. It is sickening to watch such fires, with the smoke darkening the sky for hundreds of miles. True, such fires used to burn occasionally before the coming of man, but they were relatively rare, even serving a function, and nature had time to repair the damage. People are now setting fires so quickly that reforestation can never keep pace. No one who is careless with fire has any business in the wilds. Take care of your own fires, and if you see someone else who doesn't, do something about it. They are your woods, and there won't be anything left of them if too many idiots are allowed to burn them up.

Make sure your fire is *dead out* before you leave. Drown it with water, except where there isn't any available, in which case it must be spread and smothered far enough in advance to let it cool before you leave. Stir it and feel it after you're finished. If you burn your hand, you'll have learned a worthwhile lesson in what it takes to put out a fire. Don't leave a fire that isn't cold to the touch, even after stirring.

Burning the fire out will simplify the job of putting it out and cleaning up afterward. Ashes disintegrate readily; charcoal and soot last and last. Pick out the remains of any of your trash which didn't burn and take it with you in your trash bag. Scatter the rest of the fire and the fireplace as inconspicuously as possible, and replace the duff if you removed any. The exception in heavily used spots may be to leave a permanent fireplace so that every stone around the lake doesn't eventually become sooty. If you do, build a good fireplace, so that others will use it. If one is already built, use it yourself rather than make a new scar.

Spare wood should be scattered, too, unless a fireplace is left. Leave the site at least as unspoiled as you found it.

STOVES

Stoves for the backpacker are amazingly efficient devices, though they tend to suffer somewhat by comparison to campfires. The surroundings have to be pretty bleak to make snuggling up around the flames of a gasoline pressure stove sound romantic. The food, however, tastes just as good, and the woods around often look a lot more romantic than those which have supported too many campfires. Some beautiful areas that have been closed to backpackers because of excessive population could be opened with the proviso that stoves and tents would have to be used instead of fires and "natural" shelters.

Stoves have other advantages. After a long rain, you don't have to spend an hour hunting up or chopping out enough dry wood to get a fire started properly; you just pitch your shelter, crawl under it, and start cooking supper. In winter, cooking inside the tent or snow cave over a stove is often far more practical than building a fire outside atop green wood laid on the snow. Though every outdoorsman should know how to light a fire, in a lot of places he should *use* a stove.

Cooking over a stove requires several tricks. With a large party you may carry more than one and divide the labor, cooking a main dish on one stove and heating water or cooking a second dish on the other. For parties up to four, though, and sometimes larger ones, if only one stove is carried things must be cooked one at a time. This is really no hardship, once you get used to it. Try the stove out several times before you really need it, and if special accessories like prickers are needed, find some way to make sure that they are always with the stove. The merits and disadvantages of some types of stoves are discussed in some detail in Chapter 13, but the most obvious difference is between bottled-gas and liquid-fuel versions. The bottled-gas types are very easy to light, and there is little to be said about using them. You light a match and turn on the gas; that's all there is to it.

Liquid-fueled types are trickier, because the tanks aren't under pressure, and because the feeding apparatus has to get hot before the fuel will come out as a gas rather than a liquid. These problems are solved in several ways, depending on the brand, the size of the stove, and the fuel. The stove may have a pump to pressurize the tank. With a pumped gasoline stove, you pressurize the tank, open the valve so that some raw gas comes out, light it and allow it to burn and heat the generator, and finally you open up the valve all the way, and off she goes—hopefully. Kerosene stoves all have pumps, and the operation is the same, except that an alcohol primer has to be used to heat the generator. If the pressure starts to get low with a pumped stove, you just pressurize it a bit more.

The really small gasoline stoves which are most suitable for the single backpacker or small party are not equipped with pumps, and there is a certain amount of black magic associated with bending them to your will. The first thing to do is fill the tank, since they are a nuisance to relight in the middle of cooking. Opening the filling cap also assures you that you aren't fighting a slight vacuum in the tank, which will develop as the stove cools. The next step depends on the temperature and on the style of black magic you subscribe to. The idea is to create enough pressure in the tank to force some gasoline through the valve. Once the initial pressure is created, things are fairly simple. You open the valve and allow a little fuel to collect; then you close the valve, light the gasoline, allow it to burn almost out, and then open the valve again. If you give the proper incantation, the stove will now roar to life and will keep going until it is empty. If it isn't quite hot enough it may sputter for a little while, sometimes blowing itself out, but it will soon settle down to a steady roar, and after this it is rarely temperamental.

The trick is getting that initial pressure. Though it may seem odd, I have always found these stoves very simple to light in cold or cool weather. You just warm the stove with your hands (if it's really cold, put the stove in your jacket for a little while so that it doesn't freeze to your hands). After you've warmed it, open the valve and see if the gasoline comes out; then proceed as outlined above. In warmer weather your hands will not warm the stove above the air temperature enough to pressurize it, or else it will happen so slowly that you'll begin to feel like a fool sitting around clasping your stove to your heart. At this point you can heat the stove by pouring a little gasoline into one of the many recesses provided by the manufacturer and igniting this primer. Some schools of sorcery believe in pouring on gasoline and setting a match immediately in all cases, never using their hands to warm the stove. This works, but I avoid it when I can; I think this treatment tends to bring on stove trouble at a much earlier date than normal. Either way, it's an article of faith rather than reason, so suit yourself. One can also hold lighted matches or paper under the stove to heat the tank. Personally, I like to carry a cigarette lighter, which is handy for lighting fires or pressurizing stoves.

If all this seems a bit more trouble than it's worth, you may prefer the simpler bottled-gas stoves. Once you're used to them, however, the gasoline types are not really very troublesome. Don't forget to be careful with the gasoline. Frustration and cold hands should not lull you into lighting the stove while the open fuel can is sitting nearby. I always fill the stove outside the tent, and I light it there if possible.

With gasoline stoves, *use white gas* or one of the special fuels sold in camping stores at ridiculous prices. *Do not use leaded gasoline*, whatever the stove instructions say. The fumes from leaded gas are poisonous, and the effect is cumulative, so it is a good rather than a bad thing that most stoves won't function with leaded gasoline. With any stove inside a tent, make sure there is adequate ventilation, since there will always be some carbon monoxide produced. Take care about tipping, too, especially when snow camping. With a snow base, the stove can melt itself down and tip over. Besides losing your stew and making your sleeping bag uncomfortable, someone could be badly burned if the apparatus tipped over.

Stoves, whatever the type, should be protected from the wind. Whether the stove keeps burning or not, a strong breeze will blow most of the heat away before it reaches your pot. Some kind of windbreak is necessary, whether one carried for the purpose, your tent, or something improvised on the spot.

FOOD FOR WEEKEND TRIPS

Some people like to spend a lot of time planning menus for weekend trips, but I've never had enough self-discipline to bother. For longer travels, one really has to plan pretty carefully, but I generally just make up a menu for two or three days in my kitchen or in the supermarket on Thursday night. I simply count the number of meals of each kind I have to prepare for and then start mixing and filling until I have the right number of bags sitting on the counter.

Beginners may prefer getting started with the meals prepackaged for backpackers which are available at the same place you bought your sleeping bag, pack, or stove. I've always found it easier to pack my own, for a number of reasons. For one thing, most of the packages are allegedly quantities for four people. Either the manufacturers don't go out enough to know that the average party is not four, or they know they are misleading about quantities. If I have to repackage for one or two anyway, I might just as well do it myself to begin with, for a fraction of the price. The price is the second problem. With rare exceptions these foods, although quite good, are priced outrageously. Third, they are usually packaged with big air bubbles in the packages, which help cushion the food but take up a lot of unnecessary space.

As I've already said, proportions are unreliable. If you stick to one brand for a little while, you will find out how to compute portions, but every brand is different, and I find that the effort is not worth the reward. That is, once I find out that their four-man meal is really good for two, I not only have a hungry weekend behind me, in the future I know I will have to pay twice the already high price.

89

Some of the portions verge on the absurd. There are one-pot meals purporting to provide a serving for one and weighing one ounce. Presumably a one-pot meal is designed for supper, which certainly ought to provide a third of the day's rations. Now, even if the stuff were pure fat, which has the highest fuel value per pound, it would contain less than 260 calories, which would be a tenth of a rather thin diet for a small woman. With meals like that you can lose a lot of weight, but you may not get far. Some brands have generous portions, but you'll have to experiment. For these reasons it's pretty hard to shop by price until you've already tried nearly everything on the market and made notes on it.

My own solution is to get a lot of my supplies from the market, especially for weekend trips. I order my specialized dehydrated foods in bulk from one of the manufacturers, which makes it a great deal cheaper. When I want to use them, I dip the amount I want from a large container into my stew sack.

A lot of foods that are very suitable for backpacking are available in the supermarkets these days. For bases, there are instant whipped potatoes, which I often use when I want to be able to produce a meal by just pouring in hot water. There are also rice, noodles, macaroni products, bulgur wheat, flour, and various other things. These form excellent bases for one-pot meals or for more imaginative concoctions. They are the main ingredients of most ready-packaged camping foods, anyway.

The essential basis for a good cooked supper is to use a starch like the ones just mentioned, add any seasonings and vegetables that you think would go well, put in some margarine or butter for flavor and calories, and finally add a good source of protein: meat, fish, cheese, dried eggs, dried milk, or a proper combination of vegetables (see pp. 103–104).

You can carry a few fresh vegetables along if you like, or you can save weight by taking the dehydrated kind. Dehydrated vegetables can be bought quite inexpensively in bulk, or you can sometimes get some good combinations in packaged soups. Cheese travels well and isn't too expensive as a source of protein. Dried eggs and milk are nearly perfect backpacking foods in all respects. Sausages can be cut into a stew as well as eaten at lunch. There are also various vegetable protein additives, with beef, chicken, and bacon flavorings, which can be added to one-pot meals like meat. Various dried meats are also available in bulk.

Many weekend backpackers use canned meats and fish to finish off a one-pot meal of dehydrated starches and vegetables. The additional weight of a can of tuna, boned chicken, luncheon meat, or corned beef is relatively small on short trips, and they are inexpensive and easy to get.

The suggested recipes later in this chapter should give you a good idea of starting quantities, and you can make your own adjustments as you go along. More detailed information on nutritional requirements is also discussed, but one really doesn't have to worry much about them on short trips, unless it suits the fancy. The only requirements for weekend backpacking meals are that they keep until they are eaten, that they taste good, and that there is enough to go around.

BREAKFAST

There is probably less agreement on the subject of breakfast than in any other area of backpacking. Men who use the same kind of equipment and make suppers that are nearly identical will practically fall to blows over breakfast. In the interests of party harmony, if you plan the meals, check with the other members of the group and try to come up with a solution which won't offend anyone's preferences too much.

One solution to the breakfast problem is the full-scale, no-holds-barred, cooked breakfast. Bacon and eggs, pancakes, or both, are made up, and the most extreme members of this school will even get out the reflector oven and bake muffins or coffee cake. Now, I am at the other end of the breakfast spectrum, so I have to work pretty hard to give these methods a fair presentation, smacking as they do of unseemly fanaticism. Actually, it's not so difficult to make breakfasts like this, and I don't mind eating them. It's just that you have to get up at least an hour early to have that kind of meal, and I would rather stay in bed.

An intermediate course of action is to make a good cooked cereal, which doesn't take too much time and dirties only one pot. This is a fairly good technique for relatively large groups with a central commissary, providing you can agree on a cereal. Liberal lacing with raisins, nuts, butter, milk, and brown sugar increases the food value and makes most gruels palatable.

The instant hot cereals are a good possibility for people who have to have hot food but are as lazy as I am in the morning. These can be bought in bulk or in individual packets. Since they only require the addition of hot water, there is no need to dirty or clean a pot or to watch and stir the stuff. When you wake up, you put on a pot of water to heat, and this is used for cereals and hot drinks according to taste. Have a good selection of drinks and goodies to add to the cereal, and your breakfast problem is solved. Everyone can go about the business of breaking camp, waking up, and thinking his noble or ignoble early-morning thoughts with a minimum of friction and effort.

I have found that every year I take less trouble with breakfast, unless I have a bacon-and-eggs type of companion. I prefer to get on the trail fairly quickly, rather than spend a great deal of time fixing breakfast and cleaning up. Usually, though, I have some cold cereal, into which the powdered milk is already mixed, so that I just add water. Sometimes I use a commercial cereal like Grape Nuts, adding raisins and nuts. Here is the recipe for a very pleasant and highly nutritional cereal you can make up at home.

GRANOLA

½ cup honey	½ cup sesame seeds
¾ cup oil	½ cup shredded coconut
½ cup dried milk	(unsweetened)
(¾ cup if instant)	½ cup raw cashew pieces
4 cups rolled oats	or other nuts, more if
¼ teaspoon salt	you like
1⅓ cups wheat germ	

Warm the honey and oil in a pan, stir in the other ingredients, and then spread in a thin layer in shallow baking pans or cookie sheets. Roast at 350° F., stirring every 5 minutes, until lightly browned, around 10–15 minutes.

Ingredients for granola can be varied to taste. Add raisins or chopped dried fruit if you like. For breakfast I add more powdered milk when I bag the granola. Without added milk or water it makes a tasty trail food.

Another fast breakfast advocated by some of my lazy compatriots is the commerical "instant breakfast" drink. One simply shakes up the powdered milk and the contents of the envelope the night before and drinks it in the morning while rolling the sleeping bag and tent.

A final method which I recommend on those mornings when you really want to get off in a hurry is to simply start taking lunch breaks as soon as you get on the trail, forgetting about breakfast as a separate meal altogether. You can make up a quart of orange juice for liquid, as a bow to convention. This allows you to pack away all the cooking things the night before. You just drag yourself out, roll up the sleeping bag and the tent, and start walking. About the time you've waked up enough to realize that your boot laces need adjusting and your shirt is inside out, you can stop for a breather and the first of many snacks.

LUNCHES, SNACKS, AND TRAIL FOOD

Most backpackers keep themselves fueled during the day with a long series of snacks. The only distinguishing feature of "lunch" is likely to be that it gets a longer break than ten minutes, and that it is slightly larger. If the stove is handy or fire-building materials convenient, it is often pleasant to have a cup of tea or soup with lunch, especially in raw weather, but few trail walkers actually bother to cook lunch. Instead they carry various sorts of trail food in their pockets or in an accessible corner of the pack. This is eaten cold and requires little or no preparation.

There are many popular kinds of trail food, and you can adjust yours to suit your taste, mood, finances, and metabolism. From a practical point of view, when several people travel together, it is usually most convenient to prepare supper and perhaps breakfast together. Trail food is best left to the individual, though, except for very long trips when each ounce must be planned and rationed meticulously.

I plan my trail food fairly generously, allowing some flexibility, and also taking care of my emergency food supply by simply carrying a little extra salami, chocolate, nuts, and so on. This also allows for daily variations in need. I don't begin to parcel things out into daily portions until the length of a trip exceeds one week. Suit your own taste. Trail food is a good place to adjust for individual needs, simply because amounts and frequency of eating are easy to leave to each person, when all carry and purchase their own. Variety can be achieved by the age-old method of barter.

Possibilities for trail food are almost unlimited, except that most such food should be concentrated and fairly durable. Banging around in a pocket or a pack simply destroys some types of food pretty thoroughly, and the number of special protective containers you carry should be limited. Some people take the trouble to protect a few delicacies, though, whether they lean toward tomatoes, deviled eggs, or nondurable breads.

Good trail foods that will keep for the required time are the long-lasting hard salamis and sausages, candy, nuts, cheese, hard breads, jerky, pemmican, peanut butter, butter or margarine, mixes for fruit drinks, dried fruits, and special commercially made trail rations.

Some details are given below concerning nutritional requirements and packing the most energy into the least weight, but with experience, you will be the world's greatest expert on the way your body functions best. With all the modern knowledge about nutrition, there is still an incredible amount of hogwash written. A good many studies, applied to the history of the species, would conclusively prove that we could never have survived to modern times. In fact, the body is amazingly adaptable to different eating regimes, but periods of adjustment are required. Most backpackers have strange requirements, because they spend much of their lives in relatively inactive work and head for the hills on weekends. The body never really gets in proper tune for this change. A common pattern is to feel really ready to go on Monday morning, when you are back at the desk; by the following weekend you're tuned up to get as far as the coffee machine when you're trying to push up a few thousand feet with a pack on your back, and so it goes. Some people handle this transition best with a lot of small meals of sugars and starches, while others do better with less frequent doses of protein and fat. Use what works best and feels best for you, especially on short trips. On longer ones, when your body will adjust to the exercise and diet, you want to plan your menu with at least an eye to nutritional requirements.

As one additional suggestion for trail food, here is a recipe for a version of the very durable, edible, and long-lasting Logan bread. Don't plan on eating it in the desert when water is low.

LOGAN BREAD

5 cups water	2½ cups raw or dark brown sugar
4 pounds whole wheat flour	firmly packed
1 pound soy flour	1¼ teaspoons baking powder
	1½ teaspoons salt

1½ cups honey   2 cups melted shortening
1½ cups blackstrap molasses

Mix all this stuff up thoroughly. Do not use a weak spoon or try this when your arm is feeling ineffectual—this dough lets you know it's substantial food right from the start. It should be tough stuff; if it isn't add some more flour. Flours do vary in the amount of liquid they absorb. When it is all mixed, bake it in 2-inch deep baking pans for an hour at 350° F. Cut it into 2-inch squares while it is still warm. Set the oven for warm, put the bread in to dry with the door left ajar, and leave it for 8–12 hours. Time depends on temperature, humidity, and your taste. The longer you leave it, the tougher it will get. As long as this bread is dried fairly well, it keeps for a long, long time.

FOODS FOR BACKPACKING

However they are prepared, foods for backpacking have to contain plenty of nutrients in a small amount of weight. Since a lot of our foods contain large amounts of water, one of the best methods to reduce the weight of your menu is to dehydrate it. Drying has also been used for thousands of years as a method of food preservation, so that it often solves two of the backpacker's problems simultaneously. Most menus for long trips will consist primarily of dehydrated foods.

Fortunately, modern methods of dehydration have made the selection of foods available to the outdoorsman much wider and improved the quality of many items. The old-timer stuck to the 3B's—beans, bannock, and bacon, and if he was a sophisticate he added some rice for variety. World War II brought some nutritious, but often revolting, additions. The selection is now so vast that no one is likely to try all the available brands and varieties of dried food.

Besides being dried, foods may also be completely or partially precooked. Some taste very good, while others suffer somewhat from the processing. But precooked foods can often be a real boon to the backpacker for various reasons that will be discussed later in the chapter. Take a look at the label to distinguish between various types. "Instant" foods are completely precooked and need only the addition of hot water for reconstitution to a ready-to-eat condition. Read the fine print to see whether this is the case or whether a few minutes cooking is required. This latter type has also been precooked and is almost as useful for the backpacker. Foods which require fifteen minutes or more of cooking are probably not precooked. They sometimes taste better, are often cheaper, and they may be very satisfactory, but they present some problems for the camp cook.

There are several ways of dehydrating food. The oldest uses low heat, as with drying in the sun. Food can also be cooked and dried at the same time, with a higher heat. Variations of these techniques stir, flake, or somehow agitate the food so that it will reconstitute more easily when water is added. Vacuum drying works to this same end. The most modern method is freeze-drying, in which the food dries in a vacuum at temperatures below freezing. Freeze-drying maintains the original cellular structure of the food more or less intact, so that it will usually reconstitute faster and more completely than things dried by other means. This method usually preserves the texture and flavor of the food better than any other. It is also more expensive, and the food is much more fragile and more bulky, generally requiring protection by elaborate packaging.

Some types of food meet the requirements of the backpacker quite well without special processing, and these are very useful. Peanut butter, some cheeses, some sausages, nuts, and many other foods have been favorites for a long time.

NUTRITIONAL REQUIREMENTS

Even the backpacker who lives to eat rather than eats to live has to combine business with pleasure if he plans to carry a couple of weeks' food around with him. He can't afford too many pounds of food with little or no nutritional value. The first thing he needs is plain, ordinary fuel. To hump a pack up a mountain or keep warm on a cold day you have to burn up lots of digestible food. The amount of energy available in a piece of candy or a stick of celery is normally measured by nutritionists in calories, the weight-watcher's bugbear.

You are not suited, as plants are, to get energy directly from the sun, so any work you do has to be powered by burning the food you eat. Your body can store some of that food as body fat, giving you reserves, but ultimately all your energy comes from food. People's needs vary depending on many things, but you can expect to use between 3,000 and 5,000 calories per day, depending on body weight, metabolism, physical condition, air temperature, and the amount of work you do. Probably your needs will be between 4,000 and 4,500 calories for a day on the trail.

Foods are divided into three main categories: carbohydrates, proteins, and fats. Some of each category is necessary for a good diet, as are certain minerals and vitamins. First, though, let's consider these three main categories: Carbohydrates—sugars and starches—generally provide around 1,600 calories per pound, and protein used as fuel has a similar value. Fats provide over twice as many calories, about 4,000 per pound. All these values are reduced by the presence of moisture or indigestible bulk in the food.

From these figures it is obvious that fats provide far more energy, pound for pound, than any other food, and the backpacker planning a menu should make use of this fact. The most concentrated foods available do have a high proportion of fat, but most of us would not relish drinking cooking oil for an entire week, so there are limits to the amount of fat that can be used. Fats have other special virtues. More heat is produced in digesting them than other foods, and they take longer to assimilate, so they have special value in helping one to stay warm and in "sticking to the ribs." They should receive special emphasis in cold-weather diets. In cold weather most people will happily eat far more fat than they will when temperatures are warm. On the other hand, fats do not produce much quickly available energy, and they require a good blood supply in the stomach for digestion. Hence they are likely to be unappetizing, indigestible, and even nauseating under circumstances when circulation to the stomach is poor, for example when you are at very high altitudes or when you are quite cold and exhausted.

Proteins, as a fuel, have a caloric value similar to that of carbohydrates but some of the other characteristics of fat. They, too, produce more heat in digestion and take longer, so that they "stick to the ribs" and help the body stay warm, although not so much as fat.

Carbohydrates are generally the most quickly digested types of food, so they are far better for quick energy or warmth than either fats or proteins. This is especially true of glucose (dextrose), which can be used by the body without conversion.

Some carbohydrates and fats are generally desirable in a diet, and   97 they present little problem, since almost any menu concocted by the back-packer will have more than ample quantities for nonfuel needs. Proteins, on the other hand, may present a bit more of a problem, especially to the impecunious.

PROTEINS

Carbohydrates and fats really provide much better fuel than proteins, the former being more easily assimilated and the latter providing a maximum in calories per pound. Proteins, however, are essential for another reason—they are used by the body to build new tissue. A good protein intake is essential for the sedentary city-dwellers taking to the hills on the weekend. You need proteins to allow the body to rebuild those aching muscles.

When protein is used as fuel, it does not matter much whether it is animal or vegetable in origin. Like carbohydrates, there are some proteins that humans can't digest, but most are equally suitable for getting you up the hill. For rebuilding muscles, however, all proteins are not equal. Proteins contain varying quantities of different amino acids, and eight of these acids must be present in certain proportions to be used as building blocks by the body.

Since protein to be used for tissue replacement must have all eight amino acids in the right proportions, any protein which doesn't meet the requirement will be used as simple fuel. All the amino acids must be present in the right quantities at the right time, since the body cannot store them up. If only half the right amount of one acid is present, only half of each of the others will be used for tissue replacement; the rest will go for fuel.

All this detail is given because it has an important practical consequence—expense. Proteins which naturally have approximately the right proportions of amino acids are the various animal foods: meat, fish, and dairy products. Vegetable proteins are generally low in some of the essential amino acids.

To have adequate protein in your diet, you must include reasonable amounts of meat or dairy products in the menu, or alternatively, vegetables used in quantities and mixtures that assure an adequate supply of usable protein.

VITAMINS AND MINERALS

The propagandists of the pill industry have educated us all to our need for many essential vitamins and minerals. Fortunately, almost any reasonable menu provides an adequate supply of them and you are unlikely to need any supplementary supply. Some backpackers on long trips prefer to take pills to ensure against a deficiency. There are also advocates of supplements of the water-soluble vitamins even on short trips, since these cannot be stored by the body and may run short when unusual strain occurs. Follow your own prejudices.

FILLING YOUR SHOPPING BASKET

What you buy for supplies will depend to some extent on the length of your trip, how often you go off, and what sort of cooking you plan to do, but it will probably depend mostly on how much money you can afford to put out to keep body and soul together during your trip.

The freeze-dried meals which are now readily available from many suppliers are often very good and convenient. The biggest problem with them is cost, which is sometimes just high and sometimes ridiculous. Another problem with them is bulk and poorly conceived packaging. But basically, they are very good if you can afford them. Their greatest advantage is that most of them need very little cooking—you can pour in hot water and they're done. This has special virtues in some situations, which will be discussed later.

There is little need for instructions if you are buying any of the ready-made meals from backpacking suppliers. Once you've decided the true proportions needed for each person, the directions on the package will take care of you. An increasing number of such meals are available in supermarkets, sometimes costing less than the ones at the specialty shops, but not always offering greater value.

The beginner looking for an easy introduction to camp cooking should pick meals with one or two hearty courses rather than the six-dish ones that take too much time and too many pots to make a bad reproduction of similar meals at home.

If you buy foods at the supermarket or dehydrated foods in bulk, they will often need repackaging. Dried food can be packed simply enough in plastic bags sealed with rubber bands. Peanut butter, butter, margarine, jams, and similar foods can be carried either in screwtop containers made to be tight or in plastic squeeze-tubes with removable sealing strips. Both types of containers are available in backpacking shops. Eggs can be broken into these same containers, and hard-boiled eggs can be carried in special cases made for them.

Most backpackers soon find that the biggest problem in shopping is protein. Good starch bases have been available for years, and there are even more available now. A good instant base is even available in the supermarkets in the form of mashed-potato flakes. Rice, spaghetti, and noodles are old standbys, and many more exotic grain products can be found to satisfy the most jaded palate. Vegetables are also pretty easy to get at reasonable prices, although you may have to go to a special supplier for these. I order about a year's supply at once from a large supplier of dehydrated foods.

Flavoring is also easy to manage. Judicious use of spices will get you off to a good start, and you can get interest and variety by using various kinds of sauces. Many are available in packages at the store or, more cheaply, from a mail-order supplier. Open the packages at home and dump the contents into your stew bag. You can get by even more cheaply by using some of the extracts and flavorings available in larger quantities at reduced prices, especially since you'll probably repackage the stuff anyway.

The actual protein is the expensive part if you stick to meat products. You can buy dehydrated ground beef or chicken or ham pieces, freeze-dried patties or steaks or chops. One of the best ingredients for stews is Wilson's meat bar, and if you can afford it this is a good alternative. They cost about $1.50 each for a three-ounce bar, which works out to $8.00 per pound. Although each bar is the equivalent of about ½ pound of raw meat, it's still expensive for my budget. If the price seems cheap to you, read no further. Wilson's also makes a bacon bar, at a slightly lower price.

Some alternatives have already been mentioned. Working powdered milk into your menus will give you lots of high-quality protein. Cheese is an excellent flavoring and protein source, and the harder cheeses keep very well. Dried cheeses keep best, and for long trips dried cheddar can be got from specialty houses to supplement conventional dry jack, Parmesan, and

Romano. For economy, though, vegetable protein is the best solution by far. In the proper mixtures, vegetable protein is as high in quality as meat protein, and with the proper use of flavorings, it tastes just as good in one-pot meals. You can buy vegetable protein concentrates, already mixed in the proper quantities, either in meal form (often called multipurpose food, or MPF) or in a textured, flavored form designed to replace meats. Some of the dehydrated-food suppliers carry these.

Another alternative is to simply make dishes with approximately the right combinations of sources of vegetable protein. See the reading list at the back of this book for a good book giving lots of combinations.

A list of a few good backpacking foods follows. It is far from complete, but it should help you to get started. Cooking times have to be adjusted for altitude. See the discussion on high-altitude cooking (page 108). Look at the directions on the package. Products vary, and the comments on preparation here are meant as a rough guide to help you plan meals and order food.

STARCHES, GRAINS, AND SUCH

Dehydrated potatoes have become one of the most widely used bases because one simply adds hot water. Repackage the potatoes before the trip, adding 2 tablespoons of powdered milk to each cup of flakes. Use $1\frac{1}{3}$ cups of water for each cup of flakes. Dehydrated potatoes are also available in nuggets and slices, neither of which reconstitutes right away. Plan on cooking these about the same length of time as other dehydrated vegetables. The mashed potatoes go well with cheese, gravy, and some meat or meat substitute, or made in a fairly dry mixture and fried as potato cakes, perhaps with a bit of bacon.

Noodles of various kinds and shapes make an excellent start for innumerable one-pot meals, and they are one of my favorite bases. They cook in about 8 minutes of boiling, and they are quite nourishing, since they are generally made with egg as well as flour. For camp cooking with limited amounts of heat, I generally cook them in just enough water to cover them all through the cooking. Frequent stirring keeps them from sticking. Then other ingredients for the meal can be added when the noodles are done. If vegetables are part of the dish, they may need to be cooked for a while before adding noodles. Noodles go with almost any sort of protein and sauce combination. If you are cooking over a fire and have plenty of water, it is a good idea to cook them in more water and drain some of it. The main defect of noodles is their bulk; they take up more space than spaghetti or macaroni, and this may be important on long trips.

Spaghetti, macaroni, and other similar products have always been favorites for the camp cook. They generally require more cooking time than noodles, around ten to fifteen minutes, but this is not excessive in most situations. Tomato sauces are traditional, but macaroni products go very well with many flavor combinations. Cook them the same way as noodles, only longer.

Rice is an old wilderness standby. It tastes good for supper and even makes a good breakfast cereal. It is compact and almost indestructible. Plain rice requires about twenty minutes to cook. Pour the rice into twice its volume of boiling water, cover and keep barely boiling with the cover on for the required time. If other ingredients are to be added, more water can be used. Rice goes with nearly everything. Quick-cooking and instant rice are available, and are useful to the backpacker who needs their special features, although I don't like the texture as well as that of plain rice. Brown rice is usually not suitable for general backpacking menus because it takes twice as long as white rice to cook. You might plan on using it occasionally where this wouldn't matter.

Various other grains make good bases and provide variety, but unless you can find quick-cooking kinds, they are usually impractical for the backpacker, requiring at least forty-five minutes' cooking time. Health-food stores are often good shopping places for foods like this, and if you can discover a source for quick-cooking wheat or other grains, you will find them pleasant. (Quick-cooking grains are simply those which have been precooked by one of several processes.)

One very good grain product that cooks rapidly enough to be useful to the camp cook is bulgur wheat, a very old wheat preparation that is readily available in health-food stores and in many supermarkets. It is wheat which has been precooked, dried, and cracked. Cook it and use it like rice. Cooking takes about fifteen minutes.

Legumes like beans, peas, lentils, and garbanzos are excellent food, and were the staple of most of the trappers, prospectors, and other assorted pioneers. They provide lots of protein, especially when combined with grain products or animal protein. They also have almost any other virtue that the backpacker could wish, except that they take so long to cook that they are nearly useless in their normal form. You can, however, get several kinds of precooked beans which cook quickly and can be used in innumerable dishes. Bean and pea flours make fine soups or thickeners if you can find them. They are usually marketed now as soup mixes. There are good instant pea-soup mixes which are filling and which provide a good source of protein, especially if rice, noodles, or some other grain is included in the meal.

Flours are actually merely other forms of grain, but they cook more quickly than whole grains, so they are useful to the backpacker who learns to cook with them in camp. The various wheat flours are the most common, but almost any other flour you can find can be used in the same ways, and will provide interesting variety. Soy flour, made from soybeans rather than grain, is particularly useful for its nutty flavor and its richness in protein. It can be used for thickenings or added to other flours. Flour can be used to thicken gravy. If you buy a gravy mix in the store you will get meat flavoring and flour. You can make the same thing with instant bouillon, flour, and water. I use a lot of flour for dumplings and bannock. Both of these can be made from the same mixture, which you concoct at home in short order. At camp, just stir in water and add to stews or bake in a pan or on a stick. See the recipe later in this chapter.

VEGETABLES

A great variety of vegetables can now be bought in good dehydrated versions. Freeze-drying produces the best taste, and also makes vegetables which reconstitute more quickly, but it is expensive. Quite a few vegetables turn out very nicely with less expensive processing. Cooking time can be reduced by carrying a wide-mouth screwtop container. When you stop at a stream around lunchtime, put the evening vegetables in the container with some water to soak. They can then be cooked that evening almost like fresh vegetables. Dried green peas, onions, flaked cabbage make excellent material for stews or soups. Carrots, green beans, beets, and corn are also good, but they take somewhat longer to cook, except for freeze-dried varieties. Flaked green peppers and onions make good seasonings and can be added to nearly anything. Powdered yams cook instantly, and mixed with some butter and brown sugar, they make a very good second dish for occasional variety. Tomato flakes mix with water to make paste, sauce, or juice. They are one of the best flavorings available to the camp cook for many kinds of dishes. When buying dried vegetables, check the label for cooking times and make sure that they are suitable for the dishes you have in mind. Different processing methods make a lot of difference in cooking times. Aside from freeze-dried vegetables, you will find that some carrots take four times as long as others to cook. Certain vegetables need to be partially precooked to be practical, since they aren't very suitable for backpacking meals if left raw. If you're buying in bulk, be sure to ask about cooking times when you write a processor for his price list.

FRUITS

Dried fruits make good trail food eaten as they are, and they can also be used at supper and breakfast in various other ways. Raisins, dried apricots, dried apples, figs, prunes, and dried peaches are familiar items in any supermarket. All can be stewed or eaten in cereals, besides being used as trail food. Many backpackers like to stew some for desert at suppertime, making extra to be eaten cold at the next morning's breakfast.

Quite a few other fruits can be bought from houses that specialize in dried foods. Banana flakes are useful crunchy trail food, and they can be added to other dishes. Various fruit mixtures are available, some of them quite tasty, including citrus fruits, strawberries, and fruit cocktail, good for a treat at the end of a week on the trail.

Dehydrated citrus juices are also very good and not terribly expensive when they are bought in quantity. Dehydrated orange, lemon, lime, grapefruit, and pineapple crystals produce a beverage at least as acceptable as other means of preservation.

Oranges are one of the most popular extravagances of weekend backpackers, and there is no doubt that an orange is a particularly fine way to finish a lunch on a trail or the top of a peak. You should carry the peels out, however. The refuse from most fruit is easily disposed of—if it is not burned or eaten by animals it returns quickly to the earth. Orange peels don't burn, and they seem to last almost forever, so don't toss them on the side of the trail.

BEVERAGES

Instant coffee has gotten better, and outdoorsmen have gotten lazier, so few backpackers carry ground coffee anymore. Pack a bag of your favorite instant and make it by the cup. If you are like me and drink it black, don't forget your companions' preferences when you are packing. After spending one trip facing cream-and-sugar drinkers in the morning with no cream (substitute) and sugar, I've always remembered to ask. If you really want to make coffee from scratch you can avoid taking a pot by making "boiled coffee" in a regular pan. Bring the water to a rolling boil, dump in the proper measure of coffee, put on a cover, and set aside for a few minutes. Add a little cold water to settle the grounds. It takes a little while to get the technique, and there are variations in method, but you can make very good coffee this way.

Tea, for some reason, is a much more popular beverage in the woods than coffee. You'll have to experiment, but as a rule take more tea and less coffee than tastes at home would lead you to think you will want. You can make it by the pot, but most people handle the beverage problem with hot water and a choice of additives. Tea bags permit brewing in individual cups.

Hot chocolate is another good wilderness beverage. Though the "real" kind is certainly nicer, a bag of instant hot chocolate allows people to make their own from the common hot-water pot.

Bouillon is another excellent beverage for the woods, especially just after getting into camp. For one thing, it helps to replace the salt you have been sweating away, and so it often stops a thirst that other drinks won't quench.

An unlikely hot drink that is particularly fine in winter and popular with some at other times is gelatin desert. Make it according to directions, but don't bother to cool it; drink it hot instead.

Cold drinks are popular but optional. They consist of things to add to your water bottle, contributing flavor and sugar to lunch. Citrus juices have been mentioned already, but there are also numerous artificially flavored drinks ranging from lemonade to iced tea. Many are good, particularly if water-purification tablets have left a flavor to be covered.

MISCELLANY

There is a long list of popular condiments, spices, side dishes, and so on, which are popular with many backpackers. Only a few will be mentioned here, and you will find many of your own.

Margarine or butter or a substitute is essential. Add to everything, especially one-pot meals and hot cereal. I use margarine because it is cheaper and keeps better. Either can be carried in a screwtop or tube container, but in hot weather make sure it is tight and cover with an extra plastic bag for extra protection. Some backpackers prefer to use a bottle of liquid oil instead of margarine or butter.

Carry salt and pepper in a shaker which has covers. On longer trips carry extra salt, which you will use heavily if you are perspiring.

I add my spices to dishes at home and rarely carry any loose ones on the trail. I use many, and you should suit your own taste, but a few that are especially useful to me are: garlic powder, oregano, sage, marjoram, parsley flakes, freeze-dried chives, cayenne, chili powder, and cumin.

Sweet condiments can be added to beverages, eaten at lunch, added to cereals, and even combined with snow to make sherbert. Take a few that are appropriate for the trip. Sugar and brown sugar are the most convenient to carry, but some people like to carry syrup, molasses, jam, or honey.

If you like desserts, you can use a bit of candy or some fruit, or you can take some instant pudding. Those who like to produce culinary masterpieces at camp can make a tolerable apple pie in a reflector oven, using reconstituted dried apples. The affluent looking for something original can try one of Trail Chef's dried cheesecakes. (I'm not kidding; they make up quickly and taste fairly good.)

THE WATER PROBLEM

There are several different kinds of water problems: the no-water problem, the frozen-water problem, the saltwater problem, and the downstream water problem. Right now we're talking about the last. Mountaineers may not have to worry about this one, but most other backpackers do. The problem is that most of the water in this country is now in such condition that if you drink it you'll get very sick. You may be in a real wilderness, but if there is a human habitation upstream, chances are the water is unfit to drink. I know of rivers in Alaska in very sparsely populated areas, which in a sane world would certainly be good, drinkable water. They aren't, be cause although there are very few people living on them, they dump their sewage directly into the river.

You must purify water if there is any doubt about its potability. Contaminated water can be really debilitating, so it is important to be sure. Most water can be assumed to be safe if there is no human habitation upstream. Stagnant water or other water supporting much algal growth is immediately suspect, but don't assume the water is good just because it looks that way. Although a stream will purify itself after some distance, there is no practical way to test it in the field, so if there are people uphill, even hundreds of miles away, you must decontaminate the water.

There are several ways of purifying water: boiling, chemical treatment, and microfiltration. The last is of interest mainly to expeditions in primitive areas, and will not be discussed here. Boiling water for twenty minutes will kill all harmful organisms, and this is obviously very convenient for cooking water. *Boil*, don't simmer. For purifying drinking water on the trail, boiling may be inconvenient, and either iodine or chlorine is used to kill any microorganisms likely to be found in North America. The most convenient way to carry these purifying agents is in soluble tablets: Halazone tablets liberate chlorine and Globaline tablets release iodine. In either case, dissolve one tablet per quart of clear water or two tablets per quart of murky water, shake until the tablets are dissolved, and leave for a half-hour before drinking. Water containing a lot of sediment should be filtered before adding chemicals. Several layers of cloth will clear heavy sediment.

Remember that decontamination of doubtful water is very important in the backcountry. Intestinal disturbances are especially common results from drinking tainted water, and they will put you flat on your back, which is not a good place to be if you are a week's walk from help. With virulent organisms, a small amount of bad water is sufficient, so swish the cover and lips of the container with treated water, use good water for brushing teeth, and heat your pans after washing them with suspect water. Being overcautious is worthwhile in this area.

COOKING AT HIGH ALTITUDES

Camp cooking is generally done by boiling, and the boiling temperature of water drops around 2° F. for every thousand feet of altitude gain. This may sound rather abstract and unimportant, but for the backpacker at high altitudes it is critical. I still remember very vividly a trip I took when I was ten years old with a friend at an altitude of eleven thousand feet. I was the perpetrator, and we camped around sunset in some army-surplus horror with the cold rain pouring down. We were undaunted, since we would soon have some hot supper. We built a fire in front of the shelter and started to cook the staple of the stew—fresh carrots. They boiled and boiled and boiled and the damned things stayed as hard as they had been in the store. We finally gave up and ate hot, raw carrots. It must have been a useful experience, because I haven't forgotten the effects of altitude on cooking since. I hope you won't either.

As a rough guide, you can figure that the cooking time for food will double with every six thousand feet or so of altitude. This is only a rough guide, though. Some foods require a relatively high heat to cook at all, and one finds that above, say ten thousand feet, you can boil them till doomsday, and not a blasted thing happens. If your trip calls for a campsite at eleven thousand feet, get quick-cooking or instant foods. Look at the label. If 45 minutes is tolerable cooking time, the label should call for 20 or 24 minutes if you're going to six thousand feet and 10 or 12 minutes for twelve thousand feet. The actual cooking time will be 45 minutes or so in all these cases. All the cooking times mentioned in this chapter are *sea-level cooking times*, as are most times you will find on packages. If you camp atop a fourteen-thousand-foot peak and try to cook some brown rice, you'll have an interesting way to spend the night—watching it boil.

Quick-cooking foods are the favorite solutions to the high-altitude cooking problem, but there are a couple of others. Frying is not much affected by the altitude, and trout caught in a lake at ten thousand feet will be ready to eat just about as fast as those hooked at sea level. Another solution which is rarely considered by backpackers is a pressure cooker. A four-quart model only weighs about 2½ pounds and generally comes equipped with separator baskets which weigh another eight ounces or so. Though not worthwhile for the average backpacker, a pressure cooker can actually mean a considerable saving in weight for a long trip at high altitude. The fuel used up in boiling water away is saved, and at the same time one gains great versatility in the variety of food available. Cooking time is greatly reduced, and in cold weather one saves condensation on tent walls. By allowing one to use ordinary foods instead of expensive freeze-dried menus, a pressure cooker can even save money. All this is not meant to recommend a pressure cooker to the camper who occasionally crosses a ten-thousand-foot pass, but for an extended trip above eight or ten thousand feet, it would be worth considering.

FRESH FOOD SUPPLEMENTS

In this book I have generally put down the idea of living off the land, both for practical reasons and from the point of view of a conservationist. I don't mean by this that you shouldn't make use of available foods, but that one shouldn't plan on living on them exclusively. A little study of local plants will often satisfy your lust for a salad or some fresh greens. In lake country, you may be able to dine on trout every night, carrying fat, flour, or corn meal, and side dishes to supplement fish suppers and breakfasts. In season, berries may liven your diet or even provide a significant amount of it. Used judiciously, natural foods will provide a welcome garnish to your meals. In some places and seasons, with the right knowledge of the country, you might be able to plan on getting most of your food from the land, but this is rarely possible in popular backpacking spots. More commonly, one would have to break the law, wreak ecological havoc, or spend all the time one planned on traveling, simply collecting food.

RECIPES

Following are a few recipes which I like. They are intended as suggestions; one-pot meals are a good place to exercise your own creativity. They are also varied in their applicability to different kinds of camping. On a weekend trip tuna fish would be a satisfactory protein source, readily available and not too heavy, but on a long trip the can and water content would rule it out. Dumplings, on the other hand, can be added to virtually any stew or soup.

CORNED BEEF AND CABBAGE (FOR ONE)

2 ounces dried flaked cabbage
2 ounces dried potato slices
1 ounce dried onions
2–4 tablespoons margarine
    salt and pepper to taste
½ can (12-ounce size) corned beef

Put everything except the meat into 4 cups of boiling water, and cook until tender, around 15 minutes. Pour off any excess water, dice the beef in and serve.

DUMPLING MIX

1 cup flour
2 tablespoons soy flour
2 tablespoons dehydrated eggs
2 tablespoons dried milk
1½ teaspoons baking powder
½ teaspoon salt
1 tablespoon shortening

Mix the ingredients at home, cutting in the shortening. In camp any amount you like can be mixed with enough water to make a soft dough. Then drop spoonfuls into the top of a cooking stew or soup, cover, and allow to cook 20 minutes. The same dough can be baked in a pan or twisted on a stick over a fire to make bannock.

STEW (FOR ONE)

4 ounces dried vegetables
4 ounces macaroni
2 ounces beef-flavored vegetable protein or freeze-dried ground beef
2 tablespoons soy flour
2 tablespoons margarine
1 tablespoon instant beef bouillon
    salt, pepper, oregano, sage, garlic to taste

Drop everything into a quart of boiling water and cook until done, depending on the longest cooking vegetables.

BULGUR AND CHEESE (FOR ONE)

1 cup bulgur wheat
1 tablespoon dried minced onion
1 bouillon cube (2 if you like)
2 tablespoons margarine
¼ pound cheddar cheese
2 tablespoons Parmesan or Romano cheese
  salt and pepper to taste

Mix the first three ingredients in advance. Cook 15 minutes with 2½ cups of water, and then add the cheese, salt, and pepper.

Part 2

Equipment: How to Buy and Make It

General Considerations   *7*

Since the backpacker's comfort and safety depend on his equipment, it obviously deserves careful choice. Good equipment is a bargain, even when the initial price is high, because it will last for years of hard use. Still, the beginner with limited finances cannot always afford long-range economy, at least not for everything. In this chapter, I will try to introduce some of the materials used for good backpacking equipment, the factors involved in choosing them, and the ways you can get equipment. Fortunately, good equipment isn't always expensive.

THE MATTER OF QUALITY

I've said that a high-quality backpacking outfit is a bargain, but this does not necessarily mean that high-priced gear is. Quality and price *do* tend to correspond better in lightweight camping equipment than in many other areas of the consumer economy, but there is plenty of room for intelligent shopping, and there are some tricks for getting bargains, for those to whom the savings are worth the effort.

The word is now out that backpacking has become big business, and the predictable flood of junk on the market has probably only begun. A lot of time will be spent in this section describing ways to cut corners and keep the expense of equipment down, but I have done this simply because a lot of people just can't afford to plunk down the amount of money it costs to completely outfit themselves at a good store. Still, don't be deluded; the bargains usually take some work to get, because good-quality equipment requires good, expensive materials and a lot of careful work, and these require money.

The ways of saving money and still getting good quality involve getting around these problems somehow, and this requires a little more trouble than walking around town and finding the cheapest stuff you can. Recently, a flood of aluminum contour packs, small tents, down equipment, and the like has started to hit the "surplus" stores, the discount houses, and the mass catalogue stores. I haven't seen them all, but in a number of searches I have yet to find a bargain among them. This merchandise is generally shoddy and overpriced. It's possible, of course, that you might find a deal, but let the buyer beware.

I really believe that if you are going to buy new merchandise off the shelf at a store, you will get a lot more for your money from one of the stores or catalogue businesses that specialize exclusively in lightweight camping equipment for wilderness travelers. They take pride in their equipment, and if something goes wrong with it, I think almost any of them will give you satisfaction. There are bargains to be had in "surplus" stores, but the bargains are in real government surplus, not in the junk specifically made to be sold at these outlets. The reason surplus can be a bargain is that the government sells it at a fraction of the original cost. Actually, it isn't a bargain at all, but since you have to pay for it on April 15 whether you get any benefit or not, you might as well recoup some of your losses.

Remember that the wilderness is a poor place to find out that your equipment is poorly made. The greater your ambitions, the more true this is. Badly made equipment for wilderness travel can ruin your vacation and even threaten your life. Personally, I put my equipment to some pretty severe tests, and I want to be sure it will stand up. I think it is far better to economize on other things than quality. I would rather have a couple of good wool sweaters and a tough, water-repellent wind shell than a poorly made expedition down parka. The reason is that they are dependable, and this is important in the backcountry.

For all these reasons, if money is not too much of a problem for you, the best way to get equipment is probably either to buy from one of the backpacking-mountaineering stores or to order from the catalogue of one of the mail-order specialists listed in the appendix or advertising in a magazine that caters to wilderness travelers. Send for a number of catalogues if you want to comparison shop; you can save quite a bit that way and get better equipment in the bargain. You may be able to get significant quantity discounts, especially if you get together with friends.

Some of these stores and manufacturers make better equipment than others, and prices vary somewhat, but you can be fairly sure that they won't sell you junk. Buying elsewhere will require that you know a great deal about construction to buy intelligently, and this isn't always possible. You can learn a bit by studying the sections here on the construction of equipment and choice of materials, but you can't see into the insulation layer of a sleeping bag—you have to judge from outside details. Shortcuts like using low-thread count nylon materials are becoming common in cut-rate sleeping bags. Buying from a store that caters to wilderness travelers will save you some of these headaches.

SAVING MONEY ON EQUIPMENT

False economy has been mentioned, but there are a lot of perfectly good ways to save money on your equipment if you need to. Buying surplus has been mentioned. Many former good buys are no longer available, but there are still some bargains to be had in the surplus market. The best one is in clothing. You can buy good wool clothing on the surplus market for a tenth of the cost of equivalent quality anywhere else. In a pinch you may have to pay a quarter of the ordinary cost, but this is still one of the best bargains around. Depending on the garment and your size, you may need or want alterations, but these are usually of a simple kind, requiring little skill. Some other good deals are available in surplus stores, and a few of them will be mentioned elsewhere in this section of the book. A couple of trustworthy mail-order outlets are listed in the appendix.

A few cautions are in order for shopping at surplus sources. The first is to beware of imitations. I have nothing against things made in Japan, but the imitation surplus gear which finds its way across the Pacific to the "surplus" outlets is rarely even worth inspecting. Equipment which bears all the litany of government codes may be surplus or it may be a rejected lot containing defects. These rejects may be fine for your purposes, but careful inspection is mandatory. The same caution applies to used surplus. Some very good items are available only in used condition, but make sure you check everything carefully before buying. Surplus stores are rarely the kinds of operations which will cheerfully refund your money if you find the trouble later.

Another good way to get equipment cheaply is to buy it secondhand. Bulletin boards, want ads, and garage sales occasionally offer good equipment at low prices, especially in college communities. Obvious cautions apply in buying secondhand equipment, but as more and more high-quality gear enters the market, this becomes an increasingly good way of saving money. The brand name and a few current catalogues will tell you a lot about the value of your prospective purchase.

The best deals of all result from the entry of the lightweight equipment stores into the full swing of the American economy. With yearly model changes, catalogues to get out on schedule, and so on, most dealers in backpacking equipment now have periodic sales of last year's models, items with slight defects, rental equipment, discontinued styles, and similar stuff. This is when the poor but knowledgeable backpacker gets his gear. The down jacket with the off-color pockets or the crooked seam goes for half-price, as does the parka with last year's snap pockets instead of this year's Velcro. The main problems with these sales are that you have to be in town, instead of mail ordering, and you often have to get to the store early. It's usually possible to find out well in advance when the sales will be held, and if you are convenient to a store you may be able to save a lot on your equipment this way.

Finally, comes the old-timer's favorite route—make your own. The cost of materials for good equipment is high, but the cost of labor is higher still. Lightweight gear demands lots of sewing time, and you can save money by doing the construction yourself. Doing your own sewing has other advantages, too. It often allows you to save money on materials, a possibility discussed below. It also can be its own reward: there is a particular satisfaction in designing and making your own equipment, especially when you can create it to suit your needs better than any commercially manufactured gear.

There are several possible methods for making your own outfit. You can start from scratch, designing and executing everything to meet your particular needs. You can follow someone else's pattern, modifying particular features if you want to. You can remodel a piece of equipment designed for some other use—surplus, for example. Finally, you can buy a kit, and put it together yourself. Which method you choose will depend on circumstances, including your own experience and feeling of confidence.

Kits are now available for many of the more difficult types of equipment, which formerly struck fear into the hearts of all but the most experienced. Even down bags of sophisticated design are available with the pieces precut and marked for sewing and the down packaged in separate bags for each compartment, a most welcome innovation. For someone who feels nervous about the very idea of sewing his own equipment, this is certainly the ideal way to get started.

Patterns for some items are included in this book. Many patterns and recommendations on designs and materials are to be found in Gerry Cunningham and Margaret Hansson's *Light Weight Camping Equipment and How to Make It,* a really useful book for anyone interested in making his own equipment. Various older books include some designs, especially for tents intended for use in the forest. One of the best and easiest ways to get patterns is from old equipment. If you have a parka or tent of an ideal design which is finally giving up the ghost, you need only rip out the seams to get a pattern for a new one. For clothing, the same method can be used to get a correct fit in basic pants and shirt patterns. Go up to your local secondhand clothing store, find an item of clothing with the correct generous dimensions for outdoor use, and you have a pattern which can be used with any material by just ripping out the seams.

Materials can be bought from many of the catalogues of lightweight outfitters, but before you pay full price, check your local mountaineering outlet and see if they have any remnants for sale. Most companies that make their own equipment periodically sell discontinued colors, small pieces, and bolts with discolorations or other unimportant defects. Such materials can often be bought at well below cost, especially when shops are having regular clearance sales.

PATTERNS AND INSTRUCTIONS FOR HEAVY-DUTY SHELL PARKA

The parka described here is constructed with a double layer of fabric throughout. If you make it with fairly heavy 60-40 cloth (60 per cent cotton

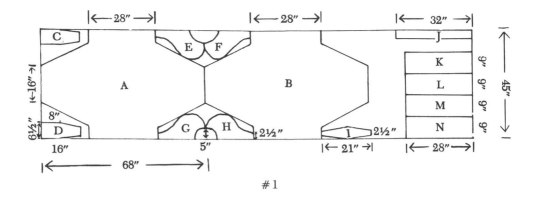

#1

and 40 per cent nylon), it should be quite durable and weatherproof. Basically, two parkas are made, and these are sewn together at the cuffs, the front opening, the bottom, and the drawstring at the waist. Seams joining the two are avoided elsewhere to make it more watertight. Many modifications are possible. The front can be cut only part way down the throat to make the parka a pullover. A rain parka can be made from this pattern by using coated fabric, either in a double or single layer.

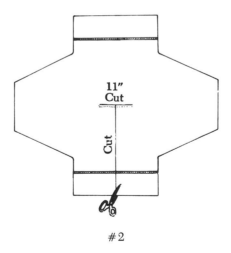

#2

MATERIALS: 4⅓ yards 45″ wide 60-40 fabric, 100″ drawstring cord, 30″ zipper for front, opening at both ends, snaps or 15″ of ½″ wide Velcro tape for storm flap closure, other closure hardware as desired for cuffs and pockets.

INSTRUCTIONS: Lay out the pattern on paper, lightweight plastic, or some other material, cut it, put it together, and check for fit. It should fit loosely. Be sure the hood fits well, and make any necessary adjustments in the length of the arms. Then lay the pattern out on your material, check carefully, and cut it out.

Sew C, E, and F into a hood, using finished fell seams; the narrow end of C faces forward. Assemble, D, G, and H in the same manner.

The 28″ edges of A and B will form the waistline of the parka. There are four such edges. Sew K to one of these edges with a finished

This type of cuff has a drawstring and a leather friction tab.

fell seam lapped so that it will shingle downwards on the final garment. Sew L, M, and N onto the other three edges in the same manner.

Cut the two resulting pieces as shown. The crosswise neck cut (11″ long) should be at the same place on each large piece, equidistant from the skirts. The long cut running up to the neck opening is for the front zipper, and it goes straight up the front.

You now have two parka bodies. Fold each one over, so that the skirts and sides are together and the creases run in the same line as the neck cut, but keep the two bodies still separate. On each one, sew the sides and lower parts of the arms together with finished fell seams (two seams on each of the two bodies).

Fit one of the parka bodies inside the other, and sew the bottoms together with a finished seam. Two grommets may now be installed on the inside layer of the jacket at the waistline, each two inches back from the still unfinished front, to provide for a drawstring. Make sure you pick a waistline low enough to leave the top of the parka loose and roomy. Sew two seams around the sides and back of the jacket along the waistline, forming an envelope for the drawstring running between the two grommets.

The cuffs may now be completed, using Velcro, buttons, snaps, elastic, or whatever sort of closure you prefer. One method I like is shown in the illustration. The drawstring goes around through the cuff and through the stiff leather friction tab cut for the purpose from a scrap of leather.

The hood should now be sewn in. First cut the neck opening out slightly to round off the corners, then pin the hood in before sewing. Sew the inside hood to the inside jacket body with a finished seam. Then sew the outside hood to the outside body with a finished fell seam lapped downward. Check the fit. Install a grommet 1½″ from each end of piece I, for the hood drawstring. Fold I down the center lengthwise, pin it onto the hood to form a visor and to finish the edges around the face of the hood.

The parka is now finished except for the front zipper, installation of the drawstrings, and installation of any pockets you may want. Piece J is a storm flap to cover the zipper. Iron a crease in it down the middle lengthwise to make pinning simpler. Pin the two sides of the zipper and the storm flap into the front opening of the jacket, with the fabric edges going between the jacket layers. Start pinning from the top on each side—a few inches space is deliberately left at the bottom to prevent excessive strain on the zipper. The jacket edges should be folded in while you are pinning, so that all seams will be finished. The storm flap is pinned along one side with the zipper, so that it will extend across the entire zipper when it is closed. Install Velcro or snap closures for the storm flap, removing and replacing pins as you go. Sew the front of the parka, and finish off any details at the top and bottom of the opening that may have been left.

The drawstrings can now be cut to length and installed by attaching a small safety pin to one end and working it through the pocket. Tie large knots to prevent the ends of the strings from being pulled through the grommets.

Whatever pockets you want can be installed quite easily, using scrap material for either the entire pocket or the flap only. Pockets can be made by sewing the two shells together and then making a slash opening. Pockets like this can be made in the upper front and the back by sewing two seams from the armpits down to the waist and making slash openings in the sides of the front of the jacket and one side of the back. Pockets between the waist and the bottom of the parka can be made in the same

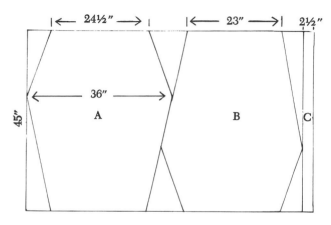

Rain or Wind Pants Pattern

way. Pockets can also simply be sewn onto the outside of the parka, but if they will carry much weight, they have to be sewn through both layers.

PATTERN AND INSTRUCTIONS FOR RAIN OR WIND PANTS

The pants shown here can be made of 60-40 cloth for a very tough set of overpants which will shed wind and quite a bit of rain, or they can be made with a coated fabric for true rain pants. For a very tough set of rain pants, the fabric can be doubled, with the coated sides facing one another.

MATERIALS: Two yards 45″ fabric, one yard elastic for waist, six inches 1″ Velcro tape for cuffs.

INSTRUCTIONS: The pattern is quite simple, but those who aren't confident should still lay it out first on paper, light plastic, or scrap, cut it out, and

123

check it. A and B form the body of the pants, while C is the waistband. Several dimensions should be checked by everyone. Make sure the 22″ cuff will fit over your boots—it is annoying to have to remove them to put on rain pants. Make sure the pants will be long enough. They will fit average-sized people, and shorter backpackers can cut them down, but tall hikers may need to change the pattern a bit. Remember that if you are working with coated fabric, you must avoid unnecessary holes; use paperclips rather than pins, and remember that the coated side faces *in*.

For assembly, sew the inside seams on the legs first, that is, the longer diagonal edges of A are sewn together with a finished fell seam. Then sew the long diagonal edges of B the same way. You now have two leg tubes. Next sew the two tubes together into pants with another finished fell seam. Sew the seam very strongly at the bottom of the crotch.

Now check the pants for fit. If the waist is too high, you should adjust it when the waistband is sewn on, because otherwise the crotch will be too low and will tend to bind. Lay the waistband along the waist and make corresponding chalk marks on each at 4″ intervals. Ascertain how long the elastic should be to hold the pants up without being too tight. Make ink marks on the elastic to show the section you will need. Now stretch the elastic out on a yardstick so that the ink marks are stretched to the length of the waist band. Fold the band in half lengthwise, put it over the elastic, and sew an envelope around the elastic down the middle of the band. Overlap the ends, sew everything together securely, and cut off the extra elastic. Sew the waistband to the pants, using your chalk marks to line things up so that the tucks are evenly distributed all the way around.

Check for fit again. The cuffs should be about the right length so they won't bind when they are closed tight and you take a high step, but they should not drag on the ground if you open them for ventilation. When you get the length right, make a small finished hem on each one, and sew the Velcro strips on the bottom so that they will close tightly over your stockinged ankle or your heaviest pants and boots.

DESIGN OF EQUIPMENT FOR BACKPACKING

The main requirements for backpacking equipment are fairly obvious, after a little consideration. It has to be tough and durable, since it will necessarily receive rough use and has to withstand the knocks and snags of the trail. It must be as lightweight as possible consistent with reliability and durability. Bulk must be controlled along with weight, so most equipment should be designed to pack into a compact, convenient bundle. Finally, it is nice if things don't cost so much that no one can afford them.

There is a good deal of contradiction in these requirements, but not so much as there used to be before the advent of plastics and modern fabrics. Even now, a certain amount of balancing is necessary, between weight and durability, for example. Rain gear that is used only occasionally can be much lighter weight than designs for constant use.

Other requirements will be discussed in the sections on specific types of equipment, but one consideration should always be the impact that a particular type of equipment will have on the wilderness. Tents that need trenching are becoming less and less appropriate, as are those which require the cutting of poles on the site. All the backpacker's equipment should be as self-contained as possible. Requirements vary with the country in which you camp, but the most versatile equipment is that which requires no materials from the surrounding woods.

In designing and choosing equipment for the wilderness, simple, old-fashioned, durable designs and construction methods should be given preference. Seams should be well sewn, with finished methods that leave no edges to ravel. Synthetic threads are stronger, and are always preferable. Hardware should be simple and strong, and should function smoothly. Unnecessary gadgetry which would be hard to repair ought to be avoided. Outside clothing and packs should be reasonably smooth, snag-resistant, and tough.

Avoid designs whose essential functioning depends on an easily broken or lost piece of hardware for which a replacement cannot be improvised. Tents with oddly-shaped, easily bent frames, stoves with removable valve knobs which fit into inaccessible recesses, and all their cousins should be looked on with a jaundiced eye.

FABRICS

Most camping equipment is made primarily of fabric, and the quality and durability of the finished product depends on the cloth that is used. There are many different kinds of weaves that are useful for lightweight equipment, but only a few will be mentioned here. The material used can also vary, and there are various ways that the cloth may be treated after weaving. Synthetic fabrics are generally much stronger and more durable than fabrics made with natural fibers, so equipment made with synthetics, particularly nylon, can be of lighter weight than cotton. Natural fibers also have certain advantages, however, which are not matched by the synthetics.

Nylon has become standard for many types of lightweight camping equipment. It is very strong and elastic, so that very lightweight nylon fabrics are resistant to both tearing and abrasion. But because each filament of the nylon is round and hard-surfaced, it is difficult to weave into tight fabrics, and good nylon cloth tends to be quite expensive. Nylon also will not absorb liquids, and it is very difficult to treat nylon so that it is water-repellent enough for outer garments that have to shed any rain. Making nylon waterproof is done by coating the whole surface of the fabric with urethane or other flexible plastic substances. In either case because of the smooth surface of each filament and the conductivity of the cloth, nylon fabric tends to condense moisture on its surface easily, and since the fabric is not absorbent, the condensed moisture is cast off quickly. In a tent, that means it drips in your ear.

Cotton still has a strong place in equipment manufacture because it can be easily made into a tightly woven cloth that is relatively watertight, though it will still breathe. Cotton will condense less moisture than even uncoated nylon, and it is absorbent enough to take waterproofing compounds well. Thus cotton is very useful for equipment intended to shed some rain, because those items will still breathe and pass out the water vapor evaporated by the body. Cotton is also considerably cheaper than nylon. Sometimes cotton is mixed with nylon to make a fabric with many of the wearing qualities of the synthetic and the water-resistant qualities of the cotton.

Wool has a special virtue when used for garments like pants, sweaters, and shirts, because it retains some of its insulating quality even when it gets wet. No other fabric or insulating material will do this nearly so well. Synthetic fluffed *Orlon* has this virtue to a lesser degree, and it is sometimes used as a substitute for wool.

INSULATING MATERIALS

Insulation in clothing, sleeping bags, and similar items is provided by air. Air is an excellent insulator, providing it is broken up into small cells and protected from disturbance by outside air currents. Gerry Cunningham is fond of pointing out that the material which cuts the air into cells will work as well whether it is goosedown or steel wool. Wool has been mentioned as a good insulator for a specific purpose. The other insulator that has special value to the backpacker is *down*, the layer of water fowl that grows under the feathers. It consists of many pods, each of which has a central nucleus with many filaments radiating from the center. It doesn't have a quill like a feather, though you may be misled because a few feathers are always mixed with down, and it is the feathers that tend to work through the fabric. Down is special because it will deaden a larger volume of air, and thus provide more insulation than an equal weight of any other material. It will also compress to a very small volume, but will pop quickly back when the compressing force is released. These two characteristics make down nearly ideal as an insulating material for sleeping bags and some other items. Special methods of construction are needed with down, and they are discussed in the chapter on sleeping bags. The best down is plucked from mature geese that have been raised in a cold climate.

In the last few years a combination of increased demand and market changes have made the best down very hard to get. Geese for the meat market are being killed at a younger age. The down from these birds is greatly inferior in quality. Modern culling methods have made it possible to extract fairly good down from this lower grade, and the same culling methods can be applied to duck down. The upshot of all this is that you must increasingly rely on your source for down quality. A label such as "goose down" no longer means what it once did.

CONSTRUCTION

Most camping equipment is put together by sewing. Synthetic thread is stronger than that made from natural fibers, so it should be used throughout. Nylon is the most common material for thread, but some people who have trouble adjusting their sewing machines to work with nylon use Dacron instead. Dacron doesn't have the stretchiness that is the troublesome

127

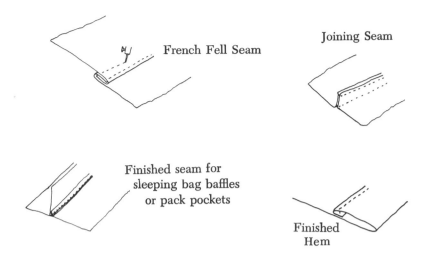

A few useful seams for the construction of backpacking equipment. The French fell seam is the most commonly used for joining pieces of cloth.

quality of nylon. Anyone willing to spend the time to learn to use a sewing machine can successfully make many items of equipment, and a home sewing machine will do most of the work quite successfully. Some parts of packs will require hand sewing with a heavy sewing awl, an item that can be purchased inexpensively from many backpacking stores.

Seams on backpacking equipment do not have to be pretty, but they should be sturdy and stay sewn. To prevent raveling, they should be finished seams, that is, double sewn. Fell seams on garments and tents should be lapped downward to prevent their catching the water. Any garment meant to shed water should be sewn with the smallest practical needle, and care should be taken not to make extra holes. This is especially important with coated fabrics, since the coating is punctured at each needle hole.

You should make a full-size pattern before you cut any expensive fabric. The pattern can be made from newspaper or old worn cloth like ripped sheets. Pin it together and make sure everything fits. Then lay the pattern out on your cloth, and figure the most economical way to cut it. With coated fabrics remember that there is an outside and an inside. The coated side of the fabric should usually be faced so that it receives the least wear. Friction will eventually rub the coating off and make the garment leak.

Boots, Socks, and Other Footwear   8

On a backpacking trip you travel on your feet. During a fairly level fifteen-mile hike each one of your feet has to be picked up and put down something like sixteen or twenty thousand times. This fact provides ample justification for special attention to your footwear. If you are careless enough to get a blister on one heel halfway through the hike, that still leaves eight or ten thousand times you have to come down on that heel before the day is out. If your boots are each a pound heavier than they need to be, you have to lift an extra pound thirty or forty thousand times on your hike, which is a lot of work, in case you haven't tried it.

The function of your footwear is, first, to protect your feet—from sharp stones, cold snow, hot sand, wet water, stinging insects, the broken glass of some fisherman's beer bottle, and a host of other hazards. Second, you may demand extra duties from the same footwear, such as boots stiff enough to kick steps in firm snow. You may want the soles to grip well on sloping rock. You should consider all these functions before buying footwear, because they are important. Cheap socks or poorly chosen boots will make your trip miserable and possibly hazardous as well.

Obviously, the same kind of footwear may not be ideal for every kind of terrain, but there are quite a few common characteristics that should be discussed before we consider special requirements. In general, since increased protection usually results in heavier boots and socks, you simply choose the lightest footwear you can find which also gives you the protection and secondary qualities you need. Foot protection together with qualities like good traction and durability come first, and when your real needs are met, you should go to great lengths to avoid every extra ounce on the feet. Remember that, unlike an extra weight in the pack, excess boot leather has to be lifted at every step, even on flat ground.

Good-quality heavy wool socks are even more important for foot comfort than boots.

SOCKS

The characteristics of good hiking socks are pretty much the same, regardless of the season or the terrain. Heavier socks are used with heavier boots, in colder weather, or to provide better cushioning, but otherwise there really isn't much difference between a good hiking sock for summer or winter, desert, beach, or mountain. The socks need to absorb perspiration without becoming matted or soggy, they should cushion the feet from the pounding of heavy packs and rough terrain, they have to protect the skin from too much blister-raising friction, be free of irritating spots themselves, and finally, keep the feet warm in cold weather.

Traditionally, two pairs of socks are worn to help perform all these tasks—usually a lightweight pair next to the feet with a heavier pair worn over them. Many materials have been advocated for the inner pair: silk, nylon, wool, and so on. Try various kinds and find out what suits you best. I prefer a soft wool or bulked Orlon inner sock; they're cheap and comfortable. If you're hooked on "space-age" developments, you might want to try the special "wick-dry" inner socks, which are reputedly quite good and cost about twice as much as wool or bulked Orlon. Avoid cotton like the plague. It becomes soaked with sweat, clammy, uncomfortable, and is almost guaranteed to cause blisters as it rubs, rubs, rubs on your feet.

Outer socks should be much heavier than any normal street sock or most athletic socks. Exactly how heavy they should be depends on the various considerations already mentioned as well as on personal preference. When in doubt, it's better to get heavier socks than lighter ones. Quality is even more important than weight. You don't need to get expensive socks, but you must absolutely get good ones. Socks that are scratchy, mat easily, have sloppy weaves, and so on are a curse to the hiker. A good thick sock feels firm, resilient, and even; the pattern of the weave should not be easily felt by squeezing the sole or the heel with the fingers—if you can feel it with your fingers, you'll feel it with your feet.

I am an unreconstructed wool man when it comes to hiking socks, at least for the heavy outer pair. Wool stays springy, and thus warm and cushiony, even when it becomes wet from water or perspiration. A good pair of heavy wool socks can be wrung out and worn even after an accidental dunking in the river. Other fibers are often added to wool socks to make them wear better, but these should make up no more than 15 per cent of the fiber content. There are several types of good heavy wool socks. I prefer the Norwegian "ragg" type, which are very good and quite cheap. A more expensive type is the "thermal" sock, which has a smooth woven outside and a terry woven lining. The thermal type is fine, but check the fiber composition, and don't get one with a lot of cotton. Finally, for a summer heavy sock some people like the new "wick-dry" ones. They are made with two layers. The inside wicks the moisture to the outside, keeping your feet fairly dry. Thus, through the miracle of modern technology, you have a sock that does what a wool sock does—almost. As I mentioned, I'm prejudiced. Those allergic to wool may want to try the synthetic socks, but Orlon liners generally protect the feet pretty well from wool outers.

Buy your socks first, because you'll need them when you get around to trying on boots. Most good stores have a box of heavy socks around in case you don't bring your own, but until you get used to buying boots it's best to be able to tell exactly how they're going to feel with your socks. Never try to fit boots with street socks; you won't be able to judge either size or comfort.

BOOTS

Boots that are going to be used for a lot of hiking and backpacking are similar in design regardless of where you hike. A good heavy-duty mountaineering boot looks pretty much like a beefed-up version of a good lightweight trail boot. A few kinds of specialized footwear will be discussed later in the chapter.

A hiking boot stands five to eight inches high from the floor to the top of the upper, with six inches a good general height. High boots, especially if they are over ten inches, are heavy without providing additional protection, support, or durability. They restrict circulation of air, cramp the calf, and, as they get older, are likely to fold at the back of the ankle and irritate the Achilles' tendon. This last item is more serious than it sounds. It can keep you flat on your back for weeks and leave the spot sensitive for months.

I suppose there are a lot of good reasons for wearing high boots if you want to lead a cavalry charge, a paratrooper squadron, or a bunch of Hell's Angels, but I have been unable to discover any good reason to wear them hiking. More ankle support can be built into a low boot, because the ankle of a high one has to be made very flexible. Stones and snow can be kept out with anklets or gaiters, which are discussed elsewhere. Only a few of the specialized boots mentioned later in the chapter may need to be made higher.*

The most satisfactory boot sole is made of hard rubber with molded lugs. (Vibram is the trade name of the most common brand, but there are many other acceptable ones.) These soles wear very well, absorb shock satisfactorily, and are good insulation for walking on snow. They give excellent traction on dry rock, and they are as satisfactory as anything except nailed boots on various other surfaces. They are superior to nailed boots in so many respects that they have replaced the latter even among alpinists. Incidentally, hiking boots should have raised heels; the light heelless boots you may see in backpacking stores are designed for technical rock climbing.

Proper height, good soles, and a comfortable fit are the most important requirements in boots designed for backpacking, but there are various other desirable features that are worth looking at when you buy boots. Most of the best models are completely lined with smooth leather, and they are often padded, especially around the ankle and the tongue. The importance of these features depends to some extent on the general design of the boot, and they are more important with heavier boots. Padding generally extends only through the ankle and does not make the boot warmer. Some people avoid padding because it retains water if the boots get wet.

Check the tongue of the boot and the fit around it. Gusseted sides which will exclude water and dirt are desirable, but if they are not included be sure the tongue is sewn on straight so that it won't flop to the side and admit debris while you are wearing it. If it tends to move to the side it won't get better; it will get worse and be a pain in the neck until the day you junk the boots.

Obviously, good leather is important to a good boot. Leather of high quality is recognizable because it *feels* good: tough and dense, not dry and papery as though it was overprocessed reject material from a ladies glove manufacturer. A really well-made boot will have good leather, since manufacturers of good boots are not stupid enough to waste their labor by the use of shoddy material. For this reason, perhaps the easiest way to guess leather quality is to inspect the construction details of the boot.

° One other excuse sometimes given for making boots higher is for use in snake country. Personally, I prefer to watch my step (and reach, and seat) in country frequented by poisonous snakes, but if you're really worried about that sort of thing, I suggest that strap-on shields for the calves would be as good as high boots in very dangerous areas, and they could be taken off when they were not needed, unlike the tops of high boots.

The type of leather which should be used is a more complicated question, since it depends largely on the uses to which you intend to put the boots. Most lightweight trail boots and rock-climbing shoes intended for dry regions and seasons are made from a good-quality thick suede. It is cheaper than other boot leathers, breathes well, and is very tough and abrasion resistant. Its use is restricted in the ways mentioned because it cannot be made very watertight. Boots made with top grain leather can be constructed with the rough side facing out or in. Construction with the rough side out unquestionably gives much better resistance to abrasion, so it is usually the choice for boots that will be used for a lot of rock climbing or scrambling in talus and scree. Leather with the smooth side out is generally tighter against water penetration, and so it is frequently chosen when this quality is important. However, boots of very well-tanned rough out leather have been manufactured which can be made quite water resistant, combining the advantages of watertightness and abrasion resistance. This rough out design is preferable to having the smooth side out where it can be scraped off, eliminating the boots' resistance to water.

It is convenient to have loops attached at the back of the ankle to help you pull the boots on, and these become particularly important in cold weather, when you may have to pull on frozen boots in the morning. One other item worth considering in boots which are expected to be used a lot in wet conditions is the placement of seams, which are the natural weak points to water seepage. The fewer the seams on the lower part of the boot, the better. Check the hardware for leak points, too. On boots intended mainly for dry hiking this is of no consequence.

WHAT KIND OF BOOT?

Despite the fact that the signs of good design and quality are similar in all hiking boots, you must still make the choice of the general type of boot you want before you start hunting for a good fit. Do you want a 6-pound pair of heavy-duty mountaineering boots, a 2½-pound pair of trail shoes, or something in between? Do you expect a lot of wet going or snow so that you have to worry about watertightness, or will you encounter only occasional stream crossings and small snow patches? Finally, are there any special characteristics your boot will need? If you expect to do rock climbing in your boots, you need to take their feel on rock into account. Mountaineers need boots tough enough for step kicking in snow and rigid enough to protect the feet from crampon straps.

The main principle of selection has already been mentioned: get the lightest boot which will fulfill your needs. If you need a heavy mountaineering boot, then nothing else will do, but unless you expect to be doing a lot of work on snow, or generally to be giving the boot such a workout that a lighter boot wouldn't take the beating, you would be better off settling on a boot of moderate weight.

Unfortunately, it is difficult to define "heavy" or "light" meaningfully in terms of exact weights that would be of any use to the prospective boot buyer. Different suppliers use different sizes to figure their "average weight" listed in their catalogues, and only a few bother to tell you which size they use. This allows you to compare weights among their offerings, but not to judge them easily against anyone else's selection. Two catalogues frequently list the same boot with weights varying by more than a pound. Added to this situation is the notorious inconsistency in the ideas of sizes held by various European boots manufacturers; a Pivetta size eight is about the same as a Galibier size nine, and so on. If you decide what general type of boot you need, heavy, light, or medium, and there are two types which seem otherwise comparable in features and fit, you can always ask the store(s) to weigh them.

A medium-heavy pair of mountaineering boots with the smooth side of the leather facing out. Though this pair has had only moderate wear, the leather looks quite worn, a common problem with boots having the smooth side out.

Heavy-duty mountaineering boots are the sovereigns of wilderness travel, since they will carry you over almost any sort of terrain and will withstand an unbelievable amount of punishment. They also have the stiffness and ponderousness suited to their regal status. Like kingly robes, they are likely to be a heavy burden to bear. A man's size-ten pair is likely to weigh over six pounds. Choose them only for trips involving a lot of travel in very rugged terrain without trails. Stiff steel shanks that prevent the boots from bending are good for certain kinds of mountaineering, but they make the boots less comfortable for backpacking. Heavy boots do not have to be too stiff for walking.

Medium-weight mountaineering boots, rough side out. This pair is on its third set of soles.

Medium-weight mountaineering boots are lighter and more flexible than their royal cousins and are much more suitable for general backpacking use, since they are easier on both the legs and the feet, require much less breaking in and will still do anything the average backpacker will ask of them. The beginner will still find them rather stiff, but both the sole and the upper are much more flexible than those of a heavy mountain boot, allowing for more comfort on the trail, but still providing enough support to prevent the feet from being bruised in talus hopping with a heavy pack. This type of boot is ideal for the backpacker who expects to be doing a lot of cross-country traveling in rugged terrain or making spring and fall trips where lots of snow and meltwater may be encountered, but who is willing to sacrifice the ability to do extensive cramponing and step-kicking for a little comfort on the trails he'll be walking 90 per cent of the time. A man's size-ten pair generally weighs four or five pounds.

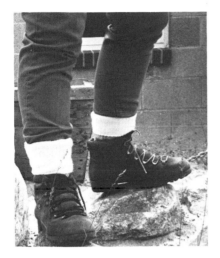

Two types of light trail boots, excellent for summer hiking in relatively dry country.

Medium-weight trail boots or light mountaineering boots are much more suitable for most backpackers than the heavier boots just mentioned. Hikers staying mainly on trails or moderate cross-country terrain do not usually need the support and protection of a mountaineering boot. Good medium-weight trail boots give plenty of purchase for climbing occasional rock slides or walking through patches of snow that does not lie at a steep angle, yet they are much lighter and more comfortable than mountain boots. Many trail boots can be made to shed water quite well, and these are good in wet areas like New England or the Northwest. The weight range for a man's size ten is around 3½ to 4½ pounds.

Light trail boots have the same advantages as medium-weight ones, except that they can rarely be waterproofed well, and are best restricted to summer hiking in fairly dry country. They will not last so long as equally well-constructed boots that are heavier, but the cost is correspondingly less. Trail hikers who avoid snow and continuous rain will prefer this type of footwear for inexpensive and comfortable service. Light trail boots are most frequently made of a tough suede which is comfortable and long-wearing. A man's size ten weighs around three pounds.

CHOOSING YOUR BOOTS

Plan to spend some time buying your boots. If you know what you're doing, you may be able to pick a sleeping bag or a tent in ten minutes, but the more experience you have, the more time you are likely to take choosing boots. If you have to buy your boots by mail, follow the directions of the catalogue carefully. Most suppliers have you trace the outline of your sole with your socks on and half your weight on the foot. Using this outline, they can often give you a good fit, but since boots are made differently, it is always easier to get a proper fit by trying the boots on. If you buy by mail, don't hesitate to send the boots back, and keep sending them back until you get a good fit. *Never* buy a pair of boots from anyone unless they will take the boots back, providing, of course, that you haven't worn them outside.

The most critical requirement for boots is that they fit. There are enough different stores and manufacturers around so that you should be able to get a pair which has all the features you want and which also fits well. If you're in a hurry and you have to choose, however, remember that a good fit comes first. A leaky boot will make your feet uncomfortable when it rains, a pair that is too light will be uncomfortable on rough ground, but a pair that fits badly will hurt all the time.

The first rule in fitting boots is that they should be large. After you have pounded along the trail for a while your feet will get bigger because of increased blood supply. They don't just seem bigger; they really are, even if you don't have any extra swelling from injury, bruises, and the like. People who hike a lot every day will have their feet expand permanently to a constant size, but weekend tourists should expect some swelling during the day. Boots that fit like gloves will feel like sophisticated instruments of torture by the end of a hard day on the trail.

The extra room is needed around the front of your foot. The heel should be snug, though not constricting. The front part of the boot should be roomy enough so that when it is laced firmly it does not bind anywhere and allows enough room for your toes to be curled up. Try to push your foot forward inside the boot when it is properly laced. If your toes can touch the toe of the boot, it is too short. Especially after expansion of your foot, when you are going downhill your toes will hit at every step, which gets to be pure agony after a while. The boot should be long enough and hold your foot firmly enough to prevent your toes from hitting even when you jam your foot forward—that's just what you'll be doing on a steep downhill trail. The only people who may want to modify this rule are mountaineers who want to use their boots on difficult technical rock or ice —this means roped climbing of sustained difficulty, not an afternoon scramble—and they will have to decide whether the added security of shorter boots is worth the torture going downhill and some extra risk of frostbite.

Roominess in front doesn't mean sloppiness, however. If your feet slide around inside the boots in any direction, you'll have blisters for sure after a couple of miles. These requirements may sound contradictory but they are met by well-designed and properly fitted boots. Don't settle for less.

If the boots seem to fit, put them both on and walk around the store (or your living room if they are mail order). Any reputable boot supplier wants you to do this. Wear them for a while, scrunch your feet around in them, jump up and down, and try them out on something that slopes so that you can feel what they'll be like going uphill, downhill, and sidehill. Heavy boots will feel stiff since they are not broken in, especially if you're not accustomed to wearing boots, but they shouldn't hurt or irritate your feet anywhere. If they do, reject them and try another pair. If the store doesn't have another pair, go somewhere else, order from a catalogue, or order from another catalogue. Good boots last a long time and they will either become cherished friends or hated possessions before you wear them out.

Remember, a pair of boots that fits well will feel good. A pair that doesn't feel good will feel worse and worse and worse as the miles add up. *Do not* fall for any stories to the effect that the boots will stretch if they are too small or have a tight spot. Boots do stretch in spots as they are broken in, but there are limits and force is required. If you set up a competition for toughness between a pair of boots and your feet, the boots will win.

Do not get roped into buying a set of unsatisfactory boots because they are all the store has. Even assuming the store is fully stocked, everyone has feet that are shaped differently and that move differently, and boots are made with widely varying shapes and designs. It is not rare at all to find that one make of boot just won't fit you properly. If Jones's won't fit, try Smith's. I usually have trouble getting a good fit because my feet are wide, but my latest pair is a French design that is too narrow for most people. It just happens to be wide where my feet are and narrow where other people's feet are wide. Keep trying.

The final step in fitting the boots is to wear them around for at least a couple of hours. If you've bought them by mail, this is no trouble. Just wear them while you're walking around the house doing chores. Any reputable backpacking or climbing store will let you bring the boots back if you take them home and find them unsatisfactory. Psychologically, though, I think it's better to make this check at the store, before it becomes inconvenient to decide that they really don't fit so well. Just try on boots when you first go into the store, and do your browsing while you're trying them. The idea of wearing them for this length of time is that stiff new boots gradually feel better or feel worse. If they feel better, clutch them to your breast and buy them. If they feel worse, start over. Choose your boots with the care you would like to use in choosing a spouse or a roommate.

BREAKING THEM IN

The only way to break in boots is to walk in them, preferably in small enough doses to avoid much blistering of your feet. If your feet are tough enough, you can just start wearing them on trips, but remember to take some moleskin. The amount of walking it takes to break in a boot depends on how tough it is and how tough the walking is. Some of the lightweight trail boots require practically no breaking in, but heavy boots can take many miles to reach an understanding with your feet. Actually, breaking in is less important with heavy boots than it once was. Heavy boots have to fit properly to begin with, since they will not move around very much to conform with your feet. If it should turn out that your boots don't quite fit, you might try finding a ski shop with a boot stretcher. Failing this, you may finally find that you have lost the battle to the boots—sell them to someone they fit, and buy another pair—carefully.

TAKING CARE OF YOUR BOOTS

A good pair of boots will stand an almost incredible amount of rough treatment, lasting through several pairs of soles, providing they are given reasonable care. The greatest single enemy of boot leather is heat, and this is the most frequent cause when the soles part prematurely from the uppers. Leather is damaged by excessive heat just as your skin is, but it lacks nerves to warn of burning and has no recuperative powers. Holding your boots near the fire or leaving them to dry in the heat is a sure way to shorten their life. Boots should be allowed to dry at normal room temperature. If possible, it is a good idea to stuff them with newspaper or special drying packets when you get home. Resist the temptation to speed up the drying process by warming them next to a stove, in front of a heat vent, or in the sun. Boot trees are not necessary, but they do prevent curling soles if your boots are very wet.

Boots should be cleaned of mud and dust. When mine are wet and muddy, I sponge them off when I get home. A stiff brush will remove most dry mud and dust. If the dirt seems to have worked into the leather, the boots should be cleaned with saddle soap before applying any waterproofing or preservative, otherwise these will just imbed the dirt deeper, to the detriment of the boots. There is no need to be fussy about all this, but occasional cleaning is needed.

All boots need to be treated occasionally to restore oils that are washed or dusted out of the leather on the trail. Generally, the same compound is used both to preserve the boot and to waterproof it. The amount and frequency of treatment depend strictly on the conditions in which you hike. For summer hiking in dry areas, a few light applications will get you through a whole season. In wet country, as much preservative as possible is rubbed into the boots whenever they manage to dry out long enough. (There isn't much point in treating wet boots.)

Excessive applications are undesirable except in very wet conditions, since the pores of the boot are closed off, making it hotter and more quickly soaked with perspiration. Where you are slogging through rain, mud, and snow all the time, however, you want a practically waterproof boot, and you should use as much waterproofing compound as the boot will hold. For intermediate conditions, simply try to find a happy medium.

There are several good waterproofing and preservative compounds for boots, but greases and oils should not be used. They soften the leather and cause the boot to collapse and lose its shape, which is undesirable in hiking and climbing boots. Liquid compounds penetrate the leather most easily, but check the container and steer clear of anything that purports to soften leather. The most popular compounds are silicone-based waxes like Sno-Seal, which are readily obtainable in climbing and ski shops. For a light coat, just rub the stuff into the outside of the boot, concentrating on the seams and around the welt. A cloth will serve, but the warmth of your hands works the wax in better. For better penetration, melt the wax first and then work the warm liquid into the boot. Whatever the directions on the can say, don't heat up your boots in the oven, heat the wax instead. Suede boots are best treated with a silicone liquid or spray prior to the use of wax preparations.

Good boots in normal use should need no care beyond that already mentioned until the soles wear out. If they need resoling or repairs, it is best to take or send them to someone with experience in working with lined boots. In most areas such bootmakers are a rarity, and you may have to either gamble with a local shoemaker or send your boots to one of the people listed in the appendix. Generally, someone who is competent will have lug rubber soles in stock, but these can also be purchased through many catalogues.

When your boots need resoling, don't put off the day—wear off the rubber, but avoid eating into any of the leather foundations. Most good boots have narrow welts, and there is very little leather to spare for sewing the uppers to the middle soles. Heavy wear of these middle soles is likely to result in extensive repairs or premature retirement of the boots.

For climbers and other rough country travelers whose boots suffer a lot of abrasion from rocks, there are a few additional precautions which will prolong the life of boots and avoid some repairs. All spots which are subject to a lot of rubbing and cutting can be coated with a thin layer of epoxy glue, especially along any stiching which gets chafed by the rocks. This technique is particularly helpful on boots used for technical rock climbing.

BOOTS FOR SPECIAL CONDITIONS

While some version of the standard mountain boot is suitable for nearly all situations likely to be encountered by the backpacker, a few special conditions may call for other kinds of footwear or for special considerations in buying regular boots. I'm sure that there are many such instances I have not run into, and there are certainly many outdoorsmen who wouldn't agree with my choice of equipment anyway. Still, all in all, in my own experience mountain boots are by far the most versatile hiking footwear made, and since the backpacker normally encounters widely varying terrain, he should think twice before sacrificing this jack-of-all-wilderness-trades for shoes specially adapted for wading swamps, running up good trails, skiing, or walking on snowshoes.

Climbing boots. Many of the best mountain boots are specifically made for difficult climbing, but there are many which are not. The average backpacker doesn't care whether his boots are good for edging on small holds or not, but anyone who ultimately wants to use his boots for difficult climbs as well as backpacking has to look at a few extra features. A climbing boot should have a very narrow welt; that is, the soles should not stick out beyond the uppers; such protrusions will increase adverse leverage on the feet and will also tend to roll off small holds. For climbing which involves steep snow, the boot must be fairly heavy and have a stiff sole. In any case, boots intended for difficult climbing must feel secure while the wearer edges on small holds, and this should be tried out in the store. Technical rock climbers who practice their art in areas free of snow and ice usually don't try to combine the requirements for a comfortable hiking boot and climbing footgear. They wear hiking boots for the approach and then change to very tight-fitting lightweight rock-climbing shoes.

Waterproof boots are preferred by a few backpackers who do a lot of hiking in marshy, flat country, especially in spring and fall when wetlands become passable to the walker, but where frequent breaks through the ice into a few inches of cold water make rubber-bottomed boots more comfortable than conventional lightweight hiking boots. The biggest difficulty with rubber boots is that they become clammy inside, hot in summer and cold in winter. They should be worn roomy, with heavy socks and insoles. Except where deep water may be encountered, the rubber-footed, leather-topped variety invented by L. L. Bean is more comfortable than the all-rubber kind. Either type can be bought insulated for cold weather, and either can be found with a Vibram sole for better traction. (You may not be able to find a Vibram-soled pair that fits, however; I can't.) In any case, don't expect to be able to use this type of footwear as a substitute for mountain

143

The rubber-bottom boot is good for hiking in very wet country with easy footing.

boots on difficult terrain. It is treacherous on steep slopes and should not be taken in rough country.

Sneakers are still used by some backpackers who appreciate their light weight and low price, and their use is certainly preferable to not going backpacking for those who can't afford boots. In the long run, however, they aren't cheaper, since they wear out much faster than boots. They are hot, get wet easily, dry out slowly, are brutal to the feet on rough ground with a heavy pack, and they are impossible in snow or cold weather. You may want to use them to put off the expense of buying boots in July, but don't risk a mountain trip with them in October—they might cost you your feet if you are caught in a snowstorm.

Some backpackers like to take lightweight sneakers or *moccasins* along for comfort around camp at the end of the day. They are a welcome luxury, but I prefer to save the weight, and instead I change socks and loosen my boots. Suit yourself. In a similar luxury category are *down booties and socks*, which are very nice to wear for lolling around on chilly nights and for warming your feet in the sleeping bag. They are one of life's little luxuries, but don't forget to worry about the necessities first.

Cold-weather footwear has to suit your means of transportation when deep snow requires the use of skis or snowshoes, but heavy or medium-weight mountain boots do very nicely if the snow permits hiking. Winter boots must be of a type that is easily made water repellent and they must be large enough to allow the wearing of heavy socks without cramping the feet. Remember that if an extra pair of socks makes the boots feel too tight, wearing the additional pair will make your feet colder rather than warmer, because circulation in your feet will be impaired.

The weather likely to be encountered by the normal backpacker does not require specialized footwear. Technical climbers often wear *double boots* in winter, but these are needed partly because of the need to stand for long periods on cramped spots. The backpacker's walking will enable him to cope with fairly cold temperatures without special footwear. An inner boot like that used in a double boot can also be bought separately, and it is an excellent addition if your boots are roomy enough to accommodate it.

Walkers in flat country often prefer insulated boots in cold weather, often combining the advantages of insulation with waterproof bottoms for early-spring and late-fall backpacking. Insulated boots are available with Vibram soles and all-leather uppers, with rubber bottoms and leather tops, or with all rubber from top to bottom. The all-leather type is the only one suited to walking in rough country. Of the other two, the leather-topped kind is much more comfortable to walk in.

Insulation in these boots must be examined with care, since many cheap and rather dangerous types are made. Condensation of perspiration from the feet can easily soak conventional types of insulation and render them useless, so any boot using this sort of material should be made with removable liners, of which at least two pairs should be carried. Another solution is the use of insulation completely sealed between two layers of rubber, the double-vapor barrier principle used in the U.S. Army Korea boots (Mickey Mouse boots). Finally, the method used in many of the best insulated boots being made now is to insulate with closed cell foam like Ensolite or Thermobar, in which each air pocket is sealed and thus cannot absorb water or perspiration.

For very cold weather, an alternative to insulated boots is the *overboot*, a fabric cover for the feet and lower legs with pockets for insulation, which can be put on over normal boots when the need arises. They are similar to mukluks, except that they are worn over boots. *Mukluks* are like thick, insulated fabric or skin boots, and are used in extremely cold

145

weather in the far north and for snowshoeing in dry, very cold weather. The backpacker without skis or snowshoes would be unlikely to encounter conditions requiring mukluks.

Overboots generally have leather bottoms which are slippery on rough ground, but some new types that do not cover the soles will become available about the time this book is published. These should present a less expensive alternative to double boots.

Special footwear is often needed for snowshoeing or skiing in winter, but for normal hiking, the need for it is really quite rare. The only really troublesome conditions are those mentioned earlier when cold has arrived in wet areas, but ice is not yet thick enough to prevent occasional breakthroughs. Similar circumstances sometimes prevail in winter along rivers in the far north when running water may flow over the thick ice layer but be concealed by snow. Frequent hikes in these conditions make an insulated waterproof boot welcome, because feet soaked by ice-cold water are undesirable at low temperatures. An occasional break through October stream ice is adequately handled by extra socks, though, so that marsh hikers are the most likely customers for insulated rubber bottoms.

Except in these conditions, the backpacker does not need to be much worried about a little cold or snow if he has proper clothing and roomy, sturdy boots. If he is caught by the first big snow and really cold weather while wandering the backcountry in the fall or early winter, proper observation of cold-weather rules will be more important than carrying special boots.

Clothing

Clothing for backpacking ought to be reasonably practical, loose, and strong enough so that your pants don't split the first time you squat down to light a fire. Roomy clothes are more comfortable than tight or binding ones. Sturdy outer garments will come through bushwhacking or rock-scrambling in a lot better condition than clothes that were never designed to take much abuse.

The importance of choosing your clothing depends pretty much on the type and duration of your trip. Where the climate is harsh it can be a very serious matter indeed. A lot of people die in the mountains because they are caught in bad weather with inadequate clothing.

Like everything else used by the backpacker, clothing has to serve as many uses as possible. A large wardrobe of specialized clothing can't be carried for different kinds of weather. If the elements might turn wet and cold, you should wear pants suitable for the possibility rather than blue jeans.

Leaving questions of modesty, morality, and vanity aside, the function of your clothing is to protect you from the elements and the critters you might meet on your trip. The threats to your epidermis might include hot sun, cold wind, rain, sleet, snow, hail, abrading stones and brush, insects, or all of the above. If you figure out which are likely, choosing clothing becomes relatively easy.

DRESSING IN LAYERS

It is usually best to carry a number of layers of clothing that are of light and medium weight, rather than concentrating everything in a few heavy garments. There are several reasons for this principle. It gives you better control over warmth, ventilation, and other factors. If your windbreaker is a big, heavy jacket, you'll find it isn't very versatile. When you are pulling up a long slope in the sun and a cool wind comes up, all you need is a windbreaker to stay comfortable. The heavy jacket's insulation will just make you sweat like a pig, leaving you damp and cold at the top of the hill. By the same token, in cold, still weather, a fuzzy sweater providing just insulation but no wind protection is often the most comfortable thing to wear —light and unconfining, but allowing a cooling breeze in when you start working hard.

Dressing in layers also gives you more insulation for a given amount of weight. Two light sweaters are warmer than one heavier one, because the layer of air trapped between them gives you additional insulation. Obviously, having your clothing in layers also gives you more control over what you take on a trip or a side trip. You can take one light sweater, but not half of a heavy one.

The layer principle allows you to adapt the same basic set of outdoor clothing to widely varying climates. You start off with underwear, a hat, sturdy pants and shirt, shorts, if you like, for summer hikes, and a good tough windbreaker to go over everything. You can add as many extra shirts and sweaters as you might need to keep warm where you are traveling. You may also carry lightweight rainwear to go over it all. For more severe conditions you might add a pair of windpants, which is a windbreaker for the lower part of your body, long underwear, and so forth. When you head for the desert, you leave the rain gear (sometimes) and take your wide-brimmed hat. The layer system is generally cheaper, more efficient, versatile, and comfortable than heavier, more elaborate clothing.

UNDERWEAR

Suit yourself, unless the weather is very cold, in which case you should use wool underwear. Tight, binding clothing of any kind gets quite uncomfortable, and underwear is no exception.

Net underwear is pleasant and versatile, and you might want to try a net shirt. The idea is that when you open your outer shirt for ventilation, the net allows plenty of cool air in for ventilation, but with the outer layers of clothing closed, a warm insulating layer of air is held near the skin. Even more important is the fact that the net gives the body some air space into which it can evaporate perspiration, so that your clothes don't tend to get soaked with sweat quite so quickly. The net mesh should be widely spaced.

PANTS

They should be loose, comfortable, and tough. A hard weave will shed more water and snags. If you like jeans, they are fine, except when there is a possibility of rain, wind, and cold. Wet, cold blue jeans are one of the most sophisticated instruments of torture known to man. Some wool or Orlon in the pants material is good if wet, cold weather might be expected. Excellent pants can often be gotten surplus. Just remember to keep away from cotton except for warm-weather use.

Two types of cuff closures. A snap fastening and a drawstring.

Knickers are good, the only trouble with them being that in cold weather they require expensive long socks. Their advantage is that they allow free leg movement. You can get them ready-made or easily convert a pair of trousers.

Pockets get a lot of use for odds and ends, so they should be sturdy. It's nice if at least some of them can be closed with zippers, buttons, snaps, or Velcro. If the pockets are hung from the belt rather than just sewn into holes in the fabric, they will last longer and be more comfortable. Pockets on the legs of pants, like those on some fatigues, should not be used. If you have them, don't put anything heavier than a bandana in them. Your legs lift them at every step, and it takes a lot of energy to lift all your pocket junk at every step.

Cuffs can be left plain or they can have some arrangement for closure. A closure is handy for plodding in snow, on dusty trails, and in tick country. For ventilation in hot weather, something that can be opened is nicer than a knit cuff.

SHIRTS AND SWEATERS

At least some of these should be wool if there is a possibility of cold weather. In winter they should all be wool. In summer you can take what you like, but if you are going to do any bushwhacking, wear something strong enough to survive the brush. Even on summer nights, a heavy shirt can be useful to discourage mosquitoes, and long sleeves are nice protection from both brush and bugs. Button pockets are nice.

For extra insulation, concentrate on fuzzy, bulky sweaters rather than tight, heavy ones. They are less resistant to abrasion, but they are warmer, and you can put on your parka for wet weather or rough rock.

HATS AND SUCH

I am not a hat wearer, but in the wilderness one is often essential. When it is cold, a hat is your most important item of insulation. Circulation, and thus heat loss, is not cut down to the head, as it is to the other extremities in cold weather. It is possible to lose over half the body's heat production

A balaclava helmet made of wool can be worn as a cap or over the whole head. It makes an excellent cold-weather hat.

When the weather gets bad, your shell clothing protects you and your insulation from the elements.

through the head. There is an old adage, "If your feet are cold, put on your hat." It happens to be true. If you are cold, put your hat on, and if you get hot, take it off.

A good hat for moderate to cold temperatures is a wool balaclava helmet. It folds up into a watch cap, but will also pull down for a face mask and neck covering when the snow really starts to blow. A watch cap is smaller. Either works well in conjunction with the hood of your parka.

Hats are just as important in hot weather. When the sun really starts to beat down, you need to keep your head cool and the sun out of your eyes. A light-colored, wide-brimmed hat is what you need. The crown should be well above the top of your head, and the more ventilation holes it has, the better.

A bandana is often handy for long sweaty climbs. Worn tied around the forehead, it keeps the sweat from running into the eyes and acts as a headband if you have long hair.

SHELL CLOTHING

Perhaps the most important clothing for the backpacker is his outer shell, which must protect him from wind, rain, snow, thorns, and horseflies. This layer is supposed to keep the inner one working by preventing shirts from being ripped, holding the layer of warm air in a fuzzy sweater despite a howling wind, and keeping insulation dry and warm.

The most important single item of clothing is a shell parka or anorak, made from a tough, windtight fabric. Such a parka should be roomy enough to allow all the insulation you might wear to fit underneath comfortably. It should be water repellent enough to shed a shower, but not waterproof so that it will trap perspiration and soak your insulation from within. It should not restrict movement. It can be a pullover or have a front opening, but any fasteners and hardware must be dependable and should be easily operable with numb or mittened hands. At least one large pocket is needed for odds and ends.

Windpants, when they are needed, should have similar characteristics to the parka. They are meant as a shell. They should go on and come off easily over boots, and they shouldn't weigh too much.

Material for parkas has always been the subject of considerable controversy, because of the many contradictory demands that are made on them. The best water-shedding material which still breathes is long fiber cotton in a suitable weave. Nylon is tougher, but it is impossible to waterproof it well without coating it completely and is harder to pack into a good windproof material. A good compromise is 60–40 cloth, which is woven with nylon in one direction and cotton the other. A well-made version of this mixture has many of the advantages of each of its components: tear strength, abrasion resistance, and water repellency.

A parka for all-around use should usually be made with two layers of fabric, at least on those sections subject to wear and heavy beating by the rain. Seams should be kept to a minimum, especially on the shoulders. Seams are the most common places for leakage.

Pullover and jacket-type parkas each have their advocates. The pullover has the advantage of simplicity and lighter weight. If the zipper fouls at the worst possible time, you still have some protection, whereas the jacket type flaps uselessly in the wind. On the other hand, the jacket design, opening all the way down the front, gives better ventilation control, especially on the trail, and I prefer it for general year-round use. Make sure the zipper is a good one, operating smoothly and without jamming.

RAINWEAR

Rain gear also falls into the category of shell clothing. You may not need to take separate rain clothing, depending on the weather where you are hiking. Staying dry is pleasant, however, and it is important if the weather should turn cold and windy. If you have to worry about no more than a summer squall, you might just rely on your parka, but no fabric which breathes will turn the rain forever. I carry a very light rain shell in most regions.

The problem with all rain gear is to keep the rain out without keeping all your body moisture in, a dilemma which you can never solve with complete success. Especially in cold weather, your perspiration will tend to condense on the inside of a waterproof garment.

The condensation problem can be reduced by providing adequate ventilation inside the garment in order to carry away the moisture before it condenses. This purpose is best served by a poncho, which is essentially a

A poncho turns the rain well where wind isn't too much of a problem. A long one can be worn over the pack, which helps provide ventilation. This one is made of inexpensive plastic, suitable for occasional use.

waterproof sheet with a head hole and hood in the middle. Some ponchos are made with an extra-long flap in the back which will drape over the pack frame or snap up when not in use. This type serves to keep the pack dry and improves ventilation, too.

A poncho is clearly superior to any other type of rain protection until the wind starts blowing or you are beating through heavy brush or scrambling on steep rock when the skirts get in the way or it just blows around your neck. In these circumstances a waterproof parka is much better. Choose the one which suits the kind of walking you do most. If you expect to meet the rain on a forest trail, get a poncho. If you would be more likely to find rain on a windswept mountain ridge, get a parka. A long, very roomy rain parka is called a cagoule, and I prefer it to a short parka. You can pull your knees inside it in a bivouac, and it hangs down far enough so that full rain pants aren't necessary.

Whatever kind of rain top you choose, make sure that you can get as much ventilation as possible. Cuffs should have fasteners which allow them to be opened, rather than elastic which keeps them closed tight. The neck should have some means of getting air in and out, a drawstring, zipper, or

A rain parka or a cagoule like this one is better protection from wind-blown rain. Rain pants or chaps protect the legs.

Velcro flap. The bottom should be wide and left open except when the wind necessitates pulling it tight.

For any extended walking in the rain, you will also want protection for your legs. Even if you aren't pushing through wet brush, enough rain will drip off your poncho or parka to soak your trousers. The same watertight material as is used for a top can be used for rain pants. They should be fairly loose. If you wear a parka, you will need full rain pants. Generally, with a poncho or a cagoule, rain chaps are adequate, and they are lighter and take much less space. Rain chaps have no seat or crotch. They consist just of the legs with loops to tie onto your belt.

Material for rainwear should be of coated nylon. There are many good types. The heaviness of the material and the number of layers simply depend on your planned use. Lightweight material made into a garment of single thickness is very compact and will turn a lot of rain, but it is not so durable as heavier material or two thicknesses of lighter material without overlapping seams. I use a single layer of coated ripstop nylon for light-

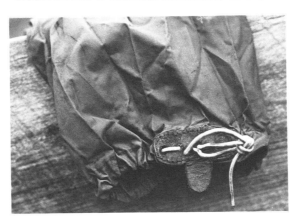

A good home-made wrist closure for rain gear. The leather friction tab holds the cuff at any diameter.

weight garments. Seams should be painted with a sealer. For more durable items, I use two layers of the same material with the uncoated sides facing out, the coating sandwiched inside where it cannot be abraded. Plastic rain gear is inexpensive and adequate for infrequent use.

A hat somewhat like those in the old sou'wester outfits is sometimes more pleasant to wear than the hood of a parka or poncho. It sheds water away from the face and allows more ventilation around the neck.

DOWN CLOTHING

In other chapters the special advantages of down as an insulator are pointed out. Down provides more insulation with less weight and in less packed space than any other material. It is the ideal insulator for use in sleeping bags and also for clothing to be used in extremely cold weather and at very high altitudes, where sufficient insulation in traditional form would be too bulky and constraining and where there is little danger of the clothing getting wet.

Down clothing is also a pleasant bit of luxury. A down vest or jacket brings a lot of warmth with little weight and bulk. It is unsurpassed for comfort in lounging around camp. For most general backpacking, however, down items are unnecessary, and they should be placed well down on the list of things to be purchased or carried. Lighter down items like vests and light jackets are usually more useful than big expedition parkas.

Too many people in the last few years have been relying almost completely on down clothing for warmth, ignoring the fact that down becomes absolutely useless when it gets wet. Some basic wool clothing should be carried wherever there is danger of wet, cold weather. Use down clothing for supplementary warmth, in really cold weather, or as a substitute for a sleeping bag. Down clothing is pleasant and convenient, but get a wool sweater, wool pants, and a good shell parka first.

Construction methods with down are described in the chapter on sleeping bags. For supplementary garments such as light jackets and vests, the most useful pieces of down equipment for backpacking, sewn-through tube construction can be used. Heavier down clothing requires full use of differential cut and baffling to prevent compression of the down. Proper tailoring in down parkas is even more important than in sleeping bags, because body movement will compress the down unless the design prevents it.

Since basic design and construction methods for down clothing are the same as in sleeping bags, there is little need to repeat them here. Material should be tightly woven nylon, but it should be the lightest weight consistent with durability. Heavier weight fabrics will tend to compress the down. Down garments usually need more down than sleeping bags to fill a given amount of space, since they have to withstand compression by wind.

MISCELLANEOUS ITEMS

In cold weather *gloves* or *mittens* are essential. Gloves allow more dexterity, but mittens are warmer. Wool liners and overmitts or overgloves are good, and surplus ones are inexpensive. Various other types are also available.

Gaiters or *anklets* are necessary in soft snow and sometimes useful to keep out scree or sand. Gaiters are long tubes of fabric covering the upper boot and lower leg and closed with laces or zippers. Anklets are shorter versions just covering the ankle and upper boot. Either prevents snow and debris from getting into the boots, and gaiters also help keep the lower leg warm in snow.

10 *Packs*

Presumably you should have a backpack in order to be a backpacker, and the variety of designs that are offered may be somewhat confusing to the beginner. There are many very good types available at any backpacking or climbing shop. There is also an increasing volume of shoddily made junk flooding many surplus, hardware, department, and sporting-goods stores. Choosing between the better types of packs is largely a matter of deciding what you're going to use one for.

TYPES OF PACKS

In order to consider their characteristics, it will be helpful to break the various packs down into broad categories, although there are some that overlap. All of them are designed to hang on the back, so that the wearer will be able to carry his load and still have a good deal of freedom to move about and use his hands. Only very small loads can be carried practically in pockets, belly packs, shoulder bags, and the like. Modern packs are all hung from the shoulders or a combination of the shoulders and the waist or hips. Tumplines, which hang the load from the head, limit movement of the neck severely, and it requires years to develop the neck muscles to use them properly, hardly a worthwhile enterprise when the loading point can

A simple frameless rucksack. A good, inexpensive day pack or children's pack, but unsuited for overnight trips.

be moved down the spine to the hips. Tumplines still have value to the canoeist for portaging, but they can be ignored by the backpacker.

The simplest pack is the *frameless rucksack,* which in its most rudimentary form is nothing more than a sack hung from two straps. Simple ones can be made from trousers and pillowcases. All the load in this kind of pack is carried by the shoulders, and any waist strap that is provided serves mainly to keep the pack from swinging around. As the most basic pack, the frameless rucksack has the virtues of simplicity but also all the defects that people have tried to correct with other designs. One is that the wearer's back has no protection. Hard, sharp, or irregularly shaped objects will gouge into your back unless you can put them on the other side of the pack. If there are only a few objects in the pack, they fall to the bottom, which isn't always the most comfortable place to carry them. As it is stuffed full the pack will start to bulge in all directions, tending toward the shape of a sphere, or if it is a long pack, a cylinder. Carrying a small, frameless rucksack packed tightly is like carrying a medicine ball hung on shoulder straps. This bulging creates the dual problem of an uncomfortably shaped pack and one which sticks far out behind, tending to pull the walker over backward, and forcing him to lean far forward against the straps.

The bulging problems can be partly solved by shaping the pack care-

A compartmentalized frameless day pack. The load is better controlled in this type of pack.

fully, by not overstuffing it, and by making it in separate compartments. Separate compartments control the shape of the pack well—several small cylinders sewn together properly make a pack of the desired shape—and they also allow the wearer to hold objects in particular places, heavy objects on top or hard things in back. Small compartments won't hold large pieces of gear, however, and all the weight of the pack still hangs from the shoulders. Also the frameless rucksack makes your back sweat badly in warm weather because there is no ventilation.

The *frame rucksack* was for many years the main answer to the problems mentioned above. The pack was attached to a large frame, basically triangular in shape, and the frame was hung on the shoulder straps. This solved several problems immediately. Hard objects were kept away from the back, no matter where they were put in the pack, the frame held at least one side of the pack in the desired shape, and the frame kept the pack away from the back, providing an air space for cooling and evaporation of sweat. However, the older rucksacks like the U.S. Army ski-mountaineering pack in the picture still bulge out a lot at the bottom, which forces the wearer to lean far forward against the weight.

Major improvements were made in the frame rucksack when the Bergans Company of Norway began to make frame rucksacks with a narrow

A standard frame rucksack. This one is a U.S. Army ski-mountaineering pack, still available at good prices in the surplus stores. Note that the load tends to bulge far from the back, forcing the wearer to lean forward. With careful packing this can be a good pack.

bottom and wide top, retaining the volume of the pack, but preventing the load from sticking so far out from the back. With the load carried higher, a smaller forward lean put the center of gravity over the feet. Since the wearer didn't have to lean so hard against the pack, carrying was easier.

Most of the weight of the frame rucksacks still goes on the shoulders, though some is transferred by the frame to the hips. This limits the load that can be carried by the average person in the frame rucksack. Training the shoulders to carry heavy loads requires a lot of miles and a lot of aches.

An improved frame rucksack, shaped so that the load rides higher, so that the wearer does not have to lean forward so much.

161

The frames of the two rucksacks shown above. The Bergans design on the left is wide at the top, so that the load in the sack can be pushed higher.

Another solution to the disadvantages of the frameless rucksack was the *packframe*, a rectangular frame with carrying straps, generally made of wood. The packframe could be used for carrying all kinds of irregular loads, since they could simply be lashed on, or it could be used with an attached bag. It usually extended above the top of the shoulder straps, allowing the load to be placed higher, so that a slight forward lean would put the center of gravity over the feet. The exaggerated lean required by some rucksacks was avoided. The packframe was also completely adjustable in the volume of the loads carried, because one could simply wrap the load in a tarp and lash it on. A small load could be placed high on the frame or a large one distributed along it in the most comfortable possible arrangement. The load still hung mainly from the shoulders, however, and if the lashing method was used, the whole pack had to be undone to get at anything inside.

It remained for A. I. Kelty to design the closest thing to an ideal pack for the average backpacker, the *contour frame pack*. The original Kelty pack is still one of the best of these, although other manufacturers are now making very good ones. As this is by far the best pack for most of the people most of the time, it is worth considering in detail.

CONTOUR FRAME PACKS

The contour frame is made of aluminum or magnesium tubing bent to follow the contour of the back. The curve brings the load closer to the back and enables the frame to be made longer, so that a pack of the same size can be made thinner while retaining the same volume, again keeping the weight closer to the back. The height of the frame makes it possible to pack the weight very high, putting the center of gravity of the pack over the feet with only a very slight forward lean.

A contour frame pack. Heavy objects are high and close to the back, with the sleeping bag and pad strapped lower down. The whole load can be transferred to the hips with a very slight forward lean.

All of these features make possible the most important feature of the Kelty-type pack, which is the use of a waistband to transfer most or all of the weight of the pack to the hips. This can be done only with the center of gravity high and close to the back and with a rigid frame that extends below the waist. It is a tremendous boon to the weekend backpacker, because the hips are well suited to carrying a lot of weight without special training of the muscles. Thus, with a good contour frame pack, any refugee from the city in reasonably good health can comfortably carry supplies for a week or two of backpacking, a feat which is much harder with a rucksack.

The frame can be used to lash irregular loads on, but it is normally used with a matching bag attached tightly to the frame with metal pins.

163

A contour pack frame with a 360° belt, far superior to the belt and backband arrangement. The complete belt can be like this one or it can be padded. The width of the shoulder straps at the top is adjustable by moving the clevis pins.

The bag can be full length, but a practical arrangement for most purposes is a bag that extends from the top of the frame two-thirds of the way down. Sleeping bag and pad are then strapped on below. The bags are made in many sizes and with many differences in detail. Shop around with the following points in mind. Get the smallest bag that will suit your purposes. There is a tendency to use bags that are far larger than needed. A narrow bag keeps the weight close to the frame where you want it. An "expedition-style" bag is designed for very large loads, and if you need it for one person's gear on a week's backpacking trip, you are carrying too much.

Dividing the bag into compartments has the advantages of holding the bag in shape and enabling you to control the load, keeping heavy objects up high. On the other hand, compartments that are too small for some of your equipment—cooksets, for example—are a damned nuisance. Many other features that add convenience are pretty obvious. Pockets are nice for lunch and miscellaneous small gear that gets lost in the main part of the pack.

More important in the long run are the details of construction. A pack that is heavy nylon throughout will last much longer than any other material. The hardware attaching the pack to the frame should hold it positively. If the pack can move around, the rubbing will soon cause some points to fail. Seams should be strong and finished so that they won't ravel out. Zippers should operate smoothly and be placed so that they don't bear heavy strains. Check all the construction details. Packs take very heavy wear, and there is no way to nurse them. If there are any weak points in the manufacture, they will cause the pack to fall apart in short order.

The frame itself should be as strong as possible. Check it as best you can, but you might as well recognize that weak points in the frame are not always visible. The belt has to be wide and very sturdy—it will carry a lot of weight. A little, dinky belt will cut you in half before long. Padded belts are nice, but they aren't necessary. A wide, plain belt will do the job. The belt can either extend around the front only, using the lower backband to support the weight in the rear, or go all the way around the hips, with the pack hung on side tabs. The half-belt is all right for moderate loads, but the 360° belt is so far superior that I wouldn't be without it. One kind is shown in the picture. The more common and expensive variety is padded. Shoulder straps should be padded, sturdy, and designed in the standard fashion. Some improved shoulder harnesses have been made, but their importance on contour frames is minimal, since most of the load is transferred to the hips.

OTHER PACKS

Although the contour frame pack is the standard backpacker's carrying case, it does have a few disadvantages, so that other packs are better for some purposes. As a general rule I would recommend that the beginner get a frame pack, adding to his collection as he becomes a connoisseur. A few beginners will have good reasons to choose other packs.

The high, rigid frame of the contour pack will not move around easily with the body. This is no disadvantage on open trails, but if you have to do a lot of bending it can be a real nuisance. The high center of gravity then tries hard to pull you over, and the frame catches on brush, rock outcrops, and fallen logs. For bushwhacking in heavy brush, a frame is a pain in the neck, and a rucksack is far superior. Other places with little headroom are equally difficult to negotiate with a frame. I remember all too well the experience of trying to get through a series of caves with a frame pack.

The extension of the frame behind the head also makes looking up rather difficult, and the climber may find the frame a nuisance in this respect. A final objection made by some people to the frame is that it makes footing a bit more difficult because of the high center of gravity. I find this to be true only in cases where you are forced to lean or bend a lot, in rock-climbing for example. Most of the time you can learn to keep the frame from throwing you off balance, and even use it to advantage, but this takes a little practice.

Frame rucksacks have the advantage when you have to carry quite a bit of weight, if the contour frame has been ruled out for some reason. Skiers, climbers, and those who backpack in brushy country often prefer rucksacks. They are pleasant to carry with reasonable loads once your shoulders are in shape, though with really heavy loads there is no substitute for a frame.

Frameless rucksacks allow even more natural body movement and weigh less than those with frames. They are favorites with bivouac specialists and with many mountaineers, but they must be packed carefully, and the load must be kept to a minimum.

An intermediate pack is the *flexible-framed rucksack*. It allows a little of the load to be transferred to the hips like the regular frame rucksack, and controls the shape of the pack somewhat, but the weight is less, and much of the flexible feeling of the frameless pack is retained. Usually stays of aluminum or magnesium are used for the flexible frame.

DESIGN FEATURES IN PACKS

There are some common requirements in the design of a good pack, no matter what the type. The most obvious is that it has to be sturdy. Packs are almost invariably *stuffed*. Strain is put on the fabric and the seams. If they aren't very tough the pack won't last long. Shoulder straps and waistbands have to carry the weight of the pack. They must be very strong, and their points of attachment to the pack have to be, too. These points should be heavily reinforced. The bottom of the pack needs to be reinforced, too, if the pack will rest on it when set down.

Shoulder straps also have to be designed for comfort. They should be wide where they pass over the shoulders to distribute the load—narrow straps or straps that curl and become narrow will cut unmercifully into the shoulders. Padding of shoulder straps is very helpful. The straps must taper as they go under the armpits or they will chafe badly. The tops of the straps should be close together, so that they will pass over the shoulders as close to the neck as possible. This is usually achieved by hanging them from a single D-ring or sewn patch. With frames, it is a good feature for the distance between the straps to be adjustable at the top for different builds.

Straps and pockets can be chosen or designed to suit the preferences and needs of the user. They have to be sturdy to do any good, and they should be carefully sewn and reinforced at points of stress.

It is helpful if packs are waterproof, but coating a fabric also makes it weaker, and the coating on pack material has to be fairly heavy or it will be worn off quickly by the constant friction that a pack suffers. For these reasons, pack material that is waterproof has to be made much heavier than equally durable material that is not waterproof. Some manufacturers like Kelty prefer to make a separate lightweight waterproof cover for use in the rain.

USING PACKS

Remember that the best pack has to be used properly to take advantage of its design. Pack it so that the cook kit doesn't dig into your back. The weight should be as high and as close to the back as possible, so that you don't have to lean against the straps in the wasted exercise of simply staying upright. For skiing, climbing, or difficult footing, you want to get the weight lower, but this makes it even more important that it be kept close to the back. A waist strap is essential for these purposes to keep the pack close to the body and prevent it from swinging. On some contour frames the pack can be lowered to bring the weight lower.

SAVING MONEY ON PACKS

It isn't really feasible for you to make your own contour frame, though you can buy a frame separately and make the bag for it if you like, either from your own design or with a kit. Study commercial ones carefully before you design your own. Shop around a little and you'll find there are a few good combinations available at reasonable prices.

Pack Layout

Fabric approximately 42″ wide

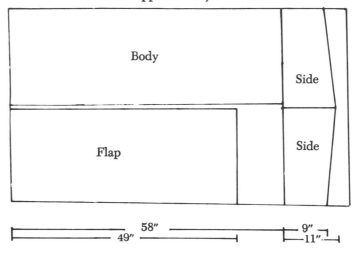

You can make your own frameless and flexible framed rucksacks, but rigid frames are pretty hard. The Army ski-mountaineering packs are still floating around, and they are good rucksacks if they are packed properly, even though they are not so well designed as some modern ones. The price has been going up, but you can still get some good ones for eight dollars or so. Don't get stuck with a bad imitation.

Packs are a good place to tap the used market, especially for frames. A top-brand frame can be gotten for half- or quarter-price, and as long as it isn't bent it will probably be in just as good a condition as when it was new. Frames last indefinitely, although some attachments need occasional mending or replacement.

INSTRUCTIONS FOR MAKING
A FLEXIBLE-FRAMED RUCKSACK

This pack is a good compromise for someone traveling fairly light. It molds well to the body, but is fairly comfortable for carrying loads. In making your own pack, you should regard patterns and instructions as suggestions. Change the pack around to fit your body and your needs.

The design is fairly simple. The basic sack is made by sewing two sides on one piece which wraps around to form the front, back, and bottom. Another piece doubles the bottom and the section which fits next to your back, forming a pocket into which the frame will be sewn, and then it continues over the top to form a flap.

The frame is formed by three aluminum bars 3/4-inch wide and 1/8-inch thick. These are drilled at the ends for machine screws or rivets, and they can be formed into a triangular frame that can be bent to fit the back, after it is sewed between the two layers of cloth on the front of the pack. The machine screws go through the stays and the fabric, with leather reinforcing pieces and washers on either side to prevent ripping of the cloth.

The pack is carried by means of both shoulder straps and a waistband. The waistband is 2 inches wide and sewed to the pack along the lower stay for a length that makes the pack comfortable for you. The shoulder straps go all the way over the shoulders. At the front they attach to the bottom of the triangular frame. At the back each strap attaches both to the top of the triangle and the top of the pack.

Much of the pack can be sewn on a sewing machine, but you will get a stronger pack by stitching throughout with a sewing awl (speedy stitcher) using heavy nylon thread.

The pack is designed without pockets, but they can be easily attached to the sides or back of the pack, if you want them.

When cutting nylon webbing, melt the cut ends to prevent fraying.

MATERIALS LIST

2 yards coated nylon pack fabric
4 feet 2″ webbing, flat type
1 buckle for 2″ webbing
3 aluminum stays, $\frac{1}{8}$″ x $\frac{3}{4}$″, two 17$\frac{1}{2}$″ long, and one 13″ long. Round ends with a
    file and drill for $\frac{1}{8}$″ machine screws $\frac{1}{2}$″ from each end of each stay.
18 feet 1″ nylon webbing (medium weight flat)
6 buckles for 1″ webbing
2 pieces sponge rubber 2″ x $\frac{1}{2}$″ x 12″
15 grommets and setting tool
6 scrap-leather patches, approximately 2″ square
3 brass, round-head machine screws $\frac{1}{8}$″ x 1$\frac{1}{2}$″ with nuts

6 ½" washers for screws
1 boot lace, 5 or 6 feet long
sewing awl and thread

1. Sew the sides into the body, making sure that the coated side of the fabric will face toward the inside of the pack. The narrow ends of the sides are at the bottom and the slanting edges at the back. The pattern allows for 1" margins. The coating will prevent raveling, but double-stitching is still wise. Make a narrow finished hem at the top edge of the pack, and install grommets along it for a drawstring, about every 4".

2. Sew the flap onto the pack. Begin at the bottom of the pack, where the flap wraps around to form a double bottom. The flap is proportioned to extend 3" up the back of the pack and 1" up each side. Sew it onto the body of the pack with a single line of stitching, folding 1" of each edge under and making tucks as you go around corners. Sew the flap all the way around the front of the pack, to within an inch of the top. Three sides should be sewn, with an opening at the top between the body and the flap, so that the frame can be inserted. The top part of the flap which protrudes above the pack should be hemmed all the way around.

3. Cut two lengths of 1" webbing, each 50" long. These are to be sewn on the flap so that they will be on the inside of the pack. Each should run 5" in from the outside edge of the flap. Start sewing them so that the ends are 2" inside the space between the body of the pack and the flap. The ends will hang out from the end of the flap. Cut two more lengths of webbing, each 6" long. Sew a buckle on the end of each. Sew these to the bottom of the pack, with the buckles protruding just up onto the back to meet the flap straps. Each will be about 4" in from the edge of the bottom.

4. Screw the frame together temporarily. Place it in the pocket between the body and the flap so that the lower stay is about 1" above the bottom of the pack and the top juncture is in the center. Melt holes in the fabric with a hot knife for the screws to go through. Punch holes in the centers of each of the leather patches. Cut two lengths of webbing each 20" long. Make a small hole in the center of each, about ½" from one end, with the hot knife, and another hole 16½" along each one from the first hole. Cut two more lengths each 10" long, install a buckle at one end of each, and make a small hole in the center, 1" from the opposite end.

Now it is time to install the frame. The bottom two screws go toward the inside of the pack. Each screw passes through the pieces in the following order: washer, leather patch, short buckle strap, short end of 20″ strap, hole in flap, two metal stays, hole in body, leather patch, washer, nut. The top screw goes through: washer, leather patch, long ends of two 20″ straps, hole in flap, two metal stays, hole in body, leather patch, washer, nut.

The 20″ straps should now run along the stays, but on the outside of the pack, with ends protruding from the upper leather patch. The two buckles should stick out from the lower junctures. Position the buckle straps so that they point upward, sticking out at an angle of 20° or so from the pack. Now sew around all the leather patches, going through both patches and both pieces of webbing, and criss-crossing back and forth so that each junction is very strong. Then sew along each side of each of the 20″ straps between the leather patches, sewing through strap, flap, and body, forming an envelope around each of the upper stays. When the frame is sewn in, sew the flap and body together at the top, just below the line of grommets, reinforcing the seam near the flap straps. Tighten the machine screws, cut off the protruding ends, and peen them down with a hammer.

5. With the scrap pieces of fabric, make tubes to sew around the foam-rubber pads. Each tube should be 18″ long and should fit tightly around the pad, with no seams on one side (which will rest on the shoulder). Coated side of the fabric should face in toward the rubber. Place a piece of sponge rubber in the center of each tube, and then sew them in with seams close to the ends of the rubber. Fold the ends of one end of a pad envelope over and sew it to the end of one of the 20″ straps. Do the same with the other pad. Two things should be noted here. These are shoulder straps, so care should be taken to make the sides which will rest on the shoulders fairly smooth—keep the folds and rough spots on top. Also note that the two 20″ straps cross at the frame apex; the strap coming from one side of the pack goes over the opposite shoulder.

Cut two more pieces of webbing each 16″ long. Sew these to the opposite ends of the shoulder pads from the pack. They fit into the buckles at the bottom of the frame.

6. Sew the 2″ buckle on one end of the 2″ webbing. Sew the center section of this waistband onto the pack along the line of the lower frame piece. It is usually most comfortable to sew it a total of 11″ to just short of each end junction, but try it out. Sew this firmly, with plenty of reinforcing.

7. Sew one 12″ piece of webbing on the top of each shoulder pad, sewing

about 2″ of an end to the pad, so that the free end points toward the pack. Cut two 5″ pieces of webbing and install a buckle on each. Sew the opposite end of each onto the top of the flap, on the line of the flap strap about 5″ back, with the buckle pointed forward. These can be connected to the straps coming back from the shoulder pads, giving you control over the lean of the pack.

8. Install the boot lace as a drawstring through the grommets. The pack is now finished. Experiment with various packings and loadings, and reinforce any points that seem to come under a lot of strain. Bend the frame to fit your back.

Tents and Other Shelters 11

The shelters used commonly by backpackers vary a great deal. Prejudices play their part, but forms and materials are dictated largely by the conditions that prevail in different seasons and parts of the country. A backpacker may use natural shelters or accommodations already built along the trail. He may improvise a shelter from natural materials or he may carry his house on his back. Semipermanent shelters such as lean-tos have special virtues for areas of heavy use. They lighten the load on the back and confine camping to spots which can be controlled, though by definition they are not wilderness.

In some places natural shelters can be relied on. One camps in the shelter of an overhanging rock if the weather threatens, and that is that. Planning on using a natural shelter requires that there be one and that you know it exists, conditions that rarely occur.

Improvising shelters is rarely practical these days, at least not without using some materials which you carry in. Shingling lean-tos with live boughs in most wilderness areas ought to be punished with thumbscrews and hot irons. Areas and seasons suited to snow shelters are about the only places where one can still plan on using strictly natural materials very often.

We are left with the tents, ponchos, tarps, and plastic sheets the backpacker brings with him, and they are the subject of this chapter. The choice between them must rely first on your particular requirements. What

173

do you need to be sheltered from? Rain? Wind? Sleet? Cold? Insects? A combination? Is the rain of the afternoon-shower variety or of the pouring-down-for-weeks-without-end kind?

Take the California Sierra Nevada Range as an example. It does rain there in the summer, but not very often. One can backpack dozens of times there from June to September and only get caught by rain on a couple of occasions. Insects are not too bad either, and they can generally be controlled fairly well with repellent. In that sort of situation, it is just plain silly to carry a lot of tent around on every trip. Take the lightest serviceable emergency shelter, and be done with it. If I backpacked only in summer and only in that area, I doubt that I would even buy or make a tent. A tube tent would be a fine contingency shelter, except above timberline; so would a tarp or a poncho or a bivouac tent.

On the other hand, winter in the same mountain range brings quite a different story. The storms are frequent, dumping large amounts of snow and bringing respectable winds. If a snow shelter was not to be used, the backpacker would have to carry a good, weathertight tent, capable of withstanding high winds. Summer in other spots requires better protection, too. Rain may come down as the rule rather than the exception. Insects are often as much of a problem as the weather, and a tent may be preferred to a tarp or other open shelter, simply because it can be designed to keep the bugs out.

Like other items of backpacking equipment, shelters are the result of compromise. Pick the best type for your temperament, needs, and pocketbook, and then make do with it in those situations for which it is not ideally suited. You may eventually own more than one type, but the number of well-made tents you can wear out in one backpacking career is quite limited. A good tent lasts a long time.

TARPS AND PONCHOS

The most elementary kind of shelter is a flat piece of waterproof material, usually with grommets along the sides and some ties here and there for convenience in use. If a hole and a hood are put in the middle, the tarp is a poncho and can be worn as well as pitched. This arrangement is still preferred by many experienced backpackers because of its simplicity, light weight, versatility, and low cost. A tarp can be pitched in an almost infinite variety of ways, just a few of which are shown in the drawing. Dimensions vary a good deal, each having its advocates. There are 9- and 10-foot square men and defenders of 7' x 9' or 9' x 11'. For two people 11' x 14' works well.

A tarp-tent is very simple to make, requiring only that you sew the material into a square or rectangle, hem the edges and put on attachment points. Along the edges these can be grommets, loops of nylon tape, or D-rings. In the body of the tarp one simply sews on enough tape ties to suit the fancy. A 9' x 11' tarp tied to itself the long way also makes a good one-man tube tent. Coated nylon makes the best material for tarps.

TUBE TENTS

The original tube tent was simply a tube of plastic, usually three mils thick. This can be easily pitched by stringing a line between two objects to hold up the tube, which is normally about nine feet long. They are made in diameters for one and two people, weighing about a pound per person.

The tube tent is an excellent emergency rain shelter for relatively sheltered areas. All that is needed is the tube, a length of parachute cord, and

A plastic tube tent like this is a good shelter to carry below timberline in mild weather, in case of unexpected rain.

A two-man tube tent folded. Weight is about two pounds.

two objects from which to suspend the tube. The weight of the body holds the arrangement down, so that there is no need for stakes. The arrangement is light, simple, and cheap, and thus has become very popular in regions to which it is suited.

I carry a few spring-type clothespins with the tube tent for use in the wind to partially close an end if necessary and to hold the tent at the proper place on the line. On threatening evenings, when I want to sleep under the stars but am worried about rain coming up in the night, I string out the tube tent between two trees with a sliding friction knot on the line. I leave the line loose, using the tent as a ground cloth. If sprinkling wakes me in the middle of the night, I stuff my gear inside, pull the line taut, and hop back in bed, the whole operation taking no more than a minute.

Tube tents are basically emergency protection against the rain. They are short-lived, are no protection against insects, will not withstand high winds, and are completely unsuitable for snow camping or very cold weather. They require ties, and although one can improvise supports, they are suitable mainly for use in places where there are trees. Used properly, they are a great boon to the backpacker, but they are not substitutes for mountain tents and should not be used as such. During long periods of rain, they will not keep you dry.

A tube tent can also be made of light coated fabric which weighs about the same as a plastic tube tent. The cost is much higher, but the product is much more durable. Although these can be sewn with small awnings and other improvements, they have basically the same advantages and defects as the plastic tube tent.

PLASTIC SHEETS

A plastic sheet around three mils thick can be used in the same ways as a tarp, but it will not last so long. Several devices are available for gripping a plastic tarp without starting a rip. You can also simply place a small stone or other object at the place you want to tie, twist it into the tarp, and tie a line around the twist.

Plastic sheets serve as ground cloths and useful emergency shelters, although tubes are more versatile. One plea about both: if you take them in, take them out again. Shredded plastic sheets are starting to appear everywhere, draped over rocks and lean-tos and then abandoned. Really, no one wants to look at the remains of your bivouac next year!

INSECT BARS

If you have an insect problem but you are using a shelter with no closure against the bugs, or no shelter at all, you can either rely on repellents or use an insect bar. This is simply a large piece of netting which you put over your sleeping bag.

There are various ways you can make a bar fasten to your bag, but it is simpler to get a large piece and drape it. A 3-yard piece of nylon netting 45 inches wide will weigh only 5 ounces. The sides can be weighted with stones. Prop the section over your head up with a stick or pack, or tie it up with cord. If you let it rest on your cheek the little beasts will bite right through.

TENTS

Tents are more durable and stable structures than the ones just mentioned. Instead of allowing dozens of forms of pitching like the tarp tent, a normal

A typical open-front forest tent. This one is a modified Baker design with an awning pitched as a double roof for snow camping. Such tents are not suited for use in the mountains or outside forested areas.

tent permits only one or two, but it pitches much more efficiently in that way, excelling in those respects for which it was designed. Most tent designs are very poor, and even many of the good ones are completely unsuitable for the backpacker, so it will be easy to narrow the field down.

There are many excellent designs of tents for forest camping, usually with open fronts, without sewn-in floors, and designed to be pitched from lines tied to surrounding trees or perhaps from poles cut or found in the surrounding forest. The open fronts of such tents make them a joy to pitch in front of a fire, especially during long rains. They also enclose a lot of space for a given weight of material. They are not generally all-weather tents, however, not easily pitched away from trees, unstable in high winds, often unsuitable for snow camping. Moreover, few of them are made in modern fabrics, so that if you want one, you may have to make it yourself.

Most modern backpacking tents are designed to be self-contained, whereas most of the best of the older styles depended on locally cut poles or on guy lines strung between trees for pitching. Such a stable, closed, self-contained tent gives the backpacker a lot of freedom, because it can be pitched almost anywhere without damaging the site. The main disadvantage is that most such tents are somewhat cramped.

THE MOUNTAIN TENT

The prototype for most modern backpacking tents was the mountain tent, itself a more sophisticated version of the pup tent. The cross section of this type of tent is a triangle, and the standard size, perhaps 7½ feet long and 5 feet wide at the front, is about right for two men and their equipment. Originally, one pole was used at each end, but this has been abandoned for the more convenient design using two poles inserted in sleeves and meeting at the top, so that no pole blocks the entrance. Some mountain tents have only one entrance at the front, with a low rear end propped by a single pole at the back. Others are full height throughout, and these often have entrances held up by two poles at either end.

Many modifications have been made in the mountain tent in the last few years, and special features will be found in many versions. Vestibules can be included at one end or both for equipment storage, different kinds of ventilation flaps and accessories can be added, and various types of entrances may be featured. More important developments have used tents designed with semicircular or other modified cross sections which are lighter, require fewer stakes and guy lines, and are more stable in winds than older tents—as well as being considerably more expensive. Most important, however, are certain basic design features that should be considered whenever you are buying or building a tent.

A typical two-man, all-weather mountain tent, made of a nylon-cotton mixture.

FEATURES OF AN ALL-WEATHER WILDERNESS TENT

Some of the requirements for an all-around backpacking tent have been mentioned. It must be self-contained. If you do all your camping in forested areas, you might not need an all-purpose tent. One of the older designs might suit you better. If, however, you expect one tent to serve you in the woods, above timberline, in snow and mountain meadow, in exposed and windy places as well as those which are well protected, you will find that the older designs won't work very well.

A tent meant to meet the requirements just mentioned has to be closed. Whatever side flaps it may have, when the wind comes up and really starts blowing, you have to be able to close everything down. An open-front tent just isn't the thing to have in a windy, exposed place. Poles have to be carried. They may serve other purposes on the way in—ski-poles, for example—but any tent requiring poles so large they have to be found or cut at the site is not an all-purpose tent.

An all-weather tent should have a waterproof floor, and the waterproofing should preferably extend six inches or so up the walls. If both the floor and lower sides are waterproof, all need for trenching around the tent is eliminated. This is essential in soggy mountain meadows and similar places where drainage is poor but trenching shouldn't be used.

There are a great many possible arrangements of poles, wands, and tie-outs, but the net effect should be a tent which pitches with a smooth surface, as little sagging as possible, and a reasonable wind profile. Sagging folds indicate poor design, and large vertical walls will catch the wind like a sail. A less essential feature of some of the best new tents is that they can be pitched with only a few stakes and guys, because of aerodynamic design and superior placement of poles. This lessens the real weight that has to be carried when stakes can't be found locally, and it greatly simplifies pitching the tent on hard ground and on snow and ice. Some of the best such designs require only three or four stakes and no guy lines. Extra staking points should be provided for use in case of extreme winds, however.

FABRICS, FLIES, AND BREATHING

The biggest problem in designing tents is finding a way to shed any rain

CHARLES SCRIBNER'S SONS

PUBLISHERS SINCE 1846

597 FIFTH AVENUE
NEW YORK, N.Y. 10017

We take pleasure in sending you this review copy of

AMERICA'S BACKPACKING BOOK

by

Raymond Bridge

Publication Date: January 14, 1974

Price: $12.50

Direct quotation in reviews is limited to 500 words unless special permission is given.

Please send us two copies of your review

Please do not release reviews before publication date

The price listed here is the suggested retail list price

g heavy condensation of
ree feet from the roof of
n several thousand feet.
cooking, breathing, and
tent fairly humid. If the
e, the tent wall will tend
s or a cold window will.
densation to a minimum,
tion can eventually soak
ious matter if they cannot

densation problem alto-
d as a lean-to, you won't
circulates away before it
rs can be made of coated
fortunately, ventilation is
one sometimes wants a

f a single layer of coated

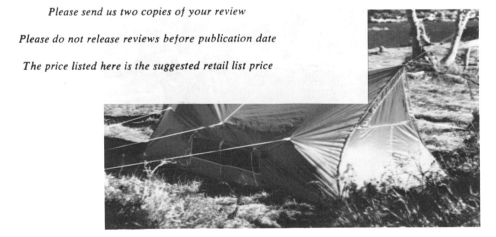

An example of a single-layer tent of coated fabric. Side vents are necessary to minimize condensation. Good for use only in mild weather.

fabric practical, but not as an all-weather tent. Some good inexpensive tents are made with large side flaps that can be opened to give a lot of ventilation. Such a tent can protect you from heavy summer rains, be screened against insects, and provide a good shelter with light weight and low cost. In cold weather, though, condensation will occur even with the vents open, snow will blow through them if they are open, and the ventilation will chill the tent, even though it doesn't solve the condensation problem.

There are two normal solutions used in all-weather tents. The tent can be made of a cotton fabric or a good cotton-nylon mixture. When such a fabric is properly chosen, it will breathe well and will minimize condensation, and yet it will shed most rain. Cotton takes waterproofing well, and the cotton fibers will swell when they get wet, tightening the tent wall. In a downpour which goes on for days or weeks, such a tent will *eventually* leak, but it will keep you quite dry in all but the wettest climates. Because of the conductivity and surface of the fabric, a cotton or cotton nylon surface always condenses less moisture and frost than synthetics, even uncoated ones. A single-layer tent of cotton or 60-40 cloth (with a coated floor) is the least expensive way to make a good all-weather tent.

The second solution to the problem is to make a tent which is really two tents, one pitched inside the other. The inside tent should be complete in itself, with a coated floor sewn in, mosquito netting, and so forth. The top of this tent can be made of uncoated nylon fabric, strong, lightweight, and capable of breathing. When there is no danger of rain, this tent can even be used alone, protecting against wind, insects, and somewhat against cold. For rain protection and additional warmth, a coated roof called a fly is pitched over the inside tent, leaving a space of a couple of inches between the two. The roof sheds the water, but the inside tent still breathes. Since both layers can be made of pure nylon, a lighter fabric can be used than in cotton or cotton-nylon tents, and the whole double tent will probably weigh no more than the single one.

The uncoated tent with a coated fly has several special advantages. The fly need only provide a roof to shed the force of the rain, and it can be used to provide an extra alcove at the front or rear of the tent for equipment storage, giving protection, but requiring little extra weight. Sealing of the seams of the fly is less critical than in a single-layer tent, since a few drips getting through will be shed by the inner tent, rather than falling on your nose. These advantages of the fly system have resulted in its displacing the single-layer tent in most of the best equipment lines in the last few years. Many manufacturers have dropped single-layer tents altogether. This is because of the greater affluence of the clientele, however, as well as the advantages of the double tent.

There are several disadvantages to the uncoated nylon tent with a fly. For one thing, it is expensive. The price of a good two-man mountain tent with a fly is quite high, even if you use a kit. Condensation is greater on nylon than on cotton or cotton-nylon mixture, so that even with the fly, a nylon tent is not usually any better, and in very cold weather frost formation is usually worse. Though wicking will eventually cause leaks in an uncoated tent, especially a small one in which rubbing against the walls is impossible to avoid, this problem should not be overemphasized. My small two-man mountain tent is made of 60-40 cloth, and in ten years of camping over much of the continent, it has kept me quite dry. A large tent which I made of Oxford weave cotton has been through downpours lasting weeks and never leaked. Nylon has tremendous advantages for making lightweight equipment, but if you should decide to make a small tent to save money, you might be better off using a single layer of cotton.

In cold weather, instead of condensing in liquid droplets on the tent wall, water forms frost. This is less bothersome with cotton and its mixtures than with nylon, but it will occur with either. For very cold weather, a frost liner is used to help solve this problem. It is a very light liner hung a few inches inside the main tent. It is not necessary for normal backpacking trips.

DESIGNING OR BUYING YOUR TENT

As with all other equipment, tent selection starts with an analysis of your own needs. I feel that for most people, purchase of a tent can wait a while. Sleeping bags, packs, and boots ought to come first. You can take a lot of good trips in nice weather using a tube tent or similar shelter in case you get caught by the rain. Later you will want a tent, and by that time you will know your needs better. If you camp mostly in the woods and use fires a lot, you may prefer one of the old designs like the Whelen tent. An open-front tent like this is a lot more pleasant to sit in on a rainy afternoon than a cramped mountain tent. See the book list at the end for details on where to find some of these designs.

Most modern backpackers, however, will be happiest with a tarp, tube tent, or a closed tent. A closed tent for one or two people should be a mountain tent or some variation of it. Dimensions depend on your preferences. The most efficient design will be about 7 or 7½ feet long with an entrance in front, but tapering in height and width toward the back to save weight. A tent wide enough for two is best except for inveterate soloers. You don't save that much weight in a one-man tent. A two-man tent which doesn't taper has a lot of advantages for long trips, especially in winter. Two entrances can be included, allowing one man to get in and out while the other is cooking, without kicking over the pot.

A four-man modified pyramid tent on the left, all nylon with a separate fly, and a two-man mountain tent on the right.

Such designs can also be enlarged for three or four people, but some kind of modified pyramid is generally used for these larger tents. A central pole or suspension line is used for the major support.

All tents are made of relatively light fabric suspended from some kind of frame, and certain standard problems in design should be considered by anyone making one or buying one. A suspension line or edge carrying the weight of the fabric, and perhaps strain from the wind as well, will tend to sag. There is no way to avoid some sagging. Pulling the fabric tight enough to avoid most of it requires a great deal of tension force. All such edges and lines need extra strength. A seam which has several layers of fabric folded together can be deliberately placed where it can take one of the lines of strain. Strength can also be provided by sewing tape along such a line. Sag

An example of a well designed pull-out tab. This one is sewn at the intersection of two seams, so that the strain is widely distributed.

These poles fit together at the top and extend through sleeves sewn on the outside of the tent. This prevents sag and leaves the entrance clear.

185

can be reduced by the use of extra suspension points and pull-out tabs to which guy lines can be rigged. A pull-out has to be strengthened or it will rip out on the first gusty night. See the illustration for an example of reinforcement. A ridge line which is not supported by a rigid pole will always sag, and a curve is often cut right into the line to prevent folds in the fabric below. This is called a catenary cut.

All other points subject to strain and wear must be reinforced, just as pull-outs are. Loops for stakes must be sewn so that a large area of fabric takes the strain. Poles should attach to reinforced points.

The bottom points of the poles fit into grommets in tabs sewn to the tent, preventing the poles from sinking into the snow and holding the tent in shape.

Except for pyramid tents, poles are best fitted *outside* the tent. Two poles which join together at the top make a good support for the front of the tent. They can fit into sleeves on the outside edges, and the lower ends can fit into a grommet in a piece of tape (see the illustration). Some newer designs may use poles which fit together to form a curve, which is then slipped into a sleeve. Support for the walls of a tent may be achieved with pull-outs or wands. Wands are like lightweight poles which slip into sleeves along the sides of the tent. They are generally made of light fiberglass sections, like those used in fishing rods.

If you are designing your own tent, get as much literature and go to as many stores as you can. By studying the best commercially made tents, you will get ideas to incorporate in your own tent. At the same time, don't be cowed. A tent made commercially, even by the best manufacturer, must be a compromise which may not best suit your needs. Designing your own

Mosquito netting is a desirable feature in any backpacking tent.

tent can be satisfying and you can often produce a far better tent for your purposes than anyone else.

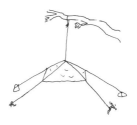

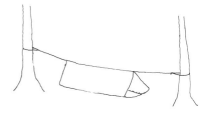

A few ways of pitching a tarp. Methods are limited only by your imagination and by the anchors that are available.

12 Sleeping Bags, Pads, and Air Mattresses

A sleeping bag is the most expensive item that most backpackers ever buy, and it is one of the most important. The days of all-night fires to keep warm by are pretty well over, and the sleeping bag is the piece of equipment that enables you to camp in a wide variety of conditions and still sleep comfortably. A night out without one will not kill you, but it will not usually be very cozy either. I like to bivouac without sleeping bags occasionally, but most of the time I wouldn't be without one. With far less bulk and weight than the old blanket roll, a modern sleeping bag keeps you genuinely warm.

HOW MUCH INSULATION DO YOU NEED?

Just as with other equipment, there is no *best* sleeping bag for all climates and all purposes. A lightweight, inexpensively constructed bag would be completely inadequate for camping in really cold weather, but the most expensive bag offered by a mountaineering shop is just as inappropriate for a summer on the Appalachian Trail. The purpose of a sleeping bag is to provide the extra insulation you need to sleep comfortably at night, when temperatures are coldest and the body's production of heat is at its lowest level.

Before thinking about the bag itself, you should decide what you want it to do. What are the warmest and coldest conditions you *normally* want to use it in, and what are the extreme conditions you would like it to withstand? Temperature ranges are very rough approximations, and many factors besides temperature have to be considered. If you do all your winter camping inside well-protected shelters, you may not need as heavy a bag as if you pitch a tent in very windy spots. Protection from wind, overhead shelter, altitude, and difficulty of trips are all important in choosing sleeping bags. Your other equipment and your clothing are important. Finally, *you* are important. The difference in the amount of insulation that people need is amazing. Some "sleep cold" and some "sleep warm," so you will have to gauge your needs from your knowledge of your own body.

My general rule for buying a sleeping bag is that it should be comfortable in the coldest conditions one normally meets, without wearing extra clothing inside. That is, if you sleep in pajamas, you should be comfortable in them; if in your underwear, you should be comfortable in that; and so forth. I save the possibility of donning every last sweater for the times when I meet extremely cold conditions, when I am run down, when the insulation is starting to get damp, and for similar difficulties. Usually, a bag that is just adequate in your coldest normal conditions will be all right the rest of the time, too. Zippers can be opened in warmer weather, or a cover can be used as described later in this chapter. Some may prefer the extra versatility of a double bag, one fitting inside the other. If summer temperatures where you camp are in the 70's at night, but down to −30 in winter, you might need two bags. Get one medium weight one that is fairly roomy, and one very light close-fitting bag for the heat of the summer. The light one goes inside the other in bitter cold.

INSULATION REQUIREMENTS

The backpacker has rather stringent requirements for his sleeping equipment. It must be light. I have carried some of the heavy car camping bags around the backcountry. It's better than not going at all, but it doesn't contribute to the enjoyment of the trip. They are horribly heavy and not very warm. The backpacker's sleeping equipment should provide as much insulation as possible for the least amount of weight. It should also have a reasonably small packed size, since bulk presents carrying problems. This means that the equipment should be quite compressible. The insulation between the sleeper and the ground, however, cannot be too compressible, because otherwise it would do no good. The body weight would squash it down, leaving no protection from heat loss to the cold ground.

The basic principles of insulation were discussed in an earlier chapter, but we might as well recapitulate them briefly here. So much nonsense has been written about sleeping bags that it is important to clear some away right at the beginning. The actual insulating material of any sleeping bag is air. Down, foam, Dacron, or whatever serves to hold the air in small, still cells. The amount of insulation is dependent on the thickness of the insulating layer. Period. There are other design considerations. The bag with the most insulation isn't necessarily the warmest, but the insulation is provided by that layer of air, and a bag with inadequate insulation can't be warm. If the insulation layer is two inches thick it provides twice the insulation of a layer one inch thick.

For all this to be true, the layer of air has to be immobilized to prevent convection currents, so that, for example, one type of insulator might maintain its effectiveness in a ten-mile-per-hour wind, while another might not. There are, however, no miracle insulators that will provide more insulation with less thickness. Thickness is the basic factor in maintaining warmth.

INSULATION MATERIALS

The three main possibilities for insulation in sleeping equipment are down, foam, and synthetic fiber batting. Since Dacron is the most effective of the synthetic fibers for this purpose, I'll stick to that; the remarks about Dacron apply to other synthetic fibers as well. Several types of foam are used for sleeping bags and sleeping pads, with different purposes and priorities in mind. Down comes in various qualities, as discussed earlier, and it may also be mixed with feathers.

Except for special circumstances, down is by far the best insulator for sleeping bags designed for backpacking, throughout those parts of the bag not bearing the body weight. It meets all the major criteria for this insulation. A given weight of down will expand to fill much more space, and thus provide much more insulation than any other material. It will also compress into a smaller space, but it will return to full volume quickly again and again. Down also has minor advantages. Its major disadvantages are in the area of cost. Down is expensive. The best down, that which is plucked from geese grown in a cold climate, is the most expensive. In addition, the characteristics of down make expensive construction necessary to make proper use of the good insulating qualities.

Thus for any given amount of insulation needed, a down bag can be built which is more efficient than any other type. On the other hand, if most of your camping is done in a fairly mild climate, you may want to buy or make a less expensive bag, using Dacron or foam. Before you do, though, be sure that they are adequate to your needs.

Dacron has to be sewn into batts to be used as insulation, because otherwise the material mats and leaves cold spots in the bag. Foam also presents some construction problems, because it is difficult to sew. One solution is to glue the foam into the shape you want and then to cover it with fabric.

THE SHAPE OF THE BAG

The large rectangular shape of most car-camping bags is a very inefficient shape for a sleeping bag. A good deal of the material lies in useless folds and represents wasted weight and money. It also presents a greater surface area to the cold air, and so loses more heat. Thus thicker insulation is needed in a rectangular bag than in a more compact bag. The most efficient bag is one which fits the body closely, following its contours, a shape commonly known as the mummy style. Most backpackers prefer to leave a little room for shifting around and choose some slightly more roomy modification of the mummy design. The bag should be roomy enough to allow you to sleep comfortably without suffering attacks of claustrophobia, but no larger. Most of the standard designs these days strike a reasonable compromise, but several manufacturers carry a special lightweight bag which is cut more closely and efficiently, a true mummy design.

All too often foam and Dacron bags are cut to a pattern which is far less efficient than most down bags. This is silly. Since these bags are colder and heavier to begin with, they need to be shaped properly even more than a down bag does.

ADVANTAGES AND DESIGN OF FOAM BAGS

Several manufacturers are now producing foam bags, although there is nothing particularly new about them. They are especially useful on boats when the temperature doesn't drop too low, since foam bags retain most (not all) of their insulating qualities when wet. The top layer of foam should be relatively soft, so that it will drape over the body somewhat. Draping is often improved by using two thinner layers of foam rather than one thick one. A foam bag should have a drawstring at the top and a zipper on the side for temperature and ventilation control.

In general, foam is stiff enough to stand out from the body and to move as a unit when one end is disturbed. As a result, foam bags tend to pump the warm air inside the bag away and suck in cold air from outside. A foam bag has a bottom which insulates the user better from the ground than other insulating materials, and a foam bag won't require additional padding in warm weather. The same can be said of a foam-bottom down bag, however. The characteristics that make foam a good ground pad make it a poor top.

I don't advise purchasing a new foam bag unless its special advantages are what you need. The current prices will buy you a better bag made of other materials or will get you a kit for a high-quality down bag. It might be worthwhile to *make* a foam bag. An excellent design is given in Paul Cardwell's *America's Camping Book*, pages 139–141. It is inexpensive to make but not anywhere near as warm as a good down bag. I want my bag to be warm enough so that my teeth won't chatter all night when I'm tired and temperatures start to plunge. However, I also sleep very warm, so if I get cold in a bag, most other people would, too. My own preferences probably stem partly from the fact that I often backpack in fairly extreme weather conditions. The claims made for some bags are absurd and are often based on one wearing a lot of insulation inside the bag. With an expedition down parka and thick insulation on my legs I can sleep at $-20°$ F. with a bedsheet over me, but that does not make the bedsheet good down to 20 below. An active man can stay warm in cold weather with relatively light clothing, and though he may carry some extra, the winter camper often depends on his sleeping bag to provide most of the insulation he needs when he stops for the night, when his body is inactive and temperatures are dropping. Furthermore, in cold weather, some emergency reserves are necessary. There *is* a good argument for carrying more insulation in the form of clothing and less in the sleeping bag, but when this is done, it is the clothing which provides the insulation, not the sleeping bag.

The great advantage of foam bags is their performance when wet, but their temperature range is limited, so this only applies in fairly mild weather. The claim that a foam bag acts like a diver's wet suit might be impressive if you want to sleep on the floor of the Atlantic, but it won't help much on Mount Whitney. A diver doesn't encounter subfreezing temperatures, evaporative cooling, or high winds. The backpacker does.

I think that someone who doesn't expect a lot of extreme cold and wants to make an inexpensive, versatile bag for himself should consider Cardwell's design. Before you do, though, compare its cost with that of making a down bag with a foam bottom or foam pad. There is a price difference, but it is not very large when you are using new materials.

DACRON BAGS

A few well-designed Dacron bags can be found on the market for $20–$30. For people who sleep fairly warm, these should be adequate for all conditions short of snow-camping and extreme cold weather. They can be extended to the latter uses with enough extra clothing, but this is a less efficient way of providing nighttime warmth than having a thicker sleeping bag. Dacron bags should probably be used only by those who rarely go out in cold weather or who need a stop-gap until they can afford a better bag. They are also good for anyone allergic to down. I think the better commercially made Dacron bags are a better economy choice than foam bags.

Dacron bags can be constructed by sewing directly through the outside fabric, the batt, and the inside fabric. This leaves cold seams, but these are not as bad as the cold seams in down or down-and-feather bags, because the Dacron doesn't compress so much. A warmer bag can be made by using two layers of batts, each sewn between one of the shells, and a thin layer of netting, then put together with no overlapping seams.

DOWN BAGS

I am giving details on the construction of down bags because I think they are a better choice for the backpacker and because construction methods are necessarily more complicated. Some of these methods are also applicable to the construction of bags using other materials.

A typical down bag suitable for most backpacking. This one has a liner to keep the bag from getting dirty.

Down is made up of tiny nuclei with filaments radiating in all directions. Although all down contains some small feathers, down pods are not feathers. The filaments can be compressed, pushing the air from between them, but when pressure is released they will spring back to shape. To provide an insulating layer, enough down must be stuffed into a compartment both to fill that compartment and to push the sides out to their full extension. Getting the maximum possible insulation from a given amount of down requires careful design to avoid loading the down and necessitating more fill to expand a compartment.

Down also shifts readily, and if it is sewn in large compartments, it will tend to bunch in one corner of a compartment unless an overfill of down is used. For the most efficient design then, many relatively small compartments are required, and they must be designed carefully to avoid loading.

The drawing shows a cross section of a few types of baffling. In the simplest, with sewn-through seams, a cold spot is left at each seam, where there is no insulation. This method of construction is suitable for some clothing but only for the very lightest sleeping bags, designed for warm-weather use. A second method was designed to eliminate this problem, and

194

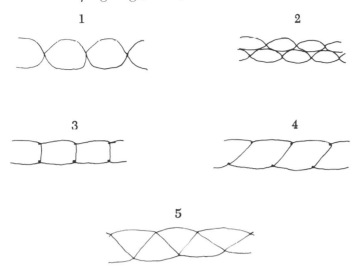

Some methods of construction for down insulating layers. 1. Sewn-through seams, which leave cold spots at the stitching. 2. Two layers of sewn-through construction, with the cold seams staggered. 3. Rectangular down compartments are formed by baffles sewn between the two sides. Baffles are made of very light fabric or netting. 4. Similar to 3, but with the baffles tilted, generally known as slant-tube construction. 5. Triangular baffling, which gives the most efficient use of the down, but is also the most expensive type of construction.

it uses two sleeping bags, either sewn together or not, with the tubes overlapping. It works well, but a lot of weight in fabric is wasted. The third and fourth methods use baffles sewn to the outside and inside layers of fabric to form tubes for the down. These are very good methods, but twisting will still tend to load the down. The best method of all, and the most expensive, is the triangular baffling method, in which a baffling layer goes back and forth between the inside and outside layers.

In addition to the methods of forming tubes for the down, the tubes themselves need to be baffled at intervals to prevent down shifting along them. The best bags are normally made with the tubes running across the bag horizontally or in a chevron pattern.

MATERIALS

Down bags should be made of lightweight nylon. It is stronger than cotton, more wear-resistant, and lighter, so that it doesn't tend to load the down. The inside of a nylon bag is slipperier and tends to bind less, which is important with closely fitting bags. Baffling material can be made of netting or a very light nylon fabric. The latter is better, allowing less shifting of the down. Thread should be synthetic throughout. Cotton thread inevitably wears out quickly, and the repairs are a nuisance.

Down is available in many grades. Judging among manufacturers is difficult because they rarely use the same systems for describing their down. Northern goose down from mature birds raised in a cold climate produces by far the best grade, but *some* duck downs are better than *some* goose downs. Within a particular line, you will often notice that several grades are used, but this is of limited help in comparing manufacturers. You will have to make a choice using other features as a guide. Remember that the weight of down in a bag means nothing by itself. Construction is more important, and down quality is at least as significant.

Since European poultry farmers are now killing geese at a younger age, the best down is no longer readily available. Quality is now achieved mainly by culling techniques. Goose down is no longer a guarantee of quality, nor is duck down necessarily an indication of inferiority. You must rely heavily on the integrity of the manufacturer.

Zippers and hardware should be of the best quality. Some good metal zippers were used in the past, but most high-quality bags today use over-size zippers of nylon or other synthetic materials, which have less tendency to jam or freeze and which are less brutal to the skin in cold weather.

OTHER CONSTRUCTION FEATURES

Any sleeping bag should have a good hood arrangement for protecting the head and preventing air circulation, while still permitting the sleeper to breathe outside the bag. The design can be simple or complicated, providing that it works. Zippers should not be cold spots, as they will be if they are left open to both the outside and the inside. This is usually solved (sort of) by the addition of a down-filled tube to cover the zipper. The zipper side of the tube should have a good, tough tape attached to prevent the zipper from catching. A better method is to have two closures with a baffle in between, either two zippers, Velcro and zippers, or another arrangement. Unfortunately, I think only one manufacturer uses this method at the moment.

A differential cut is an advantage when it is properly used. The illustration shows how this works. The idea is that if the inside of the bag is cut to the same size as the outside, you will press the two shells together every time you scrunch up or stick out an elbow. With a differential cut the inside is a smaller diameter, so that even when you stretch it tight, you don't press it against the outside and compress the insulation. The contour should be sewn in at the sides of the bag to prevent the bag from barreling and standing away from the body.

 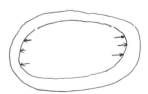

The advantages of a differential cut. At the left, the bag uses inside and outside shells of the same size, and when the body presses against the inner surfaces they are compressed against the outer ones, forming cold spots. At the right, the inner shell is cut to a smaller diameter, so that pressure cannot push it against the outer bag.

Generally, bags for the backpacker are constructed with down insulation throughout, even though the down which is compressed below serves no useful purpose. This practice is simpler to use than building ground insulation into the bag, and it prevents the bag from sustaining ground wear. Some manufacturers have started to build ground insulation directly into the bag, using a foam pad or shredded foam in the bottom part of the bag instead of down. This results in a more efficiently designed bag if it is done well. Make sure there are no cold seams at the juncture of the two forms of insulation. If a pad is included in the bag, the material surrounding the pad should be of waterproof-coated material. Material coated on one side only should be used on the inside, with the coating facing the pad (plastic coating is most unpleasant against the skin). A hole for the air to get out and into the pad area must also be included.

The standard practice in making down bags is to use permeable (uncoated) fabric both outside and inside the bag. The idea is that water vapor from the body passes out through the insulation to the outside air. The body is always evaporating some moisture even without the sweating that you feel. Sweating occurs when the body becomes too hot and perspires to cool itself by evaporation. Insensible perspiration, which you do not feel, occurs simply because your skin is more moist than the air around it.

The difficulty with permeable materials is that when moist air works out through the bag it reaches colder and colder regions, often condensing as dew before it gets out of the bag, causing the down to become damp. This particular problem is worst in extended periods of cold weather. One solution is used by Stephenson's. They make the inside of their bags from impermeable fabric so that moisture from the body cannot filter into the down. This keeps the down dry and also reduces evaporative heat loss. It is an interesting method, not yet used by anyone else. A great problem with the technique is that if heavy clothing is worn inside the bag in cold weather as supplementary insulation, moisture will condense in the clothing. For some purposes, however, this innovation offers much promise.

In any case, impermeable materials must *never* be used on the outside of a bag to make it shed water. Moisture moving through the bag from the inside will then condense on meeting the outer surface, soaking the insulation in short order.

Zippers or other closures are essential in any bag except an ultralight one designed for a very narrow temperature range. When the bag is too warm, the zipper can be opened for ventilation. For this reason, I have always preferred side zippers, which allow ventilation without causing the bag to fall off your chest. Top zippers allow less expensive construction, however, so you might prefer one. A full-length zipper makes the bag slightly heavier and less efficient, but it allows making zip-together bags, permits easier drying on sunny mornings, and allows the bag to be opened and used as a quilt.

Zip-together bags are pleasant for couples, although they are not as efficient as they seem. They require more material than one bag made for two people, and their gain in efficiency is nearly always lost by extra ventilation around the neck. Various methods have been tried to control this, but no one has come up with a good one yet. Double bags, made for two people, are more efficient, and the neck closures are usually a little better. They can be used only by couples who are truly inseparable, though.

COMPARING BAGS

In buying a sleeping bag, it is often difficult to compare the bags made by different manufacturers, since everyone uses different standards in describing comparable features. The first thing you might do is to send for catalogues from a number of mail-order houses. A few that don't make their own bags will have useful comparisons among bags made by different suppliers. Temperature ratings will give you a rough idea of the differences between the bags of a single manufacturer, but they don't help much in comparing one maker's with another's.

Look at the construction, baffling methods, size of down compartments, and amount of down. The amount of *loft* is useful. It represents the thickness to which the insulation expands, but some companies quote the thickness of the whole bag, top and bottom, while others refer to the top alone. Also, don't compare lofts too literally; there are different ways to measure it.

Since you can't look at the internal construction of down bags, you will have to judge it by externals. Be especially careful to examine workmanship. Bags with sloppy outside construction will be even sloppier inside. Beware of the new bargain bags appearing in stores that don't specialize in supplying backpackers or mountaineers. Many of them use inferior cloth (a lower thread count per inch which won't stand up to wear), and their materials and workmanship are often sloppy.

AIR MATTRESSES AND FOAM PADS

Unless you have a bag which includes a ground pad, you will have to get a separate one. They are more comfortable than sleeping on the hard ground, but this is not really the main point. If you sleep on the bare ground in a down bag, you have essentially no insulation on the bottom, so you have to have a lot more on the top, and that is a waste of money and weight. There are three commonly used types of ground beds: *air mattresses, open-cell foam pads,* and *closed-cell foam pads.*

Three types of ground beds: an air mattress, which folds to a very compact size; an open-cell foam pad with a coated fabric cover, a light and very comfortable bed; and a closed-cell foam pad, which provides maximum insulation for the least weight and expense.

Air mattresses are convenient some of the time, but they are used much less than they used to be. A few people find them more comfortable than foam pads, but most find them less pleasant to sleep on; it's mostly a matter of what you are used to. There is no question that they are colder than foam, because air currents carry heat rapidly through the mattress, and so they should not be used for snow-camping. The greatest advantage in an air mattress is that it deflates into a more compact package than a pad. Unfortunately, it may occasionally do this in the middle of the night.

If you get an air mattress, make sure that it is of good quality, made of coated nylon fabric. The plastic kind will not stand up to the rough use a backpacker gives an air mattress. The heavy rubberized fabric kind is strong enough, but is rather heavy. Be sure to carry a repair kit. An air mattress is most comfortable when inflated just enough so that no part of your body touches the ground. Overinflation makes the mattress uncomfortable and increases chances of puncture.

An open-cell foam pad is more comfortable to most people than an air mattress; it is lighter and warmer. The pad can be 1½ or 2 inches thick, depending on the amount of padding and warmth you want. It should be covered with fabric to protect the pad from dirt, abrasion, and moisture, and the covering should be waterproof on at least one side. A 2-inch foam pad is a real luxury bed.

Closed-cell foam, such as Ensolite, Thermobar, or Voltek, provides a slightly more Spartan bed than a regular foam pad. Closed-cell foam is blown so that each air pocket is closed from all the others. Thus there can be no air circulation through the foam, and a thinner bed will provide more warmth. A closed-cell foam pad is less bulky than an open-cell one that provides the same warmth. It weighs less and is cheaper because no cover is required (it can't soak up moisture). A thickness of ¼-inch will do, but ⅜-inch is warmer and gives more comfort.

Whether you use a pad or an air mattress, get a short one. There is no need for a full-length ground bed, even in the winter. Put some of your clothing in the sleeping bag stuff sack for a pillow, and use your parka, pack, or some combination for your feet. A bed around 20 inches wide and 40 inches long is adequate; get one a little larger if you like.

OTHER SLEEPING ACCESSORIES

Unless you are camping in a tent with a floor, a *ground sheet* is essential to protect your pad and sleeping bag from moisture and dirt. You can carry a sheet of coated nylon, but most people use a plastic sheet, which is discarded after it starts to wear out. Such sheets can often be gotten as scrap, eliminating cost and waste. It is not generally a good practice to use a poncho as a ground sheet, because small holes will soon develop.

A *sleeping-bag liner* is very worthwhile to help keep the bag clean. The less often you have to wash your bag, the longer it will last. Some manufacturers sell them to go with their bags, or you can make them yourself. A flannel liner will add warmth. I prefer a very light nylon ripstop: it weighs almost nothing, is slippery and doesn't bind, and it is so sheer it can be washed on the trail and dried very quickly. The cheapest liner is made from bedsheets that have worn out in some spot—usually enough material can be salvaged for a sleeping-bag liner. Sew ties into your bag and matching ones on the liner, and make sure that the head of the bag, which gets the most dirt, is well covered.

A *sleeping-bag cover* will substitute for a ground sheet, protect the bag from dirt, extend the temperature range about another 10° F., and will serve as an emergency shelter bag. Some sleeping-bag covers are fitted to the bag. I prefer a big, loose-fitting sack, which can be held up to give me some breathing space and which will accommodate my equipment as well. The ground side of the cover should be waterproof, and the top should breathe. (Unless you have a sleeping bag with the inside of impermeable fabric, in which case a completely coated cover could be used.) Plans for a cover are included in the patterns. In warm weather you can use the cover to sleep in, with or without the bag as a blanket.

MAKING SLEEPING BAGS

A down sleeping bag is probably the most difficult project you could choose to undertake, so unless you have already had some practice or are very confident, it is best to use a kit for this one. Excellent kits are available at a moderate price. A good foam-bag plan can be found in Cardwell, and Gerry's book gives an excellent general discussion and fine plans for Dacron bags and lightweight down ones. The plans presented for foam and down bags should be studied carefully before any cutting is done. Make a mock-up and check the size first, altering where necessary.

Miscellaneous Equipment   13

There are a host of small items which, if not essential to the backpacker's existence, at least help keep him comfortable and happy. Some of them are required for safety, some for bodily well being, and some to preserve the character of the wilderness. This chapter is a sort of buyers' and users' guide, designed to help you to get the things you really need into your pack without breaking your back or your wallet in the process. A number of improvisations are suggested for temporary or permanent use to keep initial expenses down.

Backpacking equipment should be light and easy to pack. This spin-fly rod has good action, but it weighs only ounces and breaks into a short package.

POTS, PANS, AND COOKSETS

This is a good place to make do when your budget is tight, but it is also an area to exercise care if and when you do get around to spending a few dollars on cooking equipment. Making do can be accomplished by a raid on the kitchen pantry or on your local Salvation Army store, where old pots can usually be got for a dime or so apiece. My personal preference for a cheap cooking set is the hobo's standby—a kit made of tin cans. This method has enough virtues so that I occasionally use it in preference to my regular pots. Tin cans don't last very long, but they are free, can be tossed away at the end of the trip, and they are quite light. They fit well into the pack, and the sizes and numbers of cans can be readily adjusted for the size

A salt and pepper shaker with sealing lids is handy.

of the group. For one person a two-pound coffee can, one smaller can (say a No. 2 or 2½), and a cup make a positively luxurious kit. You might have to pay for the cup, but the rest is free. Utensils consist of your pocketknife and a soup spoon—you certainly should be able to scavenge a soup spoon. Salt and pepper can be carried in plastic bags or in the little paper packets dispensed by hamburger stands, airlines, and other gourmet establishments. Tin-can pots should be equipped with wire bails after punching holes on either side of each pot. You make the wire bails out of wire, the kind without insulation. If you go out and buy a cookset, make sure to get one that will fit conveniently in your pack. Short, wide pots are more stable and heat more efficiently. They also slop water all over the place while you are carrying them up from the stream, and they don't always fit into the

The wide bail on this pot locks into position so that the
pot won't tip when it is hanging and pouring is easy.
The cover fits in either way and also serves as a dish.

pack compartments where you want them. Tall, narrow pots have the opposite set of vices and virtues. Two pots holding about 1½ or 2 quarts each
do nicely for parties up to about five. Covers which double as plates and
makeshift frying pans are a good idea, but if you plan to do much frying,
make sure you have a steel frying pan. Thin aluminum burns but does not
cook well. A Teflon lining is not a bad idea either.

There is a real virtue in pots with bail handles that lock in place. They
can be hung over the fire without the danger that they will suddenly decide to tip, and they are easy to handle without a special gripper. The one
shown is excellent—and expensive.

I always carry one or two of the aluminum pot grippers, and I maintain that they are a necessity of life, but some people manage very well
with a long shirtsleeve as hot-pan holder.

Pots that are used over fires are much more conveniently handled if
you have a little sack for each one. The soot doesn't get spread over the inside of the pack or smeared on the inside of the next pot, yet you don't
have to wash it off either. You don't need to buy the sacks; they can be easily made of scrap cloth. The kind of material is unimportant, since they are
only covers.

For cooking primarily with a stove, you may prefer a cookset designed
to stack in an efficient combination. The one shown in the illustration in-

Pot grippers like this clamp onto any pot or cover, greatly simplifying the handling of hot pans.

cludes a stand for the stove, a windscreen, two pots, and a cover. These work very nicely, and they are recommended for high altitude and for winter especially. If you buy one, check the joints between each of the sections, especially each of the pans and the stand. Don't buy a set that has any tightly fitting joints—as soon as wear dents them a bit you will find them stuck together while you are trying to get a hot pot of stew off the stove. You can buy these sets with the stove included, but I think it is better to buy them separately. Though you pay a little more, if you buy the stove by itself you get a cover and windscreen so that you can use it with other pans when you like.

This type of cooker fits together into a compact unit and makes cooking with a stove very efficient. The second pot can be stacked in also.

STOVES

Though many types of stove are available to the backpacker, the choice for most purposes can be narrowed to that between those burning unleaded gasoline and those using propane or butane cartridges. I suspect that most newcomers to backpacking will pick the propane or butane types, because of simplicity of operation. Gasoline stoves take some getting used to and have certain disadvantages, but they are also superior in some respects. Before discussing individual models, I'll summarize the pros and cons of each of the two types of stove.

Stoves using unleaded gasoline. Advantages: fuel is readily available—even in remote localities; the fuel is inexpensive; large containers of fuel can be carried on long trips, saving weight, and the exact amount of fuel needed for a trip can be measured into the can; the stove burns at full pressure and temperature until it is empty; it can be filled at the beginning of a meal, so that it doesn't go out in the middle of cooking.

A typical backpacking stove. This one is fueled with white gasoline and generates its own pressure once it is burning.

Disadvantages: gasoline stoves are tricky to light, especially if the wind blows the flame out; they are especially inconvenient if you should just want to light one for a few minutes to reheat food or fix a hot beverage beside the trail.

Stoves using propane or butane cartridges. Advantages: the stove lights easily and quickly—you just hold out a match and turn on the burner, and it can be turned off and relighted with no trouble; putting on a new cylinder is simple and requires no careful pouring of a flammable liquid.

Disadvantages: fuel may be impossible to obtain except at specialized stores, unless you get a stove using standard propane cylinders, and the stove is absolutely useless without the proper cartridges; the fuel is considerably more expensive than white gasoline; a cartridge that is half-empty cannot be filled at the beginning of a trip or a meal; the stove runs poorly during the last ten minutes or so of a cartridge; the empty cartridges have to be carried out—they have become a new source of joy for the litterbug.

Essentially, the cartridge stoves are clear winners for convenience, but gasoline stoves are cheaper to run, will usually result in a smaller load in your pack, and it will be a lot easier to get fuel for one in that small town near the trailhead in Wyoming.

Except for large groups, gasoline stoves for backpacking should be the kind that generate their own pressure instead of using pumps. The ones with pumps put out more heat, but they are much heavier. Some gasoline stoves are Primus (the old standard), Svea, and Optimus, all of which are very good. There are dozens of models. The champion for weight and output is the Svea 123, which packs stove, windscreen, stand for a pan, and even a tiny pot into 18 ounces. The Primus 71L and the Optimus 80 weigh a couple of ounces more and have a bit more fuel capacity, which can be an advantage in winter and with larger parties. I also like the Optimus 8R and Primus 8R, which sit flat and are more stable than any of the upright stoves just mentioned. They weigh about 8 ounces more than the Svea.

The cartridge stoves are latecomers, and there are new entries every year, all the more complicated because each one manages to bring its own type of cartridge with it. The first one to become popular in this country was the French-made Bleuet, which burns butane gas and uses its own special cartridges. It is rather tall, and hence somewhat top-heavy for cooking in tents. This would probably be the best choice for a butane stove, because cartridges are available at nearly all mountaineering and backpacking suppliers. Other entries that burn butane are likely to cause you trouble unless you carry a lot of cartridges on any trips away from the store where you bought it.

Primus makes stoves called "Grasshoppers" for both propane and butane. Propane has the advantage in cold weather, because it becomes liquid at a much lower temperature. In winter you may have to warm a butane stove before lighting it. The Primus Grasshopper that is made for use with propane also uses standard cylinders, which are generally available in hardware and department stores. It gives more burning time for the weight than the Bleuet, and the cylinder can be removed when half-full, so you can take a full cylinder on a week trip or a partly empty one for a weekend. The cylinder is heavier but the stove is lighter, so that on the return trip a Bleuet with an empty cartridge weighs about the same as a Primus with an empty cartridge. The Grasshopper is also more stable; it rests on the wide tripod formed by two folding legs and the cartridge. Of the two, the only real disadvantage of the Primus is that with a full cylinder it weighs more than a Bleuet with a full cylinder. However, the Primus cartridge lasts about a week to the Bleuet's three days. And the Primus cylinder can be removed.

Whatever kind of stove you get be sure to get a windscreen if it comes separately (as it does with the Bleuet, for example). Most of your heat will be blown away by a light breeze without one. Even with it, you must use any backpacking stove in a sheltered spot if you want to cook your food rather than simply heat the outdoors. You should also be sure to carry any prickers that might be necessary to clean the burner jet. Don't let prickers or valve stems get lost. If a funnel is needed for filling, pack that with the stove, too.

Keep any stove clean, so that it will work when you need it. Empty the fuel tank if you are storing the stove for the season; otherwise varnish tends to form inside. I don't know about the butane and propane stoves, but eventually, after long use, the gasoline stoves start to get cranky. When this happens, buy a new one. I know from personal experience that when they start to go you'll have nothing but trouble, and one of my friends had one blow up because he tried to nurse it too long. Luckily, he managed to throw the flaming mess out into the rain before it caused real trouble, but you might not be so lucky. These stoves last a long time. When yours decides to retire, give it a decent burial.

FLASHLIGHTS, CARBIDE LAMPS, AND CANDLE LANTERNS

A flashlight is one of the essential pieces of equipment, even if you become a devout early-to-bed-and-early-to-riser. There is always the possibility of

Various flashlights. A headlamp, which can be strapped on the head with the batteries kept in a pocket, freeing both hands; a penlight; and a small Mallory flashlight. Tape must be kept on the switch of the Mallory when it is not in use to prevent accidental discharge of the batteries.

an emergency or unforeseen contingency that will make it necessary for you to follow a trail in complete darkness. The size of flashlight you choose will depend on the length and circumstances of your trips.

The amount of light that a flashlight puts out is determined by the bulb and the voltage of the battery combination. Most flashlights use two 1½-volt cells in series, giving a total of 3 volts, whether the size is AA, C, or D batteries. The amount of light getting to the ground where you are looking for the dropped matches is determined also by the design of the reflector.

Of the normal flashlights the Mallory lights are currently the best around for putting the most usable light where you want it with the smallest amount of weight. The reflectors are efficient and the case and switching gimmickry is light in weight. Unfortunately, the switches get cranky after a while.

If you are using a flashlight much, getting into camp late every night so that you have to cook by artificial illumination, for example, a headlamp is a lot more convenient than a flashlight. Trying to serve the stew or tie a guy line with a flashlight clamped between your teeth is really annoying after a while. A headlamp has an elastic band that holds the light and reflector on your head, with a wire going to the battery pack in your pocket. Anything that requires using both hands is a lot easier to do with a headlamp. The main trouble with them is that most currently available ones are too heavy, because they use three or four D cells. The most commonly available one is also notorious for its sloppy construction, but for some reason the backpacking stores continue to carry it.

You can find a lightweight headlamp if you look for it. If you decide to buy a heavier one, get the kind with three D cells lined up side by side—there are a couple of good ones on the market which use this design. Do *not* get the kind that uses four cells in two stacks of two each. The springs in this model are too weak, and the light will go off and on in rhythm with your step—until it quits altogether.

The length of time your flashlight goes on shining depends on the kind of bulb and the size of batteries you use. It also depends on the kind of batteries and the temperature. The bulb part is simple: the brighter the light, the less time it will last. A PR-4 bulb requires about half the current of a PR-2, and it will last about twice as long; it will also give less light. The useful life of batteries increases with their size, unless you also increase the bulb size, and hence the drain on the batteries.

Alkaline batteries last many times longer than regular batteries, though exact figures mean little because of the many variables involved. The alkaline types cost more initially, but less over their total life. They also work better under heavy load (as when you are following a trail at night), have a longer shelf life, and are not as affected by the cold. They last somewhere between five and ten times as long as regular cells.

Always carry a spare set of batteries and a spare bulb for your flashlight. In situations where you have to use the batteries for long periods, they will last longer if you switch the two sets of batteries every hour or so, allowing one pair to rest. They will also last longer if you keep them warm. Really cold weather can make regular batteries stop working altogether, and it affects alkaline batteries as well. This is one advantage to a headlamp. The battery case can be kept in an inside pocket to keep the cells warm.

Always inactivate the flashlight before you put it in your pack or your pocket, unless you're going to use it again soon. A flashlight accidentally switched on in the pack will nearly always prove a source of considerable annoyance, and it may be a really serious mistake. With a standard type of light reverse half the cells; with the Mallory or other light, where taking the case apart is inconvenient, use a large piece of tape to immobilize the switch.

For summer trips when I don't plan to use a light very much, I now carry one of the small Mallory flashlights with one spare pair of AA cells, using a PR-4 bulb. When I tested this combination, two fresh pairs of alkaline batteries switched every hour lasted ten hours in reasonably warm weather. That would enable me to walk all night even after some previous use of the light in camp. On trips when I expect to be on the trail in the dark, and on winter trips, I generally carry a headlamp using larger cells.

Some people like candle lanterns, and they are pleasant to light a tent with on a long winter night. They are nice for romantic suppers or to light your way out of camp on short journeys in the night. They won't substitute for a flashlight, though, and I find that I rarely carry one.

A carbide lamp is a much more practical alternative to a flashlight, although most people aren't familiar with them. It is the lamp often used in caves and mines, where an electric light might cause a dangerous spark. A carbide lamp has a small pressure chamber which is filled with dry fuel, calcium carbide. When water drips on this fuel, acetylene gas is released, and this escapes through a jet in the center of the lamp reflector. A small sparking device like the one on a cigarette lighter is attached to the reflector. You simply rotate the wheel, the jet lights, and you have a very brilliant light. The flame is not very hot, so it doesn't pose a fire hazard.

A carbide lamp produces lots of light, and the fuel is much lighter than batteries, so for some kinds of trips it might be a very useful substitute for a large flashlight. It can be hung in the tent and will produce enough light for reading. There are some serious problems, however, which make it quite impractical in winter and in the mountains. The lamp requires water and is made of metal, and in cold weather the water freezes and the lamp stops working. Strong wind also makes trouble, because it affects the gas jet. If you're making long trips in forested areas, though, and you would like to have a good source of light in the evenings, a carbide lamp is ideal. A standard one weighs about 7 or 8 ounces. If you use a carbide lamp, the fuel must be kept absolutely dry. Pill cases make good waterproof containers, and some sizes are just right to carry a filling for the lamp. Keep the parts properly cleaned, replace the felts when necessary, and carry a cleaning brush for the jet.

MATCHES AND FIRE STARTERS

Get wooden kitchen matches—the big, nonsafety kind. If you find matchbooks convenient to carry, they're all right, but when the weather turns damp and the wind starts blowing, they get wet and worn, and the flame won't hold long enough, so have some kitchen matches, too. Carry plenty of matches in several waterproof containers distributed in different places. You can use plastic pill bottles, double plastic bags sealed with rubber bands, or a host of other containers. Unless you have something on your person that makes a good striking surface, pack a little piece of fine sandpaper in each container (everything around always happens to be wet when you need to light a fire). Matches can be waterproofed by dipping them in melted paraffin. A few of the windproof kind with long-burning heads may be helpful in some circumstances. They can be purchased in backpacking stores.

Many commercial fire-starters are available. Carry a few in your emergency kit, if you like. I have a candle stub which will serve as a light or get a fire going easily. Some people carry hexamine tablets or rolled-up newspaper soaked in paraffin to get the fire going in wet weather. The hexamine is available in surplus stores at a dime for a tube of five or six.

For lighting fires, a cigarette lighter can be very handy. It's easy to light and keeps burning like a candle rather than a match. Carry a few matches, too, just in case. A lighter is also good for getting a gasoline stove going. You just hold the lighter under the stove for a minute, and you have your needed pressure.

Flint and steel kits are now available in a variety of very good small designs that throw a fine, hot spark. If you want to carry one for emergency fire making, by all means do so, but don't bother unless you are going to take the time to learn to use it. There is a knack.

A piece of steel wool makes excellent tinder for emergencies, as well as being useful as an abrasive. It burns only once, so make sure everything else is ready before you use your only piece.

CONTAINERS

At least one water bottle is usually necessary, depending on the availability of water. It is convenient to have a fairly wide mouth on the bottle so that you can get it full in shallow streams and trickles and so that you can pour things like dry milk or instant breakfast in if you want to. A quart- or liter-size polyethylene bottle is tough and convenient. You can mark measurements on the side with a hot knife (not too deep!). You can save money by salvaging a bottle that contained dishwashing detergent or some similar stuff. In the desert, make sure any bottle you are going to stuff in the pack is tough.

For large containers for water, half-gallon and gallon plastic bleach bottles work fairly well, or you can buy tougher polyethylene jugs. Make sure they include some way to attach them to your pack. Treat bleach bottles with reasonable care when they are full—they aren't thick enough to stand a lot of beating.

A wineskin (bota) is a good substitute for a bottle. Wineskins are available in one- and two-quart sizes. They are flexible and pack easily, and in

A wineskin is a handy container for water. It is especially good in cold weather, when the water bottle has to be taken to bed to prevent freezing, being a more comfortable sleeping companion than a canteen.

cold weather they are lots more pleasant to sleep with than a bottle. I wouldn't trust one in the desert, though. Modern ones are manufactured using cheap split leather on the outside and a thin plastic liner inside. When the plastic liner finally goes, there is no warning—and no water.

For gasoline, a metal container is advisable. Two types are generally used: a round anodized aluminum bottle or a rectangular tin-alloy fuel can with two spouts. Get the rectangular kind. It is impossible to pour from the round ones without spilling until they're partly empty. (A new pouring

One type of fuel can.

spout has just been put on the market to correct the trouble, but you might as well get the rectangular kind with spout attached). The rectangular ones also fit into pack pockets more easily. They are available in 1-, 1½- and 2-pint sizes. The 1½-pint can plus what is in your stove should get you through a full week easily, unless you are melting snow.

KNIVES

The backpacker can get along very nicely with a small pocketknife. Get a good one; that is not the same as an expensive one. All that is needed is a pair of decent carbon steel blades that will hold an edge. If yours has a can opener, that's fine, but you can get a teeny, super-efficient GI can opener for fifteen cents and use it for a zipper pull. There are good three-dollar

A good pocket knife like this can be quite inexpensive.

pocketknives that will hold a fine edge and twenty-dollar pocketknives that won't. Try yours out in the store.

The backpacker doesn't really have much need for a sheath knife, but some people do prefer to carry them for help with kindling. There is absolutely no point in having one with a blade longer than four or five inches. You can do anything for which a camp knife is needed with that length, in-

An excellent design for a sheath knife.

cluding skinning out a grizzly bear. The swords that some people carry on their hips might be good in hand-to-hand combat, but they are certainly useless in camp. If you want a sheath knife, the rules about prices and knives apply here, too. The knife shown in the illustration is an excellent design for a sheath knife, and I have seen knives on this pattern selling for eighteen dollars. Mine cost two bucks, plus a dollar for the sheath.

Outdoor knives are best made from carbon steel rather than stainless. Stainless is hard to sharpen, and usually doesn't hold an edge particularly well.

SHARPENING A KNIFE

Dull knives aren't much help in building a fire or repairing a ski, but they are very dangerous. A dull knife requires too much force to cut, so that you

Sharpening a knife. The blade is drawn in the direction shown by the pointing finger. A much smaller stone can be used.

tend to lose control. It also tends to glance off tough spots in wood, and with all your extra pushing behind it, it is likely to end up in your leg. Keep your knife sharp.

Sharpening a knife is simple enough. You need a sharpening stone. The best ones are made of a fine artificial stone on one side and "soft Arkansas" on the other, but these are getting expensive and hard to find. Don't get just a "hard Arkansas" in any case; it is a finishing stone designed to put a razor edge on an already sharp knife. A pocket double stone of medium and fine Crystolon is good. Most people will probably be satisfied with a little pocket carborundum stone for a pocket or sheath knife. You can use a fine cutting oil or just water on it. Lay your knife diagonally across on the coarse side. Lift the back of the blade about a quarter-inch for a sheath knife or an eighth-inch for a pocket knife. Grind the edge with a pulling stroke for about twenty seconds or so on each side, depending on how dull the blade is. The cutting action is diagonal. Then turn the stone over and repeat the process on the fine grit side of the stone. Now pull the knife straight along the stone, as if cutting, with the blade at the same angle, two or three times on each side to remove the wire edge. The knife

217

should now be fairly sharp; you can test it lightly against a fingernail. If you want it really sharp, strop it on a belt or a leather pack strap. Strop in the opposite direction from cutting. This will remove the last traces of a feather edge.

AXES

The ax is the traditional woodsman's tool, which is one reason there aren't as many woods as there used to be. For most backpackers today, there really isn't much need for the ax, but if you go off on a trip into seldom traveled woods and you want to split logs for all-night fires, you might want one. Similarly, if you do a lot of camping in a very wet, wooded region, you might only be able to get dry wood out of the deadfall by splitting open good-sized logs. The ax is the tool for this kind of job, but it is heavy enough so that it isn't worth carrying unless you really need it.

Many disagree, but I haven't any use for hatchets. (An exception is for clearing trails, but that isn't our subject here.) The heavy part of an ax is not the handle, it's the head. If you are going to carry all that weight

An ax and a folding saw. A saw like this, a pruning saw, and a saw with a rectangular frame can be used for any wood-gathering chores except splitting, but they are much lighter than the ax.

around in the head, it's ridiculous not to have a handle long enough to use the weight effectively. A 28-inch handle is long enough to enable you to get a full swing. With a 2-pound Hudson's Bay head the ax will weigh about 2¾ pounds, but it will be a really effective ax. A 1¾-pound head will bring the weight down even further.

An ax is dangerous. It requires practice to learn to use one well, and only one mistake can bring an accident that is really serious in the wilderness. A 28-inch handle is short enough to cause the head to bounce into your leg unless you position yourself carefully. Learn to swing the ax in a relaxed way, and let the head do the work. Clear away anything that might catch the ax before you start swinging; many accidents are caused by the ax deflecting on a branch that the chopper didn't notice. Don't hold the piece of wood you are splitting in your hand or try to hurry your swing because it is falling. Practice with the length handle you will use. Suddenly switching to a shorter handle can be dangerous unless you are careful. Finally, keep the ax sharp. Using a dull ax in the wilderness is an excellent way to commit suicide; it's dull enough to glance off a knot, but plenty sharp enough to go halfway through your leg.

SAWS

A saw is generally a far better choice for the woodland backpacker than an ax or hatchet. It is lighter and more effective for getting firewood from deadfall, except in very wet places where dry wood has to be split out of logs.

Hacksaw blades and wire saws can be carried conveniently and are very light, and they are good emergency tools. If you really plan to use the saw to get wood, though, you should get a pruning saw or a frame saw. The pruning saw is cheap and light. You can get one with a folding handle that will cut wood up to 4 inches in diameter easily, weighing about 7 ounces with a 10-inch blade.

For larger wood, you can carry a folding saw that uses a flexible bow saw blade. Frames can be triangular or rectangular. The rectangular type may not be as strong, but it will cut a larger log. You can pay six or seven dollars for this type of saw, weighing from 12–18 ounces, or you can make one of about the same weight for two or three dollars.

MISCELLANEOUS MISCELLANY

You should carry sunglasses or goggles unless you know from experience that you won't need them. Snow, sand, and high altitude are especially hard on the eyes. Prescription sunglasses are a lot more pleasant for those who need glasses. On snow, side visors are desirable.

I wear glasses, and they do create some special problems. If you can get used to the kind with wire loops behind your ears rather than the regular plastic kind, you'll find that they do better at keeping the glasses from sliding down your sweaty nose. In some situations you'll probably want a safety band. You can buy them in sports stores or make your own. Safety glasses are a wise precaution.

Fogging is always a problem, especially when you're pushing up a long trail in cold weather. There are several antifogging compounds available that help a little. Finally, depending on how bad your eyesight is and the nature of the trip, you should consider carrying a spare pair of glasses.

Part 3

Special Skills

Finding Your Way   14

Finding one's way in the wilderness has a traditional and almost mystical significance attached to it. According to the romantic notion, if you can find your way through the great north woods and build a fire in any weather you are a woodsman. If not you are a tenderfoot. Despite this, backpackers often have only rudimentary skill at route finding. For many people, even experienced campers, getting lost in the woods is a rather terrifying possibility, the more so because route-finding techniques tend to be neglected. The modern backpacker generally follows trails which are fairly well marked, and he may have only the foggiest idea of how to use a compass. His map reading is likely to be a transposition of methods from road maps to trail maps: "Turn left at the next fork, Mabel."

Actually, backpackers in many areas have little need for general path-finding techniques, so the neglect of these skills is understandable. Still, your freedom of travel will always be limited if you stick to trails cut and marked by others. So will your confidence in your own ability to cope with some emergencies and your performance if you are actually confronted with them. You can get along as a beginner with simple route-finding skills, but you won't really achieve the freedom of the wild places until you learn to find your way around them.

The basics of making your way around the woods or the mountains are the same as those used in steering a path through the streets of New York City. They consist of ways of relating your own position to various features of your surroundings. If you want to go somewhere, you must know the relative location of that spot, a feasible path around intervening obstacles, and some way of guiding yourself along the route.

People who are very much at home in a particular environment often find their way without paying any conscious attention to their methods. It is important to note that this is an acquired skill. No one has any "natural sense of direction," or any other kind either, except for a false sense of confidence. It has been proven on numerous occasions that without some reference to the outside world, people circle aimlessly while convinced they are walking a straight line. Many "old woodsmen," dumped in an unfamiliar environment, would have just as much trouble finding their way as a city slicker. An old-timer may have literally hundreds of tricks for getting around, but they are all based on reference points in his surroundings. It is these reference points that you learn to use in finding your way, together with the description of them we call a map and the direction-finding tools you may carry, especially the pocket compass.

MAPS

Maps are *the* basic route-finding tools in wilderness travel, and learning to use them skillfully will contribute greatly to your freedom to move about easily in wild areas. You will probably rely heavily on them, from the rudimentary inspection of a road map that will place you at the trailhead to the planning of trips over trackless regions. The amount of detail you inspect will vary with the kind of trip, but journeys that don't depend on some map use are rare indeed.

All maps are designed to represent the features of the earth's surface graphically, but there are as many kinds of maps as there are purposes for using them. The first consideration in map making is *scale*. A small-scale map covers a lot of country on a small amount of paper, and so it is obviously the most convenient and inexpensive to use, providing it conveys all the necessary information. Larger-scale maps include more detail, but are more cumbersome. If you want to find out where Chicago is located in the United States, you would look on a map of the country, but if you wanted to find your way to the Field Museum, you would want a street map of the city. Neither map would be of much use for the other purpose.

Fairly large-scale maps are generally most suitable for wilderness use, since the backpacker covers ground rather slowly and needs to know about detailed landforms in planning and executing trips.

Aside from scale, different maps also vary widely in the information they try to convey and the methods used. Road maps show roads, but they generally include very little information on the land surrounding automobile corridors. Maps intended for canoeists give great detail on rapids, portages, dams, and so forth, but they too are apt to be scanty on landforms. Very good maps exist for dozens of other purposes, showing the geology of an area, the legal ownership, or the tribes of Indians that once inhabited it, but none of these is of much use in planning a backpacking trip.

The most suitable maps for the backpacker are the topographic ("topo") maps published by the U. S. Geological Survey. They show the outline of terrain by means of contour lines, are drawn on a scale appropriate for the wilderness traveler, and can often be obtained in editions showing vegetation patterns as well.

READING A TOPOGRAPHIC MAP

There are a number of ways to show the general relief of the land on a map, all designed to give a three-dimensional view on a two-dimensional surface. Various relief shadings are easy to visualize, but the most accurate way is to use contour lines. Once you have learned to read contour maps, you can visualize terrain you have never seen with relative ease, and you can get precise information on grades, watersheds, whether one point can be seen from another, and a host of other questions, the answers to which can greatly simplify route finding.

The map in the illustration is part of a U.S.G.S. topo map. Designation of lakes, trails, snowfields, administrative boundaries, and so on is fairly standard and obvious. The lines are contour lines. They are lines of constant elevation—that is, if you were to follow one of these lines as though it were a trail, you would never go up or down. On a hill, you would stay at the same height and eventually walk all the way around the hill to arrive at your starting point.

The edge of the ocean forms a boundary at zero altitude above sea level, ignoring the variation of the tides and waves. Looking at a map of

A section of a topographic map published by the U.S. Geological Survey. This one is in the fifteen-minute series, and the scale is approximately one inch to the mile. The area shown is rugged and mountainous, but gradients are not nearly as steep as some others near the area shown. The contour interval is fifty feet. There are numerous lakes and a flat, marshy meadow in the upper center at Washakie Park.

the shoreline, the water's edge would form a contour line. Now, if you imagine the ocean rising, say fifty feet, a new contour would be formed representing an altitude fifty feet above sea level. In some places with long sloping beaches and marshes, the water would come miles inland, and the contours would be quite far apart. At cliffs or bluffs they would be packed close together. High points in the land would form islands, and these would appear as closed curves describing the new shorelines. If we kept raising the ocean fifty feet at a time until all the land was covered, we would have a contour map of the area. Of course, there might be depressions protected by hills which would have to be filled to the proper levels at the same time the ocean was raised, with a siphon if you like.

This analogy may help you to visualize the terrain represented by a contour map, since any contour line can be thought of as an imaginary shoreline. Naturally, if we are standing on a hill, and there is another one across the valley, it will have a shoreline corresponding to ours, a contour at the same level.

The illustration shows a few common contour patterns and the features they represent. Note that the contours don't just tell you that there is a slope or a hill; within the limits of scale, they show you the shape and gradient of the slope or hill. The closer the lines are together, the steeper the slope, and the farther apart, the more gentle the slope. If the lines get closer together toward the top of the slope, it is concave; if they get farther apart, it is convex.

A few facts about contour lines follow from the description of them. Followed out, a contour line always meets itself eventually, forming a closed curve. Thus each line will either disappear off the edge of the map or will double-back on itself.

Contour lines cannot normally cross one another. If they do, they show an overhanging cliff. When the lines get so close together that they cannot be distinguished they represent a near-vertical cliff, and some U.S.G.S. maps leave such a space blank instead of dark. The meaning is always clear with a little study. This is only a printing problem; the actual contour extends across the cliff.

SCALES, INTERVALS, AND SUCH

As mentioned previously, the scale of a map must be appropriate to your purpose, and for the backpacker the usual rule is that the larger the scale, 227

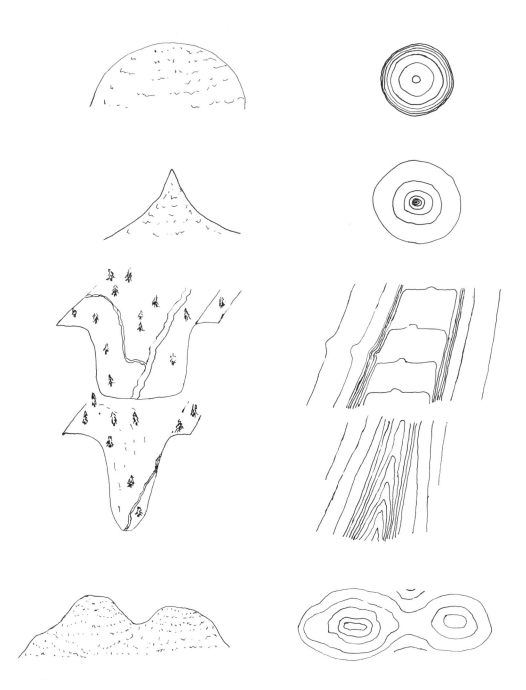

228

the better. Most of the United States is now covered by the new 15-minute quadrangle maps series, the 7½-minute series, or both. These cover areas of 15 minutes of longitude by 15 minutes of latitude (or 7½′ by 7½′), and they both show admirable detail with the tremendous accuracy allowed in trackless regions by the wonders of stereoscopic aerial photography. The 15-minute series is drawn on a scale of 1:62,500, that is, one finger width on the map equals 62,500 finger widths on the ground, not counting ups and downs. The scale works out to be very close to 1 inch: 1 mile (1:62,360 for the precision minded), close enough for the difference to be ignored by backpacking types. This series is quite adequate for most wilderness travel, showing considerable detail, but covering enough country so that the maps don't become unmanageable.

The 7½-minute series is on a 1:24,000 scale (1 inch: 2,000 feet) and it sometimes seems so detailed one could find an anthill. These maps are excellent, but for longer trips they can become both cumbersome and expensive. Even here, though, the expense is only comparative, since all the U.S.G.S. maps are bargains. Maps from either of these series are all the wilderness traveler could ask.

For those areas where the 7½- or 15-minute quads are available, they serve the purposes of the backpacker so well that there is rarely much point in considering other maps, except supplemental trail guides. There are, however, some parts of the country which are not yet mapped in these series, and many of them have great interest for the wilderness traveler. This is not coincidental, because wilderness regions tend to rank low on the list of bureaucratic priorities (mercifully), so they have been left until last for mapping. In such places wilderness travelers have to depend on various other series. In Wyoming, for example, the new series are far from complete, but the whole state is mapped on a scale of 1:250,000 (1 inch: 4 miles). These small-scale maps are very well done, but they necessarily give considerably less information than one might wish. The old 30-minute quads, which are somewhat more detailed at a scale of 1:125,000, are being allowed to go out of print by the Survey, though some are still available.

Some simplified contour patterns. The top two contrast the appearances of convex and concave slopes, and the next two show the different representations of U- and V-shaped valleys. At the bottom is a typical rounded hill or mountain with two summits separated by a saddle.

These were made around 1900, and they must be treated much more circumspectly than the modern maps made with aerial photographs, since the guesswork which often went into them did not always correspond to the realities of the landforms.

Various special prints are available from the U.S.G.S. on some regions of particular interest to backpackers, especially of the national parks and of various river systems. The scales vary considerably.

Contour intervals—the changes in elevation represented by successive contour lines—vary just as scales do, and the interval used depends on the map scale, the surveying method, and the terrain. A smaller-scale map necessarily has larger contour intervals, because it becomes difficult and pointless to fit many lines into a small space. Surveying methods influence the contour interval and have differing allowances for error, although on older maps the contours are frequently interpolated by informed guesswork. Finally, terrain affects the choice of interval. Precipitous terrain would make 2-foot contour lines run together into a continuous blur, while some parts of the country are so flat that a 200-foot interval would never show from one end of a map to another.

Most of the new 7½-minute series use 40-foot intervals for mountainous terrain, and they may use 2-foot intervals for gently rolling country. Thus one of the first things to look for in reading a map is the contour interval. Do those closely packed lines represent a 50° face or a gentle slope? The answer is a function of the scale and the contour interval.

Usually, contours are arranged in groups of five for convenience in reading the map. Every fifth contour is heavier and is marked somewhere with its altitude. With 40-foot contours each heavy line represents a 200-foot change in elevation.

In regions with extreme variations in terrain, say a quadrangle where mountains meet plains, supplemental contours may be used to show detail. These are usually shown by dotted contour lines between the solid ones, and they simply represent intermediate elevations. In the example mentioned, the steep mountain slope might make contours closer together than 40 feet impractical to use, while 20-foot levels are required to show some hills on the level land below.

Another important type of information on the U.S.G.S. maps is shown in the cultural features. These include buildings, roads, trails, and other man-made additions to and subtractions from the terrain. Clearly, the cultural features are those most likely to be out of date on an old map, so the survey date is important in evaluating the accuracy of such a map. A separate date may be shown for an updating of cultural features. Buildings may have been built or demolished. Trails and roads may have been cut or grown over since the survey was done. One other change which is less obvious is the addition of lakes to some regions. As you puzzle from a mountaintop over the identity of a large lake in the distance, don't forget that it may have been created by a dam since the mapping was done.

Unfortunately, one special problem for the backpacker concerned with trails is that the Survey is rather inconsistent about the ones it shows. Mappers are faced with the problem outlined above—namely that the maps, once made, are likely to remain unrevised for some time. Obviously, the surveyor does not want to include a path that will be obliterated within a couple of years. The judgments made vary a good deal from map to map, and as a result the hiker will find that on two maps of recent vintage, one will show every trail while the other shows nothing less substantial than a well-established, graded road. The only safe rule is that in a recently surveyed area all the trails shown on the map will exist.

U.S.G.S. EDITIONS

Various editions with different overlays are available for the standard U.S.G.S. maps. The most common are the contour and the shaded relief editions. The contour edition is far more useful, once you have taken the time to learn to read it. For beginners it may be helpful to pick up both editions for some area and compare them. The shaded relief is a bit easier to read at first and may help you to learn to interpret the contours.

Different overlays may also be available, but the only important one is the green woodland overprint. If the map you want is available with this overprint, it is to be preferred, since it shows which portions of the area covered by the map are forested.

OTHER MAPS

There are many other kinds and sources of maps, and only a few will be mentioned here. Since the U.S.G.S. maps are so well suited to the purposes of the wilderness traveler, they are usually preferred. Even in areas where the final editions have not yet become available, preliminary working editions can often be purchased from the Survey. If the region you are interested in is not covered by current large-scale maps, you can find out the status of the mapping by requesting status maps (free) from the U.S. Geological Survey, Washington, D.C. 20242. Ask for "Topographic Mapping—Status and Progress of Operations," which is updated every six months.

Aside from Survey maps, there are many other government agencies which publish maps of the areas they administer. The ones of most interest to backpackers are the Forest Service maps, but these vary tremendously in quality. There are rumors that high-quality maps made from aerial surveys and with a large scale are going to become available for sale, but so far only those for a few forests in the Northwest have appeared. Most of the current maps are rather small in scale. Some are useful supplements to the U.S.G.S. maps, showing trails more accurately. Since these maps are less expensive to make than detailed topo maps, they could be updated regularly to provide current trail and road information, and that would be really useful. The real situation, however, is that the trails shown are less reliable than those on the Survey maps. In some forests, they are generally accurate. In others you may find the trail shown has been overgrown for a couple of decades, while in still others the carefully drawn trails are proposed routes to be built and maintained if money and manpower ever become available. In defense of the Forest Service, it should be noted that most of these problems stem from lack or misallocation of money and manpower, problems which will be resolved only as a result of your pressure.

The situations in different wilderness and recreation areas are so variable, that it is impossible to generalize. Good trail maps are available from park departments, state conservation agencies, and so on, but you may have to write some letters to find them. Frequently, "sportsman's maps" are available in stores. These vary in quality, since they are usually copies of the maps of some state agency, which you can get free elsewhere.

Generally the best source of trail information for the backpacker is the trail guide or trail map published either commercially or by some local club. These are available for many popular hiking and climbing areas. In some cases these maps and guides are so good that no supplementary information is needed. Those published by the Appalachian Mountain Club are a good example. More commonly, the guides are designed to be used in conjunction with topo maps. The guide or trail map tells you where the trails are cut, but gives only enough detail to enable you to locate it on a U.S.G.S. map.

Finally, there are still areas in this country for which no good guides or U.S.G.S. maps are available. If you want prior information for a trip in one of these, you'll have to work just a little, getting a sampling of the uncertainties, joys, and frustrations of having to dig what information you can out of old accounts and inadequate maps. The U.S.G.S. may still be able to help, however. You may be able to get advance proof maps. These have unlabeled contours and elevations and the outlines of lakes and snowfields, but that's all. You have to fill in names and other information yourself. They are also subject to correction. Failing even advance maps, you can purchase aerial photos. Information on available aerial photographs and photomaps can be had free by writing the U.S. Geological Survey, Washington, D.C. 20242, and requesting "Status of Aerial Photography" and "Status of Aerial Mosaics" maps.

LEARNING TO USE MAPS

If you're one of those rare souls who was taught to use terrain maps as a child, you won't need any practice, but otherwise it's a good idea to spend some time learning the skills before you really need them. This can be done on a Sunday walk in some local hills or on a leisurely weekend backpack along well-marked trails. Get topo maps of the area beforehand, and then keep them handy while you're walking. Look at the features around you, and match them up with their representations on the map. Try to visualize some of the landmarks ahead from the map, and then see how far off you were when you reach them. Keep up your map practice on subsequent trips, and you will be able to use the map effectively when you need it.

KNOWING WHERE YOU ARE

Having obtained a decent map of the region in which you're traveling, you're ready to start the business of skillfully piloting yourself across vast and trackless regions without getting lost. Only start with small trackless regions. Oddly enough, it's sometimes easier to get lost when you're following a trail than when you really are in a pathless area. The reason is simple —when you're following those trail markers you don't really pay any attention to where you're going, and if you lose them you don't know where you are or which way is up. The obvious conclusion, for all types of hiking and backpacking, in true wilderness or on the trail, is to know where you are.

There are a lot of ways to keep track of your position, using a trail or topo map, drawing your own map as you go along, or simply keeping a mental map. In all three cases, you have to relate your own route and position to the terrain through which you're traveling. If you do this well enough, along your entire route, you can retrace it whenever you choose to do so. Being able to do it well is a matter of training, though, and training yourself requires some self-discipline. This can be as true for the experienced walker as the beginner, since when he steps into a new sort of country he may get lost by not going back to basic rules. The mountain man may get so used to working by well-defined watersheds that he gets lost after walking a mile in level forest.

With a topo map in fairly well-defined terrain, you can use the easiest and best way of knowing where you are just by occasionally glancing at the map and keeping track of your position. If you're traveling up a long valley, you simply note the landmarks as you pass by them. Having a topo map, knowing that you're traveling northwest in Big Water Valley and that you passed Bareface Bluff forty-five minutes back is as good a location as you could ask. If a blinding snow or fog suddenly appears, you can pull out your trusty compass (about which more later) and steer from where you are to where you want to be.

In the absence of such strongly delineated landforms, or a good map, or both, things get a little more complicated. If, for example, Big Water Valley is just a wide trough filled by a meandering stream and Bareface Bluff is ten miles off to one side, your casual attitude of thinking you know where you are may turn out to be quite unjustified when the fog rolls in. Even if you find the stream you won't know which direction it is traveling at that point, since it curls back and forth.

There are a host of position-finding methods, and in any particular situation only some of them will be applicable or necessary. It is important to learn to apply them and to always be aware of what you would have to know to get out of any difficulties that might occur.

The first and most satisfactory position-finding method has already been mentioned, that of keeping track of your location on a good map of the region. It is easy to do in many sorts of country, requires little or no written record-keeping, and except in difficult terrain it will enable you to steer your way out with a compass in case of need.

Lacking an accurate, detailed map or the sort of landforms that can be constantly matched with it, one method of keeping track of your position is simply watching your own trail. You may draw a crude map, keep track of walking times between landmarks or locations on the topo map, and write or mentally record various identifiable features along the way, especially at junctions.

Several rules are frequently missed by beginners in watching their own trail. The first is to *look back over your shoulder*. Any route looks very different when approached from the opposite direction. A second is to *write things down*. Memory may be relied on in many cases, especially when it is well trained, but we all tend to place far too much faith in a recollection which is likely to be under considerable strain when it is actually needed. The next day or week, with a storm raging and the fear of being lost added to natural forgetfulness, you may find your critical gully to be much less distinctive than you thought. Writing down your trail signs is also salutary in forcing you to *pick really distinctive features*. A tree that seems unmistakable when you first see it may well merge its image with hundreds of others by the next day or week. By trying to put its unique qualities on paper, you may find out just how easy it will really be to recognize them.

There are a number of special techniques for finding your way, and most of them rely on one additional piece of information to those we have already mentioned—direction. For the backpacker the normal direction finding device is a pocket compass.

DIRECTION FINDERS

The basic element of a pocket compass is a magnetized needle or a magnet attached to a face, either of which is free to rotate on a pivot. The magnet aligns itself with the earth's magnetic field, and thus tells us the direction of the field at the point where the magnet is situated.

There are a few standard fallacies about the earth's field and about compasses which we have to get out of the way, since they are rather widespread. The earth's magnetic field is not perfectly regular. Though it has a north and south pole, these do not happen to coincide with the geographic poles, and they are large shifting areas rather than well-defined points. Even if you consider the needle of the compass as pointing to the magnetic pole rather than the geographic one, you will be ignoring the irregularities in the earth's field owing to mineral deposits and other influences. Remember that the field is somewhat distorted and that it changes slowly. Remember also that the field is greatly distorted in the vicinity of iron or steel. Almost everyone knows that a compass will not point accurately if it is laid on a car fender, held next to a steel belt buckle, or rested on the pack just over the steel frypan, but people keep making these same errors anyway.

The normal way to find out the direction of the earth's magnetic field in the area where you are is by looking at your topo map, which should have a declination diagram along the margin somewhere.

DECLINATION

By declination we mean the amount that a compass needle declines from pointing true north in a particular place. It is not negligible and should not be ignored. Within the contiguous United States it varies from over 20° west, to over 20° east, and in Canada and Alaska it may be even greater. For example, in the Indian Peaks in Colorado the declination is 14½° east, which is not especially large. Even so, steering a compass course for only five miles and ignoring the declination would have you 1¼ miles off your intended route, quite enough to get you thoroughly lost. The error might be even greater, because in this kind of country one usually steers by watersheds, and the common use for a compass would be to get you down into the right one from a peak or a ridge, after which you would follow the slopes. Coming down in the wrong drainage system can head you off in the opposite direction from the one you want to go, and it may lead you to impassable cliffs.

Proper use of a compass is really an important skill for a backpacker to master. In some kinds of country the compass will be in daily use. In many other regions you may go for years without taking it out of your pack, but when you do take it out your life may depend on it. Backpacking in the Sierra Nevada range in California, I can remember few occasions when I used my compass. At least one time, however, as I was coming out of a large round valley in blizzard conditions, the difference between magnetic and true directions was also the difference between hitting the route out on the other side of the ridge or climbing a local peak. The storm was severe and the wrong route would have been extremely dangerous. The difficulty in judging distance in such conditions makes it doubly important that directions be correct and that you have the confidence to know they are correct.

Back to declination then, a confusing correction until you are used to it, but one that is important to understand. You can think of your compass needle as aligning itself with a magnetic line which itself is wandering, with an occasional drunken stagger, toward the north magnetic pole. The

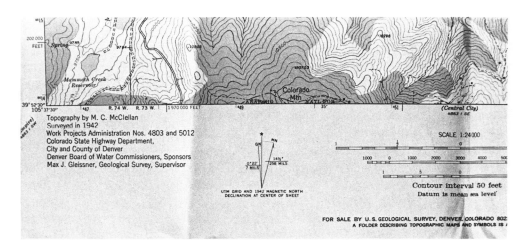

Various information is given in the margins of the U.S.G.S. maps. In the center here is the declination diagram. The star indicates true north. "MN" means magnetic north, and this angle is the declination. The arrow to MN shows the direction your compass will point. "GN" refers to the direction of a grid system which is of no particular use for backpacking. To the right are graphic and ratio scales and the information on the contour interval used.

difference between the direction of this line and the direction of true north is the declination. If the declination is 17° west, then the compass needle will point 17° to the west of true north.

In the eastern parts of the United States and Canada declination will always be west, but in the western parts of those two countries it will be east. For the inexact purposes of the backpacker, the declination can be considered constant within the limits of a 15-minute quadrangle map, and the declination at the center of the map will be shown in the diagram at the border. On some larger-scale maps or on maps of areas with wide variations in declination, a diagram showing declination at various points on the map may be substituted for the single value of center or average declination.

Though declination varies with both time and distance, the changes are generally of little consequence for the foot traveler except on very long trips or in unusual regions. You can check your maps beforehand to see what the total change in declination will be over your route, and then if it seems necessary make daily or weekly adjustments. It will rarely be necessary. Variation with time is a problem only with out-of-print maps, since on current maps declination is generally brought up to date periodically even on an old survey. Thus, on a U.S.G.S. map you will often find a more recent date under the declination diagram than under the map name. Declination changes slowly enough so that the variation is unlikely to be a problem for the backpacker.

All the foot traveler generally needs to do about declination is to make sure he knows the proper figure at the beginning of a trip. If his compass allows mechanical correction, the adjustment is made at the trailhead and can then be ignored. With less elaborate compasses the adjustment must be made in readings each time the compass is used. We'll go into more detail on this adjustment later in the chapter, but to make it you ought to know the declination of an area before you take off. This will usually be shown on any adequate map, but there are exceptions. You might have unthinkingly made one yourself by cutting off the margins of the map at home. When you do that, make sure you have all the information you need first.

WHAT THE COMPASS TELLS YOU

Even though the actual information given by a compass is pretty well understood by most hikers and campers when they are pressed, it's amazing how many of them harbor a kind of mystical faith in its abilities. People wander off into the woods with only the foggiest idea of where they are or where they are going, and they expect their native instincts and their compasses to lead them back if they get lost. When they realize they *are* lost panic sets in.

A compass gives you a directional frame of reference independent of your map and of your ability to see landmarks or celestial directional guides. Since it is independent, the compass can be used separately from the map or to supplement it. The compass can be used to orient the map when this can't be done visually. It can be used to keep you on a specific course independent of visible, identifiable, well-placed landmarks. It can be used for readily choosing natural landmarks with which to set a course. It can be used for keeping track of your route over confusing terrain or for drawing your own map of your trail, which can then be retraced if the map was properly made. The compass can be used for fixing positions, providing appropriate distant sighting points are available.

A compass is a directional guide. It can't tell you where you are, where your compass is, or where a road is. You must have other information to tell you those things, and the only way to make sure that you have that other information when you need it is to make sure you have it all the time. In one fashion or another you have to keep track of where you are and how you got there whenever you are traveling in wilderness or semiwilderness areas.

KEEPING TRACK OF WHERE YOU ARE

There are lots of ways of knowing where you are, all of them relative and useful only some of the time. The trick is to be aware of lots of ways and to choose those most appropriate to a particular situation. One of the best has already been mentioned. You carry a topo map, and in a more or less formal way, you follow your progress on it. In regions where this method works well, it is easy, fast, and interesting. It requires no tedious sightings and recording of compass readings. If the fog comes in and obscures everything more than twenty feet away, you dig out the compass, figure your desired course on the map, and start walking in the right direction.

Generally, this method is used in mountainous regions effectively, and it is often applicable in other places like deserts, where visibility is good and landmarks available.

Things are different in heavily forested regions, especially those which are relatively flat, which have confused drainage patterns and the like. Tundra, prairie, rolling fields, featureless deserts, and a host of other such places do not lend themselves to this kind of route finding. One can't keep continuous track of where he is from the map, because there is not a continuous set of natural guideposts for him to use for reference. All but the most skillful map readers may have this same difficulty in some hilly and even mountainous country, where each rise looks much like every other and a single missed stream can throw one off completely. In adverse weather conditions, landmarks disappear in any terrain.

Think a little about the ways you can keep track of where you are in a city. You can carry an adequate map, and providing you know your home address, you can wander aimlessly as you choose. When you want to go home, you find a street sign, establish a direction from numbers or the sequence of intersections, and figure out the way back. With a less adequate map you might simply find one main artery which extends a long way in either direction. Knowing a nearby number on that street you can simply wander about to one side of it or another, keeping track only of the direction of your base street. To return you simply have to cut across to the artery and follow it home. With an identifiable skyscraper or two as guide, you might choose to wander at will, heading back for Old Faithful Bank Tower when your feet got sore, knowing that you were living at the opposite end of the park from it. With a city set in a grid, you could simply keep track of the number of blocks in each direction and come back the same number by any route. Finally, in a strange city with no map and irregular streets, you might just keep track of your path—left after two blocks, right after three more, 45° left at a star intersection, and so forth— retracing the sequence to come back. A long walk by the latter method would probably require taking a few notes.

Most of these methods have corresponding wilderness techniques, although there is no friendly cop or taxi stand on the corner in case you get mixed up. With some care and a good mixture of methods you can find your way around the woods without much difficulty. The terrain is more rugged, of course, and you might have to walk farther to get around a river than a freeway. On the other hand, you won't get mugged while you're trying to find the ford, you won't have to walk five miles in discomfort to find a place to go to the bathroom, and you won't get arrested if you get tired and lie down to go to sleep.

BASELINES

One of the most useful ways to orient yourself in the backcountry is by using a baseline of some sort. This is the method which corresponds to finding a long street in the city to which you can always cut over. In the wilds a baseline can be the road where your car is parked; it can be a long river, valley, or creek; it can be a ridge, a power-line cut, a railroad track, a trail, a lake shore; it can be an imaginary line between two landmarks or a compass bearing on one; it can even be a line which you temporarily mark yourself.

The advantage to the baseline is pretty obvious. Even in dense forest, you don't have to keep careful track of every twist and turn in your wanderings. You only need to glance at the compass occasionally to maintain a rough idea of the direction you are going, and when it's time to go back, head for the line. When you hit the line you follow it back to camp or to your car.

There are some fundamental qualifications in using a baseline for your wanderings. To begin with, the baseline has to be long enough in proportion to the distance you're going to go, and it should run more or less perpendicular to your line of travel. A mile-long trail is a fine baseline for an afternoon's berry-picking expedition, but it's not so good for a three-day trek. This may seem obvious, but remember that unless you *know* your road or lakeshore extends five miles past your car or camp, you had better make sure. I know people who have planned to hit roads which made right-angle bends half a mile past where their cars were parked. One of them got very tired indeed going through five miles of heavy snow as he walked parallel to a road a hundred yards away. When the road finally turned again and he hit it, he had to go back the same five miles. Winding roads, lakeshores, and rivers can be very confusing if you don't know about the bends.

In addition to being sure your baseline is long enough, you must learn

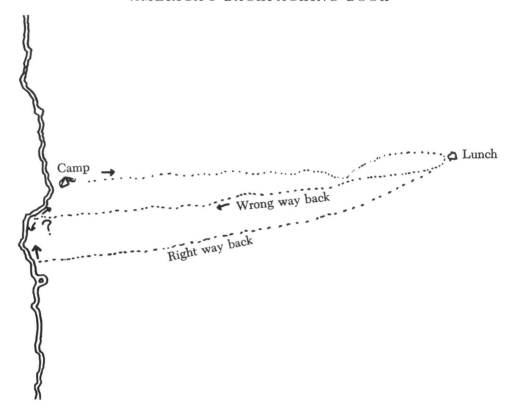

Using a creek for a baseline. The party follows a general bearing on a day hike, and then tries to retrace the bearing. When they get to the creek, they don't know which way to turn for their camp. By intentionally bearing slightly left of the proper route they would know that when the water was reached, a right turn would get them back.

to locate your objective along it. If you are familiar with the baseline in both directions, you may hit it anywhere, knowing which way to go. More commonly, you would be in the position of the party whose route is illustrated. Camped along a creek, they steer back to their camp, but on reaching the creek have no idea which way to turn. The proper method is to aim deliberately to one side. Then the direction of camp is known when the baseline is reached.

TAKING BEARINGS

Taking bearings means using the compass (or some other method) to determine the direction of an object from your position. Determining that Mount Highspire is due north of your camp is done by taking a bearing on Mt. H. The normal method of listing directions these days is to use the *azimuth* system, which simply divides the compass face into 360 degrees, running clockwise, with north=0°=360°. Thus east is 90°, south is 180°, and west is 270°. There are other methods, of course, but if you want to get into working with bearings like *north-northeast by east,* you're on your own. For more precise measurements degrees can be divided into mils or minutes and seconds, but for work with a pocket compass, you don't have to worry about them—working to an accuracy of ½° would be exceptional.

The mechanical details of taking a bearing are different depending on the type of compass you have, but the process is fairly simple in practice. Let's suppose you have a very simple kind of compass. The kind shown in the illustration is the sort that is most familiar. (It is not the easiest to use.) The first thing you have to do to get a bearing is to orient the compass. Suppose you are in the Colorado Rockies where the declination is 14° east. That means the needle on this simple compass points 14° east of true north. If you turn the compass so that the north-seeking end of the needle is on 14, the compass face will be properly oriented. All you need to do now to take the bearing is to sight across the face of the compass and read the number of degrees. Since the compass shown does not have a sighting device, you might use a couple of matchsticks or pine needles to get the most accurate possible reading. Place one above the center of the compass and move the other around the edge until they line up with the distant object. Then you can read your bearing.

TYPES OF COMPASSES

While normal backpacking trips do not require the precision of surveying instruments, a rugged, fairly accurate hand compass is really worthwhile. The example just given referred to the sort of pocket compass which lacks any means for sighting, but these are not really good instruments for the outdoorsman. Any compass *may* be better than none, but not if you rely on its presence only to find it broken and useless in the bottom of the pack when you really need it.

In my opinion any compass that is going to be used for route finding ought to have some provision for sighting, even if it is only a lubber's line (see the illustration). Sights and a sighting mirror are an advantage. The compass has to be ruggedly constructed. You might bang it around for years before you really need it, but if it isn't working when that time comes, you might just as well have not bothered. You should be able to take azimuth readings to within a degree or two to provide reasonable accuracy. The little things that can't be read closer than five degrees may help guide you to a baseline, but they are inadequate for many jobs. As a final minimum requirement, the needle or compass card (moving face) must be either liquid damped or held rigid when the compass is not in use, so that the bearing is saved excessive banging and wear.

There are a lot of other desirable features for compasses; the ones listed above are minimum requirements. Before going any further in listing special attributes, though, we need to look at some of the types of compasses that are made. The most basic one is the one we used for our bearing. More adequate compasses will have some provision for making sightings. The most obvious way to do this is to attach sights to the simple pocket compass used for taking bearings in the example above. This solution will cause certain complications in calculating bearings, though, as we will see. These problems have been solved in several ways, and probably the easiest way to explain the problem and solutions is to show how a bearing would be taken with each of several types of compass.

In the illustration a bearing is being taken on a mountain at azimuth 36° in an area with a declination of 14° east. Compass A is a standard pocket compass with a sight attached so that it is aligned with the north-south markings on the face. This is a very common type of compass. When the sights are pointing at the mountain, the bearing is obtained by the following process of calculation: the north-seeking end of the needle points at 338°, but since the needle points 14° east of true bearing, a needle pointing true north would point 14° farther west, or 338° − 14° = 324°; the bearing is the same number of degrees clockwise from zero as 324° is counterclockwise, so the bearing is 360° − 324° = 36°.

Now it is possible to train yourself to make these complicated corrections automatically, but it really shouldn't be necessary, and it isn't. The

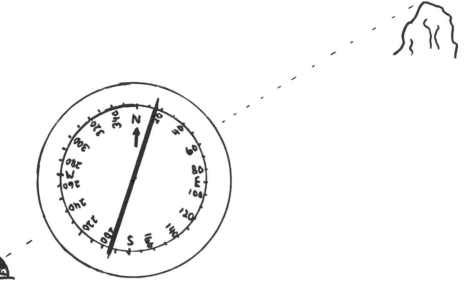

Sighting a bearing with a very simple compass. The compass needle is set on the declination, 14°, and a sighting taken across the compass. It is impossible to sight with much accuracy using this arrangement.

first thing to eliminate is the need to make the correction 360° minus the true needle reading equals the bearing. This can be done in several ways. The first is that used on compass B, a cruiser's compass. The azimuth readings run counterclockwise instead of clockwise on the dial.

The bearing calculation would go this way for compass B: the needle points to 22°, but since it is pointing 14° too far east, the true azimuth reading is 22° + 14° = 36°. We are still correcting for declination, but things have gotten a lot simpler.

A second method for simplifying bearing calculations is to use a compass card instead of a needle, as on compass C. A compass card is simply a calibrated face with a magnet permanently attached, which is free to turn on the pivot in place of a needle. The sights are still fixed to the case, but the azimuth scale is not. Again we can read the magnetic bearing directly, add the declination, and have our true bearing: 22° + 14° = 36°.

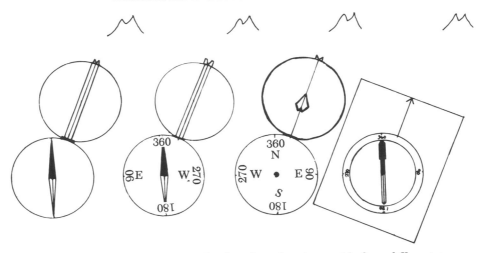

A simplified drawing of the method of reading bearings with four different types of compasses. See the text for explanation.

The third method of eliminating this calculation is to add an additional moving part to the simple compass, giving a system with a magnetized needle free pivot inside a clockwise azimuth scale, with a sight attached to the scale but free to turn around it. A compass of this type is shown in figure D. With this system, we simply turn the scale so that the needle points at the proper declination, 14°, and then we turn the sights to point at the mountain and read the declination directly, 36°.

OTHER COMPASS FEATURES

All these types of compass are made in more expensive versions which have provisions for setting off declination. A screw may be turned or another mechanical device set at the trailhead, so that you don't have to worry about declination until you've traveled far enough for it to have changed, something you won't do on a weekend backpack. This adjustment is helpful in preventing confusion in difficult situations when your mind may be a bit fogged.

A few other compass features need to be mentioned as particularly worthwhile. Walking on a bearing is much easier to do if the needle

A good hand compass. This one is rather old-fashioned, dating back to the early part of the century, but it is more effective than many modern compasses. The mirror in the lid reflects degree readings from the face (written in mirror-image figures) so that a reading can be taken at the same time as a sighting. The brass case and dial lock make the compass sturdy enough to ensure that it will be working when you need it. The line across the cover is called a lubber's line, providing a rough sighting device if the compass is held at waist level.

doesn't joggle with every step, requiring five minutes to settle down. Liquid-filled compasses solve this problem best, providing they don't contain any bubbles to interfere with the action. A cheaper method of damping needle motion is effective, though not quite as good. It is called induction damping and uses the electromagnetic field generated by the moving needle to damp it.

A map can be oriented much more easily if some kind of straight edge is fixed on the compass. The same purpose may be served by scribed lines on the bottom of a compass with a transparent plastic base. Such transparent bases are a fine feature anyway, allowing the compass to be used as a protractor, and eliminating several steps in various triangulation procedures.

Small mirrors and lenses are often attached to sights so as to allow the compass dial to be read while the sight is being taken. If mirrors are used, the dial is usually printed with both normal and mirror image figures. Large mirrors, which may be attached to the top or bottom of the compass, serve this purpose and also make bearings more convenient and accurate. With such a mirror, one can take sightings forward and backward along the trail without moving the compass placed on a steady surface, since the mirror can be angled to allow sighting from a wide range of angles.

Two recent compasses use a completely different sighting system than any normal pocket compasses, eliminating the major problem with most of them—the difficulty of getting accurate readings from the hand-held compass. It often is impossible to rest a compass on a solid object when you are taking bearings in the field, yet most compasses require the eye to focus on several points in different places to get a reading. With a hand-held compass, the needle always moves while your eye goes from the sight to the numbers, resulting in an inaccurate reading. The new Wilkie bearing compass and the Suunto KB-14 eliminate this problem with a lens allowing you to read the bearing while sighting, and they are accurate to under a degree even when hand held. The Suunto is better, since it also has a straight edge, but the Wilkie costs half as much. If you're buying a new compass one of these two would be by far the best buy for wilderness use.°

Other conveniences such as measuring scales may be included on the compass, and their utility is obvious, but beyond this point we begin to enter the regions charted by the secret rings you used to get for fifteen boxtops. Any day I expect the advent of a compass with a secret decoder and a concealed poison dart for subduing grizzly bears.

MORE ON DECLINATION

Declination tends to be more confusing to beginners than any other feature of compass work. Since the needle may point east or west of true north, one may have to add or subtract the declination figure. Most of your trav-

---

° A recent article by D. B. Richards, which appeared in the January 1972 issue of *Wilderness Camping*, after this was written, finds the Wilkie greatly inferior. Apparently Mr. Richard's sample had an inaccurately set face, indicating poor quality control. I agree with him on the Suunto, and interestingly he found the old U.S. Army Corps of Engineers compass more accurate for hand-held readings than anything but the Suunto. This is the compass shown in the photograph, one I've carried and relied on for years.

Compass sightings usually have to be taken with the compass held in the hand, and one should be bought with that fact in mind. Systems which require you to focus on several places at the same time are impractical.

eling will probably be in the same general region, though, so you shouldn't have to go back and forth every weekend. In any case you should try to get used to adjusting for declination in the same way each time, whether it is by making a mechanical adjustment on your compass at the trailhead or making a final addition or subtraction at the end of each bearing. Adjusting for declination at the end of a calculation may be the easiest way to handle declination arithmetically. To do this you take your bearing as if the needle pointed to true north, making whatever other calculations your compass technique requires. This gives you a *magnetic bearing*. Now if you are in the East, having a *west declination, subtract* the declination figure from your magnetic bearing. If you are in the West, having an *east declination, add* the declination to your magnetic bearing. Always adjust for declination at the same point in your calculation to avoid confusion.

If you are simply recording a series of bearings along a trail in case of storm, or making your own map as you go along, you may choose to use magnetic bearings exclusively, ignoring the problem of declination. This is all right, because the problem of declination only arises when you have to relate your directional system to a map or the stars or some other outside frame. Assuming you don't travel far enough for declination to change significantly, it isn't important if you use *only* magnetic bearings. If you do use such a method, however, I suggest you label all bearings to prevent later confusion. One can use *m* and *t* to indicate magnetic and true bearings. Then if later comparison with a map is needed, there won't be any awkward questions.

WHAT BEARINGS ARE GOOD FOR

Having gotten through some of the confusing preliminaries, we can go on to the actual use of map and compass as guides for travel over terrain with few landmarks or poor visibility. Perhaps the most obvious such use would be to pick out one's location and a goal on the map and to use the compass to steer the course between them, ignoring intermediate features. In practice, this method is avoided whenever possible, because of the difficulty of doing it with accuracy. Obstacles intervene and require detours, staying on a compass direction is hard while one is bobbing along on his feet and trying to watch his path, and continuous observation of the compass is irritating even when it is possible. This method is used in some circumstances, though, and many variations of it are frequent. So to begin with, the map procedure for this method will be described.

In the illustration the goal is Walleye Lake, and fortunately the end of the road is shown on the map. A line has been drawn between the two places and another line due north, so the bearing can be easily measured with a protractor or transparent-bottomed compass. In this case the proper bearing is 45°. One possible method of getting to Walleye Lake would be to follow a compass bearing of 45°. The declination diagram at the bottom of the map shows that the compass will point 17° west of true north. Thus magnetic bearings will be 17° greater than true ones,

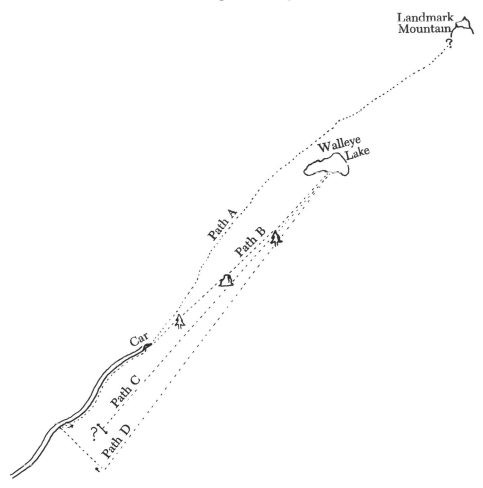

Steering a course with a bearing on a distant landmark. Using intermediate features in line with the mountain ensures a straight course. On return, deliberately heading to one side of the road is wise, so that one knows which way to turn in order to find it.

and to follow a true bearing of 45° to Walleye Lake, a magnetic bearing of 62° will be required.

The backpackers who want to go to Walleye Lake don't want to try to watch their compasses every second, so they would normally try to pick the most distant visible landmarks along the bearing 62°m. It is best to pick out two marks that line up, rather than only one; this method gives a continuous line of correction to the hiker as he weaves around obstacles. Also, if two points on a line are picked, as the nearer one is approached it may be possible to pick another landmark along the line without the need of a new compass bearing.

In the illustration, there is a large mountain on the other side of Walleye Lake from the car, and we'll assume that it is visible most of the way. Of course if the mountain was right behind the lake, the backpackers might simply be able to head straight for its summit and be assured of hitting the lake on the way. Landmark Mountain is really a good five miles on the other side of the lake, though, and if the hikers head for it, they might well take path A. Their detours around obstacles have caused them to miss the lake altogether even though they had a landmark. The way to follow path B instead is to pick intermediate landmarks, perhaps trees or rocks, to line up with Landmark Mountain. As each intermediate point is approached another farther one is picked which lies along the same line with Landmark Mountain. Occasionally the compass may be pulled out to make sure that there hasn't been significant drifting.

This same basic method might have been used if no particular goal was intended and the party was just off for a few days in the woods. A course of 62°m might have been followed, using the same method of staying on course. When the time came to return, the bearing would be reversed (62°m + 180° = 242°m).

Actually, to hit the road end the hikers would not want to try to follow an exact course of 242°m the whole way, because it would probably lead them on a course like C. It would be unlikely that they would hit the end of the road exactly, and when they realized they had missed it they would have no idea which way to turn. Instead, they should bear intentionally to one side or another. The party following course D figured that they had traveled about ten miles from their car along a fairly accurate course of 62°m. Instead of following 242°m, they took a course of 237°m, figuring that the 5° difference would leave them a little less than a mile from the road. When they were sure they had gone far enough (by traveling 1 hour longer than they had taken on the trip in) they turned right and soon hit the road. Turning right again on the road they were soon back at the car.

If they had been less sure of their accuracy going in they might have allowed a 10° leeway instead of a 5° one.

The examples given so far have been concerned with situations where a compass course is being followed, but there are many other more common occasions when compass bearings are used. When following a topo map, the experienced wilderness traveler is likely to notice certain places along the route where the returning party might have difficulty. On rounded summits above timberline, for example, the rocky terrain takes on a confusing sameness in snow or fog. In weather that is even slightly threatening, it is often prudent to jot down a bearing on the summit from the point where the route would become recognizable if the party returned in bad weather. If this has been done, clouds closing in quickly at the summit need not bring apprehension. The party can simply reverse its compass course to get back to the trail or gully.

There are many similar situations when individual bearings may be needed, even though the party is not following a continuous compass course. A portion of a trail may be unclear. A route down a hill which avoids cliffs may not be visible from above. Several watersheds may take off from one point, and a bearing may be required to get started down the right one.

ESTABLISHING A POSITION

Especially with the availability of modern maps, the main problem in finding your way is often determining where you are in the first place. You may be able to establish your own location by the use of a topo map alone, but this is not always possible; many kinds of terrain just aren't that distinctive. In the example used above, the road on which the car was parked was clearly shown on the map, but many approaches follow networks of logging roads that are unlikely to be accurately represented. You cannot determine a good bearing to follow from a map if you don't know where your starting point is. Trying to follow terrain is even more confusing when you start with a misconception of your position.

Position can be determined in a number of ways. If you are camped beside a lake, you can follow the shoreline with confidence in your ability to return, because your position relative to the lake is clear. A more general reference system will give you far more freedom to travel, though, and this is why orienting oneself on a map is generally preferred.

The principles and information used for orientation are easily listed. You may have a map, and if you do it tells you the relative position of a number of features on the landscape. Sitting out in the landscape somewhere, you will have some information about the relative positions of any existing landmarks because they are there, too, and even their absence tells you something. If the map shows a mountain beside Lake Enigma, but there isn't any mountain near the lake where you're sitting, it isn't Lake Enigma.

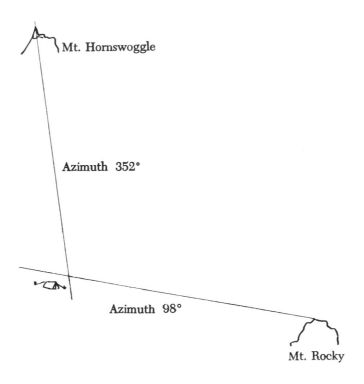

Triangulation enables you to determine your position from bearings on two known landmarks.

You have a device which gives you a directional frame of reference, your compass. (Make sure you carry it—always. Some natural direction finders will be mentioned elsewhere in the book, but depending on them is foolish. If you have limited space in your memory, fill it with the imperative ALWAYS CARRY A COMPASS IN THE BACKCOUNTRY, rather than the fact that the first star in Orion's belt rises in the east.)

The final item in your route-finding bag is simply your knowledge of elementary geometry. From it comes the method of *triangulation*, which establishes your position from the direction of two landmarks. Triangulation is used in many ways, one of which is shown in the illustration. The camp shown is within sight of two easily recognized mountains, Mount Hornswoggle and Mount Rocky. Taking bearings from camp, the backpacker determines that Hornswoggle is at azimuth 352° and Rocky is at 98°. Since there is nowhere else except the spot he is standing from which the two peaks will appear at these angles, the position is established. The backpacker can wander around as much as he likes within sight of Mt. H. and Mt. R., and he will always be able to find his way back to camp within the error limit of his compass.

If the backpacker wants to fix his position on a map, he can draw in these same bearings, using a protractor and straight edge (some compasses will serve both functions). Through the point on the map labeled "Mt. Hornswoggle" he draws a line 8° counterclockwise from due north and through Mount Rocky a line 98° clockwise. When these two lines are extended they will intersect at the campsite.

Positions are generally fixed through the use of several methods. If one is traveling along a river, a bearing on a distant landmark often gives a well-defined position along the river. The same is true of any other baseline combined with a bearing. Bearings in fact establish usable baselines. If only one landmark is visible from a distance a bearing on it may be used as a baseline to which one can always return after travel roughly perpendicular to it.

It should be apparent that proper use of a compass will allow almost complete freedom of travel in any area where there are a reasonable number of recognizable landmarks. These do not have to be continuously visible. One might confidently travel a considerable distance on a bearing with no visible landmarks, as long as he knew that Mount Hornswoggle and Mount Rocky would eventually show themselves.

The use of bearings as guides requires an understanding of their limitations, however. Any bearing includes some error. With precise surveying instruments this error is very small, but even a good pocket compass used carefully is not a precise surveying instrument. It is worthwhile to try to find how accurate your sightings are. With a very good compass, readings can be obtained which are accurate to within less than a degree, but most compasses and operators are less exact than this, and readings which are consistently within a couple of degrees of true are fairly good for most purposes. Such an error would amount to one-third of a mile in each ten. In country where landmarks are visible for long distances, you could depend on keeping within this error, but if new bearings were being taken every few hundred yards, a much larger error might accumulate.

Errors can be reduced in many ways. Multiple sights on one point will reduce an individual error on that sighting. Triangulation errors are reduced by sightings on three or more landmarks. Triangulation with only two landmarks is most accurate when the sightings are approximately at right angles. The reason for this is shown in the illustration. The best way to reduce errors in following courses or mapping your own is by periodically establishing new starting points and thus reducing errors to zero.

WALKING A COURSE

Suppose you are camped in a wooded area and you are planning to climb a mountain on a day trip away from camp. Finding your way to the mountain is simple, since it is frequently visible through the trees. The only route-finding problem will be in making your way back to camp, because there are no very good landmarks nearby. The mountain is seven or eight miles away, and if you simply take a bearing on it in the morning with the idea of reversing that course on the way home, you will probably miss the camp on the way back.

You can improve your chances of hitting the camp enormously by marking out a baseline perpendicular to your line of travel. From a standard red bandana I've torn enough strips to mark a line every hundred feet for a mile. Anyone coming back to the camp and getting within a half-mile of it would pass within fifty feet of one of these markers. With careful compass work, it is fairly easy to hit a mile-long target.

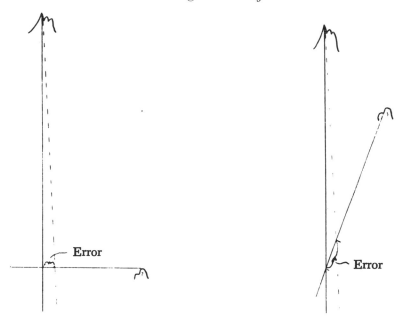

Triangulation errors from the same degree inaccuracy are much less when landmarks are roughly at right angles to one another.

An even shorter line would probably do, however, if the groups made frequent zeroing operations, an easy matter in most terrain. If, for example, a creek was crossed a couple of miles out of camp, it could be used as a new baseline. A cairn or some other marker is placed beside the creek, a new bearing taken on the mountain, and on the return the creek is crossed at the cairn, rather than wherever it is reached. When you get to the creek, you find the cairn before going on. By thus separating the journey into a number of legs, large errors are not generated. In areas with good visibility and much featureless ground, one can accomplish similar ends by traveling from one landmark to another or even building cairns.

There are times when there is no alternative but to stay on a compass bearing with no visible landmarks available. In heavy snowstorms, for example, or in fog, it may be impossible to see any appreciable distance. In such cases, if one is traveling with others, the last one in line holds the compass and directs travel. The line should be stretched out as far as visibility permits. The compass man then sights along the line at the front man, directing him whenever he begins to veer off course. On flat ground without obstacles an amazingly accurate course can be steered this way. You can even keep fairly good track of distances if you learn a pacing stride and find out what its length is. More commonly, one simply keeps track of the time he took to cover a distance over similar terrain before and estimates the distance covered by the time taken, with any needed allowances for wind, new snow, or other factors that may slow the pace.

Rounding obstacles is the usual source of error when a party is trying to walk on a particular bearing. The remedy is simply to make accurate

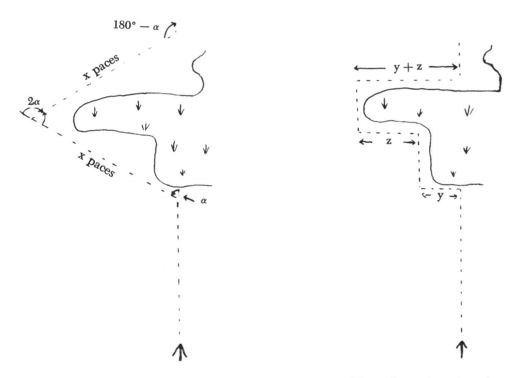

Using combinations of right angles greatly simplifies the problem of rounding obstacles. You need only keep track of a distance figure.

marches around the blockades, whenever this is possible. The illustration shows two ways to turn an intervening obstruction. The shortest way is to angle around as shown in the first example, but this requires some care in keeping the deviation and the return leg symmetrical. For foggy minds the right angle turns of the second example are simpler, and the central leg of such a course doesn't have to be paced off. For crossing ponds and creeks, one can simply take note of a landmark on either side, returning to the proper point on the opposite shore without the need for keeping track of turns along the way.

MARKING A TRAIL OR BASELINE

One occasion for marking out a line was mentioned above, where an artificial baseline was mentioned as a method for finding a camp on the return journey from a long hike. One may also wish to mark trails, junctions, or landmarks for a return journey. This is commonly done for you on maintained trails, especially in areas where the path would not show, above timberline in rocky areas, for example. On some occasions you may wish to follow suit by temporarily marking your own route or a few spots along it. While this is rarely necessary, there are occasions when it can save a great deal of time and trouble.

The traditional means for marking forest trails is by blazing trees. It is a good method for permanent routes, but it has no place in the methods of the backpacker marking a temporary passage. You should aim to leave as few signs of your visit as possible, rather than a record that will last for decades or centuries. Obviously the same comments apply to paint marks on rocks and similar defacements.

In open rocky places, ducks serve the backpacker's purposes well. A duck is simply a small cairn, a little pile of stones set in a prominent place. These show up remarkably well, and the only caution that the user may have to observe is to beware of old ducks set by others. In some places you may wish to make larger cairns and to travel from one to the other by compass bearings. Notes and bearings will help when there might be confusion in your mind on return after several days absence. Ducks and cairns are particularly useful in finding return routes down mountains topped by broad rocky plateaus but surrounded by steep sides.

In forests the best temporary markers are brightly colored plastic strips like those used by surveying parties. They can be quickly tied to twigs and are visible for long distances. I admit to writing this paragraph with trepidation, though, with visions of fluorescent orange forests dancing in my head. For God's sake take any of those things you put up back home with you. They are useful markers, but as trash left in the woods they are both obscene and everlasting. Pull them all down on your way back, and stow them carefully in pack or pocket. One substitute for plastic strips has been mentioned—a shredded bandana. You can think of others if the need arises.

WORRYING ABOUT YOUR COMPASS

There *are* places where the compass is unreliable, but they are really pretty uncommon, and "something wrong with the compass" usually translates accurately as "creeping panic and confusion in the operator." If you are planning on a trip in the regions near the magnetic pole where a normal compass is useless, you'll have to use specialized instruments, but elsewhere you are unlikely to run into areas of magnetic irregularity. Your map may make note of any that exist within its boundaries.

If you do have doubts about the compass, try to pick landmarks a couple of hundred yards apart. Take a bearing from one to the other, then walk to the second and take a back bearing. If the two bearings are 180° apart within the normal accuracy of your readings, there is no magnetic irregularity causing problems, and you can trust the compass readings.

In case you are having compass trouble, make sure you are not causing erratic readings with a piece of iron or steel on your person or somewhere else near the compass. Another possible source of error is a lock on the face or needle which is not releasing completely.

True magnetic irregularities rarely extend very far, so there is a good chance of leaving them behind by simply following a straight course in the direction of your best guess. A straight course can usually be maintained by lining up trees, rocks, or your companions. Back sights along the course can be taken periodically, and when they begin to agree, the compass can again be trusted. If you have paced off the distance traveled, this information can be combined with the backsight to give you a good estimate of the direction and distance of your blind march.

Remember, 99 per cent of all erratic compass readings are due to erratic readers. Trust your compass unless you have carefully tested reason not to; in a contest between your instinct and the compass, always assume your instinct is faulty.

NATURAL ROUTE FINDERS: STARS, MOSS, AND ALL THAT

There is a common assumption that route-finding ability starts with vast stores of information about moss growing on trees, shadow sticks, and such. It doesn't. Spend your time learning to use maps, compasses, and your own eyes, and when you've learned, spend some more time learning to use them better. Obviously, it is possible to use natural route finders to get around— people did it for millennia before the discovery of the magnetic compass, and the stars are still the most accurate directional indicators. For precise position finding when large distances are involved, specialized instruments for celestial navigation are needed. The reading list at the back of this book will tell you where to get more information on the use of transits, sextants, and similar instruments. Celestial route finding with a transit or sextant is a different matter from picking your way along by the sun and the tree rings, however.

The reason I am cynical about such methods is that they are all very unreliable. The first difficulty is remembering them. If you can't remember to bring a compass when you head for the woods, you'll probably forget which way to point your watch, especially in the panic that usually accompanies the realization that you're lost. Such methods are even more unreliable because all the good ones require fair weather, and in my experience the time you really need to know which way is north is when the visibility is poor. If you're in a comfortable enough position to wait out the snowstorm and watch for Polaris, chances are you don't really need to anyway.

There is a function for such knowledge in survival manuals, and some of it is nice to know, but although a prisoner of war will not have a compass and may need to follow the sun, you should have a compass and map that are unaffected by the cloud cover.

Without a compass or map one generally does have to use celestial bodies as guides. There may be land features which will give you directional hints, but they are of a local nature and are not likely to be of much

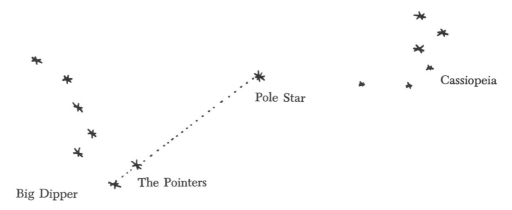

The location of the North Star, Polaris.

use unless you are quite familiar with the area. Such signs include water flow, topography, wind direction and signs of it like blown snow or plant growth, and pattern of vegetation growth.

The best celestial guide is the North Star, Polaris, which is never more than about one degree from true north. The drawing shows the common methods for locating it, but the more familiar with the night sky you become, the better able you will be to interpolate on evenings when clouds or hills obscure parts of the sky. Another possible guide at night is Orion. The star on the front of his belt is on the celestial equator, so it rises in the east and sets in the west. However, in the wilderness you are unlikely to see the rise over a true horizon, so this is a rough and unreliable guide. Those really familiar with the night sky can find other rough directional signals, but since travel at night is usually inadvisable, all you can do is set two sticks in the ground sighted at Polaris and wait until morning for some landmarks to appear.

Many methods of getting the direction from the sun have appeared from time to time. Most of them are useless, either because they are not reliable (the watch method, for example), or because they use up long periods of time, usually at a particular time of the day. The only method worthy of much attention is the one devised by Robert Owendoff.

THE OWENDOFF SHADOW-STICK METHOD

For the Owendoff method you need the shadow of some object with a steady point three or more feet above the ground. The shadow point should fall on a spot that is fairly level for a few inches around. A shadow can be that of a rock or tree (one not being moved by the wind) or one can be made by planting a stick in the ground. A stick around four feet long is a good size. Mark the point of the shadow with a twig, a matchstick, or something similar. Wait until the shadow has moved a couple of inches and mark its position again. A line between the two points you have just marked will run roughly east-west with the east end at the second mark.

Like all rough shadow methods, the Owendoff technique is subject to considerable error, but it will give an approximate direction fairly quickly. It is most accurate around noon and least accurate around sunrise and sunset. It is accurate all day around the spring and fall equinoxes, while maximum error is reached on the summer and winter solstices. If you're going to get lost and break your compass on a sunny day, make sure to pick one of the equinoxes. Owendoff also points out (Robert S. Owendoff, *Better Ways of Pathfinding*) that his method has the advantage that the errors in it will cancel out to zero through the day, a characteristic not possessed by some other methods.

In using any celestial method, try to set your course with landmarks that will carry you in a straight line for good distances between checks. Line up two trees along the course, for example, and before you reach the nearer one pick another along the same line.

TRIANGULATION WITHOUT A COMPASS

If you think a little about the method of triangulation, you will realize that it does not depend on a compass for accuracy. If a compass is used to orient the map, then only two landmarks are needed to determine your position. If you have no compass you need three landmarks. I think the easiest method is by using a piece of tracing paper, which I carry with my map. The tracing paper is laid on a flat spot from which three landmarks are visible. I then take sights using needles from the repair kit, but matchsticks, pine needles, or twigs will do. One needle is stuck at approximately the center of the paper. Another is lined up between the first needle and a landmark and stuck in the margin of the paper. A line is drawn between the two needles. The outside needle is taken out, and without moving the paper it is lined up with the center needle and the second landmark. A second line is drawn, and then the procedure is repeated for the third landmark. The paper now has three lines on it, intersecting near the center of the paper where the central needle was.

The tracing paper can now be laid on the map and moved around until each of the three lines passes through the landmark it represents. (The landmarks will not be at any particular distance along the position lines.) There is only one position that this will occur, when the intersection rests over your location on the map.

The tracing paper method can be used even if you are not certain which landmarks you see, providing you have some notion of where you are. The paper can be moved around to test different combinations. When you find one that seems to fit, you can orient the map with one landmark and test the hypothetical position against the terrain. More than three landmarks can be used when they are available.

GENERAL

Finding your way in the wilderness, at least for reasonable distances in regions mapped by modern methods, isn't really very difficult. Exploration in remote areas where maps are inadequate is another matter, but even that shouldn't intimidate anyone who has come to feel at home in wild places.

The fundamentals in getting around beyond the well-marked trails are the training of your own powers of observation, learning to write important things down, developing skill at reading maps, and learning to use a compass properly. With those skills, you'll have little difficulty in meeting emergencies. The likelihood of breaking your compass at the same time that you can't get out using a map alone is pretty small. Besides, the more experience you get in guiding yourself around through the woods, with and without trails, the fewer the occasions will be when you don't know just where you are. Personally, I get lost a lot, but somehow it always happens on the roads leading to the trailhead rather than in the paths and gullies beyond.

Emergencies and Survival Techniques 15

There is an emphasis throughout this book on intelligent preparation as the best way to avoid serious trouble in the wilderness. This readiness is more a state of mind than a particular piece of equipment or safety precaution taken in advance. Wilderness travel is an activity that depends for its enjoyment and safety on the self-reliance of the people or person doing it. Equipment of a particular kind may be necessary or desirable, but it won't make you safe. The determined idiot can manage to get hurt anywhere, and the wilderness will provide him with plenty of opportunity for getting lost, breaking a leg, or having his strength sapped by weather conditions.

STAYING OUT OF TROUBLE

The way to stay out of trouble in the backcountry is to get to know yourself and the wilderness you are traveling and then to confine your travel to situations you can handle. When you won't know what you're getting into, make your decisions in a conservative frame of mind. In the mountains, don't try to explore a long and possibly impassable route when you don't have adequate food and clothing. In the desert, don't push on to an uncertain waterhole when you are carrying a minimal supply of water. In the woods, don't take strong chances of breaking a leg when you are a long way from help.

It would be pointless to catalogue a great list of possible mistakes that one can make in the woods; they are numberless, anyhow. Following good camping and hiking practices will keep you out of most trouble. If you are to avoid getting lost, you need to use good route-finding methods. Adequate clothing and shelter will protect you from the weather, while poorly chosen equipment will not. If you don't take enough food, you may expect to get hungry.

SOLO TRAVEL

The rule that one should "Never travel alone!" has been written many times. I can't very well repeat it because I frequently travel in the wilderness alone. Personally, I think it is a silly rule. It is important to recognize the element of truth in it, however. Solo travel away from the beaten path requires far more care than trips with other people. The lone traveler must rely on his own resources without help for an extended period. This self-reliance can be very exhilarating, but it can also be burdensome.

Most of the North American wilderness is quite hospitable in temperate seasons. If you are traveling with a friend and you slip and break your leg, the situation isn't usually serious. He can help you to get comfortable and fetch whatever you might need during his absence, and then he can go out for help. Your situation when you are alone is quite a bit more serious. You have to splint the leg yourself and to manage water, food, and shelter until a search party comes on you or until your leg has knit well enough to allow you to get out.

If you think a little about situations like this, you will realize that the solo traveler often has to carry far more equipment and supplies than a member of a large party. He must not only take all his own basic equipment, he must also carry larger reserves. This is particularly true when the environment is inhospitable—in winter, in the desert, on high mountains.

In referring to solo travel here, I'm talking about trips into true wilderness, on infrequently traveled paths, or wandering out of season. You don't need to take company on popular trails in the summer to have the advantages and disadvantages of other people. The John Muir or the Appalachian Trails on an August weekend are well enough traveled so that you would have help in short order, and thus you would not need to apply more caution than if you were traveling in a group. The equivalency applies only as long as you are on the traveled trail, though. A side trip of a couple of miles changes the picture completely.

Traveling by yourself in the backcountry can provide some of your most memorable wilderness experiences, but reasonable safety requires that you be aware of the special dangers of being alone. You have to use more care in planning trips and choosing equipment and provisions. You must leave wider safety margins. Finally, you should pay particular attention to the advisability of leaving word of your plans with someone in case of accident, a subject discussed in more detail later in the chapter.

EMERGENCIES

One thing that every sensible wilderness lover has to realize is that no matter what precautions are taken, the possibilities of an accident always exist. Life in the wilds is at least as uncertain as it is elsewhere. That is the reason for taking various precautions to ensure that one is fairly well prepared for contingencies. The best mountaineer can be caught by a storm and the best woodsman can slip and break a leg.

One of the implications of the discussion at the beginning of the chapter was that it is generally possible to prevent emergencies by avoiding accidents. It is equally important, though, to prevent difficulties and accidents from becoming emergencies. Getting lost is not an emergency. Many outdoorsmen have become temporarily lost. At worst, the result is a chilly night and a growling stomach, and in return, the lost man has received a few good lessons. Getting lost only creates an emergency when combined with other problems: panic, accidents, and so on. The additional ingredients which create the emergency usually result from the actions of the people in trouble.

The one essential ingredient in every formula for dealing with difficulties in the backcountry is a cool head. If you keep your wits there is rarely a serious problem and almost never an insurmountable one. If you lose your good sense, you can get into real trouble in a woodlot. A second very useful quality for dealing with difficulties is a sense of humor. If you can sit down and have a good laugh (not to be confused with an hysterical giggle) at yourself for getting into your predicament, you have practically guaranteed that you will follow a sensible procedure in getting out of it.

An evaluation of your situation is important if you want to follow a sensible course, and that evaluation has to include all the information you have, including that about yourself—you are, after all, the most important ingredient. The need for haste is rare in the wilderness, whether in emergencies or not. Timetables are usually determined more by when you have to be back at the office than they are by your surroundings, and when real problems arise they have the virtue of enabling you to forget external irrelevancies. In difficulty in the wilds careful consideration is usually far more valuable than a thirty-minute head start.

People usually fear their problem to be much greater than it actually is. The body will stand a good deal more punishment than its owner generally thinks, and a bit of hunger, cold, or thirst, uncomfortable as it may be, hardly makes an emergency by itself. Even injuries are not always particularly serious. A broken arm can be set just as well in five or six days as tomorrow, providing its owner acts sensibly and avoids breaking a leg in his panic to get out.

The other side of the coin shows itself in the underestimation of certain kinds of trouble. Wet clothing in cold weather is a more serious problem than many others which appear much more alarming. A deep snowfall can reduce travel without skis or snowshoes to a tenth or twentieth of the speed of the party before its occurrence. Careful evaluation is the key to getting out of trouble in the wilds. Panic and the calm bred of ignorance are the main pitfalls to avoid.

SURVIVAL

Remember that whenever you get in trouble in the woods, survival is not usually the issue at hand. You can live and function for quite a while in most wildernesses with adequate clothing, even if you are completely out of food. With care you can even last for some time without water.

In either case, though, you cannot afford to squander your body's reserves of food, heat, and water. If you spend the night out, don't get cold and wet when you can easily build shelter and a fire. If you are in the des-

Survival depends a great deal on the equipment you carry with you. A waterproof cagoule like this covers the whole body with the knees drawn up. It can be a lifesaver in wet, cold conditions.

ert without water, travel when the sun is down to conserve your body's moisture. Such advice follows from common sense, but don't forget to use yours when you need it.

The problem in most emergencies in the backcountry is getting out, not surviving for months at a time in the same place. Most of the survival literature is designed for the military and has only slight relevance to the problems faced by the outdoorsman in trouble. You will not have your parachute or the fuselage of your plane handy. It will do you little good in British Columbia to know which part of a cashew to eat, and hopefully enemy troops will not be searching you out. Thus while it is understandable that an escaping prisoner of war will not have a compass handy, there is certainly no reason why you shouldn't. The principles of travel and survival in the wilderness in case of trouble are pretty much the same as they are when you're just having a good time.

A word about finding food is in order here, but I am not going to give a list of drawings and designs for snares, as I think they would be a waste of time. Living off the land is a fascinating technique to learn, but I don't believe that it has much to do with the survival problems faced by the average wilderness traveler in trouble. If you're traveling for months at a time in the far reaches of the north woods and you're living off the land, fine. Just keep doing it. Similarly, if you have fishing equipment along and your trip out from a fine chain of lakes is slowed by a sprained ankle, you would be a fool not to keep on fishing.

The methods for finding and getting hold of wild food in a particular kind of country usually require detailed local knowledge. You may learn every edible plant in Pennsylvania, but the knowledge will do you no good if you are stranded in the mountains of Colorado. The study of edible plants is worthwhile, but you should start with a guide for the region where you live, and not expect to apply the same guide to a different region.

The advice to try a little of an unfamiliar plant has been frequently repeated. If your problem is truly that you are starving, this might be wise, but under most circumstances I think it would be stupid. There are several plants in North America besides mushrooms which are highly poisonous even in small quantities and there are many others which can produce quite disagreeable effects. Aside from the possibility of killing yourself, the last thing you need when you are trying to walk out of the wilderness is an energy-depleting digestive upset. If you find a patch of raspberries, that is dandy, but I think that experimenting with unfamiliar plants is one of the more foolish courses of action in the emergencies you are likely to encounter. If you want to learn how to live off the land in your area, you had better get some plant guides and start learning.

Animal life, including insects, is generally safer and more nutritious than plant food for the neophyte suddenly thrown out on his own, providing he avoids sick animals. He generally won't have much trouble avoiding them, however, because they will avoid him. You may be able to net fish, snare rabbits, and beat porcupines over the head with clubs, but you may not. If it's only a forty-mile walk out, you'd probably be better off using your energy to do that. The most likely source of concentrated food is the insect population, but even that depends very much on location.

It has always seemed to me that the biggest problem with living-off-the-land techniques as an answer to wilderness emergencies is that real trouble generally occurs when they are not very applicable. If I am caught by a deep early snow, I am not going to waste my energy trying to dig out some miner's lettuce. Blizzard conditions are a time to hole up, not to go out tracking rabbits that are sensibly curled up at home. At the times and places where food is relatively simple to scrounge up, there is rarely any real need to do so. When the woods are friendly and the food is flitting around, you aren't likely to have an emergency. When the wind is howling and the sleet is blowing and freezing and you slip and break your hip on the icy rockfield you're crossing, *then* you have an emergency, and also more important and useful things to do than setting snares. That is the time for which I carry emergency food.

INJURIES

First aid is discussed in another chapter, but some of the difficulties surrounding an injury will be considered here. Once the necessary first aid has been given, one is faced with the question of what to do next. Is the injured person well enough to walk out with or without help? Will he be well enough tomorrow or the next day?

There is no way to set up a formula to deal with the problems created by an injury, but some general principles can be mentioned. Complicating factors need to be taken into account, as do the consequences that can be expected from the delay in obtaining medical care for the injured person. The effects of shock and cold in particular must be anticipated. In a wilderness situation, where blood transfusions and warm rooms are not readily available, vigorous treatment to prevent shock and body chilling have to be started as soon as possible.

Once first aid has been given and the victim made as comfortable as possible, the problem of obtaining help or evacuation arises. With a large group the problem is greatly simplified. The group may be large enough to evacuate the victim without outside help. This should be done in an orderly fashion, avoiding any unseemly haste that is not required by the condition of the victim.

Smaller groups are placed in a more difficult position. The number of people required to carry an injured man out should not be underestimated, although it will vary with the situation. Sending for additional help or waiting a few days until the victim is well enough to aid in his own retreat should be considered.

In case of trouble on the way out, two people should be sent out wherever possible. In their haste they must take especial care that they can find their way back and that they do not become totally exhausted. They will need to bring back help besides reaching it. A man going out for assistance is also obviously not doing his injured companion any good by breaking his own leg. Will power needs to be exercised to prevent carelessness during emergencies. More care is needed, not less.

With a party of three, one of whom is severely injured, obviously one person goes for help, while the other stays with the victim. The most difficult decisions must be made by the person whose single companion has been badly hurt: whether to stay and nurse the victim or go for help—the decision must be made on the basis of whatever knowledge of the situation he has. It may be possible to get food, water, and fuel in sufficient quantities for the person to take care of himself if he is not too badly hurt; the judgment has to be made on the spot.

Fortunately, the kinds of injuries that result in such dilemmas are rare in the backcountry. A sprained ankle, broken leg, or flesh wound would be far more likely. Wounds heal themselves if they are kept clean, and infecting bacteria are much rarer in the wilds than in civilization. A victim of a broken leg will usually be able to take care of himself while waiting for help, once the leg is splinted and supplies are gathered and conveniently placed.

GETTING LOST

The first thing to think about when you find you are lost is that this state is always only relative. You will invariably know *something* about where you are. If you sit down and think about it, you will probably find that you know a lot more than you first realized. Narrow your position down as much as possible, and figure out any information you have about landmarks and boundaries and watersheds in the area in which you are lost. Very often the idea of following water out works very well, though following the *watershed* would be a better way of putting it. This is because in many kinds of country following the ridgelines will get you out much faster than fighting along the creek bottoms. In any case, don't blindly follow either one; think about the area you are lost in first.

You are unlikely to travel very far between the time you feel you know where you are and the time you decide you are lost. Figure out a systematic way to return to your position. Use your map and compass if you have

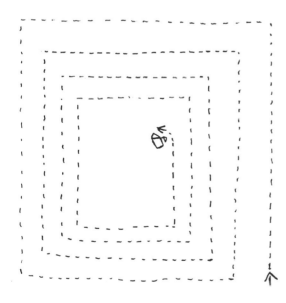

A search pattern which can be used if you are near camp but visibility is poor. Make the initial square much larger than you think necessary, so that you can be sure the perimeter surrounds your camp. Make the reduction in size on each sweep small enough so that you won't miss the camp.

273

them. Do not go running back trying to find a familiar place, which will probably just leave you more confused. You are almost certain to have enough information to find your way back—*if* you proceed systematically and avoid attempted shortcuts. If you are near your camp in forest or similar terrain, follow a search pattern like that shown in the diagram.

Don't guess where you are or what direction you should go and then gamble heavily on that guess. Allow yourself the widest possible latitude for error, and then follow a plan that allows for it. Don't thrash around for two days looking for a trail when you are not sure you're even in the right valley. Instead, head for a road that you can't miss, and then follow it out.

Remember that the general principles of route finding are the same whether you are lost or not. Keep a record of your bearings on the way out, so that you won't get more confused. Without a compass, you can still maintain a straight line of travel by lining up two objects at different distances. Find a third object on the same line before you reach the first.

WALKING OUT

If you get lost, lose your equipment, run out of supplies, or have some similar crisis, don't immediately start working up images of the Donner Party trapped by the great blizzard in the Sierras. The North American wilderness is generally a fairly friendly place. In the woods, you can build a fire every night and stay reasonably comfortable even without food for a few days. You can walk a long way in that time if you keep your wits about you. In really remote areas, you could start eating grubs, lizards, frogs, or something else easy to trap, and keep going for the better part of the summer. The point is simply that in most wilderness in temperate seasons, a sensible person will always manage to get out—a little the worse (or better) for wear, perhaps, but he will get out.

In difficult environments and seasons you may have to be a little more clever. If you are lost in the desert and you find a nice waterhole, don't take a drink and wander on—at least until you have planned out a good course of action. If you leave it, mark your trail back. In winter with a broken ski or snowshoe in a storm, dig yourself a snowhole for a shelter, and then stay where it's warm while the storm blows over and you fix your transportation. A good shelter in a bad mountain storm is the place to stay while the weather is bad, unless you're well equipped for anything. In all these cases, remember that your body has a good reserve supply of essentials, but they can be depleted in a hurry by the weather. If you can outlast the elements, do so rather than trying to challenge them at their worst. When you are in difficulty don't try to fight nature; you will lose. In the desert, for example, if your water container is too small and you get dehydrated making it to your waterhole, spend a day there tanking up and allowing your body to recover before you try to make another leg of your journey.

All this desperate-situation advice is quite unnecessary for the well-prepared wilderness traveler under most circumstances. Follow normal safety rules in preparing your trips, and you are unlikely to run into such problems. Most such survival crises don't happen to backpackers but to mechanized travelers when their machines break down.

LEAVING WORD WHEN YOU GO IN

It is only prudent and courteous when you head for the backcountry to leave word with some responsible person. Tell him where you are going, side trips you might make, when you plan to be out, and when to assume you are in trouble. This precaution should not be ignored unless your passing would never be noticed. If your wife or your job is expecting you on Tuesday, they will let someone know when you don't get back. If your car is left sitting by the trailhead, someone will eventually come looking. Be reasonable enough to let them know where to look, so that they won't have an army searching an area of hundreds of square miles. Also, as long as they're going to be looking anyway, why not give them a chance to find you in a day or two, instead of your body a month later?

Backpackers tend to feel naturally reluctant about cramping themselves with registration systems, but the proper response is to improve the methods rather than ignore them and provoke responsible authorities into tightening up. Personally, I think there is a lot to be said in favor of removing the responsibility for rescues from the shoulders of the Park Service, the Forest Service, and similar administrators—it too often tempts them into promulgating books full of rules, and every citizen over the age of consent ought to have the right to be a fool and get killed if he wants to. How

275

ever, as long as administrators are expected by the public to mount searches and rescue efforts, it behooves those of us who want to roam to make those rescues as inexpensive as possible. The alternative is idiotic regulation like that in Grand Teton National Park, where travel alone off the trails is illegal.

A solo traveler especially, might want someone to know where to pick him up in case he should happen to break a leg. If you know that a friend will come looking when you're not back on Tuesday, you can lie back and relax and eat your spare food while you wait. Allow enough leeway in your schedule to take care of unforseen delays, and be sure to mention all possible changes in plans. Don't forget that if you change your mind at the trailhead, all you have to do is leave a note with the car.

Besides calling friends or family to leave word, there are various formal systems of reporting. The oldest is to leave a note on your automobile. Many wilderness areas have registration systems along the trail, but these don't allow for much detail and they aren't usually checked in the off seasons. So leave word somewhere else, too. Registration with the rangers is a common system, especially in the national parks, and this is one of the methods which arouses the most opposition among climbers and backpackers, creating many unfortunate hostilities and misunderstandings. In remote areas, leave word with law-enforcement officers or a storekeeper in the last town you pass.

Objectionable registration systems need to be changed, but their virtues and purpose in aiding rescues ought to be mentioned here. Try to cooperate with the rangers where registration systems exist, and if you ignore them, at least leave word with a friend who can tell someone where you went in case you get hurt. Some registration systems also have the admirable purpose of preventing excessive pressure on delicate areas. Cooperate, please!

One of the best systems going is the kind operated by the Rocky Mountain Rescue Group in Boulder, Colorado. There is a phone number with which one can register at any time of the day or night. This is cheap, since it can use a recording, and it doesn't require anyone to drive a hundred miles out of their way to register somewhere. You just call the number when you wake up at four in the morning and decide to climb a mountain, and then you call back when you return. It is particularly worthwhile in a town where there are many college students or out-of-town visitors who don't have any friends to leave word with.

However you leave word of your intentions, don't forget to let whoever was responsible know when you are out. Every rescue group remembers a few thoughtless individuals who got back from the mountains, forgot to let Aunt Tillie know they had come home, and took off for a wild weekend in Mexico with six-dozen searchers and four helicopters combing the hills in blowing sleet.

EMERGENCY SUPPLIES

The equipment and provisions which you will need in case of an emergency vary with the sort of trip you are taking, its remoteness, the kind of country, and the season. Potable water is plentiful in some places, but not in others. Low temperatures that might be expected will obviously influence your choice of basic and extra clothing. Even on day hikes, however, there are essentials you should never travel without:

    First-aid kit
    Pocket knife
    Matches in waterproof container and candle or other fire-starter
    Compass
    Map
    Flashlight
    Extra food
    Windtight parka
    Rain gear where needed
    Water bottle(s)
    Water-purification tablets where needed

Each person will add his own essentials: a whistle for signaling, parachute cord for many purposes, and so on. I include some of these in my first-aid kit. A generous emergency supply of matches should be carried separately and must be left untouched by daily needs. Even if you're a great fire builder, wet and windy weather combined with cold hands can use a lot of matches getting a flame going. Special equipment like skis may require special repair items, and these are obviously essential for emergencies. Extra food should be of a type which can be eaten uncooked if necessary. A piece of steel wool makes very good kindling. Use it well—it only goes once.

In some places—the mountains, for example—sunglasses and sunburn preventatives rank as essential, since snow blindness or serious sunburn may result from forgetting them. A suitable hat is vital in the desert, and extra clothes are important survival items whenever the weather may turn cold.

First Aid and Emergency Medicine 16

It is a cliché that the best cure for accidents is prevention, but it is true nevertheless. I don't happen to believe in safety at any cost, but anyone who does a lot of traveling in the wilderness will take his risks with some premeditation rather than out of sheer ignorance. Five days travel from the road is a long way from help.

There isn't much reason to be frightened about wilderness travel. The hazards to a healthy person in most types of terrain are pretty minimal. The point is simply that self-reliance applies to medical problems as well as other aspects of life when you are in the backcountry. The more that you and your companions know about first aid and subsequent care the better off you will be. You may never have to use what you know, or the use may be confined to patching up the victims of auto accidents while you are driving to and from the hills. But you'll never regret any time you invest in learning first aid.

PHYSICAL CONDITION

Sensible backpacking requires that you have some idea of what shape you are in before you start. A checkup by a doctor from time to time is a good idea, and it is mandatory for older people who are taking up backpacking after a long sedentary period. A remote wilderness peak is not the place to find out that you have a heart condition. If you have any unusual problems which require special attention or drugs, it is important to carry whatever you might need on the trip. It is also essential that your companions know about your condition and what to do in case of difficulties. A diabetic, for example, needs to pay special attention to his diet on a strenuous trip, and it is important that his companions be able to recognize and treat coma and insulin shock. Someone allergic to bee stings might have to carry adrenalin, and again his companions should know what to do in an emergency.

There is very little information in this chapter on the treatment of problems which might arise from a preexisting condition that would have been detected in a physical examination. Ask your doctor, and tell the other members of your party anything they might need to know. With limited space, it's impossible to discuss all the possible accidental injuries that might arise in the woods with normal, healthy people. While at the doctor's you should get a tetanus booster. Trails traveled by animals are full of the microorganisms that cause tetanus.

I strongly recommend that anyone interested in wilderness travel learn as much first aid as possible. Take the Red Cross courses, and check with any mountaineering clubs in your area to see if they give advanced courses beyond what the Red Cross teaches. The Seattle Mountaineers give a particularly outstanding course, and the textbook for it, *Medicine for Mountaineering*, edited by James A. Wilkerson, is excellent.

First aid is what you do under normal circumstances until the doctor comes. Since no layman has enough training to understand all he should about injuries, the Red Cross courses wisely limit themselves to the care that would be advisable under the assumption that a doctor will be available in a short time. Obviously, this is not the case if you are thirty or forty hard miles from the nearest road. Under such conditions, you must at the very least plan on nursing a seriously injured person for some time.

CARING FOR AN INJURED PERSON

Some general principles apply to the care of anyone who is sick or injured. The first is to think. Obvious as this may seem from the vantage point of an easy chair, it often takes a good deal of self-discipline in an actual accident situation. The first thing you have to do is to evaluate the situation, which may take a matter of an hour or a few seconds. In case of severe persisting danger, the first thing you might have to do is to get yourself and the victim to a safe place. Such situations are rare, and it is never good to move an injured person before examining him carefully. But if he has been hit on the head with a rock you will do him no good by getting knocked on the skull yourself.

Aside from dangerous positions, the thing to check first is the possible presence of one of the medical emergency cases: severe bleeding, cessation of breathing, or poisoning. The last is unlikely in wilderness circumstances, although it happens. The first two are quite possible, and they require immediate action on your part—stopping the bleeding and giving artificial respiration if breathing has stopped.

Having taken care of the emergency cases and removed yourself and your victim from imminent danger of lightning strikes, drowning, or falling off cliffs, take a few minutes to really take stock of the situation. There are a lot of things you are going to have to do, and your patient will be better off if you take time to plan them. You have to:

1. Thoroughly examine the injured person to find out what is wrong, as best you can.
2. Get help, send someone else for it, or decide that circumstances make this unnecessary or impractical.
3. Give whatever first aid is necessary to the injured person, splinting broken bones and so forth.
4. Give supportive care to the injured person, and perhaps move him to a better spot, especially if the weather is cold or stormy.
5. Talk to the victim, who is presumably your friend; calming him and comforting him is as important as taking care of physical injuries.
6. Write down all pertinent information, including what happened, what you found, what you did, and when each occurred. The sequence may be very important to the diagnosis of a doctor taking over. Don't rely on memory.

Deciding on the order of these steps, priorities, and thoroughness is a matter of judgment and the particular situation, but make sure you exercise that judgment rather than simply go on at random. If you are dealing with a serious injury but have plenty of people, and help is a couple of hours down the trail, you should have a couple of people on their way as soon as you've taken care of the hurry cases. On the other hand, if there is only one other healthy person and help is a long way off, you may need his assistance in moving the victim and getting him into a shelter before he goes for help. Variations are infinite, and you are bound to make mistakes. The important thing is to think everything out before you go off half-cocked and make the situation worse. Force yourself to be cool and methodical.

TRAUMATIC INJURIES

Most people engaged in backpacking are fairly healthy, whether they are young or old. If someone does get suddenly sick, it is usually from the kind of infectious diseases that don't flourish in the wilderness. After one has walked into the woods for a week, any medical problems that arise will probably be from falling off a cliff, being hit on the head by a branch, cutting oneself with an ax, or something similar. Such injuries are *traumatic* injuries, those which result from some violence done to the body.

Traumatic injuries are also the cause of the major first-aid *emergency*, severe bleeding. Blood is essential to the body's functioning, it is under a good deal of pressure as it leaves the heart, and there is a limited amount of the stuff in the body. It follows that SEVERE BLEEDING MUST BE STOPPED RIGHT AWAY. Get something on the wound and apply pressure with your hand. Sterile dressings are ideal, but they are rarely at hand, and stopping the bleeding immediately is more important than sterility, so grab anything, slap it on the wound, and clamp down. Then hang onto it, and the bleeding will stop. *Don't peek*. Maintain the pressure without trying to look for around fifteen minutes after the major bleeding stops. Otherwise you will dislodge the clot that has been forming, and you'll have to start all over.

There are a lot of suggested ways to tell the difference between venous and arterial bleeding, but direct pressure is the way to stop either one, so if you are in doubt, don't worry about it, just put pressure on the wound. The essential difference is clear: arterial pressure is much greater.

An arterial wound spurts hard, and you have to press hard to stop it. It may squirt a considerable distance with each beat of the heart. Venous bleeding is slower, steadier, under much less pressure, and much easier to stop.

Remember that *the treatment for bleeding is direct pressure with whatever is immediately at hand.* Elevation of an arm or a leg will be of some additional help. Unless you know the pressure points from lots of practice, don't worry about them; you'll just waste time. Everyone has learned something about tourniquets somewhere. Don't use them. The need for them is rare, and they are very dangerous. It is unlikely that you would ever have to use one.

While you are holding onto that wound, or after you have found that there isn't any severe bleeding, you can start thinking about the other things that are or might be wrong with your friend. Traumatic injuries include burns, wounds, broken bones and injuries to the joints, and various kinds of internal injuries. If you are hurt, or if someone you are backpacking with is hurt, you probably already know a lot about what happened, so you should be able to tell what sorts of injuries are likely. Have a talk with your friend and see what he can tell about what happened and what is the matter. Even if he is unconscious, you know a lot. If he fell off a cliff and he isn't conscious, chances are pretty good that he hit his head.

SHOCK

One of the common characteristics of traumatic injuries is shock. Basically, traumatic shock results from a loss of blood pressure, and you can expect some shock with any injury. It is vitally important that you treat for shock from the very beginning. Shock is no joke—it is what kills most people who die from accidents. In a wilderness situation rapid treatment is even more important than on a city street, because no blood transfusions are going to be available an hour later. Shock is the kind of disorder that keeps building and feeding on its own symptoms, so you have to stop it as soon as you can.

Since there is a drop in blood pressure with shock, it stands to reason that not as much blood will get up to the brain of a standing person. One way or another, he is quite likely to go down, so you should get him to lie down before he falls over and hits his head in the bargain. Feet can be raised slightly unless you have reason to suspect head or internal injuries. Keep the victim lying down.

Again, if blood pressure is lowered, you can expect that circulation is going to be impaired and that he is going to have a hard time keeping warm. You have to help him to retain his body heat. How vigorous the treatment should be depends on conditions. If it is a pleasant temperature out, just cover your friend with a couple of sweaters, but if there is snow on the ground and a cold wind is blowing, you may have to get into a sleeping bag with him inside a tent. You don't want to make him hot and sweaty, but it is vital that you keep him from getting chilled. A person in shock is likely to be thirsty. He has usually lost blood or fluid from the blood, and his body needs to replace it. If your friend is conscious, let him have sips of water or (better) warm bouillon or soup. If you use water, put a pinch of salt in each cup. Don't give any liquids orally to an unconscious or semiconscious person, who may inhale them. Also avoid giving liquids to anyone who is nauseated (common in shock) or if you suspect internal injuries. If the liquid makes him throw up, he will lose more than he has gained.

Finally, psychological factors are very important in shock. If your friend is really hurt, he isn't going to be too happy. It is up to you to reassure him and give him confidence by talking to him and handling the situation calmly and well. Don't make tactless comments which will make things worse, and don't let anyone else do so. If you have a hysterical type in the company, get him away from the injured person. On the other hand, don't make inane comments to the victim like "Everything is okay." He may be woozy, but he knows everything is not okay. Tell him what you're doing, and be sensibly optimistic.

Symptoms of shock include general pallor, cold skin, sweating when the person isn't hot, fainting, a panicky, alarmed, incoherent state of mind, listlessness, dilated pupils, and a weak, thready pulse. However, don't wait for symptoms to appear. Treat for shock in the case of any traumatic injury.

BURNS

Burns other than minor ones are not very common in the wilderness, but they do happen. Treatment is simple, although the injury is not. Minor burns can be immersed in cold water until they feel more comfortable, and then bandaged. With serious burns, expect severe shock and treat for it. Burns are very painful—and this alone can induce shock—and fluids from the blood are lost in quantity through the damaged cell walls. The burn should be covered with a sterile dressing, and the victim should be gotten to medical care as soon as possible.

WOUNDS

Wounds are the most common sort of injury in the woods. The major danger is bleeding, which has already been discussed. Some bleeding is a good thing. With puncture wounds, it may be a good idea to induce bleeding to clean the wound out, particularly if the puncture is from some object that may have come in contact with animal dung.

Once the bleeding has been stopped and the victim is under care for shock, you have to worry about infection. This is one area where the wilderness has good advantages. Harmful bacteria are considerably less common than they are back home, but they are around nonetheless. What you actually do will depend on the wound. The best first step is probably to wash your hands well. If the wound is dirty, wash it too. The body can handle a certain number of outside bacteria, but large quantities of germs are carried in with dirt, and the dirt particles are irritants in themselves. Get the wound clean as soon as possible. There is some natural anesthesia at the beginning, and cleaning will hurt more later. Once the wound is clean, cover it with a clean sterile dressing and fasten that with tape or bandages. If you don't have a sterile dressing in the first-aid kit, make one from the cleanest lint-free cloth you have. You can sterilize it by boiling or singeing it in a flame for a while. Don't get a lot of fancy ideas about stitching up the wound. That is a good way to seal in pockets of infection, causing them to spread. The wound will heal faster if it is stitched and *if* there is no infection, but it will heal more surely if it is left open and covered with a dressing.

BROKEN BONES

Besides wounds, broken bones, sprains, and other joint injuries are the most likely medical problems in the backcountry. First aid is treatment for shock and immobilization of the injury. If a bone is broken completely the rigidity of the limb has been destroyed, and motion will cause the jagged ends of the bones to injure the surrounding tissue. A splint should hold the limb rigid so that this can't occur. There are many bones and joints in the body and many kinds of injuries that can occur. A few general rules apply.

Some fractures are open, that is, the skin has been broken either by the end of the broken bone or by the impact that caused the break. In either case infection is a strong possibility. You should treat the wound like any other wound, stopping any bleeding, cleaning, and applying a sterile dressing. At the same time, however, you should recognize that this is an especially dangerous wound, since an infection could involve the bone, and bone infections are dangerous. If the bone end is protruding, it is not generally advisable to pull the bone back under the skin, but this will be necessary if you can't get the person out within a day or two. Clean a protruding bone end off with a sterile pad and Phisohex or Zepharin. Once the wound is dressed, a compound fracture should be splinted like other fractures.

While splinting a fracture, move the affected part as little as possible. Don't try to set it—that's what doctors get paid for, and they can do it just as well next week if you don't get out today. You may have to straighten a limb to splint it. Do the moving gently and slowly, with some tension on the end of the limb. It will hurt the victim, but use his pain as a guide to whether you are doing more damage. Extreme pain means you're injuring tissue. Finding splints where you are may require some imagination on your part, but it usually isn't too hard. The basic principle is to immobilize the joints above and below the injury, so that the fracture won't be moved around. Other parts of the body can be used as splints. A leg can be splinted to the other leg, a finger to another finger, the arm to the upper part of the body, with the upper arm along the side and the forearm and hand across the chest—the same position as in pledging allegiance to the flag. You can use sticks, air mattresses, ski poles, and pack frames for splints. Get the limb in a position that is fairly comfortable for the victim. His pain is your best guide to whether the bone end is pressing somewhere it shouldn't. Try to splint things in their normal positions of rest. Fingers curve and elbows and knees are slightly bent, not straight. If you splint to another part of the body, have some cloth preventing two layers of skin from touching, and pad joints where they press together—knees, ankles, finger joints.

Severe sprains and joint injuries should be treated like fractures. They may be breaks, and you can't tell. The general rule is to treat any suspected fracture as though it were one. Dislocations should generally be treated the same way. Fingers and shoulders are the most common. Fingers can just be splinted and left alone. A dislocated shoulder may need treatment. If a doctor can be reached by hiking on out, just put the injured arm in a sling and walk. If you won't get out for a few days and the circulation to the hand is impaired, you may have to do something to prevent damage to the limb. Have the victim lie down, and sit down on his injured side facing him. Take off one of your boots, put your foot in his armpit, and pull on the arm. Just pull steadily, and look at the scenery or something. You have to overcome his muscle spasm. This won't occur until *his* muscle gets tired, and that won't occur until *your* muscles get tired. Keep pulling, and after around ten or twenty minutes his joint will pop back in and he'll heave a sigh of relief. Then put on the sling. Don't ever try to reduce a fracture like this unless you have to. A bone can be chipped or a nerve pinched.

Whenever you are applying a splint, allow for adjustments of the ties or tape in case of swelling. Swelling will normally occur after a fracture, and you don't want circulation to be cut off. If possible, you should be able to get at the toes or fingers occasionally to check for circulation problems.

Fractures of the spinal column are very special cases. The spinal cord runs down the middle of the spine, and if this cord is severed, the victim will be permanently paralyzed. If the injury is in the neck, he will die. If you have any reason to suspect a back injury, you must not move the person in a way that could cause further injury. Very careful movement and splinting is necessary to prevent possible severing of the spinal cord.

Symptoms of a back injury include local tenderness, inability to move one or both the lower extremities, inability to feel your touch or pinch on one or both of the lower extremities, a prickling sensation on one or both of the lower extremities. The abnormalities just mentioned occur when the spinal cord is already damaged or under pressure, but their absence does not mean there has been no back injury. It simply means that the spinal cord has not yet been damaged. Don't be the one to damage it. If you sus-

287

pect a back injury, assume there is one and splint it. All this applies even more to neck injuries. A neck injury must be supported with a small pad behind the neck, about the size of a pair of street socks rolled up, and then the whole head must be held immobile. The sleeping bag makes a good splint for the head. The victim has to be placed on something rigid like a pack frame. His head goes on top of the middle of the sleeping bag on top of the frame. Don't forget the pad under the neck. Then half the bag can be rolled on each side of his head to form a large pad. The head and chest are then strapped down so that the neck cannot be moved. The greatest care should be taken in moving the victim onto the splint. Several people are needed to raise the person a few inches while the pack frame, pad, and sleeping bag are slid under him. One person should hold the head, very carefully and under slight tension as the lift is made together on his command. The same sort of procedure and the same rigid splint are needed for any back injury, and a pack frame with a sleeping pad is an excellent splint.

Rib fractures are rarely serious, and they don't require any splinting. Normally, the chest muscles become rigid around the injury and splint it fairly well. If the victim is in considerable pain from breathing, but isn't short of breath, you can tape along the line of the ribs from breastbone to splint, just below the nipple and just after the victim has exhaled completely. This prevents the injured side of the chest from moving so much, but for this reason the tape should be removed after a day or so if you are still in the backcountry.

Don't forget about shock with fractures. Even without an open fracture, there is always bleeding—that's what the swelling is. Loss of a quart of blood is normal with a break in a large bone like the thigh or pelvis. Multiple breaks cause a lot of bleeding. In a wilderness situation you must be very careful of this. Your friend won't die of a broken leg, but if you aren't careful he might die of the resulting shock.

INJURIES TO THE VITAL ORGANS

Traumatic injuries can also result in damage to the organs in the body cavity or to the head, with or without an outside wound. Such injuries are not common in normal backpacking circumstances. You may slip and break your leg on the trail or open up your hand with a knife, but unless you took a long fall, you would not be likely to suffer internal injuries. You should recognize the possibility, however, if someone has received a bad blow to some part of the body. Chest and head injuries will be considered separately.

The symptoms you should look for in circumstances that might result in internal injury are pain, nausea, bloody excretions or vomit, and most important, shock. Internal bleeding is just as serious as external, but there is nothing you can do to stop it. If an internal injury is indicated your friend will need surgery. Treat him for shock, don't give him anything by mouth, and do something to get him to a hospital.

Chest injuries other than a broken rib are also pretty unlikely. In rare cases a broken rib may penetrate into the chest cavity and puncture a lung, causing severe pain, some difficulty in breathing, and coughing up of frothy blood. Have the victim lie on the *injured* side. If he lies on the other side, the blood will run into the good lung and cause trouble there. Another uncommon chest injury is caused by a complete puncture of the chest wall, say by a ski pole or ice ax. This causes what is known as a sucking chest wound. The action of the breathing muscles forces air in and out of the wound, and the victim cannot get any air into the good lung. The hole has to be sealed up so that the victim can breathe. Use a piece of plastic, a gauze pad covered with Vaseline, or something, but don't delay. One final injury about which you can do something is known as flail chest. If the chest receives a massive blow in a fall, the ribs on one side may be so shattered that the whole chest wall loses its rigidity, even though there is no puncture. It flaps uselessly in and out, and again the victim can't breathe. Roll him onto the injured side, with a rolled-up jacket or a day pack under the injury. The other side of the chest will then be able to pump air in and out of the lung, and the breathing difficulty will decrease.

There are some other types of chest injury which won't be mentioned in detail here, because there is nothing you can do except to get the victim in a position where breathing is most comfortable. With any chest injury, the victim must have medical help quickly.

HEAD INJURIES

The brain is a unique organ both because of its function and the way it is enclosed in a rigid case of bone. The skull is intended as protection for the brain, and obviously any injury to it is a matter of concern. Basically, there isn't anything you can do for skull or brain damage except to get the victim evacuated, but there are a few special problems you should be aware of. If a person receives a blow to the head and is unconscious, this is a sign that his brain has been injured. Like any other part of the body, the brain may swell up after an injury, but since it is encased in the skull, there is no place for it to swell, and pressure will build up. For this reason, a person may be unconscious from a blow to the head, recover completely, and then start showing signs of a head injury again minutes or hours later. After any period of unconsciousness, this should be watched for, since it indicates a very dangerous situation.

Normal signs of head injury include irrationality, grogginess, nausea, unequal pupil size, complete or partial paralysis, or leaking blood or straw-colored liquid from the nose or ears. Bleeding may be local however, rather than indicating skull damage.

CARE OF AN UNCONSCIOUS VICTIM

Unconsciousness may result from head injury, electrical shock, suffocation, or various other things, but the first concern of the person giving care (after severe bleeding) must always be the victim's breathing. If he isn't breathing, you have to give artificial respiration. This is simple enough with the mouth-to-mouth method, but you ought to practice it on one of the Red Cross dummies. To perform resuscitation, turn the victim on his back, clear any vomit or other debris from his mouth, get the tongue away from the back of the throat by tilting the head back or pulling the jaw forward, pinch the nostrils shut, and blow into the victim's mouth. Remove your mouth, take another breath, and do it again. You should hear the air coming out of his lungs, and see his chest rising when you blow. If you don't, something is stuck in the airway. Roll him over, hit him in the back, clear the mouth, and try again. Continue artificial respiration as long as there is any chance the victim is alive.

Even if the unconscious person is breathing, you must still worry about the airway. In a coma, the muscles may relax more than in sleep, and the tongue may drop to the back of the throat, suffocating the victim. Place the unconscious person on his side, the head tilted down to prevent

290

the tongue dropping, and to allow any vomit to escape without choking the victim. If the victim must be kept on his back, he should be attended all the time. Don't forget to keep him warm.

HEAT AND COLD

The temperature of the environment can cause problems for anyone who is caught unprepared. Too much sun can cause overheating. If you're out in the sun too long, you or one of your companions may start to feel faint and look pale, suffering from heat exhaustion. Skin temperature will be about normal. The solution is to rest in the shade, drink some liquids, and get some salt. Heat exhaustion is not serious, and a little rest will bring you back to normal. Heat stroke is very serious and must be treated immediately. The victim collapses or feels dizzy, and the skin is hot, red, and dry. Heat stroke is fatal unless the victim is cooled off right away. Wet cloths or immersion in cool water would be possible methods.

Don't get sunburned. Use a skin preparation and put on clothing before you burn. For complete protection of exposed parts of the body zinc oxide ointment can be used.

Cooling of the body can also be a problem. Inadequate clothing and not enough food can easily result in chilling when a cold wind comes up, especially if the clothing is wet. If the body core becomes chilled, the victim can die from exposure. Watch your companions, and be especially alert to someone who has suffered an accident. If the person starts to become short-tempered or irrational, look for signs that he is getting cold, perhaps bluish lips or nails. He needs warming and some sugary foods. As the body temperature drops, the victim will start to be clumsy, will become listless and incoherent, and will finally start to cough up froth and become unconscious. He has to be made warm. Get into a sleeping bag with him. Give him warm sugary liquids if he is conscious. This cooling of the body core is known as hypothermia, or exposure. For an accident victim during cold weather it is an especially dangerous possibility in combination with shock.

Frostbite will not occur in backpacking situations, unless the victim is already suffering from hypothermia or from another injury that has affected circulation to a limb. The best cure is prevention, warming extremities when they start to feel numb, changing socks, and so forth. The old advice to rub a frostbitten part with snow is so grotesquely absurd, I can't imagine where it started. Rubbing shouldn't be used at all once a part is actually frozen. Proper treatment of frostbite is rapid rewarming in water of 108°–112° F., but it must be no hotter and checked with a thermometer, and possibilities for this treatment in a backpacking situation are limited. Usually, it would be best to walk out on a frozen foot and get to a hospital. After thawing, a person whose foot was frostbitten is a litter case. Any friction will cause severe tissue damage. True frostbite with deep freezing is quite unusual and unnecessary in any normal backpacking situation. Frost-nip of the face, ears, and nose in very cold winds should be watched for, and warmed right away without rubbing.

BITES

There are a lot of little critters out there waiting to bite you, but fortunately most won't do you any permanent damage. Snakes and black widows get the most publicity, but the species in the United States are rarely lethal. Multiple bites or bites of children account for nearly all fatalities. Carry a snake-bite kit in snake country and season. A small incision is made over each fang mark with a sterile razor or knife blade, and as much venom as possible is drawn out by suction. Meanwhile, spreading of venom should be slowed by keeping the victim quiet and tying a wide constriction band above the bite. The constriction band is not a tourniquet and should not cut off circulation. As the swelling moves up the limb, another set of incisions can be made four inches or so above the first and suction applied there, but don't do any more cutting after that. Infection is likely to be a worse problem than the bite if a long line of cuts is made.

Remember that poisonous snakes in the United States are not terribly dangerous. Keep the victim calm and reassure him. Incisions should be only about one-half inch long and the same depth. On the hand or foot, they should be even shallower, and great care should be taken to avoid cutting nerves or blood vessels. There is little chance of death even with an untreated bite. Keeping the victim quiet is probably more important than incision and suction.

Scorpions and black widows are also not likely to be lethal in this country except rarely to children and older people. Again the victim should be kept quiet and given care, and medical help should be sent for if spasms and other symptoms indicate the bite or sting was poisonous. But incision and suction will not help and should not be performed.

Ticks can carry several diseases. In tick country, keep pants legs tucked in or closed and use repellents. Alternatively, the body can be inspected every few hours, since ticks take some time to settle down and start biting. In removing a tick, the head of which has become imbedded, be sure to get the whole tick out by pulling very gently, and then wash the wound well. If any parts of the head are left in the bite a doctor should be visited when you return from the trip.

Animal bites carry the danger of rabies, and the animal should be captured if possible, followed by a visit to the doctor. Even though the chance of rabies may be remote, it is fatal once it appears, so this is not an area to take chances.

CARE AND TRANSPORTATION

No hard and fast rules can be laid down for the problem of how to get an injured person out of the woods. A few general comments are worth making, however. The first is that haste is only rarely necessary. If your friend breaks his leg, take care of him. Don't try a lot of breakneck heroics. He will be in a lot better shape if you nurse him for a week where you are than if you try to pick him up and carry him out that night. Internal injuries and the like are urgent, but there is still the matter of balancing the advantages of speed against the damage that may be done in getting the victim out a day earlier. Don't underestimate the difficulty of carrying out someone who is really hurt.

A man with a broken arm isn't an emergency at all. Get a good night's sleep, and then you carry the gear and he can carry himself. Someone who can't walk will have to be carried out on a stretcher. If you have a large party, you can improvise a litter out of packframes and manage all right, but with a small party, send for help. Sloppy transportation is the cause of more injuries than any other mistake in first aid. Back and neck injuries especially demand getting help if at all possible. You can splint them with packframes, but getting the victim out should be done with proper equipment and methods. A treated wound or splinted fracture can wait. Internal injuries or head injuries may require fast treatment.

If you have to care for an injured person for a few days while someone goes out for help or while you wait to be missed, you have a lot of work on your hands. Cleaning a wound and changing dressings daily are important. You will probably have to sterilize cloths to do it, since your first-aid kit is bound to be of limited size. An injured person may repress the need to eliminate because of the problems involved, and extra difficulties will arise. Ultimately, for example, he won't be able to urinate if he waits too long. Ask him if he needs to go to the bathroom, and figure out a system for managing it with some kind of improvised bedpan.

Bed sores and pneumonia have to be prevented with an injured person. Lying on the same parts of the body for long periods cuts off circulation and ultimately results in tissue death and severe open sores. You will have to help your friend shift position every two hours, without fail, if he is laid out so that he can't move. At the same time, you should make him cough, especially if chest pains cause him to resist the need to do so. Fluids accumulating in the lungs make a good place for bacteria to grow, and they will cause pneumonia if they aren't coughed up.

A FINAL NOTE

Despite the many horrible possibilities discussed in this chapter, most injuries in the backcountry are not serious, and thoughtful action will take care of the situation. Panic and hasty action cause more trouble than the accidents that precipitate them.

FIRST-AID KIT

The items listed here are far from definitive. Make up your own kit and use whatever training and experience you can get as a guide. Prescription drugs are often advisable for wilderness travel, but since you will have to see a doctor for them anyway, no advice will be given here. See the book list at the end for more information:

elastic bandage—good for bandages as well as minor sprains
adhesive tape, 2″–3″ wide—the cloth kind that can be torn into narrower strips

sterile dressings
sterile razor blade
aspirin
Band-Aids
a few cotton-tipped swabs
tweezers
small bottle of aqueous Zepharin—antiseptic which doesn't sting or
   leave red coloring that masks infection
snake-bite kit (when needed)
needle
moleskin (for blisters)
soap

17 *Physical Conditioning*

Typically, at the beginning of the season the backpacker drags his winter-softened and beer-sodden body through several agonizing weekends before he begins to feel human in Saturday night's camp. One solution would be to stick to very easy trips during the first month of summer, but that would require one to make an embarrassing admission that he has fallen apart and would also severely curtail the summer program. So one puts up with aching muscles and near exhaustion.

Common as this syndrome is, nobody really advocates practicing it. So there are the annual resolutions to "stay in shape this year," sometimes carried out, but more often dropped by the wayside. This chapter is written for your time of trial—the first morning you decide to skip your situps until tomorrow. It also offers some suggestions on getting in shape for wilderness travel.

BACKPACKING AS A CONDITIONER

Backpacking itself is a good exercise, especially since it can be enjoyed at many levels of difficulty. The only problems with it are that most of us don't manage to get out often enough and that a lot of people like to do backpacking at a much more strenuous level than the one for which their daily routine prepares them. If you're satisfied with walking a few level miles to camp a couple of times a season, then you shouldn't need to undergo any special training to get in condition beforehand.

More fundamentally, most people (at least the kind of people likely to read this book) would like to stay in good physical tune. When you are out of shape, you get tired quickly, you can be injured easily, you don't feel as well, and you are subject to various unpleasantries like premature aging and heart attacks. Many sorts of exercise programs are suitable to keep you in shape, but it's more pleasant if you follow one that you enjoy. You are also more likely to keep it up. Though backpacking to me is a good deal more than a way to stay in shape, it serves that function, too.

RUNNING YOUR BODY EFFICIENTLY

Like most machines, the body operates most efficiently when it is functioning at a level well below its greatest capacity. Your car uses less gas traveling a mile at 30 mph than covering the same mile at 75 mph. Your body works the same way. A person in good shape uses fewer calories to carry a forty-pound pack ten miles than someone in poor condition does.

Both for enjoyment and safety, it is worthwhile to be in good enough shape to undertake the kind of trips you like without pushing yourself to the limit. Maintaining an extra reserve ensures that you will be able to go as well Sunday as Saturday, that you will be able to enjoy the scenery at stops instead of just lying exhausted on the turf, that the hard parts of the trip will be enjoyable rather than a torture, and that you will have a reserve in case of difficulties.

Clearly all these adjectives are relative. What is difficult terrain for the family backpacker may be an easy morning stroll for the fanatic peak bagger, and similarly what is good physical condition for one is soft for the other. This is as it should be. The governing factor is how you feel. If you're forty pounds overweight and never walk farther than your car, you have a good chance of having a cardiac arrest at an early age, and you should certainly work into backpacking slowly. If you're fit and you feel good, you can backpack as fast and as far as you want to without overtaxing your body.

STRENGTH AND ENDURANCE

The definition of good physical condition should be largely a matter of common sense. Someone spending most of his time doing hard work in the outdoors doesn't have to worry about it. He gets in good condition for his work by doing it, and he stays in condition by doing it every day. The work that most of us do these days, however, is good physical conditioning for nothing so much as lying quietly in a coffin, perhaps with martini in hand. Most people know they're in rotten shape and have a vague desire to improve. Someone is always willing to sell them a way to do it without expenditure of time or effort.

A lot of schemes that have been promoted recently of the "six-minute-a-day-do-it-in-your-office" variety are simply ludicrous. Others are all right for building up a little muscle strength, but the amount of good that this will do you in backpacking or similar activities is limited. When we talk about physical fitness we really mean many different things including strength, endurance, and flexibility. Endurance is much more likely to be a problem for the average person than strength is. He can pick up a fifty-pound pack, but he is ready to collapse after carrying it for a hundred yards.

Isometric exercises—those which build strength by contracting a muscle completely for one short period a day—have been demonstrated to be as effective as anything in building muscle strength. Such exercises are easy and take very little time, but they don't build a capacity for endurance at all.

Endurance is built up by forcing the body to develop improved capacities for breathing and circulation in the lungs, heart, and muscles. The only way to build up endurance is to engage in activities which require you to endure. There is clearly an overlapping area of activity increasing both strength and endurance, but the two are really distinct. Doing isometric exercises or heavy weight lifting won't help you climb two thousand feet on a mountain trail, because the muscles have been pushed only in short spurts.

EXERCISE FOR THE FITNESS YOU WANT

The body follows rules so in tune with common sense that our habit of looking for tricks makes them seem too straightforward to be true. Exercising in a certain way prepares the body for the same kind of strain. If you want to be able to lift a heavy weight, train for it by lifting progressively heavier weights. If you want your spine to be flexible, bend it. If you want to be able to hike over the hills for hour after hour, do work which pushes your muscles constantly over an extended period.

There is no cheap and easy way to train for endurance. There are lots of enjoyable ways, but they all require that you keep your body working continuously for at least an hour per exercise period. You may jog and walk, run and jog, play tennis, bicycle, or climb a local hill, but you have to keep your muscles working all the time. You don't have to maintain the same pace for the whole period, but you have to keep going. Run until you're out of breath, and then slow to a fast walk, or bicycle at full tilt and then slow down a little for a while. Don't collapse for five of each fifteen minutes. It is better to keep going at a lower level of performance than to push as hard as you can and then drop. Endurance training requires you to keep working.

You may feel that you need extra strength in particular muscles, that you aren't flexible enough, that your balance is poor, or what not. It is easy enough to work on any particular difficiencies in the course of almost any exercise program. If you are training for a really long backpacking trip on which you will carry brutal loads, you can always do some jogging with a heavy pack occasionally. Jogging on rough ground will do wonders for your balance and agility. You can interrupt a bicycling trip for some one-legged deep-knee bends to improve the strength of your legs or pull-ups for your arms. Put in some occasional stretching and bending exercises for flexibility.

BY THE SWEAT OF YOUR BROW

There aren't any really hard and fast rules about what kind of exercises you have to do to get fit. They don't have to be the same ones every time. If you're training for endurance, though, you can always count on the rule that you are going to have to do some work to do any good. Increased capacity for any physical activity results from taxing the body. If you can lift a 150-pound weight in a press, regularly pressing 75 pounds will not persuade the muscles to become stronger. Similarly, running at an easy pace will not force the body to improve its capacity for sustained exercise.

When you finish a training session, you have to feel as though you have been pushing yourself, if it is to do you any good. If you haven't even worked up a sweat, you won't have worked up any more endurance either. You get what you train for.

HOW FAST

People who are young and in good physical shape can push themselves as fast as they want to. If they go too hard, they'll suffer from aching muscles for a few days, the body's way of revenging itself on excess. But this really doesn't matter much. Older people and people who are terribly out of condition should take things more slowly. The older you get, the longer your body will take to respond to training, an excellent reason for staying in shape once you get there.

Have patience. As your body develops an increased capacity, increase your demands on it. A little common sense will tell you how to balance things. You should feel tired after training, but if you don't bounce back after a reasonable amount of time, you're pushing too hard.

It should go without saying that a physical examination is mandatory before you start a program of hard physical conditioning when you are out of shape. This is especially true for people over forty. People who are overweight and in poor muscular condition should get medical advice on a combined program of exercise and dieting.

HOW OFTEN

If you're trying to build yourself up, a good training session every other day will do nicely, while two sessions a week will keep you at a given level of fitness. Whether you use a rigid schedule or a less regular one is unimportant providing you can keep it up. Some people work best by scheduling an exercise period every day or every other day. Others do better by taking opportunities that arise, sometimes going out for a run and sometimes just taking the bicycle on a thirty-mile errand instead of the car. The important thing is not to let the sedentary days drag into weeks, working out three days in a row and then stopping for ten. Good results do depend on *regular* exercise.

If you go on a backpacking trip over the weekend, two more sessions of exercise on Tuesday and Thursday will keep your capacity for work building up without costing you too much time. Weekends alone produce results much more slowly. The body is all tuned up on Monday morning, but by Friday it has lagged back into the city patterns and requires the whole weekend to get used to hard exercise again.

Another season. Backpacking on skis in the winter is a good way to stay in shape, besides having a special fascination of its own. On a ski mountaineering trip in Rocky Mountain National Park.

DO SOMETHING YOU ENJOY

Those endowed with Puritan ethics and iron will can keep up the most boring exercise routines every day for their whole lives, and I applaud them. Their superior moral fiber is an inspiration to us all. But I find that daily setting-up routines lasting an hour or so are a colossal bore. I need exercises with some inherent interest or I soon stop doing them. The trick is to find some things you like to do that are also good training, and then do one of them at least every other day.

Running and jogging are great exercises if you like them enough or if you have someplace to go that is interesting enough to keep you happy. Beaches are fantastic conditioners and interesting enough to make running a pleasure. Running to or from work is great, providing you can manage the practical problems of dressing and showers. Bicycling on some of your regular trips tends to be even better, because the bicycle has a much greater range.

Variety helps the jaded muscles to keep going. Go swimming on Monday, bicycle on Wednesday, play tennis on Friday, and go backpacking over the weekend. It's more interesting than setting-up exercises every morning, anyway.

You can avoid the winter doldrums by not putting your equipment away during the cold months. Try cross-country skiing or snowshoeing. You may find that backpacking in winter is even more enjoyable than in summer.

Mountain Walking 18

The mountains provide one of the most interesting and challenging environments for the backpacker. My own vision of paradise would not be complete without a range of jagged, snowcapped peaks. The basic principles of backpacking are the same in the mountains as anywhere else, but a little extra care and equipment may be needed by those whose experience is limited to the flatlands. Also, on more difficult mountain terrain, special skills are essential for safe travel.

THE MOUNTAIN ENVIRONMENT

It is characteristic of all mountain ranges to have weather conditions which are more variable and harsher than the gentler country around them. Higher altitude means colder temperatures, but it also means less atmospheric protection from the rays of the sun. Even more important, mountains present a barrier to catch weather systems moving toward them. By forcing the air in those systems to go over or around them, the mountains are likely to produce turbulent winds, rapid temperature changes, and often storms. Mountains may even generate their own miniature weather systems, producing thunderstorms, and then attracting the lightning from them.

Mountain terrain is generally more rugged and difficult than that of the land surrounding it, although there are exceptions. Difficulties may range from steep trails to glaciers, snow slopes, and cliffs. As a general rule, travel in mountains is slower, because of the need to do a lot of climbing. My own general rule is that each thousand feet of altitude gain takes about as much time and energy as three miles of horizontal progress. If you need to go over a couple of passes during the day, rising and dropping several thousand feet for each one, you may have a long, hard day even though the distance you cover is only five or six miles.

Since the mountains in this country range from wooded hills to sandstone monoliths and glaciated crags, generalized statements about them are hard to make, but as a rule, one can say that in the high country the weather will be rougher and more erratic, the environment will be consistently harsher, and the ecology will be more fragile than in the surrounding country.

THE VARIETY OF NORTH AMERICAN MOUNTAINS

The meaning of the word *mountain* is rather varied, depending on what part of the continent you happen to be occupying. The ancient and worn-down mountains of Virginia would be foothills in some other states. From the point of view of technique, backpacking on a mountain which is wooded all the way to the top is not very different from traveling in the surrounding country, except that the going is slower. Timberline is a good dividing point, indicating that the conditions above are too harsh to permit tree growth. Above timberline the weather is harder, shelter may be difficult to find, and fuel is generally unavailable.

Where mountains are wooded and rounded off, there is really not much need to consider special techniques. Hills are longer, weather patterns may be influenced by the mountains, and of course the tops of the hills will be cooler and more exposed to wind or snow than the country below. It is above timberline, though, that these differences in degree generally amount to a difference in kind.

Harsh mountain conditions result from a combination of altitude, latitude, and situation. Timberline in the Colorado Rockies will probably be reached between eleven thousand and twelve thousand feet; in the White Mountains of New Hampshire it may be below five thousand feet. In British Columbia and Alaska, glaciers may drop all the way to the sea. The mountains of North America are as varied as the continent itself—no book can list enough rules to cover all the situations. Watch for the special problems presented by the mountains, and avoid them if you are not equipped to cope with them. This applies to every backpacker from the rank beginner to the most experienced mountaineer. The key to safety in the mountains is respect for their power and variable temperament. As you get to know them better, you will be able to undertake more difficult routes with confidence and safety, but as you do you will gain more and more respect for mountain hazards.

DANGERS IN THE MOUNTAINS

The greatest danger in the mountains is bad weather. Anyone can fall off a cliff, and even experienced travelers do so once in a while, but only in very unusual circumstances. Bad weather can claim the lives of careful and intelligent people, because it is hard to foresee. Even the best mountain weathermen are sometimes fooled. Most important, weather is too familiar, and people tend to discount the need to prepare for it. Most backpackers have enough native good sense not to attempt a traverse of a steep snow gully without the proper equipment and experience. The mere thought of an uncontrolled slide to the rocks a thousand feet below is enough to make them think twice. Unfortunately, a cloud does not evoke the same caution. Yet it is just as important to be properly dressed when the weather deteriorates as it is to have an ice ax for arrest of a fall on a snow slope.

Weather is exceptionally dangerous in the mountains because it can change greatly in a very short time and exposed peaks may not offer any shelter or makings for a fire. Thunderstorms, for example, are very dangerous when they catch climbers high on peaks and ridges.

Besides the hazards of deteriorating weather, many mountains present the more obvious worries associated with steep terrain. If your mountain has steep rock walls and snow or ice slopes, you must either avoid them or have the equipment and knowledge to travel past them in reasonable safety. The dangers of rock walls, glaciers, and snow slopes include not only poor footing, but rockfall, avalanches, and crevasses. The experienced mountaineer is usually far more fearful of stones falling from cliffs above than he is of falling from his own stance.

Mountains, especially steep ones, are subject to tremendous pressures from the many erosive forces of weather. In terms of geological time precipitous mountains are very young, and the adage that what goes up must come down is quite true of the high peaks. Long before they even reach their greatest elevation, the mountains are being worn away, eroded, and broken down by the wind, gravity, running and freezing water, avalanches, and the pressing, exploring roots of the plants. Every mountain is always in the process of falling apart, and it is a good idea to be somewhere else when some of the pieces decide to make their downward trek. Rockfall can threaten the hiker as much as the rock gymnast, if he is standing under a loose cliff.

So much for the itemization of mountain dangers. None of them need cause particular worry if you pay adequate attention to safety during mountain travel. Like other wilderness dangers, they are generally easy to avoid.

SPECIAL EQUIPMENT FOR MOUNTAIN TRAVEL

The changeable weather of the mountains has already been mentioned, so it should be obvious that the high-country walker needs to carry spare clothes to keep reasonably warm and dry in case of a sudden storm. The principles of clothing were discussed in Chapter 9, so there isn't any need for repetition here. The point is to be alert to possibilities and to prepare for them. In the high ranges of the United States and Canada snowstorms can occur in any month of the year, and the even more dangerous combination of cold rain and high wind is common. Allowing the warm sun to persuade you that shorts and a light shirt make an adequate outfit is asking for trouble. You'll probably get away with it many times, but one day it may kill you. Wear what you like, but always carry clothing for conditions that may come in later. What is needed will vary with the range and season, but a minimum should include some woolen clothing, together with wind protection and perhaps rain gear. Wool is the only fabric that retains significant insulating power when it gets wet.

Camping at high altitudes requires warm sleeping gear or a fire, and fires can never be depended on above timberline. Cooking above timberline demands a stove and fuel and often shelter from wind. In most ranges, camping above timberline requires a mountain tent, even if it is not used on warm nights. Bivouac equipment may be substituted, but shelters that cannot be pitched in a high wind are not dependable above timberline. Mountain boots need to be sturdy and have good traction.

Most specialized climbing equipment is outside the province of this book. Climbing on rock steep enough so that a minor slip would be dangerous requires sophisticated technique and equipment, beginning with a rope. Even more elaborate methods are required for safety on extreme climbs, with various types of climbing "hardware" used to protect against the consequences of a slip and sometimes to aid the progress of a climb. This kind of mountaineering is generally categorized as *technical climbing*. Those interested in this sport should refer to the bibliography at the end of this book for literature. Serious study of technique is required for safe travel on technical terrain.

Between the worlds of the backpacker on the trail and the serious technical climbers, there is a vast amount of mountain terrain which can be safely traveled without using a rope. It is the proper province of the adventurous backpacker and also the ideal training ground for those who want to go on to bigger things one day. This is the province of the rock scrambler and the snow slogger. Rock scrambling requires no special equipment, but the backpacker venturing onto steep terrain where there are stretches covered by snow will feel the need for an *ice ax* and perhaps for *crampons*, and some of the uses for these tools will be discussed later in this chapter.

MOUNTAIN WEATHER

As with all kinds of weather prediction, local experience is invaluable for the amateur in the mountains, as is a check with TV or radio or a call to the weather bureau before departure. Despite all my cautionary notes, I don't believe in carrying stuff I don't have to, and calling the weatherman sometimes saves me a few pounds. If I really don't expect rain, I carry only emergency rain gear, whereas if I plan on it I carry the equipment I need to be comfortable.

The mountains, though, have wiles of their own, which will never be mentioned by the forecaster talking to the millions down in the flatlands. An acquaintance with the weather patterns of the ranges you frequent will mellow through the years into warm friendship and also contribute a lot to your comfort.

The first thing to remember about mountains is that they stick up a long way out of the ground. Suppose you are a reasonably friendly mass of air, rolling peacefully across the country at a sane and moderate speed. Then you come to this mountain. It is in your way, and since there are other masses of air traveling along behind you, jostling if you slow down, somehow you have to get past the mountain. You can either push up and over the barrier or perhaps around it and through a pass; in either case you'll have to speed up to maintain your rate of progress and keep from being pushed too much. Anyone on the mountain will experience high winds and air turbulence. Furthermore, you'll expand and cool in the higher altitude and lower atmospheric pressure as you go over the top of the mountain, and if you are carrying a lot of moisture most of it will fall as rain, sleet, or snow. Thus the mountain backpacker is struggling in a very real storm, despite calm, sunny weather on the plains.

Mountains also generate their own weather. The slanting rays of the sun often strike the mountainsides straight on, warming them more than the ground around them. The mountainsides, in their turn, warm the air nearby, and when this air is warmed it expands and rises. An updraft of air is created around the mountain, and it is often quite strong. Depending on the air currents involved and the moisture content of the air, winds, clouds, and thunderheads may result. A thunderhead can often be recognized as a

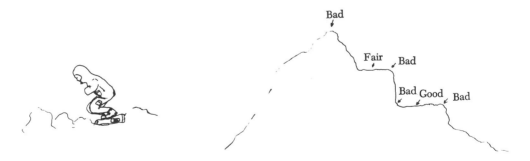

The crouching position with the feet close together is the safest one in a lightning storm; a pack under the feet helps insulate the backpacker from the ground. The cross-section of the mountain shows the relative danger from lightning strikes at various places.

billowing, heavy cloud which expands upward, often very rapidly. When it reaches its height, the top flattens off against a higher atmospheric layer, and the cloud takes on an anvil shape. Large fronts of advancing clouds also bring thunderstorms, and either kind is a signal to get off the peaks and ridges in a hurry.

The cold winds, fog, rain, and snow of an intruding frontal system can be just as dangerous to the ill-prepared, but they are no real threat to the well-equipped party. They also usually give more warning than the rapidly building summer afternoon thunderstorm. Lightning from either an isolated thunderhead or a frontal system can only be avoided, so first consideration will be given to this threat.

LIGHTNING

Electrical storms are among the most feared hazards of the mountains among experienced backpackers and climbers, not because they claim large numbers of lives, but because they are among the *objective dangers* of the mountains. Objective dangers are those which, like rockfall, can only be escaped by being somewhere else when they occur. They have frightening inevitability about them, and though the danger is not great, it can be reduced only by learning enough to take evasive action.

Lightning is a very rapid electrical discharge resulting from a large voltage between two clouds or between a cloud and the ground. Lightning bolts from the ground are the ones we are concerned with. Prior to the strike, a large difference in charge has built up between the cloud and the earth. The only way the difference can be balanced is for a current to flow between the two, but it will not flow easily, because the air between is a good insulator. The discharge only takes place when a tremendous voltage has built up, enough to overcome the insulating layer. When this happens, the lightning bolt follows the path of the least resistance, generally from the point closest to the cloud, perhaps the peak of the mountain or some sharp point along a ridge. As the discharge takes place, currents flow along the surface of the ground to the point of discharge, also flowing along the path of minimum resistance, and these ground currents are just as dangerous as the lightning bolt itself. Ground currents become stronger and more hazardous close to the strike point.

If a thunderstorm is threatening, the first thing to do is to get down off the mountain as quickly as possible, short of taking a fall. For example, suppose you have climbed a mountain along a ridge several miles in length. Another route drops off a saddle to your right, but it goes off the wrong side of the mountain. If a thunderstorm is threatening, the worst place you could possibly be except for the summit itself is along that ridge. Take the saddle route down even if it means a long walk home. If the storm clears, you can always backtrack.

Once the storm begins, it is best to find the safest location nearby and to protect yourself as best you can. If lightning is striking or threatening, continuing your climb down is likely to be dangerous if you are still high, and descending would require you to cross exposed places. The diagram shows the most dangerous and the safest places. Ridges, summits, outer sides of ledges, and outcrops are the likely strike points. Depressions and places on the inside of wide shelves are fairly safe. On a shelf, the safe spot is as far in as possible, but still well clear of the inside cliff. (See the diagram.) If a strike occurs nearby, remember the surface currents. They will not hurt you while flowing past the soles of your feet, but if your feet and hands, or both hands, or feet and head, touch the rock, your body may be the path of least resistance for the current. The best position is a squat, with only the feet touching the ground. If a rope, pack, rolled tent, or something similar is available, squat on that to get a little extra insulation from the ground. Keep your feet close together.

A cave provides excellent protection from lightning as well as rain, because the currents flow along the surface. Great caution is required here, however, since a hollow or a shallow cave is very dangerous. *Do not get under an overhang for shelter from the rain during a thunderstorm high on a mountain.* A current running along the surface and trying to get past a shallow cave or overhang will use your body as the route of least resistance from the floor to the roof. This is unhealthy. A good cave must be quite deep with no crevices in the rock running to the back of the cave.

A few warning signs might be mentioned, although they may or may not occur prior to a strike. When the charge is building up on a mountain on which you are standing, it will build up on you, too. When your hair stands up on end, you have good cause to worry. I have experienced this sensation and have no wish to repeat the experience, but I've never heard what the French call "the buzzing of the bees," a humming sound which often precedes a strike.

The most obvious warning signs are threatening clouds, and they give much better notice than the last-minute frights mentioned before. It is almost always possible to see storms building up well in advance, and being caught by surprise is usually the result of not paying attention. Watch for the buildup of thunderheads on nearby peaks, and don't underestimate the speed with which they can form once they have begun to mushroom upward. Keep an eye out for approaching frontal systems; a little study of the area will tell you the direction they usually come from at a particular time of year. Breakneck retreats off the summits should be rare. They indicate you are pushing your luck and cutting things too close. There is an occasional unavoidable situation when all the visible sky looks beautiful, but you meet the storm system coming from the other side of the hill at the top of the ridge or peak.

RAIN, SLEET, DRIVING WIND, AND ALL THAT

Although lightning tends to be the most feared element of mountain weather among experienced backpackers and climbers, far more people run afoul of the other ingredients of mountain storms. No one really knows how many deaths occur each year in the mountains from body chilling, but it is probably the most frequent form of accidental death in the high country. The chilling effects of sudden storms deserve the utmost caution of anyone who wanders in the mountains, and one should always carry adequate clothing and supplies to meet the danger.

Rules for proper clothing are simple enough, but on sunny summer days they are too often forgotten. Even in winter at high altitude, the sun is often deceptively warm when the wind isn't blowing, and the cool air is still enough so that its temperature isn't noticed. With the muscular exertion of hiking up steep slopes, the traveler will probably be sweating, and the dangers of chilling will not occur to him.

The wind alone may chill the mountain walker to the bone. Coming down from his mountain in the afternoon with his clothing soaked with sweat and his body reserves depleted by hard work, the combination of the afternoon wind and creeping shadows may chill him severely. If a cold rain is added, he may never get back.

The effects of storms carrying freezing rain and then snow are much more serious than this, especially if they catch the hiker above timberline and shelter. Without proper clothing even the strongest hikers are quickly chilled. The principles discussed in the clothing chapter are important for the mountain traveler more than any other. Windtight shell clothing is essential for mountain travel. Shell clothing is light and easily carried. Enough insulation should be taken for reasonable comfort in any weather that might blow in. Obviously, quantities will vary with range and season, but the rule remains constant—don't be lulled into a false sense of security by the weather at the trailhead or at camp in the morning. The most characteristic feature of mountain weather is rapid change.

When wet weather is a possibility, water resistant or waterproof shell garments are needed, the choice depending on various considerations mentioned elsewhere. Finally, to harp on my favorite rule, when wet, cold weather is a possibility, carry some *wool* clothing. With the affluence of many backpackers now hitting the trail, a lot more down clothing is being carried, and it is so warm that people carrying it tend to rely completely on its qualities, which are great indeed. But, when down gets wet, it is completely useless. Basic insulation in the mountains, except in places and seasons where there is never any rain or sleet, should be wool, which is the only material retaining much insulation power after it gets wet.

Clearly, it is especially important in the mountains not to get your clothes wet in the first place if you can help it, unless a change will soon be available. Take off your sweater before you soak it with sweat, and stop to get the rain gear out of the pack as soon as the drizzle starts, not after you're already beginning to feel soaked. By the time your skin starts feeling wet, your clothes are already pretty damp. Stay as dry as possible.

ROUTE FINDING IN THE MOUNTAINS

Basically, finding your way in the mountains is easier than in most terrain. Visibility is usually good, terrain and landmarks are well defined, so that following progress on a topo map is quite simple. Only a few special tricks have to be learned. The first is to avoid terrain that is too difficult. Both in planning trips on the map and looking at the scenery ahead, it is important to consider your abilities, time, equipment, and party, so that you avoid getting into trouble. Remember that there is a lot of terrain in the mountains that is impassable to the backpacker. This is especially important when you plan routes which take a different way down a peak or a pass than up. If you aren't sure of the feasibility of a route, allow enough time and energy to search for the way and turn back if necessary.

Get in the habit of planning your routes in the mountains well in advance, or at least looking for them. You can often tell a great deal from the map and from distant views about features which will be obscured once you are close to a mountain. From the trailhead it may be quite obvious that a particular ridge is easy or impossible, while from below the same ridge will be invisible or completely distorted. It is especially difficult to see the route ahead from above, and if you make a wrong choice, you have to climb back up, the thought of which may encourage you to take foolish chances.

Guidebooks may be useful for advance information on mountain trips. Once you are familiar with a particular region, maps become more useful, but in an area that is completely new to you, many mysteries will remain until you see the ground. A forty-foot cliff doesn't show on a fifty-foot contour map, and on ridge routes especially, the map may not give you any indication of what to expect.

Always be wary of the consequences of a possible slip in the mountains. Climbing sound faces with proper technique and equipment isn't too hazardous, but scrambling around unroped on easy but loose rock just above a cliff can be very dangerous. Backpackers who wouldn't think of trying difficult rock climbing sometimes manage to get themselves into far more precarious positions than the average rock climber ever does. You can often travel safely on difficult terrain, providing you keep a close eye out for the consequences of a slip. It's quite safe to climb a very difficult step when there is no place to fall, but a loose blocky slope that looks very easy may be too risky when it hangs over thin air. Care and experience are the essential ingredients. Unless you know you can manage a move safely—and come back if you have to—don't try it.

Backpackers should be especially careful about snow slopes. They provide safe avenues for the traveler on many mountains with proper care, equipment, and practice, but without one of these elements they are dangerous. In the spring, many established trails cross snow slopes, and examining them with an eye for the consequences of a slip is vital. The use of

313

the ice ax for self-arrest is discussed later in this chapter. Without an ice ax, stopping a fall on steep, hard snow is virtually impossible. You will go to the bottom in a hurry. Crossing and climbing snow slopes can be completely safe, but get your experience in places where you won't be hurt by your mistakes.

Though trails maintained by government agencies or private clubs are generally safe even for inexperienced walkers, the mountains are not a good place to blindly follow trail markers, leaving good sense behind. Sections of a trail may be washed out, maintenance may have been dropped, or snow or bad weather conditions may have turned a normally simple trail into a route for roped parties only. Cairns and worn trails do not necessarily mark an easy route either. Especially in popular climbing areas, these may simply guide the climber to an extremely difficult route. Finally, on rocky land above timberline, trail markings may be nonexistent or difficult to follow, especially if the weather deteriorates. Keep your common sense in the mountains, and let your own experience guide you in the safety of routes. If things start to get too hard, turn around and go back. There's always another weekend.

CLIMBING AND SCRAMBLING

The principle of watching for the consequences of a slip has already been mentioned several times. It provides the general dividing line between roped climbing and scrambling. Where the line will be drawn will vary with the individual and his experience, but the beginner should be careful to draw it with a generous margin for error. Where the consequences of a slip would be disastrous, the climber should be roped and have the skill to use the rope effectively. Easy footing should not lull you into false confidence—it's what is underneath you that really counts.

The use of ropes and climbing hardware is beyond the scope of this book. In this chapter I've chosen to draw my own line at the start of terrain where a rope is needed. Unfortunately, that beginning is somewhat ambiguous, and I can only advise the reader to make his own decisions conservatively—don't climb up anything unless you're sure you can get safely down. Down-climbing is almost always harder than going up.

SNOW

In many mountain ranges permanent snowfields last all summer, and even lower ranges sport them in spring and winter. Long climbs on steep snow are the province of the mountaineer who has practiced proper use of the rope, protection, step-cutting, and other skills. However, the experienced backpacker often makes trips which involve crossing or climbing occasional snow slopes. Learning the use of an ice ax for self-arrest and perhaps a little crampon technique greatly extends the range of possibilities open to the backpacker. Even if only one snow gully ten feet wide needs to be crossed on a particular trip, that gully might be an impassable barrier without an ice ax, if a slip in it would result in an uncontrolled fall.

Actual progress on snow can be made in one of several ways. On fairly flat terrain, of course, one simply walks. On the consolidated snow slopes of spring and summer, though, simple walking will usually result in a slip. If the snow is reasonably soft, steps can be kicked into the snow. One or two kicks make an adequate step if the snow is soft enough for kicking steps at all. Harder snow requires either cutting steps or wearing crampons. Routes requiring step-cutting should be avoided by all but experienced climbers. If the slope requires cutting steps, then a fall would be dangerous, and an ice ax being used for cutting cannot be held ready for self-arrest. A rope is usually required, so step-cutting is not in the province of the backpacker.

Going down should be given more attention than going up. Don't ever go up a slope unless you're sure that you can get down safely. In soft snow, the technique is to face out and walk down, plunging the heel in at each step. The natural tendency of the nervous beginner is to stay as close to the slope as possible, leaning back and almost sitting down. Learn to overcome this temptation. The safe position is standing straight up with your weight over your feet. Come down hard on your heels to dig good steps. Leaning back simply tends to break out your steps.

If you're thinking about climbing a slope, check to see if it is soft enough to heel down first. Unless you have crampons and can use them, harder slopes shouldn't be attempted. Coming down facing the slope, trying to kick steps below you, is no exercise to try without a rope.

Remember that snow conditions change during the day. If the sun is just leaving a snow slope, it is going to freeze harder in a few hours. Are you going to be coming down again? If you're working up a slope that is just soft enough to kick steps in, make sure it will be softer rather than harder on your way down. Remember the slope during the day. If the weather changes and starts to get cold, turn around before the snow gets hard.

In spring and early summer, slopes may get very soft and avalanche. If there is any avalanching on similar slopes, if large balls have been rolling down, if there are any cornices above, or if the snow is very sloppy, *stay off*. It takes years to learn to judge avalanche hazards well. Don't take chances. In winter conditions, before the snow has become consolidated, stay off steep open slopes completely, unless you have studied avalanche conditions thoroughly. Avalanches are killers.

THE ICE AX AND SELF-ARREST

The mountaineer uses the ice ax for many purposes, but only one of them will be discussed here. For the general backpacker the ax is used mainly as a walking stick and occasionally for self-arrest. The walking stick use needs no explanation.

Self-arrest is the use of the ax to stop a slide on a snow slope. In principle it is simple, but it can only be learned through practice. To learn it well, you'll have to go up to the mountains, find a snow slope with a gentle runout so that you can't get hurt, and practice for at least a day. To do any good the arrest has to become a reflexive action. You have to train yourself to use it by instinct, and that does not come naturally. Your natural instinct is to let go of the ax and claw the slope with your fingernails. Long experience has shown this instinct to be unhealthy.

If you decide to learn self-arrest, you must first buy, borrow, or rent an ice ax. Fine points of design become important in step-cutting and technical ice and snow climbing—they need not concern us here. If you expect to go on to roped climbing, I recommend you get an ax with a metal handle, but this is not important for the backpacker. The handle of the ax should be long enough so that the point reaches the floor when you hold the head in your hand. A few inches one way or the other doesn't matter. Don't get an extremely short ax that may be prominently displayed in a mountaineering store. It is excellent for climbing severe ice walls, but you aren't planning on climbing any severe ice walls, and a short ax is dangerous for self-arrest.

A standard ice ax should reach the ground when the head is held in the hand. At the bottom is the spike, or point. The head, at the top, is made up of the pick, extending in the direction of the thumb, and the adze, going the other way.

Once you have your ice ax, take plenty of warm clothes to the hills with you. A day of self-arrest practice means a day of sliding and wallowing in the snow. Be sure to wear a hat and mittens or gloves. You will get wet, and a change will be welcome at the car or in the pack. You need to find a slope that is packed and steep enough so that you would slide if you should slip, but it must run out onto a gentle flat patch with no protruding rocks in case you do indeed slip and slide.

Climb up the slope a little way and hold the ax in the position shown in the illustration. The head is held in the hand with the thumb going around the adze. The other hand holds the shaft just above the spike. The shaft goes diagonally down across the chest, with the pick sticking out away from the body and held just below the shoulder. To arrest a slip, you

317

The ice ax held ready for self-arrest. To check a slip the climber falls forward on the pick, controlling it with his hand and shoulder.

simply fall on your chest and dig the pick into the snow. For more stopping power, hunch your back up so that your weight is on the pick and your toes. This is simple in principle, but there are a lot of fine points which have to be learned with practice. Try a few practice arrests whenever you have a chance. In soft snow, you start digging with pick and feet just as fast as you can. In hard snow, when you get going fast, the pick has to be edged into the snow very quickly, but smoothly and carefully, or else it is likely to be pulled from your hands and left far above you.

In your initial practice, keep trying the same thing, climbing higher onto steeper ground as you learn the technique. Let yourself slide a little way before you start the arrest, so that you can find what it is like to stop from a faster slide. Learn to really dig in. You have to get your face down to the snow to get your weight on the ax pick and your feet. Your hand controlling the pick must hang on to prevent it from being pulled up above your shoulder, where you can no longer put weight on it. If you start to lose control of the pick, lessen the pressure on it until you regain your hold. *You must hang onto the ax!*

Once you feel you have mastered the arrest while falling forward, try falling a bit to each side. Roll onto the ax and then get your rear end up to put pressure on it. Then try facing downslope and falling forward. Finally, you will get to the point of falling backward. Start low the first few times,

Practicing self-arrest. The sliding person is trying arrest from a backwards, head-first tumble. These people are using a rope for safety because the snow here has rocks at the bottom. Find a place with a safe runoff instead unless you have been trained in the use of a rope.

and then practice from higher up. Roll over on the pick side, hanging onto the ax in the arrest position. Don't roll toward the point. It might catch in the snow and rip the ax from your hands. Once you've rolled onto the pick, a little pressure on it will make it drag, and your body will swing around so that your feet are downslope. Then you're in normal arrest position, and you do the same thing you've been doing all along. On fast snow this all has to be done very quickly or you'll get out of control.

If you manage to get through backward headfirst falls and you're still ready for more, repeat the whole sequence with a pack. Don't get overconfident. Start on an easy slope with each new step and then work onto steeper ones. And *never* practice on a slope without a good runout or one with rocks protruding in the possible line of fall. Learn self-arrest on safe slopes. Once you've become sure of yourself, you'll be able to safely traverse snow slopes that are within your capability for self-arrest. The more practice you get, the better those limits will get and the better your judgment of them will be.

A few special cautions are in order regarding snow slopes. The first is to make all your judgments about them conservatively. An uncontrolled slide down a snow slope or gully could be deadly. There is no reason to be afraid of snow, but there's very good reason not to try anything unless you *know* you can handle it. Pushing your limits is completely out of place without a rope and proper rope techniques.

An arrest requires a certain distance to work. Whenever you're deciding whether a slope is safe, look at the distance you would have available. Make sure that there is a lot more distance than you need to stop before you would reach any rocks or drop-offs. Be particularly watchful for ice patches in the snow. Arresting on snow and ice are quite different matters, and a few yards of ice can cause you to take a spill or throw an arrest out of control. Don't climb or cross any snow slope unless you know you could arrest a fall. Don't forget that it takes longer to arrest if you're wearing a pack.

CRAMPONS

After gaining some experience on snow, you will find that you could easily arrest a slip on many slopes that are too hard to permit step-kicking. Crampons permit easy footing on hard snow. They are steel frames that strap to the boot with spikes bent at right angles to stick into the snow. For short sections of snow lightweight instep crampons are available, with four or five points, designed to strap to the center of the boot. These require considerable care in use, however, and for longer snow stretches full length crampons are required. These should have points 1¼ inches to 1¾ inches long; ten points per crampon, all going straight down from the boot sole are best. Those with points projecting straight out in front of the toe are of use only on steep slopes, where the backpacker has no business.

Crampons are tricky to use until you get the knack, and you should get lots of practice in a safe place before you try to use them where a fall could be dangerous. *They must fit your boots properly.* This means that the

Strapping on a crampon. This one has horns sticking out in front which are not recommended for beginners. A good fit to the boot and secure strapping are essential.

side irons must hold the boots firmly, allowing no side to side slipping. The front points of a crampon should be just under the toe of the boot, not in front of it or very far behind. Make sure the binding is secure. A loose or badly fitted crampon is really dangerous.

In use crampons must be placed with all the points dug into the slope, which means that the ankles have to flex to the angle of the slope. Edging the foot so that only half the points go into the slope invites a fall. Practice going up, down, and across the slope. Be sure to practice switchbacking, the most insecure maneuver you are likely to make.

Be very careful not to catch one of your crampons on the other pant leg. This can cause a fall, a gash in the leg, or both. When they aren't on your feet, crampons should have some kind of guards on them and be put in the pack. They are sharp and dangerous. They should be kept sharp—dull crampons can cause slips.

Practice arresting with crampons on. On hard snow, be careful about digging your toes in while wearing crampons, especially if you have front points that stick out from the toes. A crampon catching suddenly in hard snow can flip you over and cause you to lose control completely. One other caution: soft, wet snow sometimes balls between the points of crampons, which can cause them suddenly not to bite. Be very cautious if snow starts to stick between your points. The problem can be stopped by poking the points of the crampons through a piece of plastic sheeting, and then tying it fast around the boot.

Desert Walking 19

Like the mountains, deserts are extreme environments. They have great appeal for many backpackers, and their aesthetic qualities are unique and immensely varied. They range from great mazes of red sandstone canyons to vast stretches of sand dunes, shifting endlessly in the winds. The special beauty of a shaded waterfall surrounded by cottonwoods and animal trails in the midst of the harsh clarity of the desert is unmatched by anything in nature.

The single characteristic which sets the desert apart is, of course, the scarcity of water. Definitions vary, and they need not concern us here—the essential tone of life in desert country is set by the fact that water is not readily available. There are as many kinds of desert as there are mountains. The climatic conditions which produce deserts may exist over flat plains or incredibly rugged landscapes. Rock may be granite, sandstone, or any of a host of others; plants and animal life vary even more. The saguaro cactus forests of the Sonoran Desert give way to the agave plant to the southeast and the Joshua tree to the north. Further north stretch the endless reaches of sagebrush of the Great Basin.

Common features are equally striking. Life in the desert must suit itself to short feasts and long famines. Like the life of the high mountains, growth is often crowded into one short season, and much of the structure of the plant or animal is built around the characteristics needed for survival during the rest of the year. Conservation is the basic survival requirement in the desert—conservation of water.

The backpacker in the desert has much to learn from the forms of life that survive there the year round. He must be prepared for extremes of temperature, not simply of heat but of cold as well. Without heavy vegetation cover, large bodies of water, or significant masses of water vapor in the air, the desert responds much more directly to the sun's daily cycle than other places. When the sun comes up, its radiation heats things up rapidly, and when the sun goes down, the heat is radiated to the black sky just as rapidly. Blazing days and freezing nights are quite common in the desert. Actual temperatures will vary with location and season, but it is a general rule that the daily temperature range in desert regions will be great. The desert is not the jungle, and you must be prepared for chilly nights as well as hot days.

CONSERVING WATER

The human body will function properly only within a very narrow temperature range, and it will not even survive if the temperature of the vital organs goes much above or below the level it should be. Even so, we can function well in widely varying environments but there is a price.

The price is the need to maintain the right body temperature. When it is cold, you cannot hibernate like a snake; you have to burn enough fuel to keep warm. Similarly, when it is hot, your body must be cooled to keep its temperature from going too high. Cooling is our main concern here.

There is only one way that the body can cool itself in situations like desert walking with no convenient swimming pools or air-conditioned restaurants, and that method is by evaporation. Turning liquid water into water vapor uses up lots of heat, so the body sweats when it gets too hot, and when the sweat evaporates, the skin is cooled. By increasing the circulation to the skin, the body ensures that the blood is cooled.

Clearly, this cooling method requires water—the more cooling, the more water. So if one wants to conserve water in the desert, the way to do it is to minimize the amount of cooling which is necessary and to ensure that it is as efficient as possible. The amount of water needed by the body for its other functions is small by comparison, and the possibilities for reducing it are minimal.

If the body is to remain at a constant temperature, the amount of heat lost must be exactly the same as the quantity of heat gained. If one exceeds the other, the body will get warmer or cooler, and this can go on only for a short time before trouble ensues. For a simple example, suppose the air temperature is exactly the same as body temperature—that is fairly hot, nearly 100° F. Under such conditions, there will be no heat loss or gain from the air alone. Heat loss will be due to evaporation, and heat gain will be from sunshine, touching hot objects, and the body's own heat production.

In the desert, direct sunshine can contribute a good deal of heat. This can be reduced by wearing light, loose clothing, and especially by wearing a hat with a high crown and a wide brim. Obviously, it is even more efficient to stay out of the sun in a shady spot. This may sometimes be advisable in a hot desert during the summer months—one simply camps in a shady spot during the day, confining travel to the evening, night, and early-morning hours.

During the day, hot objects will include anything in direct sunlight. The ground temperature on a hot day in the desert is much hotter than the temperature of the air. Generally, only the feet are touching the ground, so protection is provided by relatively thick lug soles on the boots. Thin-soled shoes should be avoided. If you sit down to rest on hot ground, you may need to protect yourself with your pack or sleeping pad.

Generally, the biggest contributor of heat is the body itself. The body gets energy by consuming food as fuel, but this can never be done with perfect efficiency. Some of the energy from the food is simply generated as heat, so the body is always producing heat as long as it is alive. A certain amount is produced at rest, and the more work the body does, the more extra heat is produced. If the environment is colder than the body, then the extra heat is used to maintain normal body temperature, but in the situation we are discussing, all this heat must be eliminated by evaporation of water. It follows that the more work the body does, the more heat has to be eliminated, and the more water will be required. To conserve water, keep your activities slow, steady, and efficient. Sudden bursts of energy in the desert produce great quantities of sweat which run off the body without doing their job of cooling.

These rules are also sensible for other reasons. When you are overheated, your body does not perform well. Traveling at night during really hot periods will often get you twice as far, besides keeping your water-consumption down. This is true simply because your body functions better when it isn't overheated, even though visibility is poor.

A light-colored hat with a wide brim, high crown, and good ventilation is important to keep you cool and to keep your brains from becoming addled. You need all the good sense you can muster in desert travel, and you'll have very little left after the sun has beaten down on your bare head for a few hours.

Don't risk sunburn. It is a dangerous matter in the desert. Do your sunbathing judiciously, and cover up with light, loose clothing when water is a problem—the water won't evaporate so quickly, the cooled air will remain near the skin for a little while, and your body won't be heated so much by direct sun.

WATER—HOW MUCH AND WHERE

How much water you need to carry depends on how far it is to the next sure supply. You must also allow leeway for unforeseen circumstances. Amounts will also vary with the individual and with temperatures. As a rule, figure on a minimum supply of a gallon per day for each person. Always err on the high side, even though each gallon weighs over eight pounds.

Once you have gained some experience with the amount your body needs, you may be able to reduce this amount of water somewhat, especially where safety is not a problem—hiking in hills above a water source, for example. In any case, learn the trick of tanking up on water when you stop at a supply. Your body can store quite a bit of water itself, and provides the most convenient place to carry reserves. If you are camped at a spring, start drinking as soon as you get up, taking a sip every few minutes. If you get in the habit of drinking a lot when water is available, you'll find you can go a long way before you have to break out the supply in the pack.

Don't try to reverse this coin by allowing your normal reserves to become depleted, unless it is absolutely necessary. It takes more water to replace the body's usual supply after it is overdrawn than it does to keep the supply up in the first place.

The matter of finding water should never be left to chance in the desert. In some desert regions, water supplies are relatively frequent, and practice will teach the desert rat to dig it out, but desert regions are not the same, and your basic water supply should never depend on the uncertain possibility that you will find a waterhole.

Check with someone who *knows* about water supplies. Rangers, ranchers, or other local people who have visited an area recently should be able to tell you whether you can depend on a spring or a creek. Don't depend on maps, which may be inaccurate or out of date. I have found permanent springs shown on U.S.G.S. maps dried up even in nondesert areas. Don't believe everything you hear. "Oh yeah, I was over to Buzzard Spring just last week, and it was running high" may mean just that, or it may mean your informant has never even heard of Buzzard Spring but won't admit it to some cocky city feller. Use your judgment and a large dose of skepticism; your life may depend on it.

If you are in doubt about a particular water supply, you may have to carry enough water there for the outward journey and return to the last source or continued travel to the next sure source. So for a day's journey to Dubious Creek, you would have to carry at least two gallons of water per person, one to get you there and one to get you back.

Water containers for use in the desert must be dependable. Cheap or poorly made canteens and bottles are all right where they may merely mean a couple of hours of dry going, but in the desert there is no room for wineskins with split liners or canteens with leaky rivets in the covers. Always put on the lid securely when you set the canteen down. A careless kick can be serious. Polyethylene bottles must be kept well away from the fire.

You can travel for some distance on your body's reserves of water if you are careful to conserve them in every way possible, but save this sort of endurance trial for emergencies. You will be more comfortable and use less water if you take small sips when you feel the need, rather than holding out as long as possible. Your body does not work very well when it becomes dehydrated either, and you run a much greater danger of overheating. When your mouth gets dry, take a small swig and roll it around for a while to wash away the sun.

Finding water follows fairly obvious rules, combined with any knowledge you may have of patterns in a particular area. Plant life generally indicates water, especially if there are a number of trees growing together.

Unfortunately, the water may be quite a way down, especially in a dry season. If you find good plant growth near a dry wash, try digging at the lowest point.

If you hit damp soil or sand within a foot or so, you'll probably get some water further down. If not, you've had a lesson in how far down tap roots can go. There's water under that mesquite all right, but it may be thirty or forty feet deep. Converging animal trails will also lead to water, if you can find some converging animal trails. Following a gully downhill may bring you to a point where a rock layer carries the water close to the surface. Finally, there are the various survival methods, particularly the solar still. The solar still depends on the plastic sheet trapping moisture, which the heat of the sun evaporates from the soil in which the hole is dug. When the plastic sheet cools, the humid air below condenses dew on the sheet, which then runs into the container. Under the right conditions, this condensation may occur throughout the day, since heat builds up below the sheet as it does in a greenhouse, while the air above tends to cool the plastic. The method works best where there is a wide temperature change during the day. It is a good way of getting fresh water along sunny beaches. It won't work at all if there is little or no moisture in the soil—or no soil.

The method for making a solar still is shown in the diagram. You'll need four to six going all the time the sun is up to get enough water for a day, and this means you'll have to carry the equipment for making them, weighing a pound or a pound and a half. Despite propaganda to the contrary, they do not always work.

You may have guessed that I am generally dubious about such means of finding water. It's always nice to be able to find a waterhole that you weren't anticipating, perhaps by making a short detour to a grove of cottonwoods at the bottom of a bluff, and there's no question that the more you know about finding water, the better off you'll be backpacking in desert country. The fact remains, though, that you may be forty miles from the next waterhole, and whether you can spot it from twenty miles away or not, there is just one way to make sure you'll get there. That is to know where the water is to begin with and to carry a large enough supply to get you there with plenty of room for error. I have never had to try chopping open a barrel cactus, and I don't ever want to—it isn't something you should do except in an emergency. Besides, most of the desert in the

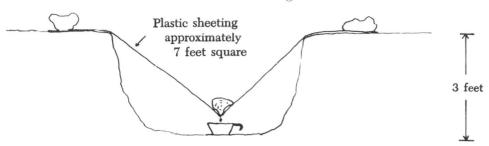

A solar still is made with a large sheet of plastic hung in a freshly dug hole, weighted around the edge with rocks, with one rock holding a drip point in the center over a container. Pieces of moist plant can be cut up and put in the hole to contribute extra moisture. The quantity of moisture that can be obtained is limited and quite variable.

United States has no large cacti. I'd hate to try sucking water from sage-brush. With my luck if I depended on a solar still, I'd actually need it on a solid sandstone rock shelf where it would be absolutely useless.

The best way to handle the hazards of desert backpacking is to be ready for them. Know what you're doing before you leave. Be *sure* to carry enough water in good containers. Take along a map which you've studied in advance, and make sure you have a compass and know how to use it. Don't take chances, and follow the normal safety rules for wilderness travel discussed elsewhere in the book.

WATER FIT TO DRINK

The desert is practically unique in that one finds there a good deal of water which is tainted, not by people but by natural circumstances. Of course, the same caution about possible human pollution applies in the desert as anywhere else. If there is any doubt about purity, don't take chances: boil or use a chemical method to protect yourself from getting sick.

Wherever there is a reasonable amount of rainfall, water collecting in a basin will finally overflow and cut out a drainage system. Thus in most parts of the continent water is running toward the sea—slowly, perhaps, but moving still. In the desert this is often not the case. Where evaporation has exceeded rainfall for eons, the hills surrounding various drainage basins may never have been cut through because water never rises high enough to spill over. In some of our deserts there are vast drainage basins which end in a lake or low point with no outlet. As the water evaporates, minerals it has leeched from the ground are left behind. After many years the deposits build up: salt flats and alkali pools. The very names in many desert regions bear witness to the disillusionment in that sterile water—Great Salt Lake, Badwater, the Alkali Lakes, Arsenic Spring, Salt Wash Valley.

Checking with someone in advance will warn you of bad water. If you do come upon water that is suspect, look around for plant and insect life. Its absence is a sure warning of trouble, and the possibility of arsenic should make you wary. Even where plants are growing, water may be too saline or full of other minerals to be potable, but where other life is flourishing, a taste will not hurt you.

TOO MUCH WATER

In desert regions plants are scattered and there is little soil. When water does fall it is usually in the form of hard thunderstorms, and runoff is rapid, because little moisture can be trapped and stored. This is when the normally dry washes and arroyos are filled with sudden torrents. Watch out for these sudden floods, even though they don't occur frequently. If great thunderheads are billowing over the hills, it is a good time to stay out of that narrow canyon leading up to them—don't forget that it was formed by the water rushing down. Above all, don't camp in the bottom of a dry wash, lest you have a sudden surprise during the night. Debris along the sides of gullies and washes will often show you how high the water rises. Camp a little higher than that.

If you are hiking in a river valley below a control dam, in Grand Canyon for example, be especially careful to camp high or to check with the authorities before you go. Such dams have completely stopped the normal river cycle; the amount of flow is controlled not by the rainfall but by the dam. If a call is put on the river downstream from you, the water level may suddenly go up five or ten feet when the dam is opened. If you happen to be camped by the side of the water when this happens in the middle of the night, you are in for an unpleasant shock.

OTHER CAMPING HINTS

The obvious search for afternoon shade should not lull you into forgetting the morrow. The early-morning sun in the desert gets hot in a hurry. If you want any sleep in the morning, you should take the morning shade into account. You might use the sun as an early alarm clock instead, but personally I hate to wake up overheated and dry. In the absence of natural shade, you may want to pitch a poncho or a tarp as an awning, a particularly useful trick at lunch and during rest stops.

In deeply carved country, cooling generally creates strong downcanyon winds in the evening, so try to pick a campsite that avoids them. If you can't stay away from them, at least weight your gear down so that you don't lose half your equipment if the wind suddenly comes up while you're down at the creek for water.

Be particularly scrupulous with sanitation and trash in the desert. Carry out anything that doesn't burn completely, choose latrines carefully, burn the toilet paper if possible, and don't pollute streams, especially small ones, by washing in them. Carry washing water away from the channel. Water in the desert is rare and precious, and even in sparsely populated country other people and animals will seek out the smallest creek. Leave it clean for them. The same rule applies to campsites. You want to camp near water, and so does everyone else. Leave the site at least as pleasant as you found it.

If you use fires for cooking or warmth, burn dead wood only. Lots of living desert plants look dead and burn easily, but that is not an excuse for breaking them off and using them for fuel. In heavily used areas, use a stove, and encourage others to do the same. Perennial plants grow very slowly in the desert, and it is disgusting to destroy a beautiful campsite for generations just for cooking fuel.

FINDING YOUR WAY

The general principles of getting around in the desert are no different than for anyplace else, but there are a few special cautions worth mentioning. In badlands, canyon country, and similar regions, watersheds and landmarks are often very confusing. One can easily become lost in a maze of

331

gullies or canyons, and special care is needed to prevent becoming lost. The practice of "following water to civilization" is particularly inapplicable in desert regions, unless careful thought is given in advance. Water may lead to a seasonal lake in the middle of nowhere, or it may follow hundreds of miles of impassable canyons. Careful mapwork and advance study of watersheds are essential.

SEASONS

Again like the high mountains, deserts frequently are out of bounds for normal backpacking during several months of the year. Study your particular region for temperatures, snowfall, water, and the like. In general, fall, winter, and spring are the best seasons for desert backpacking. Summer trips in the desert should be undertaken only after careful checking and usually only after you have had some experience. Regions like Death Valley may require night travel in the summer months.

Backpacking in Winter 20

For backpackers whose favorite wilderness lies deep under the snow during the winter months, cold-weather camping can provide a fascination matched at no other time of the year. Snow camping is also more difficult than bedding down in summer meadows, especially for the self-propelled camper, and far more skill and endurance are required than in milder seasons.

In snow country, winter brings peace and solitude to many areas that have become crowded and noisy in summer. The beauty of the winter landscape is the equal of any other season, and the quiet clarity of the air is unrivaled. Winter brings challenge for the competent and potential danger for the careless, both of a much more serious nature than trials and threats that occur in milder seasons.

Because of its unique rewards and difficulties, deep snow country is a special place for the experienced backpacker, a place where true wilderness can often be found even in regions relatively close to civilization. There is a peculiar exhilaration in the winter wilderness that can be found at no other time of year.

Special cautions must be applied, however. Except in a few particularly harsh environments, the summer backcountry rarely presents any serious danger to any traveler who takes the most elementary safety precautions. A couple of nights out in the woods at most times of year will make you hungry, and if you are not adequately clothed you will be a bit the worse for wear, but that's all, providing you keep your head. Even in the mountains in the summer, a person who is properly equipped can generally spend a night out suffering no more than moderate discomfort. In winter things are not so simple. Adequate clothing, equipment, food, and the skill to use them well are often essential for survival, not merely for comfort.

In summer, I really believe that any reasonably healthy person who has not allowed himself to dissipate completely can manage to go on a successful backpacking trip. He may have to limit his goals at first, and he certainly will need to be careful of his equipment and load if he is not in proper physical condition, but normal good health is the only qualification for easy trips. The victim of the idiot box and the reclining chair may be dog tired at the end of an easy day, but he can manage it, and he will feel good on Monday morning.

In winter this is not the case. Some winter trips are easy, and some winter activities are not strenuous. Backpacking in snow conditions that may change in a few hours is a different matter, however. Physical reserves are required that are not necessary in summer. A typical winter trip will require a heavier pack than a summer one. More clothing, heavier sleeping equipment, more food, a more comprehensive emergency kit, and various incidentals must all be carried, and either snowshoes or skis must be worn. Travelers in winter often have to break trail through powder snow or breakable crust, and this is strenuous exercise. On reaching camp, it may be necessary to stamp a platform before a tent can be pitched and before one can stand without the aid of snowshoes or skis. Days are short, weather can be severe, water may have to be melted. Simply getting up after a spill in soft snow can be quite tiring for the novice to wilderness travel on skis or snowshoes.

This partial catalogue of difficulties is not intended to discourage the prospective winter visitor to the wilderness. It is merely cautionary. A rank beginner may well enjoy easy snowshoe hikes or ski tours on trails, perhaps including overnight trips to cabins accompanied by experienced companions. True wilderness travel in deep snow country is not for the neophyte, however. Start backpacking and camping in mild weather, and take to the snowy trails when you feel physically fit and at home in the wilds. If you want to start in winter, begin with short trips of a few hours on skis or snowshoes, *with companions*, or start camping close to home or car. Cold-weather camping, like cold-water swimming, should be approached with caution. It's all right to plunge right in *after* you know you can take it.

WALKING IN THE SNOW

Backpacking with a few inches of snow on the ground is not much different from doing the same thing with no snow. You must make sure that your boots are heavy and watertight enough for the conditions and that your clothing is adequate for the weather conditions. Other equipment must also be suitable. With a light autumn snow cover it is usually best to clear a tent site of snow so that the tent can be pitched directly on the ground, but in spring the snow cover is likely to be more consolidated; a bare spot may be so wet that it is just as well to camp on top of the snow.

Occasions when it is practical to hike with snow on the ground may range from relatively mild spring conditions or moderate weather in places which do not receive a heavy winter cover to the extremely severe cold that may be found in midwinter during a light snow year in the north country. Camping techniques range accordingly between regular summer methods and the snow-camping procedure outlined below.

Besides taking special care that they have adequate clothing, shelter, and food, hikers in cold weather must beware of one particular danger, especially when engaged in fall and early winter camping in heavy-snow regions. They must remember that even though there may only be six inches of snow on the ground when they leave, a storm in the backcountry could easily bring a couple of feet or more, making the trip *out* a very different affair from the one going in. On snowshoe and ski trips when a heavy base has already been built up, an additional two or three feet is of no particular consequence and may even make the going easier, but for hikers caught by the first heavy snow of the year, a pleasant autumn hike may easily be turned into a survival ordeal. Backpackers should be wary of this possibility in fall and in early winter, particularly in the mountains, and they should go prepared. On long trips into deep wilderness, this will probably mean carrying snowshoes even if they are not needed for the trip in. Four days of good going can get you a long way in before there is much snow on the ground, and if you'd like to be sure of getting out again before spring, think about what the same trail would be like after heavy snows and drifting winds.

WINTER TRANSPORTATION: SNOWSHOES AND SKIS

In areas where the snow comes and goes and at times when the snow is shallow enough or well enough consolidated to allow normal walking, camping and hiking are simply a bit more challenging than they are when there is no snow on the ground. When the snow pack begins to build up, however, travel becomes impossible without special equipment designed to keep the traveler on top of the snow. In principle this is fairly simple: you fasten something to each foot which increases the area bearing your weight and thus prevents you from sinking too far into the snow.

There is not adequate space here to go into the selection of snowshoes and skis in great detail, and I have discussed this and other winter backpacking subjects in considerable detail in my book on snow camping. Essentially, the choice depends on the sort of country you want to travel. The first choice to be made is between skis and snowshoes. Skis are the more elegant form of transportation, and in country where they are suitable they are much faster. With skis one can slide effortlessly on downhill sections of a trip, while with snowshoes one must still walk. Properly chosen and waxed skis also allow a lot of gliding on the flat and on gentle uphill slopes, except when breaking trail though heavy snow. By comparison, snowshoes require one to slog along. Finally, on many kinds of steep, open alpine terrain, skis are much easier to use than snowshoes, whether for up- or downhill going.

Before you conclude that no one in his right mind would use snowshoes in preference to skis, though, you should consider the other side of the coin. Skis are very awkward to carry when they are not in use, whereas many kinds of snowshoes can be strapped on the back of the pack so compactly that only their weight will even be noticed. Skis require snow deep enough to provide a reasonably clear path, especially on steeper slopes, and to cover rocks and stumps enough to prevent damage to the skis. Snowshoes have considerably more latitude. This difference is of little importance in places like the Sierras which have plenty of snow and open terrain, but can be decisive in regions like the Northeast which have less snow and more brush. Skis are also generally more expensive, less adaptable in use with various sorts of footwear, and demand more preliminary practice.

As a general rule, the hiker who wants to continue backpacking after the snows fall can start snowshoeing almost immediately, and he can become a skilled snowshoer in a fairly short time. Skis take more initial practice and gradual development of skills, especially for steep slopes and alpine conditions. In regions like the Northeast, skiers are more confined in their range. For country with heavy snow cover, though, skis are by far the finest means of transportation in winter.

There are many specialized varieties of both skis and snowshoes, and there is not enough space here to go into detail about choice. For snowshoes the following general considerations apply: (1) Longer shoes are faster

Some good snowshoe designs for different conditions. At the left are modified bearpaws, good in very brushy country, and fairly good for climbing. The long shoes with tails are usually known as Michigan or Maine snowshoes, and they are very good all-around models. Second from the right are Green Mountain bearpaws, a good compromise for mountains and thick woods, but not so good for steep climbing as the regular bearpaws on the right. The latter are worst of all on regular trail travel.

337

and more comfortable to wear in open country and on good trails, but they are not good for steep slopes or brushy, rough country; (2) upturned toes are best in light, powder snow and with moderate slopes; straight toes are good for step-kicking on steep slopes, but are a pain in the neck the rest of the time; (3) tails help the shoes track and reduce dragging, but they become inconvenient in brush; (4) the area of the shoe governs flotation; smaller shoes sink deeper, and more body weight or a heavier pack should indicate a bigger shoe; a long, narrow shoe may have the same flotation as a shorter, more rounded one; (5) all snowshoes should be heavier at the back, so that the toes will lift clear of the snow without special effort; (6) the area in front of the foot which actually bears weight determines whether the shoe will tend to "dive"—the smaller the front area, the more dive; a toe-hole close to the front of the shoe will make the shoe dive and will be better for climbing, but the more true this is, the less comfortable the shoe will be for straightforward going; (7) the awkwardness of snowshoes depends mainly on how far apart the legs must spread in walking, and this depends both on the width and form of the shoes—the Michigan and Maine patterns, for example, are wide in the center, but they fit together in a walking pattern so that the feet don't have to spread far; longer shoes will do the same with a long, gliding stride.

Any well-made pair of snowshoes will do in almost any country, even though each type has particular advantages. My own preference for general use is the Maine or Michigan design, both of which are rather like the old beavertail styles except that they have toes curved up a few inches. In mountain country I use bearpaws, which have no toe lift at all and which have the toe hole well forward. In regions where the advantages of very long snowshoes are evident I almost always use skis, so my experience with long snowshoes is limited.

Like snowshoes, skis come in specialized versions, but unlike good snowshoes, they are not all equally rugged. Most of the ski-binding-boot combinations used for downhill skiing these days can be dismissed out of hand for wilderness use, but with the increasing availability of Nordic touring equipment, the self-propelled skier still has a vast variety of equipment available. Any skiing gear which will be used on the flat and uphill as well as on downward runs must be adjustable to permit the heels to lift and the ankles to move back and forth. Rigid modern downhill arrangements won't do.

Acceptable equipment for wilderness skiing with backpack can range from Nordic "light-touring" gear to slightly modified downhill equipment. The lighter the equipment, the more enjoyable it is to use, but since safety and versatility have to be major considerations for wilderness skiing, lightness must often bow to conservatism. For most backpacking trips regular Nordic touring skis, 60 millimeters (2 ⅓ inches) across in the center, are the minimum size suitable in durability for backpacking in unbroken snow on varied terrain. Experienced wilderness skiers in suitable terrain can often manage with light touring equipment, but one should be wary of using such fragile gear in deep wilderness. For alpine wilderness travel, Nordic mountain skis should be considered the minimum in sturdiness—their steel edges are a necessity on steep and icy slopes. When alpine skis are used they should be fairly soft if possible, since stiffer skis tend to bury themselves in troughs of soft snow. "Deep-powder" types are excellent.

Bindings and boots for wilderness backpacking must be such that the heel will rise easily from the ski during cross-country travel. Boots and socks should be heavy and warm enough for the conditions that may be encountered; neither ultralight Nordic shoes nor alpine molded casts are suitable for the varied demands of the generalist.

My own recommendations would be as follows: for the backpacker on really easy terrain who plans to travel mainly in groups or mainly on day tours with occasional overnight trips in good snow, standard Nordic light-touring equipment with pin bindings and insulated boots; for the person who wants to do a lot of week-long or weekend backpacking on skis, mainly along trails, roads, or rolling country, standard touring skis, Nordic cable bindings, and the best insulated Nordic touring boots he can find; for the mountain tourer who expects to go through a lot of rough country, crusty snow, and icy slopes, but who is willing to sacrifice some downhill speed and control for better mobility, ski mountaineering boots, Silvretta bindings, and mountain touring skis; for the mountain tourer who doesn't want to sacrifice any of the thrills of the downhill run, a flexible downhill ski, Ramy or Eckel bindings, and a good ski-mountaineering boot.

TRAVEL IN THE SNOW

Whatever your means of transportation, on foot, ski, or snowshoe, the most important thing to remember in planning trips for the snowy seasons is the

Ski touring in the backcountry.

variability of the snow cover. The experienced mild-weather backpacker learns to judge his capabilities pretty accurately. With some general knowledge of the country and a map he can plan to get from point A to point B with relative confidence. Except for difficult off-trail routes near the peaks even the weather is not likely to slow him too much. Even the exceptions can usually be anticipated—ridges or valley rims that may or may not turn out to be passable, and so on. Snow upsets all this easy planning: the smooth ski tour of one day becomes a hard three-day slog with different snow conditions; the easy hike through six inches of powder becomes an endurance trial after a heavy night's fall; a little sun changes simple snowshoeing atop a crust into a grueling slog through sticky, wet, soft, heavy slush.

Snow can be deposited rapidly, it can form deep drifts in minutes, and it can change quickly in important ways. This fact, combined with the severity of winter weather conditions and the more isolated circumstances which generally prevail during the winter months, makes it necessary for the wilderness traveler to allow himself much greater margins for error when

340

planning trips. One of the unavoidable consequences is a much heavier pack.

Planning winter trips will depend on your means of transportation and the area where you travel and on information which you must obtain either through experience or research. The depth of the snow cover is often a vital factor in determining what a particular tour might be like, and this will vary with region and year. By midwinter of practially any year you can confidently plan to ski almost anywhere in the High Sierras of California, but that is certainly not true in New England. A late December trip through the Rockies might slide over a snow cover a couple of yards thick or take you up a trail as dry as it was in July.

The most difficult conditions for winter travel occur when there is enough snow to make walking difficult or impossible but not enough to provide a smooth cover over which to ski or snowshoe. The rocks stick out far enough to make skiing impossible, snowshoes take a terrible beating and tend to sink and jam between boulders, and the walker finds himself plunging repeatedly through the unconsolidated snow. In these conditions, all but the most ambitious are best advised to stick to smooth valley trails, where ski touring and snowshoeing are possible long before steeper slopes are filled in.

Depth of snow is relative to terrain. On the plains, fields, and beaches, a few inches of snow makes ski touring with Nordic equipment so speedy and effortless one seems to ski in a dream. Mountain boulder fields will require many feet of snow for snowshoeing and even more for skiing. An open forest floor makes for easy travel with little snow, but brush, small growth, and deadfall take much more snow before easy travel is possible. Whatever your means of transportation, pace and ambitions have to be adapted to the prevailing snow conditions, and plans have to take into account the possible changes that may precede your return to civilization. A change for the worse will cause you to regret running your supplies down to the end.

The most important special feature of the winter trail is the much greater need for regulation of the body's temperature. Cold air requires that you dress heavily at camp and during rests, but strenuous going forces your body to produce lots of extra heat, and you may find yourself sweating almost as soon as you get going. Normal human frailty prompts most people to procrastinate at each step of stripping down –*don't wait*. Take

Warm, well-chosen clothing is vital for wilderness travel in the winter.

clothes off before you begin to sweat. Perspiration will soak into your clothing almost unnoticed until you stop, and then the chill wind will remind you that sweat-soaked clothes are poor insulators. Wet clothes in winter are dangerous, and they get wet as often from the inside as from outside.

Clothing is discussed in an earlier chapter, and it is only mentioned here to note that it is important. In summer you can get away with a lot, but cold weather is often unforgiving of such carelessness.

There are several things that summer backpackers are likely to forget when they first hit the trail in the winter. Winter days are short—remember? In summer you may be able to get away with late starts and late camps, but in winter that sun goes down early, and then it gets *cold*. Wilderness travelers tend to become dehydrated easily. You work hard, you may be panting, and you often sweat without knowing it because the perspiration evaporates quickly. Winter air tends to be dry, so that you lose more moisture, and the fact that available water is frozen may make you drink much less than you need. Whether you stop for tea, get lots of liquid at supper, or solve the problem another way, it is important to maintain an adequate liquid intake. Among other things, your body is much more vulnerable to shock in case of injury if it is dehydrated. Also, it is more important to keep the food going into your system in cold weather. If you don't, hard exercise can easily drain your ready reserves, leaving you without fuel for warmth when you need it. Eat fats and proteins for staying power and carbohydrates for quick fuel.

CAMPING ON SNOW

There are several major differences between cold-weather camping and living outside at milder times of the year. For one thing the harsher climate generally makes shelter necessary. It is possible to sleep out under the sky even in winter with sensible and efficiently designed backpacking equipment, but wind combined with cold often makes this impossible. Such shelter must also do more than simply shed rain. Winter camping in the woods may utilize the cheerful combination of a lean-to tent and a fire in front, but if you plan to venture into windswept regions with sparser vegetation

Wind-driven snow makes a closed tent desirable in winter.

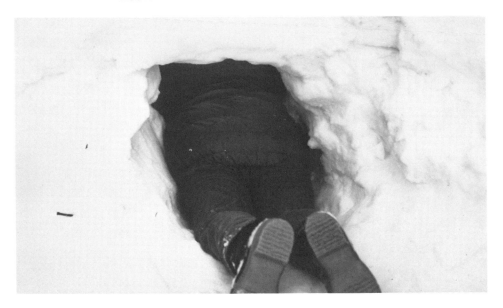

Snow shelters are good protection from the elements, although getting in and out may be chilly.

or into forests where fires would be inappropriate, you will have to build a snow shelter or have a closed tent, preferably one with a floor.

A good snow cover at least minimizes the danger of forest fire, so that there is usually no hindrance to building fires on that account. Other problems do confront the camper who wants to keep himself warm in front of a cheery fire, though. As a start, he should remember that a cooking fire is quite a different matter from a warming fire, especially when it comes to gathering wood. The mountains of wood that a healthy fire can consume have to be collected a few times before their size is adequately impressed on your mind. An ax or a saw is usually mandatory for those depending on fires for warmth in winter, both because dry wood may have to be split out of logs or stubs and because deadfall is often covered over in winter. For this purpose, emergency tools are not adequate—putting up enough wood for a good night's fire requires adequate equipment.

The problem of justification is just as relevant in winter as in summer. In some areas with plenty of fast-growing woods fuel is no problem, but in many regions it *is* a problem, and even in heavily wooded areas big fires are unjustifiable if heavy use in the summer leaves no surplus growth. Since this issue has already been mentioned, I won't belabor it here, but it is important to note that going out in the winter and proving your hardy constitution does not give you special license to cut down live trees where the cutting would be improper in summer. Deadfall may be easy enough to find where the snows don't fall too deeply, but in some places standing dead trees or stubs are the only source of deadwood. These are always good prospects for dry wood, since they will not become wet to the core until they rot out.

Cooking fires don't present the problems of all-night warming fires, and in most forested areas you can get enough wood for cooking from dead branches or deadfall, even without a good ax or saw. Squaw wood *usually* provides adequate kindling, and your pocket knife can be used to make fuzz sticks.

For any kind of fire in winter you will have to worry about the problem of a base. If the snow is only a few feet deep, digging down to the ground is the easiest expedient, but with a deep snow cover this is not practical (you don't want to have to lower pots to the fire with a line). Often the best alternative is to build on the top of a boulder when a suitable one is available, which also puts the fire at a convenient height. When this is not practical you must have a base on the snow to prevent the fire from melting its way out of sight and drowning. The traditional base uses a number of green poles, which is all right if the forest can spare them and you have the means of cutting them. A better alternative when materials are available is to use rotten chunks of logs. These are usually wet and punky enough to hold up a fire for quite a while, but they may also be buried in deep snow where you can't find them.

With a heating fire, a reflector is even more important in winter than in summer. Without a reflector, you'll need a conflagration to keep you warm and half a day to get the wood to feed it. In winter you have a ready material for building the foundation of a reflector wall—banked-up snow works to hold up a wall of logs. The snow also provides an easy method of controlling drafts. With big fire, though, you will find that melting will force frequent revision of fireplace architecture.

Backpackers using stoves for cooking in winter generally work from the comfortable interiors of their sleeping bags. Once the strenuous activity of the trail and setting up camp is over, it tends to get cold waiting around for the snow to melt and the food to heat, and the luxurious warmth of a down bag makes it a nice place to wait. Make sure you get all the chores done first. It's hard to get out of that snug bag once you're in.

When the snow cover is light, it is usually easiest to clear a spot for the tent, but with a deeper layer, a platform has to be stamped out. Start with your skis or snowshoes on; sidestep with skis and just walk around with snowshoes. Be sure to cover a large enough area, since you'll need space to walk around the tent, and you'll want a platform in front.

When you reach the point of diminishing returns with walking, start hopping up and down on the boards or webs until you are convinced that you've done all the packing you can with them on (wearing the pack will give you more oomph). Now try stepping off onto your platform to see whether you've really done all you can with the skis or snowshoes. Pack for a while with your boots. Eventually, you should end up with a fairly stable platform for the tent. Make it smooth—bumps and holes will soon freeze solid.

Set up the tent using whatever anchors are at hand that are appropriate to the snow. Sticks may work as stakes in snow of medium consistency. They can be buried and stamped down in soft snow, with the tent loops tied around them before burial. Skis, poles, ice axes, and snowshoes will all serve as anchors, but think a little beforehand. Don't use your skis to hold the main guys for the tent and then find you need them to go for water.

COOKING AND WATER

Cooking in snow camps should be kept as simple as possible, since it is usually done inside the tent or snow shelter. Stick to one-pot meals. The danger of spilling the stew in a cramped tent is bad enough without attempting any six-course suppers. In very cold weather you may be able to count on keeping some fresh food like meat without worrying about spoilage, but the main problem in winter cooking is that liquid water is often not available. Find some if at all possible. Melting snow is time-consuming and takes a lot of fuel. It takes almost as much to convert the snow to water as it does to heat that water all the way to boiling. If you must melt snow, try to find crust, ice or granular snow. Incredible quantities of light powder snow are required to get any amount of water. Melt a little snow and then keep adding more. If you start with a full pot of snow, you are liable to scorch the pan, giving a burned taste to the water and the stew. With powder snow, you are sure to scorch the pot unless the snow is added bit by bit, because the powder acts like a blotter and soaks up the water as fast as it is melted. Get plenty of liquid at meals to replace what you lost during the day, and fill your water bottle to take to bed.

A few other tips on winter cooking. Use a lot of fat. You will find that it tastes good. You need the calories, and the extra heat that is produced in digesting fat will help keep you warm. Use a cover during cooking, keep the tent door open if you can, and avoid meals that require long periods of boiling. Water vapor inside the tent in winter will condense as water or frost, and some of it will end up in your insulation.

OTHER WINTER-CAMPING NOTES

Use all of your insulation at night. Fluff up sleeping bags carefully and prepare your bed well. You may not wear your extra clothing, but you can put it in waterproof sacks or shells and use it for insulation underneath the legs and feet, as a pillow, or as extra insulation under the upper body.

Do not leave anything lying about loose outside the tent. Even a light snowfall at night will cover it up, providing it isn't blown away. Skis, poles, and snowshoes that aren't used for anchoring the tent should be stuck upright so that you won't have to dig them out.

Snow shelters are warm and protected from the wind. Learn to build them on mild afternoons. It takes practice. Igloos are hard to build except when snow conditions are right. A snow cave is generally best. It is most easily dug into the side of a large drift, preferably with a light shovel carried for the purpose. Wait for consolidated spring or wind-packed snow for your first attempt—powder snow just collapses. Make the cave just large enough to enable you to get in and make necessary movements. Dig the entrance a little lower than your sleeping spot, so that cold air will go down. Punch an air hole above you. Take your digging tools in with you in case of drifting during the night—*this is important!* Don't leave your equipment where it could be buried outside. Take it in or leave it where it could not be snowed into featureless landscape. Practice with snow shelters before you depend on using them. They are very effective, but they require experience.

347

AVALANCHES

One winter hazard of the mountains deserves special mention—avalanche danger. The mechanical properties of snow vary widely and are constantly changing, so it is always hard to judge the stability of a snow slope. A completely safe snow field of a morning may be very hazardous the same afternoon. Snow obeys the laws of gravity like any other substance; when the forces holding the snow on a slope becomes less than the force of gravity, the whole thing goes down. If you are skiing on the slope or snowshoeing under it when it decides to make its trip to the valley floor, you may not live to tell the tale.

Avalanche problems are too complicated to discuss in any detail here. The Bibliography at the back lists a number of books on the subject which should be read by anyone who travels the mountains in winter. Avalanches and other winter hazards are discussed in more detail in my book on winter camping. The beginner should beware of any slope between about 20° and 45° that is not heavily forested, especially during or after a heavy snow or blowing snow. Lee slopes are the most dangerous. Being in the runout path is almost as dangerous as being on the slope itself. An avalanche will run a long way on flat ground once it is moving.

Finally, remember that winter camping is very enjoyable, but it requires care and a conservative attitude. Allow a large safety margin in winter. The wilderness in snowy seasons is much less forgiving of stupidity or overconfidence than it is at milder times of year.

Long-Distance Walking   21

Certain basic problems become quickly obvious to anyone interested in long trips on foot, whether he inclines toward a summer journey along the Appalachian Trail or a couple of months in the Brooks Range of Alaska. Where water has to be carried it puts a very strict limit on feasible distances, but even if water is plentiful the weight of food begins to damp the enthusiasm when your ambitions stretch much beyond two weeks.

The weekend backpacker can take a fairly casual attitude toward the weight of food, even carrying fresh steaks and oranges if he likes. Long-distance travel, however, really brings him up against the problems of weight and preservation. He must also consider nutritional requirements which are not very important on short trips, ensuring that the normal vitamin and mineral needs of the body are satisfied.

On a long trip, the backpacker will work himself into excellent shape, and it is usually found that his capacity for making use of fuel will increase. During the first few weeks of a trip a caloric deficit will probably even serve the beneficial purpose of burning off accumulated city fat, but eventually an insufficient diet will slow the walker down. Besides, developing a constant craving for food is no way to enjoy a trip, so adequate food is essential.

Finally, I think that it is important to have an attractive diet on most long trips. If you are trying for some kind of endurance record you may choose to live for a couple of months on pemmican, but it's a lot more pleasant to have a varied diet which weighs slightly more per calorie. Chocolate bars and dried salami are all right for short trips, but they get awfully old after a week or two.

On a long trip a man of average size will probably need over 4,000 calories per day. It is possible to provide 4,000 calories of nutritional food with only 1½ pounds, but this requires concentrating almost exclusively on fats and protein. For most people this is likely to be a rather boring diet and also a fairly expensive one.

I would recommend planning on about 4,500 calories per man per day, at least until you are sure you can go for long periods with less—you may even find you need more. Small people may plan on a bit less. Using lightweight food, but with a reasonable amount of variety, this will probably result in a load of about 2½ pounds of food a day for each person. That adds up to 17½ pounds of food a week, and this figure may need to be increased if stoves are used and fuel must be carried.

Taking this figure, we have a load of 35 or 40 pounds for two weeks worth of food, depending on whether or not you have to carry fuel. Piled on top of your other equipment, this load will probably just about set the limit of the distance you will want to travel. It is possible to carry more, but it is not much fun.

REPLENISHING YOUR SUPPLIES

The conclusion of this discussion is that you should try to plan on replenishing your supplies at least every two weeks on a long trip. There are circumstances which may force longer intervals, and there are some methods which may enable you to lengthen your period of independence, but for most trips the two-week cutoff is reasonable.

The question then becomes how to restore your larder in the middle of your trip. This problem of logistics is the one which has always complicated the planning of expeditions into faraway places. Backpackers, like armies, march on their stomachs. Unfortunately, the problem of supply is much easier these days, because wilderness areas are shrinking.

Hikers on routes like the Appalachian Trail can use one of the simplest, cheapest, and most reliable means of resupply, since there are towns within easy reach of most of the length of the trail. One simply packages his gear in parcels of appropriate size and arranges to have a friend mail them to him, care of General Delivery at the next convenient post office. Small towns usually are poorly stocked with backpacking foods, but this system allows plenty of leeway. If you decide you want a little more food for the next leg than you had originally planned, you can purchase a few meals at the local grocery.

It is usually wise, in fact, if you are stopping at towns in this way, to buy the next day's food there. It satisfies the inevitable craving for some fresh vegetables and fruit. This method allows for lots of adjustability in your schedule. When you pick up one package, you send a postcard to your friend telling him to drop the next parcel in the mail.

There are two main defects of this admirable method. One is that the Post Office Department is not so reliable as it used to be, especially for General Delivery. Make sure to allow enough time for the packages to arrive. Sending *Special Handling* will speed their transit, and insuring them may get them treated a bit more carefully. Be sure to carry identification, because some post offices now require it, and have enough cash along to get supplies in case a package goes astray. Have all packages marked *Return Postage Guaranteed* in case you miss one.

The main problem with this method is, of course, that you have to walk into town. In many areas this may cost you a couple of extra days of travel, and in others the distance makes the whole idea impractical. You must also coordinate your schedule with that of the post office. If you arrive in town at one o'clock Saturday afternoon, you'll have to wait a day and a half to get your package. Check on the schedules of rural post offices, and then allow plenty of leeway. Maybe they shouldn't close an hour early, but it won't do you much good to know that when you find the doors locked.

Walking to town from your route may also have aesthetic disadvantages. It's often pleasant to drop off your route and have a beer after a couple of weeks, but there are some times when the continuity of the experience has real importance for you, and then it may take a week to reestablish your rapport with your line of travel. If you feel that this would be the case, use one of the other methods of resupply.

CACHING

Another good method of replenishing supplies on a long route which approaches roads occasionally is to establish caches of supplies in advance. During the planning stages of the trip, you simply take weekend jaunts to places along your route to carry in supplies. This technique has many advantages. It enables you to place your food just where you need it, eliminating the need for long side trips during your actual journey. You are independent of the schedules of local grocers and postmen. And you don't need to leave your route unless you want to. You can also establish the cache near the road or close to your path, depending on considerations of time and mood.

The defects of the cache system are fairly obvious. Lots of advance travel is necessary, a minor matter if you live within reasonable distance of the route, but not so minor if you do not. If your trip is in Wyoming and your home is in Virginia, advance trips over weekends in the spring would probably prove somewhat impractical. Under these circumstances, you may have to plant your caches just before the trip, somehow finding the extra time and patience to do it.

Caches also have to be protected from raiders, six-, four-, and two-legged. Any sturdy, tight container will do to keep out insects, but animals and people may be more determined and clever. Hide it to protect it from possible human depredation, unless the spot is exceedingly remote. A note with a moving plea may or may not be effective. Where there are trees or the right kind of rocks, hanging your supplies up should keep out four-legged scavengers. Make sure to arrange things so that squirrels cannot jump onto the top and get in that way. Metal friction-top cans will protect against rodents, and they can be buried or hung, but they are not proof against bears, so in bear country hang them well out of reach. The only major problem with metal cans is getting rid of them. Please don't toss them on the landscape just because you're on a long trip.

The degree of care and protection you give a cache should be in proportion to its importance and remoteness. Don't count on the distance from civilization alone making a food or water cache safe. In many regions food in a moving camp is relatively safe from animals, but when it is stored in one place for some time, especially when it is unattended by people, the local animal life can be expected to make a few attempts. Consider the capabilities of the local denizens when you choose sites and containers.

Don't neglect the possibilities of laying out your caches from the water. A canoe will carry far more than you ever could haul on your back, and if you are crossing rivers or lakes on your trip, you can have a pleasant advance look at the country from another point of view by bringing in some of your supplies by canoe or kayak.

Make sure that you can find your supplies when you need them. Write down the location of every cache, and be sure the location is positive. "Behind a big rock a couple of miles along the ridge north of Rabbit Ears Pass" is likely to prove vague when you come by a month later. Use bearings, markers which won't be obliterated, or some other positive means of locating the cache. All this is more important if you get someone else to lay some of your supplies out.

RENDEZVOUS

You may be able to press some of your friends into service to keep you supplied. Get one of the more dependable ones good and fired up about the trip, and then try: "Say, Harry, how about meeting me at Buchanan Pass on July 10 with a few odds and ends?" Don't tell him what the odds and ends weigh yet. In any case, once you have him hooked, drop the casual air, and make sure he'll come, through rain, sleet, or snow. Joking aside, this can be pleasant for you and your suppliers both, providing all the details are hammered out in advance so there is no chance of a foul-up. Don't pick someone who might change his mind and go on a heavy date instead.

This method can work at almost any level of difficulty and distance, although planning problems get worse as you get farther into remote areas. You might get a friend to canoe into an area with some supplies for you and spend a few days visiting. In remote areas you may be able to hire someone who will contract to bring in supplies and meet you at a certain place and date. Obviously, you have to satisfy yourself that he is reliable.

Rendezvous have great advantages in that they are adaptable to almost any kind of trip, although they require lots of advance arrangement. They provide human contact, something that might or might not attract you. Their main disadvantage is their inflexibility. You have to be there when you said you would be. If you are two days ahead of schedule, you'll have to wait, and you have to plan in such a way that there is no danger of your getting behind.

AIR SUPPLY

Rendezvous can be made with vehicles as well as people on foot, and air supply has obvious attractions for the sojourner in really remote locations. The greatest problems are those of logistics, expense, and possible interference from the weather. In many regions of the North, it is possible to arrange a meeting at a lake where the plane can land readily. This greatly simplifies packaging problems, possible confusion over location, and so on. In forested areas, lakes also provide just about the only reliable places for you and an airplane to find one another. Large snowfields and glaciers can also be used by planes equipped with skis, but this is much more complex.

For wilderness not supplied with convenient lakes, the alternative is an airdrop. You wave *hi* to the pilot from the middle of your great big visible something-or-other, and he drops your stuff attached to a parachute. I've never tried it, but it all sounds very exciting, especially if you've ever attempted to pick out a small object from a few hundred feet up, moving fast. For drops, your stuff obviously has to be packed to stand some banging, and the site and signal method from you to pilot have to be chosen with care.

In either type of air supply, make sure you have a reliable pilot who knows the country and what he is doing. If it's an airdrop, be sure he has made a few. Finding the right pilot is easier in the remote regions of the North, because small planes are more commonly used for such purposes there. A lot of bush pilots are very good, and many of them know the country they fly very well indeed. Just make *sure*.

Once you get a good pilot, don't leave any uncertainties. You're going to meet him at Big Trout Lake on such and such a date. What if he doesn't make it? Planes depend on weather and sparkplugs. What if you don't make it? Does he come back the next day, or what? If he just assures you not to worry about a thing, don't—go to someone else.

Airplanes make a lot of noise. Avoid using them, if possible. But they cost less money than you would expect. Although you have to pay for flying time both ways, from the airfield back to the same airfield, it usually

354

doesn't take very long, and sometimes you can find someone who makes regular runs to a fishing lodge or something and will give you a reduction. Rates vary a lot, somewhere between ten and twenty dollars per half-hour. Arrange everything in advance. If you haven't agreed to pay him to come looking if he misses you, he may not feel you'll reimburse him to do it. Make a definite arrangement.

PLANNING

One of the pleasures of weekend trips, once you've taken quite a few, is that you can do them on short notice. Decide to go somewhere, throw some things in your pack, and go. One of the pleasures of long trips is in the planning. The anticipation can add to your enjoyment, and the planning can be as much of a challenge as the execution. It had better be a pleasure, because there is a lot of it. Mistakes which are minor miscalculations on short trips add up to major ones when the time period extends to weeks or months. Quantities of food, water, and fuel must be calculated carefully. Menus must be planned. Socks have to be replaced and clothing washed. An inadequate sleeping bag becomes a curse rather than a small annoyance. Boots that press on the Achilles' tendons will literally cripple the wearer. Timetables have to be met, so that rendezvous are not missed or supplies allowed to run out.

Planning such a trip requires some knowledge of your equipment and yourself. You can't afford to guess how much terrain you can cover. You have to have a pretty good idea. You must also know a lot about the country to which you are going. Temperatures, terrain, water supplies, mosquito season, and a dozen other factors have to be considered. You have to be prepared for whatever problems you might encounter, so a lack of knowledge means extra weight—things you have to take because you aren't aware that you won't need them. If the snow is melted in July, you won't need an ice ax in August, but unless you find out in advance, you may end up carrying one.

You'll need maps of your whole route early in the game. How much ground are you planning to cover, and how much time do you have? What about vegetation, trails, elevation gain, and so on? Then you have to break the trip down into legs, finding places and ways to get supplies, and arranging the details. Finally, you have to buy the stuff, package it into parcels for days, weeks, and supply points, and get it where it has to go. By the time you finally get off, you'll *need* a couple of months in the wilderness.

Don't leave anything to chance in planning a long trip. Make lists, check them, and double-check them. Pay special attention to your repair kit, since wear and tear that you might normally manage at home will have to be handled on the trail. The same rule applies to certain kinds of supplies. Minor first-aid supplies get used up, as do soap, matches, film, and so forth. Plastic ground sheets wear out. Such items need periodic restocking.

Most methods of resupply can be integrated with safety checks and perhaps with chances to get extra things you might need. If you are stopping at towns, you can obviously write friends, letting them know you are all right, and perhaps requesting they mail more socks or a yellow camera filter to your next stop. A rendezvous will also serve as a safety check, and if there are several, you may also ask someone to pick up an item for you and bring it to the next meeting place. Even caches might be checked by friends for notes if you make advance plans to leave them. Your precautions depend on your taste and good sense, but give the matter some thought. At a minimum, you might leave a prearranged sequence of messages in case a search is necessary, to narrow the range down.

RELAYING

For the completely self-sufficient party, the absolutely self-contained trip or section of a trip, there is one solution other than the native porters of the pukka-sahib set: relaying. The principle is simple. You start off with a mountain of supplies and your pack frame. You pick up as large a piece of the mountain as you can carry, tie it to your frame, and carry it off in the direction you want to go, for a period that suits your taste. You leave the piece and go back for the rest of the mountain. Eventually, all of the mountain has either been eaten or carried to its new location. Repeat.

Eventually, attrition reduces the mountain to a size that will fit into one packload. By this time, if your calculations have been accurate, the remaining supplies are just about enough to carry you to the place you are going and still leave a bit for emergencies. The method is tedious and is used mainly for climbing large mountains, but it has some place in the normal repertoire of long-distance techniques. For trips where the return is over the same route, caches are left along the way for the trip back.

AND THEN THERE'S LIVING OFF THE LAND

For long-distance trips into wilderness far from any roads, the idea of living off the country has obvious attraction. If you could count on getting most of your food from the woods and waters, you could plan on a three-month trip with only what you could carry in a reasonable pack. Sometimes it is possible, but as a rule it isn't.

To begin with, the pressure of population, excessive hunting, and poor conservation has necessitated game laws which are not designed for the pot-hunter. Even where there is sufficient game, seasons are usually very limited. This is sometimes true of fishing as well. Big game is generally out of the question except in rare cases.

For someone who wants to live off the country, the best prospects are fishing, small game, and native plants. All these may be useful to supplement food you carry, but unless you have spent lots of time in a particular area and know food-gathering methods there well, it would be unwise to plan on getting a great deal of your food from the land. You would probably find that you could hunt for food or walk, but not both. In good fishing country, or at a time and place with plenty of berries, you might get a lot of your food from the land, but think twice before you count on it, and always carry a reserve of food with you for scarce times.

Techniques for living off the land should be kept in conformity with good conservation practices, whether these are legally required or not. Especially in harsh environments, the ecological system is often a fragile thing. The fact that an animal is not protected does not necessarily mean that it is plentiful. If you hunt or fish, have some concern for the animals that are providing you with food. Don't violate game laws just because there is no warden around.

Plant hunters can also be destructive. Pick your berries without pulling the plant out by the roots, and don't tear up the plant cover in places like alpine tundra, where it regenerates slowly. Heavy plant gathering

357

should usually be restricted to zones where plant life is abundant and grows quickly.

Living off the land, while it is still perfectly appropriate in areas like northern British Columbia, which are very sparsely populated, is becoming a less and less desirable activity in the wilderness areas which are easily accessible and suffering from severe population pressure. The normal ethic of the wilderness traveler in this day and age should be to leave the wilderness in the condition in which he found it, without a mark of his passage, rather than trying to harvest it. Men can no longer live as predators; there are too many of them.

Bivouac Camping: Going Extra-Light 22

Personal styles of tripping in the wilderness range over a full spectrum, from the luxury lover who won't move in the morning without his fresh-baked blueberry muffins to the half-mad saints like John Muir who cover hundreds of miles on the bread crusts and tea they carry in their pockets. Both extremes are poorly represented in this book, since I never go to either one.

Bivouac camping tends toward the Spartan side of the continuum, but thanks to modern equipment it is usually a lot more comfortable than the nights suffered by some of the hard men of the past. With down clothing, lightweight waterproof material, aluminum pots, and tiny gasoline stoves, a comfortable night can be spent with amazingly light and compact equipment.

The bivouacker attempts to reduce his load to an absolute minimum consistent with safety and reasonable comfort. The definitions of both "safety" and "reasonable comfort" will vary, but the intent is to shave them down as closely as possible. Though many campers have begun this way through lack of funds, it isn't really a technique to be recommended for the beginner, especially in cold weather, in the mountains, or in the desert. Both enjoyment and safety in this sort of camping depend on skill and good physical condition. Further, equipment for this style of travel may in fact turn out to be more expensive than for more hedonistic methods, because really good quality is essential.

EQUIPMENT

Equipment for bivouac camping must be even more carefully matched with the conditions of the area in which you plan to travel than more orthodox outfits. Generally, when the lightweight specialist sets up his "bivvy" for the night, he puts on every piece of clothing he carries. There isn't any spare sweater for a cold night—the sweater is included in the initial calculations. This applies to each item of equipment. A tent is usually not carried. A light tarp may be used as shelter, ground cloth, and fire reflector, but just as often the poncho, cagoule, or walking tent doubles for rain protection on the trail and at night. In case of rain a natural shelter is found when possible, and if not, one stretches or huddles beneath one's own.

Cooking equipment is kept simple by cooking simply. In forested areas, a coffee can for a pot, a cup, and a spoon do very nicely. Where fires can't be built, food can be eaten cold, a very light gasoline stove can be carried, or chemical fuels like heat tablets can be used for small heating jobs. I feel that fires and gasoline or bottled gas stoves are the only methods worth considering except for emergency kits. If I can't build a fire and don't want to carry a stove, I plan to eat my food cold. Heating tablets aren't worth the trouble.

Obviously the principles of choosing equipment for bivouacking are the same as for any other kind of camping. There are no miracle materials that will buy you luxury at no cost of weight and money. The lightweight specialist cuts extra ounces off by sacrificing other virtues for efficiency, versatility, and light weight. If he travels in cold regions where down sleeping equipment is needed, he may use a down parka and a half-bag for sleeping, getting a jacket as well as sleeping gear into the same package. Otherwise he picks the tightest-fitting and most efficient bag, trading roominess for light weight. Unnecessary extra clothing is left at home. The most rudimentary shelter possible is used.

The equipment needed for bivouac camping cannot be prescribed, because its choice depends on the experience of the camper. In the woods it may consist of a light ax, some matches and food, and a coffee can and spoon for eating and cooking. The mountains in winter will require a light shovel and expensive down equipment with a host of other essential items.

PUTTING UP WITH DISCOMFORTS

The main difference between bivouac camping and ordinary backpacking is that the lightweight enthusiast is willing to sacrifice some comfort in the interests of increased mobility. He may not *always* be less comfortable, but by cutting down on his reserve equipment, he must willingly face the possibility of a few wet, cold nights from time to time. On a really cold night he expects to survive unharmed but understands he will do some shivering. His menu is Spartan, planned for the least possible weight, and it may be eaten cold. He eschews a spacious tent in favor of a cranny under a rock, knowing that he can travel farther without the extra weight.

Bivouacking is not always uncomfortable by any means. Warm nights under the stars and dry nights in natural shelters are remembered with affection by every hiker who enjoys camping with an absolute minimum of equipment. On occasion, however, even the most skillful suffer a miserable night. That's not so bad when the sun rises bright and warm the next morning, but sometimes the night is followed by a raw and cheerless day. Then the bivouac camper is forced to turn philosopher to explain his devotion to the art.

EXPERIENCE AND PHYSICAL CONDITION

Bivouac camping is a delightful style of backpacking. It allows a more intimate contact with one's surroundings than more elaborately equipped methods do. The lightly equipped hiker can cover a tremendous amount of ground in a day, even in rough terrain. However, the line between effective lightweight travel and getting into trouble because of inadequate equipment is fine—that is what bivouacking is all about. The lightweight specialist has to know what he is doing. He may not be able to afford the mistakes that inexperienced people are bound to make. It is important to work into this type of backpacking gradually, as you gain experience and knowledge both of your own ability and the vagaries of the land you travel.

Bivouacking with a real minimum of equipment demands precise knowledge of the area in which you are traveling. How fast can you drop down to timberline? How easily can fires be made in the rain? How cold does it get at night four thousand feet above the highest weather observation station, and how hard do the winds blow? The average backpacker simply takes enough equipment to allow him plenty of leeway, but the bivouacker wants to cut this to an absolute minimum, and he must have a pretty good idea of the answers to such questions. The experienced wilderness traveler in an unfamiliar area will always take more than he needs, because he has to allow room for error about conditions.

The beginner also should beware of leaving basic equipment home too soon. Practice the techniques of improvising a shelter before you stake your life on being able to do it. Bivouacking safely requires skill and judgment on such matters that will come only with experience.

One other factor which is important for bivouac camping is good physical condition. Going extra-light requires a certain amount of gambling with weather conditions. If you lose the gamble, you are thrown on your body's reserves of endurance and strength. The dependability of those reserves and your proper assessment of them are even more important than your equipment as a guarantee of reasonable safety. If you are out of shape, you may be using most of your available strength to cover the distance you have traveled, and a good meal and warm sleeping bag may be essential to allow your body to recover from the day's exertions. If this is the case, a cold night may leave you in poor shape to handle any difficulties. These are the ingredients of real trouble in the backcountry.

Understanding your body is also important. Too many people, especially men, refuse to admit that their bodies have limits. The superman complex often blinds one to information that is critical for successful bivouacs. No two people's bodies work in quite the same way. Metabolism, weight, circulation, and a dozen other factors vary greatly. In consequence, tolerance of cold and different kinds of food is completely different from one person to the next. Such tolerance does not necessarily correspond with general physical condition. Thin, wiry, lightweight people tend to chill more quickly even if they are in excellent shape, because they have little fat under the skin (fat is a good insulator) and because their surface area per pound of body weight is greater, causing them to lose a higher percentage of heat.

Many other factors enter into cold tolerance, however, so that it is impossible for anyone except you to predict how many wool shirts you will need to get through a cold night, even if you use every heat-saving trick known. You will be able to predict such information only by watching how you react in different circumstances. Your responses to different kinds of food in different situations are just as important and even less predictable by an outsider. Some people can sit out a cold night, fueling themselves happily with dry salami and chocolate bars. Others cannot tolerate fats when they get cold—their circulation to the stomach is too poor to digest it —they need sugars and perhaps hot food. Find out your idiosyncrasies in advance.

A CONTINUING EXPERIMENT

Though bivouac camping is often comfortable and almost luxuriant, it is also wrapped up inextricably with a kind of self-testing and stoicism. One tests and refines his skills at taking every advantage of his knowledge of the land and the capacities of his body. A bit of care will ensure that this doesn't involve undue risk, but it will inevitably call for endurance of some discomfort. You can't find out how little you can get by with except by trying to get by with less and less. Pushing yourself to the limits is a good thing; you will usually find that they are a lot farther than you imagined. The human body is a very elastic thing, especially when it is frequently stretched so that it does not become brittle.

Still, this kind of testing is not everyone's cup of tea. It is possible for anyone in good health to backpack without sacrificing much in the way of comfort and bodily pleasure. The same cannot be said of bivouacking. If even thinking about a long, chilly night of wakeful shivering bothers you, don't try ultralight travel.

23 Backpacking with Children

Backpacking makes a really pleasant family sport, providing that a reasonable amount of common sense is used in planning family trips. Children cannot be expected to go like adults in their prime, nor can they be expected to want to repeat the experience of an unpleasant first trip. Older kids with adventurous spirits may be willing to put up with quite a few hardships and still enjoy themselves, but younger children require gradual acclimatization to an unfamiliar environment. Don't make their first trip on a weekend in October when the weather looks like it might pour cold rain down for a few days in a row. The same cautionary note applies to older kids who think that a walk in the country means a stroll in the park at the end of the subway line. A lot of young people (like a lot of old people) don't adjust easily to strange surroundings. Take them car camping and on day hikes on nice sunny weekends to break them in.

BACKPACKING INFANTS

In some ways infants are easier to handle on backpacking trips than older children are. They don't want to walk, aren't yet place-oriented, and they almost always love the movement of the carrier. A baby may fuss when you first put him in the carrier, but he will quiet down as soon as you get moving, unless he is really uncomfortable for some reason. Plan your trips in reasonably clement weather, and allow plenty of extra time for feeding and changes, and you should be able to take a pleasant trip with the baby along.

The biggest problem on trips with infants and toddlers is the bulk of their clothing, since you need to carry a lot of changes. If the weather is at all chilly or windy, you don't want to leave wet things on the child. And while the extra clothes and diapers don't weigh very much, they take up a lot of space. They can be put in a stuff sack and be attached to the outside of the pack or baby carrier.

I have little use for disposable diapers at home, but on trips where fires can be built they are a real blessing, simply because you don't have the weight of wet diapers to worry about. I think the best kind is the one without a plastic cover which is meant to go in special pants. These weigh less and take up less space than the full-sized kind, and the lack of individual plastic covers makes them a bit easier to get rid of. While you're on the trail you can drop these into a plastic sack hung on your pack. When you reach camp, set them on a rock or branch to dry as much as possible. After you're finished cooking, build the fire up and burn them. Throw in a little at a time—if you toss three or four wet diapers on top of the fire at once, they'll put it out. This method requires firewood, and in its absence, cloth diapers will probably work better. Carry cloth diapers to use at night, anyway, so that the baby won't soak its clothing and sleeping things and get cold. The cloth ones absorb much more liquid.

If you are using cloth diapers, you may be able to make your stops where water is available and rinse the diapers out (not in the stream, please). Then you can hang them on the pack to dry, and once dry they can be stored in a plastic bag. For trips longer than two or three days, you will certainly have to stop to do washes every couple of days with any child who isn't toilet trained.

Food is really less of a problem than clothing with infants and toddlers. Breast-feeding simply requires the choice of a scenic spot for a stop. For bottle-feeding, carry plastic bottles, which are lighter and don't get broken. Use one of the powdered formula preparations that makes up on the spot, like dried Enfamil or Similac. All you need is a clean bottle with the right amount of clean, tepid water. Since you make it up at the time and don't store it, sterilization isn't necessary. Water will be available at body temperature if you put the water in the bottle an hour or two ahead of time, and then carry it in your pocket.

Other food isn't too much of a problem either, although this will depend on what you are already feeding your child. Lots of dehydrated foods reconstitute in mushy form, and you can try these out on your baby at home first. Banana flakes, pea and bean powders, dried mashed potatoes and yams, puddings, custards, and cooked cereals are examples. Regular baby cereals are as easy to make in camp as at home. If you prefer, it isn't much trouble to carry jars of baby food along.

Sleeping arrangements can be managed with pinned blankets and the like, with packs and other padded objects forming a bed. One of the fluffy synthetic "sleepers" is a good garment to use inside the blankets. As the child gets older, a Dacron-filled mummy-type sleeping bag can be gotten at a reasonable price; down is a poor choice until the child can sleep dry.

SLIGHTLY OLDER

Children are hardest to manage on trips at age four or five. The exact age varies with the child and the parent, but it is reached when he gets too heavy to carry and is still too young to walk very far. You may be able to carry the child some of the time, letting him walk for the rest, but you'll probably have to plan shorter trips. Try to make the trip interesting. Children at this age are rarely enthusiastic about just hiking. They may enjoy playing outside, but they don't want to make headway on a trail. They are capable of walking a long way but get bored doing it. Getting the child interested in looking for wildflowers, insects, trees, or what have you can serve the dual purpose of teaching him something about the subject and getting him pleasantly from point A to point B. Water is a great help. Half an hour playing in a stream will renew flagging spirits.

Don't expect to make very long distances each day with children this age. Plan to stop early in the day, and use up your extra energy taking walks or climbs from camp. Everyone will be happier as a result.

SCHOOL AGE

From about the age of six or eight, children start to become good hikers. The only trick is to keep up their enthusiasm and interest. Try to make trips pleasant and interesting. Some children can take a lot of challenge, but others can't. Don't overdo things.

By this age, children are usually enthusiastic about carrying their own packs. Give them some of their own bulky things, but don't let their packs get too heavy. Kids have plenty of energy, but not too much endurance.

Watch your children's clothing carefully, especially in cold or hot weather. Because their bodies are smaller, they can become chilled or over-heated very quickly. A child needs an extra sweater when a cool breeze starts to blow and a hat to protect his head against the sun even more than an adult does. Use sunbonnets for small children in warm weather. A child also needs periodic snacks for energy. These strictures apply even to adolescents. A teen-ager generally does not have quite the reserves of an adult in similar physical condition.

Once children stay dry through the night, sleeping gear can be about the same as adults'. A few economies can be made in that younger children don't usually go on trips where really severe conditions are expected. Dacron mummy bags may be adequate during the years when they are growing fastest. A child's down bag will also double as a footsack for adult bivouac equipment. (Many manufacturers sell the same bag for both purposes.) If you do want a down bag for a younger child, you might want to consider the new kit that is being offered by Frostline. The bag is made so that extensions can be sewn on as the child grows, spreading the weight and expense of the bag over several years.

CARRIERS

Small children have to be carried, at least some of the time, and quite a few manufacturers are now making carriers. Very young infants don't get enough back support from the standard frame carriers. Several solutions are possible. The frameless carrier shown in the picture is excellent for infants, as are other similar ones. Good carriers for very young children can also be made from small frameless day packs by cutting leg holes. Finally, you can make a sort of cocoon for the child in a regular frame carrier by dropping the seat and packing the baby in receiving blankets.

One trouble with the frameless carriers is that they don't allow the child much freedom to move and look around. As the child gets older, a

367

A frameless carrier like this works well for infants. A shell parka can be worn over the whole thing, baby and all, if a cold wind should come up. A pack can also be carried on the back.

frame pack is more suitable. The parent is also likely to find the frame type more comfortable as the child gets heavier.

Frame carriers are made either so that the passenger can face forward or backward. The forward-facing type is easier to carry, but is a little hotter and gives the child less freedom to kick his legs around. Of the two sets of disadvantages, I prefer those accompanying the forward-facing style. If you buy a frame carrier, get one with the seat suspended in a larger compartment, like the one shown in the picture. These are adjustable, and they give you some space to store diapers, extra clothes, and so forth.

The problem of who carries the child for a backpacking trip of a weekend or a week is largely a matter of balancing weights and strength. All equipment can be packed on one packframe for the man to heft, while the mother carries the baby, or some combination can be worked out. One method is shown in the picture. An extension is mounted on the top of the packframe, while the pack is mounted in a low position. Then the baby carrier can be strapped to the extension. The extension can be purchased, or you can make one out of a couple of pieces of broomstick and a piece of aluminum rod. This arrangement isn't too bad when the child is really young, but it starts to get pretty heavy around age three!

Frame carriers like this are the best way to carry children once they are old enough to sit up well.

When you are picking routes for backpacking with a child in a carrier, steer as clear as possible of thick brush. It becomes quite tricky to get through without scratching the baby. Be careful about leaning forward to duck under brush and limbs, lest you run the baby right into the obstacle. The arrangement with the baby high on a packframe is only for open routes. The child is much higher than your head, and real care is required in watching for branches that might hit him.

OTHER COMMENTS

Younger children generally take to camping quite well, but the unfamiliar surroundings are apt to be rather scary at first, particularly at night. A little time and thought will prevent unpleasant experiences that leave lasting impressions. If you get up in response to the child in the middle of the night, shine the light on your face, not on his. That flashlight coming at you in

369

The carrier can be strapped on top of an extension on the frame, and the pack carried below. With an older child this makes a heavy load. This arrangement is not for brushy routes!

the middle of the night isn't very comforting. Small children should be very thoroughly diapered and sheathed in rubber pants on a cool night, so that their bedding doesn't get soaked and cold. Above all, don't push the child too hard to match your ambitions for the trip. Make it pleasant, so that he will want to go again.

Watching the World Around You

The backpacker has an unusual opportunity to s which is relatively free of people. Occasionally he m to see one which shows few signs of human influenc becoming quite rare. You can become absorbed around you without understanding too much of i' miliar with many of its other inhabitants. Person; know of the incredibly complex ecological system t ing, the more appreciation I gain for it.

In the short space of this chapter, it's imp about nature study. One of the characteristics o more you learn about it, the more aware you ar knowledge and the better your realization of t' actions that go on even in the tiniest and most around us.

One of the interesting aspects of nature that many things which might excite your c derstood. This is still an area in which the real contributions if he is so inclined, althou to satisfying our own sense of wonder. Thei wildlife in its habitat, a particular exciteme never seen before or which has never be traveling. There are also moments of vision, much harder to come by, when a vantage point combines with your own state at the moment to make you really, intuitively understand some great natural process. Whether you are looking at the strata of a mountain from a particular angle, watching a bank of clouds roll in, or studying an insect engaged in his tasks, such a moment of understanding is priceless.

In this chapter I'll try to make some suggestions on ways that you can find out about some of the workings of the country around you when you go backpacking and how to become acquainted with some of its inhabitants.

LEARNING THE NAMES OF THINGS

One aspect of nature study is inevitably the problem of identification. You can study a plant yourself, or watch an animal, without having any idea what others have called it. If you want to be able to look it up later on, however, to find out what is known about its patterns of life as an aid to future observations, you'll have to find out what it is called. Learning to identify shells or birds or grasses tends to be a nuisance and a bore at first, but it usually becomes fascinating after you have passed the first frustrating stages of finding out what to look for.

Naming things in a reasonable way actually requires a good deal of understanding, and taxonomy, the science of classification and naming, is a subject with fascinations of its own. For the beginner, books which use popular names and descriptions that aren't too obscure are obviously preferred. In many areas, this is all that is ever needed. "Red-shafted flicker" is certainly adequate and is comprehensible to more people than *Colaptes cafer* just as "sugar maple" is generally more satisfactory than *Acer saccharum.*

It is worth realizing from the beginning, though, that some disciplines have their own jargon for reasons other than obfuscation. Popular names can sometimes be very confusing because they vary so much. One flower

---

Walking the wild country, occasionally you have moments of vision when you intuitively apprehend the great natural forces around you. Junipers in the Desolation Wilderness.

can have half a dozen names, and each one of them may be applied to completely different plants in other regions. This can have amusing results, as in one argument I remember over whether a tree was a ponderosa pine or a yellow pine (the same thing), but it can be very confusing as well. There is a great advantage to a scientific system of nomenclature which is generally used throughout the literature. The standard system is in Latin, although there are standardized English lists in some specialized fields. (For North American birds, for example, there is the American Ornithologists' Union checklist.)

Amateur naturalists who get interested in certain areas will ultimately have to learn the scientific system of nomenclature for one of several reasons. Popular names simply don't exist for many plants. Conspicuous forms of life like birds, mammals, and wildflowers attract enough attention to have common names, but this is not always true of small plants or insects. The keys and literature used by professionals will be likely to use scientific names. For an introduction to standard scientific nomenclature for the plant and animal kingdoms, refer to the Bibliography at the end of this book.

FIELD GUIDES FOR THE AMATEUR

The beginner does not usually have to resort to the full paraphernalia of technical descriptions these days, because good field guides, written in fairly plain English with useful illustrations, are now available for most things you might want to begin learning about—birds, trees, shells, and so forth. The importance of this for the beginner is hard to overemphasize. Many older guides are overlarge, require a dictionary to use, need long, tedious cross-referencing to find necessary information—the list could go on and on. The best modern field guides are so well done that the beginner can actually *use* one right away.

The backpacker has to be very selective about what he carries, so he must limit himself in the subjects on which he wants to concentrate on a particular trip. You won't get very far if you pack up a geology of the area, a couple of bird guides, a flower book, a manual of woody plants, and half a dozen other volumes. Concentrate on one or two subjects at a time, and then be selective in choosing your guide to each.

Some birds are readily identified without guides, like these magnificent Canada geese at mating time.

Invariably, the best way to learn about birds or geology or clouds or trees is to get someone who is knowledgeable to show you. He can work from the specific to the general, and in thrashing through a book you have to go the other way. He can point out the pattern of flight of a flicker or a horned lark, something a book can never adequately describe. He can tell you that the plant you found varies from the norm in a particular way because of its exposure to the elements.

If you can't get someone to teach you, the next best thing is a good field guide. It is also the transition tool for the beginner who has learned the basics and is starting out on his own or the expert on his first hike in a new region. To use a field guide effectively, you have to become acquainted with it. Each guide will have a different system of identification, depending on its purpose and its author. Some guides will require only a

375

cursory glance at the beginning, while with others, long advance study will pay off when you get outside.

The guide must use some kind of a system of classification. A good one will have a system that is easy for the amateur to use in the field. If you're looking for a tree guide to New England for use on ski tours, don't pick one that relies mainly on leaf characteristics. Unless you have achieved some botanical proficiency, you will be better off with a flower guide that makes basic separations with simple-minded distinctions like color instead of anatomical classification. Many plant guides use keys, a programmed system which guides you through a series of questions, each answer taking you to a new question, until you finally arrive at your species, as if by magic. Try the key out on a few things when you first look at the guide. You may find that it works beautifully, or you may discover that it is hopelessly confusing. In general, keys are best used in narrowly based guides—for example, those designed for use in a particular region. Keys to large numbers of species become rather complex. One problem with keys is that if you make one mistake you are led down a dead-end path. Other systems are sometimes better because you end by comparing a number of characteristics.

Field guides to animals are necessarily more complicated than most plant guides. Although one usually has to consider more species of plants, a tree or flower will stand still for examination. A tree guide may be able to rely on one characteristic, say the needles of a pine. A bird guide must show many field marks—a tail band will do you no good if you saw just the front of the bird. A fox may leave only his tracks as a sign of his passage.

CHOOSING GUIDES

A number of general field guides are listed at the back of this book, but often the best solution is a pamphlet that confines itself to a particular region, perhaps even narrowing the field further to a season. For the backpacker a local guide will eliminate a lot of extra ounces, and for the beginner it will limit the headaches. Limitation of scope can greatly simplify a manual. Regional guides are often prepared under the auspices of universities or museums, and their limited scope may keep them out of standard bookstore channels, but they are well worth searching out.

Special regional guides often cover a larger range of subjects than

A lightweight local guide to plants and animals in the Rocky Mountains would enable you to identify the more common and prominent flowers like these columbine.

comprehensive field manuals for North America, the eastern United States, or similar large geographical areas. There are good guides to the wildlife and plants of the southern and northern Rockies, for example, which discuss all the more commonly encountered flora and fauna very well. One small volume thus covers a great deal of the most interesting natural history of a good-sized region.

It is worth spending some time in a library studying various field books. Try to envision their use outdoors, or take them out for a day, if this is feasible. Try to find those which most closely suit your purposes. A field guide becomes an old friend—you get far more out of it because of long acquaintance, so it is worth choosing well. Usually, modern guides are most useful. Improvements in printing technology have allowed much better use of illustrations, and of course, new authors have a chance to profit from past mistakes. Sometimes, though, you will find a very old guide which is far superior to anything recent, especially in the special regional manuals.

Field guides are necessarily very brief in their discussions. The purpose of a field guide is to enable you to identify a hawk, not to delve into its life history. Generally, only those habits will be included which will help in distinguishing the species. You will have to go to other books to make a real acquaintance after you have been introduced by a field manual.

It is usually best to start with an introduction to the natural history of the place you are traveling in. Some broad information about the ecology of the alpine zone or the Great Basin desert will give you a framework into which to fit the life cycle of a particular inhabitant. If you want to find a species, some knowledge of its habits is a great help in deciding where and when to look.

GETTING STARTED

The natural world is a complex and continuous web; there is no starting point and no end. Whatever you begin to study will ultimately lead you everywhere else. If you begin with the landforms, the history of which extend far back beyond the beginning of life and for which a thousand years is a moment, you will still find soil produced and bound together by plants. If you look, you will find great cliffs of rock made up solely of the fossilized skeletons of billions upon billions of tiny animals.

Start at the point that interests you. You might just want to be able to identify the trees in your favorite forest or along a mountain trail. You might want to make a better acquaintance with the hawk that soars on the summer thermals while you take your midmorning break. You might want to find out something about the forces that shaped and sculpted a valley you frequently camp in or to be able to make a better pattern of the stars you watch from your sleeping bag. Perhaps you would just like to find some good salad greens.

A little patience is generally required in many fields of nature study. Bird-watching or track-hunting is likely to be a bit frustrating at first, until you have beaten enough of the basics into your skull, then things will begin

A pair of lightweight binoculars is a great help to the backpacker in many kinds of nature study. These are 6 x 25, meaning that they magnify six times, and the diameter of the objective lens is 25 millimeters. 6 x 15 is even lighter and adequate for most purposes, although they would be poor in twilight.

to come much more quickly. If you don't feel patient, try learning trees or constellations first—a few satisfying results usually come a bit more quickly.

TOOLS OF THE TRADE

Some areas of nature study require nothing more than an alert pair of eyes and an inquiring mind. On the other hand, you may find yourself carrying more weight in equipment for your investigations than for staying alive and comfortable. The backpacker has to make do with lightweight equipment in order to travel freely in the wilderness. Pick your binoculars and other items with an eye toward weight and versatility. When you've learned enough of the basics, carry a notebook and paper instead of a library of guidebooks, and look up that odd flycatcher when you get home.

Very lightweight inexpensive binoculars are now available which are ideal for the backpacking wildlife watcher. The price you pay for the low weight is measured light-gathering ability; in other words, such glasses are not effective in poor light. This is rarely critical in the backcountry, at least in my experience. For even lighter weight, you can carry a monocular instead, although this is less satisfactory for some purposes. Either will double as a magnifier by looking backward through it at close range. Whatever tools you carry, try to keep their weight down while making them serve as many purposes as possible.

The study of your surroundings can enrich your backpacking trips and your life for as long as you pursue it. Whether you limit your study to a hedonistic subject like edible mushrooms or follow an arcane interest in lichens, it is sure to increase your enjoyment of your own trips and broaden your understanding of the balance of natural forces in the wilderness. It is a pursuit which brings its own rewards.

Part 4

Where to Go
and What to Do
When You Get There

Some Nice Places
to Backpack

There are so many fine places to go backpacking in Mexico, the United States, and Canada, that there is not the slightest hope of compiling a list of a very large number of them here. The best that I can hope to do is to mention a few interesting places for you to consider and to suggest a few spots that you might not think to investigate. Some are wilderness areas and some are not, while some fall in between. By definition a maintained trail is not a wilderness, but it may run through a true wilderness. Some trails, in fact, although they were built by people, are kept open mainly by animal traffic.

Several great trail systems and routes exist which should take precedence in a list of places to go backpacking, the first and best known of which is the . . .

APPALACHIAN TRAIL

The Appalachian Trail is a well-maintained and well-marked trail extending two thousand miles from the summit of Mount Katahdin in Maine to Springer Mountain in Georgia. Hundreds of side trails provide access and additional interest. The trail is described in detail in a series of trail guides describing each section in nearly perfect detail. The country along it varies from deep forests and bogs to the boulder fields above timberline in the Presidential Range. In the country through which it winds travel is often exceedingly difficult without trails. So for the long-distance walker in the eastern United States, the Appalachian Trail and its branches are a favorite refuge from the megalopolis. The fine maintenance is a real blessing in an area where the brush overgrows an unused trail very quickly indeed. There are many lean-tos and shelters along the trail.

Besides the guides listed in the Bibliography, you can get information on the trail from the Appalachian Trail Conference, 1718 N Street, N.W., Washington, D.C. 20036. Many local affiliated clubs cut and maintain hundreds of miles of other trails. Request a list of such clubs from the conference.

PACIFIC CREST TRAIL

Unlike the Appalachian Trail, which was established and is maintained by dedicated hikers on the East Coast, the Pacific Crest Trail varies tremendously in its condition and marking. From available information you could plan a trip over the length of the Appalachian Trail in a week, but setting up for the Pacific Crest would take long and careful checking.

The trail is about 2,300 miles long and traverses some of the most beautiful country in the United States. It begins in the arid mountains of southern California, winds through the beautiful Sierra Nevada Range and then through the Southern and Northern Cascades. Passing the rock walls of the Sierra and the glaciers of the Cascades, this trail presents one of the finest backpacking possibilities in the world. The trail is more rugged and not so well marked and maintained as the Appalachian Trail. Some sections, like the John Muir Trail in the Sierra, are heavily traveled in summer, but some other parts are not much visited. The trail passes through twenty-five national forests and six national parks. A description is available from the Pacific Crest Trail Conference, Green Hotel, Pasadena, California 91101.

THE ROCKY MOUNTAIN ROUTE

The longest route of all, and one which is not yet a trail, generally follows the Continental Divide from Mexico to Canada. The divide separates westward-flowing streams from eastward ones. It extends well over three thousand miles from its entry to the United States in New Mexico, through the high country of Colorado, over semidesert and glaciated peaks in Wyoming, along the Montana-Idaho border for a way, and finally through Montana and Glacier National Park to the Canadian border.

A trail route has been proposed which generally follows the divide, departing from it where it becomes too rugged, but only some sections of the trail actually exist, and the challenge of wilderness route finding is very real for any backpacker attempting a section of the divide route. The route passes through three national parks and many wilderness areas.

OTHER LONG TRAIL SYSTEMS

There are many other trail systems, formal and informal, which can occupy the backpacker for weeks. The *Long Trail* in Vermont is the oldest, extending 261 miles through the state, traveling in beautiful woods, and climbing in the northern section into fine mountain areas. A part of the Long Trail is included in the Appalachian Trail.

You might be surprised to know that the greatest system of state trails in the country is in Pennsylvania, which has well over four thousand miles of state trails. This system includes the new *Susquehannock Loop Trail*, an 85-mile trail within easy reach of New York, Philadelphia, and other teeming millions. You can get a map of the system for seventy-five cents from Keystone Trails Association, P.O. Box 144, Concordville, Pennsylvania 19331.

The *Northville–Lake Placid Trail* is an even better goal for refugees from the megalopolis, passing through some fine semiwilderness in upstate New York. There are about a dozen lean-tos along the route and many fine campsites. You can get a free pamphlet describing the trail from the New York State Department of Environmental Conservation, Bureau of Forest Recreation, Wolf Road, Albany, New York 12205.

AND OTHER PLACES

If you travel a bit farther, to the northern end of the Appalachian Trail at Maine's Mount Katahdin, you will find one of the finest backpacking areas in the eastern United States. Katahdin is in *Baxter State Park*, whose managers have mercifully protected it from would-be improvers, developers, and other assorted vultures, so that it remains a paradise for the wilderness lover. At the height of the summer season, you'll have to make reservations or take your chances, since the rangers will not permit overuse of the campgrounds. In spring or fall, which are nicer anyway, you shouldn't have much trouble. Unfortunately, the park policies toward winter travelers are still rather unenlightened and practically prohibitive of winter travel by skiers and snowshoers who can't afford a ranger as a companion and guide.

One of the most interesting spots in the East, and one of the least visited (believe it or not!), is in New Jersey. The great *pine barrens* stretch in from the shore, covering over a million acres, and most evidence of civilization you will find there consists of ruins dating back to colonial times. Although there are some developed campgrounds along roads, heading back into the woods will soon get you away from your fellow men. There are a few maintained trails, but it is more interesting to follow the remnants of ancient roads.

In Ohio you can follow the 500-mile *Buckeye Trail*, parts of which travel through interesting country. Some sections are rather urban for the backpacker, and permits may be required for entry or overnight camping from various public and private groups. Trail maps and information can be had from the Buckeye Trail Association, 913 Ohio Building, 65 South Front Street, Columbus, Ohio 43215.

Westerners have so much country to choose from that any listing is almost random. California alone has nearly sixteen thousand miles of trails on federal lands and over fifteen hundred miles of state trails. Colorado has over eleven thousand miles of trails and Idaho over ten thousand. These states and others in the West, besides having more trails than you could explore in a dozen lifetimes, have many possibilities for off-trail travel. Even a whole book of selected routes would necessarily be capricious and arbitrary, and picking a few trails and spots for this chapter seems nearly hopeless.

386   All of the national parks, all of the wilderness areas, primitive areas,

and many national forests and national monuments are fine places to back-pack. Some of the national parks are becoming crowded, but getting away from the roads will usually leave the crowds far behind. Even overburdened Yellowstone has some wonderful little-used corners, and if you head across the northern park border to the incredibly fine *Beartooth Primitive Area,* you will find one of the wildest and most rugged regions in the country, a true wilderness for the mountain-minded traveler with enough experience to find his own way.

The *Wind River Range* of Wyoming is another of the best alpine wildernesses in the West. Many trails and routes are described in Beckey's guide (see the Bibliography), but bushwhacking is common in these great mountains.

The Northwest contains some of the most rugged mountain wilderness in the country. A circuit of *Mount Rainier* is a good backpacking project, and the rugged routes in the *North Cascades* are legendary. A guide to *Routes and Rocks in the Mt. Challenger Quadrangle* is published by the Seattle Mountaineers, and serves both hikers and climbers. Washington also possesses the fantastic wilderness of *Olympic National Park* and adjoining areas on the Olympic Peninsula. This magnificent region has as much to offer the backpacker as any comparable region of the world, ranging from rain forests and peaks with good-sized glaciers to fifty miles of beaches and rugged coastline, most of it wilderness.

The Southwest offers good possibilities for backpackers in widely varied country ranging from desert to fairly well-watered mountains. The *Grand Canyon,* both in and out of the park, offers so many possibilities for the wilderness traveler that one could spend a lifetime exploring it. *Canyonlands National Park* is fascinating in a different way. In either place it is easy to get off the beaten track if you want to.

Leaving the "lower 48" in either direction by land will lead you to wide opportunities for exploration. Mexico offers many possibilities for combining backpacking with meeting people of different cultures. For the wilderness backpacker, though, the gem of the country is probably *Baja California,* the long peninsula that forms the Pacific coast south of the U.S. state of California. Baja has hundreds of miles of beaches and desert, but it also includes some fine granite peaks. A useful guide to the rarely visited mountain country is John Robinson's *Camping and Climbing in Baja.*

Canada and Alaska have so much wilderness country that listing it is absurd. Nearly all of Alaska is wilderness, some of it quite feasible for back-packing without trails and some practically impassable by foot. A visit to the *Brooks Range* might be the dream of a lifetime for many wilderness backpackers. The Forest Service and the Bureau of Land Management have literature describing some trails maintained within their jurisdictions in Alaska. Canada's national parks are perhaps even finer than ours, and other wilderness areas in the north and the west of Canada are so huge as to boggle the imagination. The average map distorts the north in Canada and Alaska, giving no accurate impression of how vast the country really is.

In eastern Canada there is a great deal of true wilderness, unlike the eastern United States, and although much of it is best traveled by canoe, there is a great deal of fine backpacking country as well. Much of the interior of Newfoundland, for example, is completely wild. There are also some excellent trail systems. The *Fundy Trail* in New Brunswick Province is one, and the *Bruce Trail* in Ontario, 480 miles long, is outstanding. For information on the latter, write the Bruce Trail Association, 33 Hardale Crescent, Hamilton, Ontario. Ultimately, the Bruce Trail will form a trail over 1,100 miles long with the Finger Lakes Trail in New York, when the latter is complete.

This short list doesn't begin to touch the possibilities open to the back-packer in North America, but I hope that some of the suggestions will get you started. Good hunting!

Saving Your Wilderness 26

Once you become interested in backpacking, you are almost certain to become a confirmed conservationist, but it may take a few years of watching your favorite spots dwindle in size and disappear before you realize how serious the possibility of the destruction of all our remaining wilderness is. Americans still tend to think there is an unlimited frontier out there somewhere, and this illusion is most prevalent around those spots that remain unspoiled. The booster mentality is still very strong in this country, despite current lip service to the environment. Tactics for destruction are sometimes more subtle now—the merits of a proposed wilderness are studied by a committee while the devastation goes on, or the virgin stands of timber are cut down to make way for roads so that more people can enjoy the scenery.

It we manage to overcome our other problems, the need for open places and wild places in this country will grow fantastically in the next few years, just as it has been growing. People from all kinds of backgrounds want to get away from the cities and away from suburbia to visit unspoiled places. Unfortunately, assorted commercial interests are hell-bent to convince them that they can't enjoy the outdoors without buying a half-dozen machines to destroy it. Population in all our parks, forests, and wildernesses is growing, but pressure is growing faster because so many people don't know how to use the backcountry without ruining it.

One of the purposes of this book is to present a method of traveling the open spaces of North America without damaging them, whether you

389

are walking trails near the great urban centers or crossing the most rugged wilderness. The time for pioneering is over. We have little enough wild country left, and the aim of every wilderness traveler should be to leave no trace of his passage, unless it be to clean up someone else's mess.

The first place to preserve the wilderness is where you encounter it. Carry your trash out. Bring a stove rather than break lovely, century-old snags to make your tea. Help to minimize the damage to delicate environments by population pressure.

Still, although there is some need for improvement in the attitudes and practices of backpackers, they are not the ones who are threatening the wilderness, and it *is* being threatened. Various commercial interests remain the great gobblers, abetted by their bureaucratic allies. The oil companies are busy in Alaska trying to destroy the last great wilderness in the United States. The highway interests have designs on so many places it would take a shelf of books to enumerate them. This kind of list could go on and on, but that would serve little purpose. The point here is simply that every inch of countryside will one day stand in the way of *something* justified in the name of growth and progress. The value of open lands and wilderness should be quite obvious from the current population pressure on them. It is time that we as a nation realized that wilderness is a resource far more precious than a highway right-of-way, an additional tract development, or even a few tons of minerals.

A host of practical arguments for the preservation of wild lands have been elaborated elsewhere, and I will not reiterate them here. One other point that I would like to make is simply that there is a moral issue involved. I don't believe that we have a *right* to destroy every other species and ecological system and place of beauty on the planet because it happens to suit the purposes of a chamber of commerce. During his period of claiming stewardship over the planet, man has been a poor caretaker, a fact that is becoming increasingly clear every time we open our eyes or take a breath. The lesson of the true significance of man's place in the universe is one thing that the wilderness can teach, and it is a lesson far more valuable than any oil field on earth.

Reflections of a more permanent reality. The preservation of the beauty of this wilderness depends on you—both when you go backpacking, and when you are acting as a citizen.

DO IT

Those people who travel in the backcountry have learned to value wild places, and if they do not do their best to ensure preservation of our remaining wilderness, no one else will. If you have come this far in this book, *they* is you. Public pressure, if it is strong and determined enough, is a great thing. You can help by joining various conservation organizations, like the Sierra Club and the Wilderness Society, but the pressure you can exert is far more important than money. Use those groups to help stay informed of places where action is important, but don't limit yourself to what someone else tells you. If you hike in the wilderness, you owe it a little protection. If you see someone building a road in it or tearing up the meadows with a trail bike, do something about it besides shaking your head. One of the defects of the Forest Service is that it is subject to local pressure, but this can also be a virtue. If you like the way the Service is handling your favorite area tell the local chief ranger and his boss. But if you don't like it, say so forcefully, and don't let them hide behind regulation books. If you let them clear-cut the finest grove in the forest, you won't get it back.

There are a lot of issues of concern to the backpacker besides the preservation of pure wilderness. I won't go into large problems of the environment and the society, but at the most immediate level of recreational use, areas of heavy utilization are as important as wilderness. They are needed to take the pressure off true wilderness, and they are required to teach citified people the value of a stream, tree, or mountain. A person who loves a city park is going to be a lot more responsive to pleas for preservation of your favorite mountain range than someone who never sees anything but concrete.

A FEW SPECIAL ISSUES

This is a particularly critical time in the preservation of many areas, because many government agencies are now required to make evaluations of lands under their jurisdictions for classification under the Wilderness Act. Recommendation by an agency that an area be considered for wilderness status gives that region protection until Congress has acted, but recommendation that it not be so considered can be disastrous. Outside Alaska, the most important such agencies are the Forest Service and the Park Service. Without public pressure, the Forest Service in some areas will follow the pressures of the local mining and timber interests. There are many glaring examples. Find out the status of wilderness areas that you know. Are they protected? What is their status? What can be done to protect them?

Semiwilderness areas need protection, too. They are often just as fine as pristine wilderness, but show considerable evidence of human habitation and exploitation. They may or may not be suited to heavy population pressure, and they should be managed to retain their quality.

Recreational use can be just as destructive as any other form of exploitation, and this is an area that really needs your good influence. Many national parks are already overdeveloped by bureaucrats who measure their success in managing a park by the number of people they have managed to cram through during the year. This trend can be reversed only by pressure on the Park Service. People who drive through the parks without stopping except at the ice cream stand cannot be blamed—most of them don't know they are being short-changed. If the rangers have a legitimate function besides enforcement of reasonable rules, it is to introduce people to the wilderness around them. That cannot be done from a car, and cars have little place in the parks. Under current circumstances, people may have to use them to get *to* the parks, but the value of creating a miniature Los Angeles within each national park isn't open to question—yet this is what many of the development projects amount to.

The current tendency in the parks is to limit entrances by upping admission prices, requiring reservations, and so forth. These solutions may be necessary, and I would rather put up with them than see a park destroyed. But usually pressures could be better reduced by getting rid of the motor vehicles. A car takes up more space, makes more noise, pollutes more air, requires more facilities, and carries more trash than a person—or a lot of people. Let the visitors walk or put them on bicycles. That is what the parks are all about anyway. Let them stick their noses in flowers, gawk at the cliffs, wonder at the sunset, and get blisters on their feet. But for God's sake, let them leave their gasoline engines somewhere else—we need parks, not parking lots.

Appendices

Where to Get It

All the companies listed here deal in mail orders. Writing for catalogues is a good idea even if you plan to buy your equipment at a local shop. A selection of these catalogues will give you a good idea of what is available and what it should cost. An asterisk indicates a house with an especially good selection of items for the backpacker:

ABC SPORT SHOP, 185 Norris Drive, Rochester, N.Y. 14610
ALASKA SLEEPING BAG CO., 334 N.W. 11th Ave., Portland, Ore. 97209
ALPINE HUT, 4725 30th Ave., N.E., Seattle, Wash. 98105
ALPINE RECREATION, Warehouse, 4–B Henshaw S.E., Woburn, Mass. 01801
BACK COUNTRY CAMP AND TRAIL EQUIPMENT, 8272 Orangethorpe Ave., Buena Park, Calif. 90620
EDDIE BAUER, Seattle, Wash. 98124
L. L. BEAN, Freeport, Me. 04032
BERNARD FOOD INDUSTRIES, Box 487, San Jose, Calif. 95103
    Dehydrated food.
BISHOP'S ULTIMATE OUTDOOR EQUIPMENT, 6804 Millwood Rd., Bethesda, Md. 20034
BLACK'S, Ogdensburg, N.Y. 13669
CAMP AND TRAIL OUTFITTERS, 21 Park Place, New York, N.Y. 10007
CHUCK WAGON, 176 Oak St., Newton, Mass. 02164
    Dehydrated food.

DRI-LITE, 11333 Atlantic, Lynwood, Calif. 93001
Dehydrated food.
°EASTERN MOUNTAIN SPORTS, 1041 Commonwealth Ave., Boston, Mass. 02315
Also has a new line of kits.
EUREKA TENT & AWNING CO., P.O. Box 966, Binghamton, N.Y. 13902
FROSTLINE, Box 2190, Boulder, Colo. 80302
Outstanding kits for tents, down clothing, and some other items that you sew yourself. Planning and instructions are very good.
GERRY, 5450 North Valley Highway, Denver, Colo. 80216
HIGHLAND OUTFITTERS, P.O. Box 121, Riverside, Calif. 92502
HIRSCH-WEIS/WHITE STAG, 5203 S.E. Johnson Creek Blvd., Portland, Ore. 97206
HOLUBAR, Box 7, Boulder, Colo. 80302
Their Carikit catalogue has their new kit line.
KELTY, 1801 Victory Blvd., Glendale, Calif. 91201
PETER LIMMER AND SONS, Intervale, N.H. 03845
Custom and ready-made boots.
MOOR AND MOUNTAIN, Concord, Mass. 01742
MOUNTAIN PRODUCTS CORP., 123 So. Wenatchee Ave., Wenatchee, Wash. 98801
MOUNTAIN SPORTS, 821 Pearl St., Boulder, Colo. 80302
NORTH FACE, 1234 5th St., Berkeley, Calif. 94710
PERMA-PAK, 40 East 2430 So., Salt Lake City, Utah 84115
Dehydrated food, including good bulk items.
°RECREATIONAL EQUIPMENT, 1525–11th Ave., Seattle, Wash. 98122
Generally the best buys around. Recreational Equipment is a cooperative which gives you a rebate on some of your purchase money at the end of the year. Membership fee is $1.
RICH-MOOR, P.O. Box 2728, Van Nuys, Calif. 91404
Dehydrated food.
SIERRA DESIGNS, 4th & Addison, Berkeley, Calif. 94710
°SKI HUT, 1615 University Avenue, Berkeley, Calif. 94703
SMILIE CO., 575 Howard St., San Francisco, Calif. 94105
STEPHENSON'S, 23206 Hatteras St., Woodland Hills, Calif. 91364
TRAIL CHEF, 1109 S. Wall St., Los Angeles, Calif. 90015

U.S. GEOLOGICAL SURVEY, Washington, D.C. 20025 or Federal Center, Denver, Colo. 80225

Index maps for any state are free on request.

WEST RIDGE, 11930 W. Olympic Blvd., West Los Angeles, Calif. 90025

Many other plant forms are particularly interesting, but available field guides to ferns and such are regional. The gourmet will find Alexander Smith's *The Mushroom Hunter's Guide* (University of Michigan Press) indispensable. Various other mushroom guides are good, but don't ever try a mushroom unless you're *sure*.

Field Book of Snakes of the U.S. and Canada by Karl Schmidt and D. Dwight Davis (Putnam) is a good guide, as is *A Field Guide to the Insects* by Donald Borror and Richard White (Houghton Mifflin).

The patterns of the stars are made easily recognizable by H. A. Rey's *The Stars* (Houghton Mifflin). *The Friendly Stars* by Martha Martin and Donald Menzel is charming; it is an older book brought out in a new edition by Dover.

There are many rock and mineral guides; Frederick Pough's *A Field Guide to Rocks and Minerals* (Houghton Mifflin) is one. Pamphlets and maps on the geology of many regions are published by the U.S. Geological Survey.

A fine introduction to the natural history of the continent is Peter Farb's *The Face of North America* (Harper and Row). Victor Shelford's *The Ecology of North America* is a comprehensive attempt to describe the life of the continent before the intervention of the Europeans.

A few of the really great books about wild places and the intricacies of nature are: *The Life and Death of the Salt Marsh* by John and Mildred Teal (Ballantine), *The Outermost House* by Henry Beston (Viking), *Desert Solitaire* by Edward Abbey (Simon and Schuster), *A Sand County Almanac* by Aldo Leopold (Ballantine), *The Man Who Walked Through Time* by Colin Fletcher (Knopf), *The Forest and the Sea* by Marston Bates (New American Library), *The Edge of the Sea* by Rachel Carson (Houghton Mifflin; Signet), Thoreau's *The Maine Woods* (Bramhall House), *The Immense Journey* by Loren Eiseley (Random House), *The Desert Year* by Joseph Wood Krutch (William Sloane), *The Mountains of California* by John Muir (Doubleday), *From Laurel Hill to Siler's Bog* by John Terres (Knopf), and *One Day on Teton Marsh* by Sally Carrighar (Houghton Mifflin).

EQUIPMENT

The indispensable guide for anyone making his own equipment is *Lightweight Camping Equipment and How to Make It* by Gerry Cunningham and Margaret Hansson, published by Colorado Outdoor Sports Corporation in Denver.

Bibliography

This section is included so that the reader who would like to pursue particular subjects or get a different viewpoint will have a starting point. Backpackers disagree on many subjects, because they have different bodies of experience to draw upon. After a few trips, the reader will have his own set of facts and prejudices with which to judge this book and the others mentioned here.

GENERAL

A good basic book on modern camping of all kinds is *America's Camping Book*, written by Paul Cardwell and published by Scribners. The best book about north woods-style camping, far from civilization, is Calvin Rutstrum's *New Way of the Wilderness* (Macmillan). For a book about modern backpacking with a slightly different viewpoint from mine, try Colin Fletcher's *The Complete Walker* (Knopf), an altogether delightful volume. The Sierra Club *Wilderness Handbook* (Ballantine), edited by David Brower, is a paperback version of the old *Going Light with Backpack or Burro*.

FOOD

Those who travel in large groups should consult Hasse Bunnelle's *Food for Knapsackers*, published by the Sierra Club. If you delight in traditional methods, you'll like Bradford Angier's *Wilderness Cookery* (Stackpole). If you like to plan your meals with scientific precision, or if you are going out on long enough trips to be concerned with nutritional requirements, two government publications will provide the information you need: *Food*, the 1959 Yearbook of the U.S. Department of Agriculture, and *Composition of Foods* by Bernice Watt and Annabel Merrill. Both are available from the U.S. Superintendant of Documents.

If you're interested in cooking with vegetable protein, substituting it for meat, eggs, and the like, a good introduction is *Diet for a Small Planet* by Frances Moore Lappé (Ballantine).

ROUTE FINDING

The best book around is Calvin Rutstrum's *Wilderness Route Finder* (Macmillan), including information on the more intricate techniques needed on extended trips in the far North. *Better Ways of Pathfinding* by Robert Owendoff (Stackpole) is worth reading.

FIRST AID AND EMERGENCY MEDICINE

The current Red Cross *First Aid Textbook* (Doubleday) is basic. The best discussion of wilderness medical problems in short compass (assuming you already know your Red Cross first aid) is the *Mountain Medicine Symposium*, reprinted from *Appalachia*, and available for one dollar from the Appalachian Mountain Club, 5 Joy St., Boston, Mass. 02108. *Emergency Care and Transportation of the Sick and Injured*, published by the American Academy of Orthopedic Surgeons, is outstanding and thorough.

Advanced techniques are covered exhaustively in *Medicine for Mountaineering*, edited by James Wilkerson and published by the Seattle Mountaineers.

Anyone interested in mountain or winter travel should try to get a copy of *Hypothermia: Killer of the Unprepared*, a booklet by Theodore Lathrop, published by the Mazamas.

THE MOUNTAINS

The best guides are *Mountaineering: The Freedom of the Hills*, edited by

Harvey Manning and published by the Seattle Mountaineers, and Alan Blackshaw's *Mountaineering* (Penguin).

WINTER

The author's *Complete Snow Camper's Guide* is also published by Scribners. The Sierra Club *Manual of Ski Mountaineering* (Ballantine), edited by David Brower, is an old standby.

THE NATURAL WORLD

It is impossible to even begin to mention the many good nature books that are available. Local field guides are often best, but they are also very numerous, and there would be no point in trying to list them here. A good introduction to the methods of the naturalist and to scientific nomenclature is Vinson Brown's *The Amateur Naturalist* (Bramhall House).

The best field guide to the birds is *Birds of North America* by Chandler Robbins, Bertel Bruun, and Herbert Zim (Golden Press). Two excellent older guides are Roger Tory Peterson's *A Field Guide to the Birds* (which covers the eastern part of the country) and *A Field Guide to the Western Birds*, both published by Houghton Mifflin. Records of songs are available, keyed to the Peterson guides. Peterson has also written a good introduction to birding, *How to Know the Birds* (New American Library).

For mammals, a good guide is *A Field Guide to the Mammals* by William Burt and Richard Grossenheider. Tracks and signs are discussed delightfully in Olaus Murie's *Field Guide to Animal Tracks*. Both are put out by Houghton Mifflin.

Flower lovers have to go to regional guides for field manuals, since no one has yet come out with a book of manageable size that takes in the whole country. A search of the local libraries and bookstores will be fruitful.

Tree guides are numerous. The best one covering all the United States and Canada is *Trees of North America* by C. Frank Brockman (Golden Press). For more leisurely and intimate acquaintance with the trees, try Donald Peattie's *A Natural History of the Trees* (about the eastern species) or *A Natural History of Western Trees* (both Houghton Mifflin).

Bibliography

WHERE TO GO

The only comprehensive guide is the *Handbook of Wilderness Travel* by George Wells. The new edition by Colorado Outdoor Sports Corporation has not been adequately revised, but there is still a lot of information.

The Appalachian Trail Council publishes a series of eleven guides to the Appalachian Trail and side trails to it. They cover Katahdin, Maine past Katahdin, New Hampshire and Vermont, Massachusetts and Connecticut, New York and New Jersey, Pennsylvania, Susquehanna to Shenandoah National Park, Shenandoah National Park, Central and Southwestern Virginia, Tennessee and North Carolina to the Great Smokies, and the Great Smokies to Georgia.

The Appalachian Mountain Club publishes comprehensive trail guides to Maine Mountains, the White Mountains, Massachusetts and Rhode Island, and to Mount Desert Island–Acadia National Park. A *Guide to the Long Trail* is published by the Green Mountain Club, and a *Guide to Adirondack Trails* by the Adirondack Mountain Club.

For trips in Washington and Oregon, the Seattle Mountaineers publish many books of short hikes besides the booklet mentioned in the text. For the Glacier Peak Wilderness Area, there is *Routes and Rocks*, also by Tabor and Crowder. The Olympic Peninsula is covered well in Robert Wood's *Trail Country*.

Wyoming is served by Orrin and Lorraine Bonney's *Guide to the Wyoming Mountains and Wilderness Areas* (Swallow), portions of which are also available in smaller editions.

Some of the best trips in California are described in two Wilderness Press books by Karl Schwenke and Thomas Winnett, *Sierra South* and *Sierra North*. Robert Wood's *The Tahoe–Yosemite Trail* and *Desolation Wilderness* cover some of my favorite trails in the Sierra.

Robert Ormes' *Guide to the Colorado Mountains* (Swallow) and Herbert Ungnade's *Guide to the New Mexico Mountains* by the same publisher are not primarily trail guides, but contain a great deal of information useful to backpackers.

Index

413